D1569534

Innovation as a social process

Elihu Thomson was a major American inventor of electric lighting and power systems. A contemporary of Thomas Edison, Thomson performed the engineering and design work necessary to make electric lighting a common product. From the 1880s to the 1930s, Thomson was employed by the General Electric Company and its predecessors. Thomson's career, working within the corporation, reveals how successful applications of inventions are based on explicit links among technological artifacts, marketing strategy, and the business organization needed for manufacturing and marketing.

STUDIES IN ECONOMIC HISTORY AND POLICY
THE UNITED STATES IN THE TWENTIETH CENTURY

Edited by
Louis Galambos and Robert Gallman

Innovation as a social process

Elihu Thomson and the rise of
General Electric, 1870–1900

W. BERNARD CARLSON

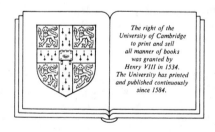

The right of the
University of Cambridge
to print and sell
all manner of books
was granted by
Henry VIII in 1534.
The University has printed
and published continuously
since 1584.

Cambridge University Press

Cambridge

New York   Port Chester   Melbourne   Sydney

Published by the Press Syndicate of the University of Cambridge
The Pitt Building, Trumpington Street, Cambridge CB2 1RP
40 West 20th Street, New York, NY 10011, USA
10 Stamford Road, Oakleigh, Melbourne 3166, Australia

First published 1991

Printed in Canada

Library of Congress Cataloging-in-Publication Data
Carlson, W. Bernard.
Innovation as a social process : Elihu Thomson and the rise of
General Electric, 1870–1900 / W. Bernard Carlson.
p. cm. — (Studies in economic history and policy)
Includes bibliographical references
Includes index
ISBN 0-521-39317-5 (hardcover)
1. Thomson, Elihu, 1853–1937. 2. Inventors – United States –
Biography. 3. General Electric Company – History. 4. Electric
industries – United States – History – 19th century.
5. Electric power systems – United States – History – 19th century.
6. Industrial organization – United States – History – 19th century.
I. Title. II. Series.
TK140.T5C37   1991
338.7'62138'092 – dc20
[B]   91–9107
                                                                    CIP

British Library Cataloguing in Publication Data
Carlson, W. Bernard
Innovation as a social process.
1. United States. Electrical engineering. General Electric
Company. Thomson, Elihu
I. Title   II. Series
621.3092

ISBN 0-521-39317-5 hardback

To Marion,
who nurtured me in my youth,

Regina,
who sustains me in the present,

and Julia Marion,
with whom the future resides.

Contents

Figures and tables

Figures

Tables

Editors' preface

During the late nineteenth century, the U.S. economy was still experiencing rapid *extensive* growth based primarily on new inputs of capital, labor, and natural resources. But even then the foundation was being constructed for a twentieth-century *intensive* economy that would grow primarily through technological and organizational improvements that would result in productivity gains. Science-based industries would play a large role in that transformation. The industries based on electricity would be especially important – as they still are today – and one of the most important innovators in the early years in that sector of the economy was Elihu Thomson.

Thomson was a brilliant inventor who held patents for lighting systems, transformers, instruments, and welding equipment. He blended craft knowledge with scientific knowledge to develop practical innovations that could be the basis of capitalist enterprises. He was a hands-on, experimental innovator, much in the style of his contemporaries George Westinghouse and Thomas Edison.

Like Edison and Westinghouse, Thomson helped build the business organizations that could produce and market his innovations. He was thus an organizational as well as a technical entrepreneur, gathering capital, developing a firm, devising marketing strategies. As always, this was a risky enterprise. Thomson was not an immediate success. But he persisted and eventually helped create two significant firms: Thomson-Houston and General Electric. The latter enterprise was one of those that built innovation into the very structure of the company, completing a transformation from the relatively individual inventor to the socially organized process of discovery – a transformation in which Thomson played a significant role. W. Bernard Carlson's study of Thomson, *Innovation as a Social Process*, is a welcome addition to

Studies in Economic History and Policy: The United States in the Twentieth Century.

Louis Galambos
Professor of History
Johns Hopkins University

Robert Gallman
Kenan Professor of Economics and History
University of North Carolina at Chapel Hill

Acknowledgments

During the past decade I have worked in many different offices, and in nearly all of them I have hung a reproduction of a painting titled *A View near Volterra,* by Jean-Baptiste Camille Corot. The painting shows a lone horseman traversing a narrow path on the side of a rocky hill; in the distance, but out of sight of the horseman, is Volterra, his destination. I chose to place that painting over my desk in graduate school because it served as a visual expression of the intellectual journey I felt I had undertaken.

When I began this study of Elihu Thomson, I assumed that my journey would be a solitary endeavor. Yet, unlike the horseman in the painting, I have been pleasantly surprised by the number of friendly and helpful people I have met along the way. Each time I thought I would have to go it alone, I discovered someone around the next bend in the road, helping me with the many tasks related to historical research and encouraging me to grow intellectually.

During my odyssey I have been the beneficiary of a number of grants and fellowships. My preliminary research on Thomson was undertaken in 1979–80 while I was a research assistant in the History and Sociology of Science Department at the University of Pennsylvania. The following summer, I inventoried the Thomson collection at the American Philosophical Society, with the support of the society and a research conference grant (RD-20023) from the National Endowment for the Humanities. During 1980–1, I received the Fellowship in Electrical History of the Institute of Electrical and Electronics Engineers, and that award permitted me to work full-time on the dissertation. In 1982, with the support of a predoctoral fellowship from the Smithsonian Institution, I supplemented my manuscript research with study of Thomson's models and artifacts at the National Museum of American History. During that same year, I benefited from a John E. Rovensky Fellowship in Business and Economic History and a research grant from the Bakken Museum of Electricity in Life, in Minneapolis. While the Rovensky fellowship provided me with the funds to search the business and corporate records, the Bakken grant supported my research on x-ray technology.

After several years of teaching, I resumed full-time work on Thomson in 1988. During that phase of revision and rewriting, I had the privilege of being a Newcomen Fellow in Business and Economic History at the Harvard Business School (1988–9). Funded by both Harvard and the Newcomen Society of the United States, that fellowship allowed me to spend a year at Harvard writing and learning from the business history group. In addition, the timely completion of this manuscript has been facilitated by support from the University of Virginia. During the summer of 1988, I received a research grant in the humanities and social sciences from the office of the associate provost for research, and during the summer of 1990 my salary was covered by the office of the dean of engineering.

Individuals at many institutions have graciously accommodated my research. At the American Philosophical Society (APS), where the largest collection of Thomson manuscripts is stored, the entire staff was friendly and helpful. Edward C. Carter, chief librarian, took a special interest in my project and helped me find a place in the APS family. Murphy Smith went out of his way to find me a private desk in the library stacks. Stephen Catlett and Elizabeth Carroll-Horrocks permitted me to work with the Thomson materials in the vault and to Xerox documents. Roy Goodman and Jeff Cohen answered my many reference questions, and Helen Black Irwin set up a special Xeroxing account for me. Marty Levitt assiduously hunted down illustrations for this book and handled the permissions.

At the National Museum of American History, Bernard S. Finn served as my fellowship adviser and encouraged my efforts to analyze electrical artifacts. Within the Division of Electricity and Modern Physics, Art Mollella, Anastasia Atsiknoudas, Ray Hutt, and Nance Briscoe helped me locate materials and provided good cheer over the years of research. At the General Electric Company (GE) in Lynn, Massachusetts, Marshall Moore and Ernest Yamartino were instrumental in helping me find previously unused Thomson manuscripts and photographs. (This valuable collection has since been transferred to the GE Hall of History Museum in Schenectady, New York.) George Wise, GE's historian in Schenectady, encouraged my electrical studies and also arranged my visit to the Hammond and Historical Files at

GE's Schenectady plant. At the New Britain Public Library, I was aided by Arlene Palmer and Barbara Hubbard of the Local History Room; in particular, Barbara was an exemplary librarian, brimming with enthusiasm and knowledge of nineteenth-century New Britain. In addition, I wish to thank the following archivists, curators, and librarians for their generous assistance: Nancy Roth and Dorina Morawetz of the Bakken Museum, Minneapolis, Minnesota; Florence Lathrop, Lizz Frost, and Charles Burgelman of the Baker Library, Harvard University Graduate School of Business Administration, Boston, Massachusetts; Scott Berger of the library of the National Museum of American History, Washington, D.C.; Gladys Breuer of the Franklin Institute, Philadelphia, Pennsylvania; Santo Diano of Central High School, Philadelphia; Janet Lane, Kenneth Turino, and Diane Shepard of the Lynn Historical Society, Lynn, Massachusetts; Janet Locatelli of the Michigan Technological University Library, Houghton, Michigan; Michael London of Northeast Utilities, Hartford, Connecticut; Warren Seamen of the Massachusetts Institute of Technology (MIT) Museum, Cambridge, Massachusetts; Helen Samuels and Kathy Jacob of the MIT Archives; Jill Papenhagen of the Case Western Reserve University Library, Cleveland, Ohio; Harold Williams of the National Archives, Washington, D.C.; Henry Williams of the Philadelphia Social History Project; Ruth Shoemaker of General Electric; and David Wright of The Pierpont Morgan Library, New York, New York.

In undertaking this research, I also wish to thank George B. Thomson, grandson of Elihu Thomson, for supplying genealogical data and for help in locating several relevant collections. At an early stage of the project, Charles Scott and Barbara Kimmelman served as my research assistants, and I am grateful to them for locating articles in nineteenth-century electrical journals. My thanks also to Ruth Kane and Mary Alice Fisher for wisdom and advice regarding life and scholarship.

As I planned and wrote this book, I had the privilege and pleasure of studying with two exceptional historians, Thomas P. Hughes and Alfred D. Chandler, Jr. Professor Hughes was my mentor at the University of Pennsylvania and taught me the history of technology. In the spring of 1979 he proposed that I write my dissertation on Thomson, but he let me decide what themes and issues I should investigate. Over the years, his gentle but firm comments helped me sharpen my analysis and adopt a more complex view of Thomson's personality. From Professor Chandler I learned business history, first through his books and then as a Newcomen Fellow. He taught me to seek out the larger patterns in human and business enterprises. From both men, I learned something more than the historical method; I saw how they integrated the scholarly, professional, and personal aspects of their lives in order to be able to treat all people with respect and gracious dignity.

Along with Professors Hughes and Chandler, other individuals have been forthcoming with advice and support. Robert Kohler taught me the importance of institutional history and served as a member of my dissertation committee at Pennsylvania. Kendall Dood of the United States Patent Office and Stuart Bennett of the University of Sheffield discussed with me the intricacies of nineteenth-century generators and feedback control devices. Susan Douglas took time to give me tips about history and the art of writing books. My close friend and research partner Michael E. Gorman has consistently supported and encouraged me in completing this book. I have also benefited from conversations about Thomson and the history of technology, business, and science with Brent Barnett, Wiebe Bijker, A. Hunter Dupree, T. R. Durham, Margaret B. W. Graham, Takashi Hikino, Paul Israel, John James, Ronald Kline, Timothy Lenoir, Steven Lubar, Patrick McGuire, Matthew Mehalik, H. V. Nelles, Larry Owens, Trevor Pinch, Terry Reynolds, Mark Rose, Merritt Roe Smith, Steven Tolliday, Steven Wheelwright, Rosalind Williams, and Olivier Zunz.

I am grateful to Louis Galambos for reading the manuscript and providing suggestions for strengthening it as a whole. Stuart W. Leslie and George Wise also read drafts and offered me crucial advice concerning the conceptual structure. Professor Chandler read an early version of the manuscript and helped me understand the larger significance of my business narrative. I wish to thank other scholars who took time to read individual chapters: John K. Brown, Glenn Bugos, Richard John, Eda Kranakis, Naomi Lamoureaux, Edwin Layton, Bayla Singer, and Mark Thomas. I owe a special debt to Jonathan Coopersmith, Thomas Misa, and Bryan Pfaffenberger for carefully critiquing my introduction and conclusion. Of course, though many have assisted me, I take full responsibility for the final text and any errors of fact or interpretation.

A number of individuals at both the University of Virginia and Cambridge University Press have been instrumental in the preparation of this book. Priscilla Critzer has graciously helped with the typing and correspondence over the years and has always been encouraging. Kim

Candee saw me through the last few months of typing, Xeroxing, and petty details, all of which she handled with grace and skill. My thanks to Marty Britt for handling several last-minute photographs. Boris Starosta and Michelle Bollinger prepared the illustrations and created the original artwork for this book, and I appreciated their creativity and enthusiasm. I am especially grateful to the Humanities Division at Virginia for subsidizing the preparation of the illustrations; the over-all appearance of this book owes much to this timely grant. At Cambridge University Press, I wish to thank Frank Smith for his advice and encouragement, Sophia Prybylski for coordinating production superbly, and Jim Mobley for his skillful copyediting.

This book is dedicated to my grandmother, my daughter, and especially my wife, Regina. From the first days to the last, Regina has shared with me the exhilarating moments of intellectual discovery, as well as the bleak hours of self-doubt and confusion. Throughout the long process of research and writing, she has stood by me, as adviser, confidante, and fan. It is to her that I owe my greatest debt.

Abbreviations used in footnotes

Frequently cited manuscript collections and repositories

CHS Archives	Central High School Archives, Philadelphia, Pennsylvania
Div. Elec., NMAH	Division of Electricity and Modern Physics, National Museum of American History, Washington, D.C.
ENHS	Thomas Edison Papers, Edison National Historic Site, West Orange, New Jersey
Hall of History Collection	Thomson Collection, General Electric Hall of History, Schenectady, New York
Hammond File	John W. Hammond File, General Electric Company, Schenectady, New York
HELCO Collection	Hartford Electric Light Company Collection, Connecticut Historical Society, Hartford, Connecticut
Higginson Papers	Henry L. Higginson Papers, Baker Library, Harvard University Graduate School of Business Administration, Boston, Massachusetts
Lynn HS	Thomson Collection, Lynn Historical Society, Lynn, Massachusetts
MIT Archives	Thomson Collection, Institute Archives and Special Collections, Massachusetts Institute of Technology, Cambridge, Massachusetts

NARS	Records of the Patent Office, RG-241, Washington Records Center, National Archives and Records Center, Suitland, Maryland
NBPL	New Britain Public Library, New Britain, Connecticut
PSHP	Philadelphia Social History Project, University of Pennsylvania, Philadelphia, Pennsylvania
R. G. Dun & Co. Collection	R. G. Dun & Co. Collection, Baker Library, Harvard University Graduate School of Business Administration, Boston, Massachusetts
TP	Elihu Thomson Papers, American Philosophical Society, Philadelphia, Pennsylvania
Villard Papers	Henry Villard Papers, Baker Library, Harvard University Graduate School of Business Administration, Boston, Massachusetts

Abbreviations used for periodicals

GE Rev.	*General Electric Review*
J. Franklin Inst.	*Journal of the Franklin Institute*
Proc. APS	*Proceedings of the American Philosophical Society*

Other abbreviations

Autobiog. Papers	Autobiographical Papers
CAC	Charles A. Coffin
CL	Collected Letters

EJH	Edwin J. Houston
ET	Elihu Thomson
LB	Letterbook
T-H	Thomson-Houston

Introduction

"There is scarcely a day passing," mused Elihu Thomson in the late 1860s, "on which some new use for electricity is not discovered. It seems destined to become at some future time the means of obtaining light, heat, and mechanical force."[1] A young man of 16, Thomson dreamt presciently of his own future, for few men in American history would discover more new uses for electricity. Thomas A. Edison, George Westinghouse, Charles Brush, and Elihu Thomson were the brilliant inventors who created the first electric lighting and power systems. The third most prolific inventor in American history, Thomson was granted 696 patents in a career that spanned five decades.[2] His inventions included arc and incandescent lighting systems, the repulsion-induction motor, electric welding equipment, a recording wattmeter, and improved transformers, all of which were central in establishing how electricity is used today.

Thomson not only furthered the development of electrical technology through his numerous inventions but also effectively linked his inventions with business organizations and marketing strategies. Closely associated with the Thomson-Houston Electric Company, and later the General Electric Company, he directed technological innovation in ways that permitted those firms to surpass their competitors and expand into new markets. During the 1880s and 1890s, Thomson helped establish a tradition of regular product improvement and scientific research that led to the creation of the General Electric Research Laboratory in 1900. The first of its kind in the United States, that industrial research laboratory converted the innovation process

---

1 Quotation is from ET, "Universal Journal," No. 10 (1869), Collected Essays, TP.
2 Measured in terms of U.S. patents granted, Thomson is the third most prolific inventor in American history. He received 696 patents in the course of his career, a figure surpassed only by Thomas Edison with 1,093 and John O'Connor (an inventor of railroad equipment) with 949. See "Meet the Champion Inventors," *Popular Science Monthly*, 128:11–13 (January 1936).

into a dependable asset of corporate capitalism. Because Thomson spent much of his career working in the corporate context, his career provides insight into how creative individuals function in large organizations.

Despite his prominent role in the formation of the electrical industry, little has been written about Thomson as an inventor and engineer. He has been the subject of one book-length biography, whose title, *Beloved Scientist,* reveals its hagiographic focus. Commissioned by the family after Thomson's death in 1937, that biography praised his personal manner, his scientific curiosity, and his genius, but explained little about how and why Thomson went about his work as an inventor. In his landmark study of the electrical manufacturing industry, Harold C. Passer briefly characterized Thomson as an imitator who built upon the work of more important pioneers such as Edison and Brush. That there has not been more written about Thomson is surprising, given the substantial collections of his correspondence at the American Philosophical Society and his artifacts at the National Museum of American History and the Franklin Institute.[3]

This book is a study of Thomson as an inventor. However, it is not a traditional biography, tracing his life from cradle to grave. Instead, this book uses Thomson's career to narrate two interrelated stories. The first is the technological tale of how Thomson helped convert electric lights, generators, and motors from lecture-hall curiosities in 1875 to commonplace products in 1900. At the outset of this story, the only electric lamps were laboratory devices that could be used only

3 See David O. Woodbury, *Beloved Scientist: Elihu Thomson, A Guiding Spirit of the Electrical Age* (New York: Whittlesey House, 1944; reprinted Cambridge, Mass.: Harvard University Press, 1960). Harold J. Abrahams has edited two volumes of Thomson's correspondence with scientists in the early twentieth century; see H. J. Abrahams and Marion B. Savin, eds., *Selections of the Scientific Correspondence of Elihu Thomson* (Cambridge, Mass.: MIT Press, 1971); and Harold J. Abrahams, ed., *Heroic Efforts at Meteor Crater, Arizona: Selected Correspondence between Daniel Moreau Barringer and Elihu Thomson* (Rutherford, N.J.: Fairleigh Dickinson University Press, 1983). See also Harold C. Passer discussing Thomson in *The Electrical Manufacturers, 1875–1900: A Study in Competition, Entrepreneurship, Technical Change, and Economic Growth* (Cambridge, Mass.: Harvard University Press, 1953), pp. 21–31, 57, 192–4. For a description of Thomson-related materials, see John L. Haney, "The Elihu Thomson Collection," *Library Bulletin of the American Philosophical Society* (1938), pp. 39–51; and W. Bernard Carlson, "The Elihu Thomson Papers: A Planning Report" (unpublished report, Library of the American Philosophical Society, 1980).

under special and favorable conditions; by its end, they had become essential to daily life and business. Thomson played an important part in that conversion from curiosity to everyday product by inventing new and efficient systems of lighting and by carefully matching his inventions to marketing and manufacturing requirements. To be sure, the history of electric lighting has been covered in earlier studies, but much of the emphasis in those studies has been on Edison and his direct-current system of incandescent lighting. Because Thomson worked on both arc lighting and alternating-current systems, his career provides a contrast (and even a corrective) to the focus on Edison.[4]

The second story is a business narrative. Thomson's career illuminates the rise of the General Electric Company, the preeminent firm in the electrical industry in the United States. By tracing how Thomson worked with several sets of backers and entrepreneurs, we can see, step by step, how the small entrepreneurial firm of nineteenth-century America was transformed into the modern corporation of the twentieth century. By combining technology, organizational arrangements, marketing strategies, and new sources of capital, Thomson, Charles A. Coffin, and others shaped General Electric into what Alfred D. Chandler, Jr., has called the modern industrial enterprise. Characterized by a managerial hierarchy that coordinates a variety of operating units for production, distribution, and research, the modern industrial enterprise is the business institution by which managers exploited the potential of new technologies and created the global economy.[5] In recounting how individuals such as Thomson and Coffin shaped General Electric as a modern industrial enterprise, this study seeks a balance between individualistic entrepreneurial history and Chandler's institutional approach. In particular, it shows how the unique characteristics of Thomson and Coffin informed the structure and strategy of General Electric. Such an approach should enrich our understanding of the appearance of managerial capitalism in late-nineteenth-century America and underscore the role played by technology in this economic drama.

4 Along with Passer's *The Electrical Manufacturers*, other major studies of the history of electric lighting include Thomas P. Hughes, *Networks of Power: Electrification in Western Society, 1880–1930* (Baltimore: Johns Hopkins University Press, 1983); and Robert Friedel and Paul Israel, *Edison's Electric Light: Biography of an Invention* (New Brunswick, N.J.: Rutgers University Press, 1986).

5 Alfred D. Chandler, Jr., *Scale and Scope: The Dynamics of Industrial Capitalism* (Cambridge, Mass.: Belknap Press of Harvard University, 1990).

Two themes – the relationship between technological innovation and knowledge, and innovation as a social process – provide a matrix for weaving together the technological and business narratives. Because of the significance of these themes for this book, each will be described in detail.

The first theme leads us to an investigation into how inventors use both scientific knowledge and craft knowledge in creating new technology. "Scientific knowledge" generally refers to information about the natural world that is organized into formal theories and legitimated through experiment and observation. Since the seventeenth century in the West, this knowledge has been created and maintained by a self-conscious community of practitioners. "Craft knowledge" denotes the ideas and insights that individuals acquire through direct, hands-on manipulation of devices.[6] Frequently this knowledge is object-oriented and nonverbal; as Jerome Ravetz suggested in his discussion of the craft aspects of science,

> the craftsman works with particular objects; he must know their properties in all their particularity; and his knowledge of them cannot be specified in a formal account. . . . Indeed, much of his technique may not even have the character of conscious knowledge; by experience his hands and eyes have taught themselves.[7]

6 To the best of my knowledge, no historian of technology has formulated an explicit definition of "craft knowledge." Instead, it has been discussed under a number of different headings, including "technical skill," "shop culture," and "craft tradition." In thinking about Thomson and craft knowledge, I have been influenced by the following studies: Eugene S. Ferguson, "The Mind's Eye: Nonverbal Thought in Technology," *Science,* 197:827 (1977); Brooke Hindle, *Emulation and Invention* (New York: Norton, 1983); A. Rupert Hall, "On Knowing, and Knowing How To . . . ," *History of Technology,* 3:91–103 (1978); Merritt Roe Smith, *Harper's Ferry Armory and the New Technology* (Ithaca, N.Y.: Cornell University Press, 1977), pp. 62–8; Monte A. Calvert, *The Mechanical Engineer in America, 1830–1910* (Baltimore: Johns Hopkins University Press, 1975), pp. 6–8; James R. Blackaby, "How the Workbench Changed the Nature of Work," *American Heritage of Invention and Technology,* 2:26–30 (Fall 1986); Thomas P. Hughes, "Model Builders and Instrument Makers," *Science in Context,* 2:59–75 (1988); Lissa Roberts, "Reuniting Mind and Body: The Role of Sensuous Technology in the Chemical Revolution" (paper presented to the History of Science Society, November 1990). I have also explored Edison's craft knowledge in "Building Thomas Edison's Laboratory in West Orange, New Jersey: A Case Study of Using Craft Knowledge for Technological Innovation," *History of Technology* (1991).
7 Jerome R. Ravetz, *Scientific Knowledge and Its Social Problems* (Oxford University Press, 1971), pp. 75–6.

Both Brooke Hindle and Eugene S. Ferguson have emphasized that firsthand, personal experience with devices is often essential for design and invention, and yet we know very little about this form of knowledge. To some extent this intellectual lacuna exists because, as Ravetz suggests, craftsmen seldom produce formal or written records in the course of their work. However, this gap is also the result of a long-standing bias among scholars that places a higher value on affairs of the mind than on actions of the hand. As Denis Diderot wrote in his *Encyclopédie,*

> I do not know why people have a low opinion of what this word implies; for we depend on the *crafts* for all the necessary things of life. Anyone who has taken the trouble to visit casually the workshops will see in all places utility allied with the greatest evidence of intelligence: antiquity made gods of those who invented the *crafts;* the following centuries threw into the mud those who perfected the same work.[8]

In investigating the knowledge utilized by inventors to create new technology, I am building on an extensive body of historical scholarship that has examined the nature of technological and engineering knowledge.[9] To date, much of this literature has been focused on the interaction between science and technology and on engineering science. In this study, I propose to complement this emphasis on science with an attempt to recover the craft component of Thomson's inventions. In doing so, this book should provide insight into how modern engineering embraces both scientific and craft knowledge.[10]

8 Denis Diderot, *The Encyclopedia: Selections,* ed. and trans. S. J. Gendizier (New York: Harper & Row, 1967), p. 85.
9 There are two useful reviews of the literature on technological knowledge: John M. Staudenmaier, *Technology's Storytellers: Reweaving the Human Fabric* (Cambridge, Mass.: MIT Press, 1985), pp. 83–120; Edwin T. Layton, Jr., "Through the Looking Glass: or, News from Lake Mirror Image," in S. H. Cutcliffe and R. C. Post, eds., *In Context: History and the History of Technology. Essays in Honor of Melvin Kranzberg (Research in Technology Studies, Vol. 1)* (Bethlehem, Pa.: Lehigh University Press, 1989), pp. 29–41.
10 The notion that modern engineering embraces both scientific and craft knowledge is one of the themes developed by Henry Petroski in *The Pencil: A History of Design and Circumstance* (New York: Knopf, 1990), pp. 76–7. For a case study of the nonscientific component of engineering, see Walter G. Vincenti, "Technological Knowledge without Science: The Innovation of Flush Riveting in American Airplanes, ca. 1930–ca. 1950," *Technology and Culture,* 25:540–76 (July 1984). J. R. Harris has argued persuasively that craft skills were essential to the innovations underlying the British Industrial Revolution in "Skills, Coal, and British Industry in the Eighteenth Century," *History,* 61:167–82 (June 1976).

At first glance, it may seem surprising to use a nineteenth-century electrical inventor as a case study to investigate the interplay of scientific and craft knowledge in modern technology, because the electrical industry generally is cited as a paradigmatic example of how science became technology. For instance, it is often assumed that once Michael Faraday discovered the principles of electromagnetic induction in 1831, it was relatively easy for Edison to invent his incandescent lighting system between 1879 and 1882. No one ever seems to be too worried about the intervening 50 years and the technological efforts required to put theory into practice.[11]

In contrast, Thomson's career reveals that the development of electrical technology in the late nineteenth century required a combination of scientific values and craft knowledge. Nowhere in his notebooks, published articles, or patents did Thomson move from scientific theory to technological practice in the way we might expect. In the course of inventing new electrical devices, Thomson drew on his scientific background not for a theoretical understanding of electricity but rather for an experimental outlook, for standards regarding publication and priority, and for social recognition from the scientific community. Indeed, he was more like the American millwrights Zebulon and Austin Parker, who, Edwin T. Layton has argued, borrowed experimental techniques, but not theory, from hydraulic science in the 1820s and 1830s.[12] Science thus provided Thomson with a set of values that guided his thinking and behavior.

Along with the values of science, Thomson's inventions were based on craft knowledge. He created new electrical technology by using the manual skills he had developed as a young man while building apparatus, conducting experiments, and performing demonstrations. He learned about electrical technology by studying machines firsthand

---

11 A typical treatment of the electrical industry as being science-based is by J. D. Bernal, *Science and Industry in the Nineteenth Century* (Bloomington: Indiana University Press, 1970). For a valuable and unfortunately partial cataloging of the technological efforts that occurred between Faraday and Edison, consult W. James King, "The Development of Electrical Technology in the 19th Century. 3: The Early Arc Light and Generator," *United States National Museum Bulletin 228*, paper 30 (Washington, D.C.: Smithsonian Institution, 1962), pp. 333–407.

12 Edwin T. Layton, Jr., "Millwrights and Engineers, Science, Social Roles, and the Evolution of the Turbine in America," in W. Krohn, E. T. Layton, and P. Weingart, eds., *The Dynamics of Science and Technology* (*Sociology of the Sciences Yearbook, Vol. 2*) (Dordrecht, Holland: D. Reidel, 1978), pp. 61–87.

and then building his own versions. At first, Thomson could only emulate (to use Brooke Hindle's term) the machines of other inventors, but gradually he honed his skills so that he was able to invent his own unique devices. At the height of his career, Thomson produced new inventions and insights into electricity by working through a series of alternative electrical and mechanical arrangements. In narrating the story of Thomson's electric lighting inventions, I shall identify the skills he possessed and show how they evolved in response to new challenges and organizational settings. Although Thomson is but one example among many, his story suggests that the electrical industry in the late nineteenth century was based as much on craft knowledge as on scientific theory. And if this is true, then the interesting question becomes why the electrical industry came to be science-based in the twentieth century, a question that will be addressed in the conclusion.

The second theme follows from the first. In creating new technology, it is not enough to possess scientific or craft knowledge; one must also locate this knowledge in a social organization that can act upon it. At different times in history, various social organizations have been created to develop and use technological knowledge. For instance, in the Middle Ages, monasteries stimulated the mechanical knowledge needed to develop waterwheels and clocks.[13] Consequently, if one wishes to understand the innovation process, one must ask not only about the knowledge base but also about the organization within which that knowledge is developed and used.

To investigate the organizational context of innovation, I have found it useful to view innovation as the synthesis of creative acts in the technical, organizational, and marketing realms.[14] First, innovation is the creation of hardware, physical objects, or artifacts. This is simply

13 On the mechanical technology used in monasteries in medieval Europe, see Lewis Mumford, *Technics and Civilization* (New York: Harcourt, Brace & World, 1934), pp. 12–14; Walter Horn and Ernest Born, *The Plan of St. Gall,* 3 vols. (Berkeley: University of California Press, 1979); and Terry S. Reynolds, *Stronger than a Hundred Men: A History of the Vertical Water Wheel* (Baltimore: Johns Hopkins University Press, 1983), pp. 109–12.

14 In developing an interpretation of innovation as including technical, organizational, and marketing components, I have been inspired by the approach used by Susan Douglas in *Inventing American Broadcasting, 1899–1922* (Baltimore: Johns Hopkins University Press, 1987). In that study, Douglas skillfully showed how the inventors of radio not only invented new technology and business arrangements but also negotiated the social meanings of their inventions through shrewd use of the press.

the popular notion of invention. In the case at hand, Thomson invented several systems or machines for efficiently generating electricity and converting electricity to light. Although obvious, it is important in a social analysis of technology to remember that technological innovation is about the creation of physical objects, in order to maintain a balanced perspective. When one is looking at technology as the result of social and cultural forces, it is tempting to assume that these forces alone determine technology. Although such forces are significant, technology is also shaped by technical considerations and natural forces. An invention has to work in the real world, and some designs, though they can be conceived and might have social meaning, might not function. By keeping in mind that inventors do indeed create physical devices, one can permit technical considerations to play a role in the analysis without having them overwhelm the social issues.[15]

Yet the process of innovation is much more than the creation of artifacts; an inventor must locate his or her creation in an organization. This is necessary so that the inventor can gain access to the capital and resources required to perfect, manufacture, and market an invention. For Thomson and electrical technology in late-nineteenth-century America, the key social organization was the business firm. Because his electric lighting inventions required substantial capital, new services, and marketing arrangements, Thomson worked with Charles A. Coffin and others in order to create new business arrangements to perform those tasks. Thus, Thomson's work on electric lighting permits us to see how technological and organizational innovations are linked.

Beyond the creation of artifacts and organizations, the innovation process requires a third creative effort. In the course of creating a new artifact, an inventor must devise a marketing strategy. Generally, an inventor has ideas about who will use an invention and why, and the inventor must continually refine and communicate these conceptions to business associates and to consumers so that they will support and purchase the invention. Frequently, conceptions about who will use an invention and why are negotiated among the individuals and groups involved in production and distribution. Within the business firm, the

15 John Law is one of the few sociologists or historians who have considered how technology is shaped by both natural and social forces: "Technology and Heterogeneous Engineering: The Case of Portuguese Expansion," in W. E. Bijker, T. P. Hughes, and T. Pinch, eds., *The Social Construction of Technological Systems* (Cambridge, Mass.: MIT Press, 1987), pp. 111–34, especially pp. 113–14.

groups responsible for innovation, manufacturing, and marketing may have their own conceptions of the invention, and they may articulate these conceptions as a marketing strategy. Furthermore, as an invention is taken up and used by consumers, conceptions may change even more; because of personal experiences, social arrangements, and general cultural values, consumers may use a device in ways that differ significantly from those anticipated by the inventor or manufacturer. In order to achieve commercial success, the inventor and manufacturer need to be sensitive to consumers' conceptions and integrate them into the marketing strategy.[16]

The introduction of electric lighting required the creation of a new marketing strategy.[17] Along with creating a system of electric lighting and a business organization, Thomson and his associates had to develop a strategy that would convince people to purchase electric lighting equipment. In particular, they chose to invent a new customer for electric lighting equipment: the central-station utility.[18] Rather

16 For a discussion of how cultural conceptions and social meanings may shape the development and diffusion of a technology, see Madeline Akrich, "How Can Technical Objects Be Described?" (unpublished paper, Centre de Sociologie de l'Innovation, Ecole Nationale Supérieure des Mines, Paris, 1987); Bryan Pfaffenberger, "The Social Meaning of the Personal Computer, Or, Why the Personal Computer Revolution Was No Revolution," *Anthropological Quarterly*, 61:39–50 (1988); and W. Bernard Carlson, "Artifacts and Frames of Meaning: Thomas A. Edison, His Managers, and the Cultural Construction of Motion Pictures," in W. E. Bijker and J. Law, eds., *Shaping Technology, Building Society: Studies in Sociotechnical Change* (Cambridge, Mass.: MIT Press, in press).

17 For many new technological devices, inventors often have utilized existing business organizations and marketing strategies to produce and distribute their creations. In fact, I suspect that inventors often choose to develop devices that fit, more or less, into the existing business scheme, because they do not wish to have to develop new business and marketing arrangements. Frequently they lack the skills necessary to innovate in those other realms. For instance, after failing to sell his first invention, an electrical vote-recording machine, Edison claimed that he avoided inventing devices that would have no clearly established market. See Matthew Josephson, *Edison: A Biography* (New York: McGraw-Hill, 1959), pp. 65–6. I am grateful to Steven Lubar for suggesting this point to me.

18 In *Networks of Power,* Thomas P. Hughes emphasized that the development of the central station was the key innovation in the evolution of the electric lighting and power industry. My argument here parallels that of Reese V. Jenkins, who has suggested that George Eastman invented a new mass market for his simple roll-film camera: "Technology and the Market: George Eastman and the Origins of Mass Amateur Photography," *Technology and Culture*, 16:1–19 (January 1975).

than sell generators, lights, and the necessary accessories outright to consumers, Thomson and his partners found that it was more profitable to persuade businessmen in towns and cities to organize utility companies that would purchase Thomson's inventions and in turn sell the service of lighting. This was a complex and risky undertaking for Thomson and his associates, requiring negotiations with numerous individual businessmen. It also required the development of new devices and organizational arrangements tailored to this strategy. What is important about Thomson, Coffin, and the other early pioneers in electric lighting is that they were able to articulate this strategy, organize their company to pursue it, and link their technology to it. Only by doing so were they able to establish electric lighting as an industry, characterized in America by large manufacturers such as General Electric and by investor-owned central-station utilities.

By viewing innovation as a synthesis of hardware, organization, and strategy, we are able to capture the complexity and richness of Thomson's career as an inventor. Many studies of inventors have concentrated exclusively on how they invented just the machines; had I done the same in this book, I would be overlooking much of Thomson's creative effort. Thomson's talent and strength lay not only in inventing new devices but also in connecting them to business organization and marketing strategy. Because we associate technological innovation with heroic inventors and moments of brilliant inspiration, we often overlook the forging of these connections between business and technology. In fact, because Thomson does not conform to the standard role of the heroic inventor, he has been perceived by some scholars as merely an imitator whose work duplicated that of the pioneering geniuses.[19] Yet Thomson's work in joining technology and business required as much talent and genius as did the creation of revolutionary technology. Moreover, it is the forging of these links that permits a new technology to become commonplace. Because of Thomson's role

---

19 For a discussion of the standard role of the heroic inventor, see Douglas, *Inventing American Broadcasting*, pp. xxiv–xxv; and Wyn Wachhorst, *Thomas A. Edison: An American Myth* (Cambridge, Mass.: MIT Press, 1981). Passer regarded Thomson as a good engineer who followed up the pioneering work of Brush and Edison with more efficient and reliable machines: *The Electrical Manufacturers*, pp. 192–4. In his biography of Samuel Insull, Forrest McDonald harshly presented Thomson as a "cowbird" inventor who stole ideas from his rivals: *Insull* (University of Chicago Press, 1962), pp. 45–6.

in the large business organization, we are able to trace these links and consequently better understand the nature of the innovation process.

By examining how Thomson joined new hardware with new business structures and marketing strategies, we gain insight into the "second industrial revolution" that swept across America in the Gilded Age. As Chandler and other business historians have demonstrated, technological innovation stimulated organizational change; utilizing improvements in transportation, communications, and production technologies, businessmen transformed the small family firm into the modern corporation. With these new organizations, managers enlarged and organized production efficiently, created new national and international markets, and generally ensured the prosperity of American society.[20] Because Thomson played a prominent role in two dynamic central firms, the Thomson-Houston Electric Company and General Electric, his career provides a window through which we can see how firms utilized new technology to bring about those significant changes.

Viewing innovation as a process combining hardware, organization, and marketing strategy builds upon a well-established scholarly tradition. During the past 50 years, interpretations of invention have moved steadily away from a focus on technical genius to an analysis of the range of activities undertaken by inventors and businessmen. An early step in this direction was taken by Joseph Schumpeter, who replaced the heroic inventor with the heroic entrepreneur, emphasizing that the ability to manufacture and market an invention was as important as the creative genius required to synthesize it. Inspired by Schumpeter, Harold C. Passer, Arthur A. Bright, and John B. Rae studied the roles of entrepreneurs in establishing new industries such as automobiles and electricity. Their work revealed that the exploitation of new technology required innovations in finance, product design, manufacture, and marketing. Studying Edison and Elmer Sperry, Thomas P. Hughes drew in part on the tradition of entrepreneurial history to show that professional inventors develop their own methods of invention that embrace a variety of technical and business activities. Stuart W. Leslie

20 Alfred D. Chandler, Jr., *The Visible Hand: The Managerial Revolution in American Business* (Cambridge, Mass.: Belknap Press of Harvard University, 1977); Louis Galambos and Joseph Pratt, *The Rise of the Corporate Commonwealth* (New York: Basic Books, 1988), pp. 17–38; David A. Hounshell, *From the American System to Mass Production, 1800–1932* (Baltimore: Johns Hopkins University Press, 1984).

and George Wise have furthered this tradition by demonstrating how
Charles Kettering and Willis Whitney succeeded in the corporate context because of their skills as managers and organizational innovators.
More recently, John Law has made explicit this notion that technological change includes social, economic, political, and technical efforts
through his discussion of "heterogeneous engineering." Emerging
from this rich body of historical scholarship is an awareness that it is
no longer satisfactory to view technological innovation as a narrow
technical enterprise; the task now is to understand how creative inventors, managers, and engineers link these varied activities together.[21]

My approach to innovation has also been influenced by the scholarship of Alfred D. Chandler, Jr. Throughout his productive career,
Chandler has demonstrated that managers have built powerful and
lasting firms by developing first a strategy and then a structure for
tapping new markets and for utilizing new production technologies.[22]
In this story of Thomson and electric lighting, we shall see that Chandler is still correct; Thomson and his business associates succeeded
only when they deliberately designed their business organizations and
products in response to their marketing strategies. Yet whereas this
case fits the Chandlerian paradigm, it should also sharpen our under-

---

21 For a guide to the literature on entrepreneurial history, see Steven A. Sass,
   *Entrepreneurial Historians and History: Leadership and Rationality in Amer-
   ican Economic Historiography, 1940–1960* (New York: Garland Press,
   1986); and Stuart W. Leslie, "Whatever Happened to Entrepreneurial History?" (unpublished paper, History of Science Department, Johns Hopkins
   University, 1986). See also Joseph Schumpeter, *Theory of Economic Development* (Cambridge, Mass.: Harvard Economic Studies, 1934); Passer, *The
   Electrical Manufacturers;* Arthur A. Bright, Jr., *The Electric-Lamp Industry: Technological Change and Economic Development from 1800 to 1947*
   (New York: Macmillan, 1949; reprinted New York: Arno, 1972); John B.
   Rae, *The American Automobile: A Brief History* (University of Chicago Press,
   1965); Thomas P. Hughes, "Edison's Method," in W. Pickett, ed., *Technology
   at the Turning Point* (San Francisco Press, 1977); Thomas P. Hughes, *Elmer
   Sperry: Inventor and Engineer* (Baltimore: Johns Hopkins University Press,
   1971); Stuart W. Leslie, *"Boss" Kettering: Wizard of General Motors* (New
   York: Columbia University Press, 1983); George Wise, *Willis R. Whitney,
   General Electric, and the Origins of U.S. Industrial Research* (New York:
   Columbia University Press, 1985); and Law, "Technology and Heterogeneous
   Engineering."
22 Alfred D. Chandler, Jr., *Strategy and Structure: Chapters in the History of
   American Industrial Enterprise* (Cambridge, Mass.: MIT Press, 1962); Chan-
   dler, *The Visible Hand.*

standing of several key elements in the rise of big business. Intent on understanding the contours of managerial capitalism, Chandler said little about either the origins of technology or market demand. Chandler also assumed that businessmen built modern business enterprises using internally generated capital and that the pioneers did not have to innovate with regard to the mobilization of capital. In this study, I shall add to Chandler's organizational analysis by looking more closely at the content of technology and the ways in which entrepreneurs shaped markets and mobilized capital.

One might well ask how this book differs from the previous studies of the electrical industry by Hughes and Passer. With regard to Hughes's seminal study, *Networks of Power*, I would cite two differences. First, Hughes investigated the evolution of systems for generation and distribution in the United States, Great Britain, and Germany from the perspective of the utility company. This book investigates electric lighting and power systems from the perspective of the manufacturer of electrical equipment. Second, Hughes began his story with Edison and the central station and moved forward in time. A major goal of this study is to identify the origins of the central station as a strategy used by electrical manufacturers to sell equipment. In one sense, this book is the "prehistory" of Hughes's story of the evolution of electrical systems.

Turning to Passer, his study can be characterized as being macroeconomic, whereas this book is a microeconomic study. Whereas Passer concentrated on identifying trends across the industry, this study investigates how decisions were made within Thomson-Houston and General Electric. I have been able to undertake this microeconomic study because I have had access to the Thomson papers, a manuscript collection probably not available to Passer. Furthermore, although Passer was thoroughly familiar with electrical technology, he was not especially concerned with investigating the process by which this technology was created. Following Schumpeter, he tended to regard the invention process as a mysterious act performed by heroic individuals, and he did not inquire into how inventors actually worked. Instead, Passer focused on understanding the role of the entrepreneur in building the industry. In contrast, I seek to comprehend the process by which inventors and entrepreneurs interweave technology, organization, and strategy. Thus, this book complements Passer's study by taking a more detailed look at the role of technology in the operation of Thomson-Houston and General Electric, but at the same time it strikes out in new directions.

As the foregoing discussion of major themes and historiographic context suggests, this book is an investigation of innovation as a social process. Although this idea will be developed throughout the book, let me briefly indicate the major ways in which I see innovation as a social activity. First, unlike many historians of invention, I am viewing innovation not as the act of a lone individual but rather as an activity in which the inventor constantly interacts with a variety of people. Thomson worked with assistants, depended on his backers and managers for guidance, and responded to the needs of customers. Second, innovation is a social process in the sense that inventors join their artifacts with social organizations. As we shall see, in linking the hardware of electric lighting to a business structure, Thomson and Coffin were obliged to modify both entities. Third, by including marketing strategy as a component of the innovation process, I wish to suggest that the innovation process is not guided solely by technical and economic criteria but is also informed by social and cultural values. In devising a marketing strategy, Thomson and his business associates had to consider not only the price of their product but also the reasons why individuals would want to buy electric lighting. To convince individuals to purchase their product, Thomson and his partners had to identify and tie social meanings to their product; they had to show that electric lighting was useful, desirable, and an expression of modernity and material progress. This negotiation of social meanings took place through the definition and creation of central stations. A fourth way in which innovation is a social process concerns the knowledge base. Inventors such as Thomson brought to their creative endeavors a body of ideas, skills, and values that certainly influenced what they invented. Significantly, they acquired their particular bodies of knowledge in response to both personal needs and their social networks. Consequently, to appreciate the social construction of Thomson's inventions, we need to understand how he came to acquire his body of knowledge.

I am striving to draw a detailed picture of how Thomson went about the business of invention. This book should reveal that we can best understand the development of new technology by simultaneously examining related technical and business developments. If we wish to know how an inventor produced a particular device, it is necessary to inquire about his skills and values, his organizational situation, and the market perceptions associated with the new invention. It is not enough simply to consider how social context informs technological content; indeed, the challenge at hand is to understand how individuals simultaneously invent both content and context.

1. The cultivation of a scientific man

The city is the teacher of the man.
Simonides of Ceos
(ca. 556–468 B.C.)

One of the many advantages to be derived from the study of general science . . . is the amount of wholesome discipline which the mind undergoes in the formation of the moral and intellectual character. By dint of application, the mind attains strength, the judgement is matured, and the individual acquires correct ideas of his own powers, and the best modes of applying them.

Imperial Journal of Art, Science, Mechanics and Engineering
(1840)

At first glance, the details of Elihu Thomson's childhood and early adulthood parallel the life stories of other American technological heroes, such as Thomas Edison and Henry Ford. Like those famous men, Thomson came from a humble family; his parents were Scottish working-class immigrants. Like Edison, Elihu was a curious child who developed an early love of nature and knowledge. As a young man, he learned much from a few books and more from close observation of the machines surrounding him; such was the way that Ford learned about the industrial world. Thomson attended public school, but was forced to curtail his education in order to help support his family. Yet through ambition and hard work Thomson overcame those limitations to become a successful inventor.[1]

Despite these parallels, there are important differences between Thomson's early years and those of other prominent inventors. Unlike

---

1 Peter Collier and David Horowitz, *The Fords: An American Epic* (New York: Summit, 1987); Robert Lacey, *Ford: The Men and the Machine* (Boston: Little, Brown, 1986); Matthew Josephson, *Edison: A Biography* (New York: McGraw-Hill, 1959); Thomas P. Hughes, *Thomas Edison: Professional Inventor* (London: Her Majesty's Stationery Office, 1976); Harold C. Livesay, *American Made: Men Who Shaped the American Economy* (Boston: Little, Brown, 1979).

16

Ford, Thomson did not grow up on a farm, but in the heart of a bustling industrial city, Philadelphia. In the city, Thomson studied a rich array of industrial technology and observed how machines were reshaping American life. Growing up in Philadelphia, he received a sound education at Central High School, and he had access to technical and scientific institutions such as the Franklin Institute and the American Philosophical Society. Philadelphia offered a host of opportunities for a bright and ambitious boy.

Thomson's early years also differed from those of other American inventors in that he was educated in science. In his youth, Thomson was an ardent student of science; studying it on his own and in high school, he was impressed with the experimental method, an ideology of self-discipline, and the rituals and rewards of the scientific community. Thomson was so taken with the intellectual order and social prestige of science that after graduating from high school he embarked on building a scientific career for himself in Philadelphia. Thomson's interest in science does not conform with the traditional image of the heroic inventor who, like Edison, is supposed to have had little use for abstract theories and elitist scientific societies.[2] Yet for Thomson, both the content and social structure of science were highly significant; as a teenager and young man, science provided employment, ideals, and a community with which to identify.

This chapter describes how Thomson became interested in science, what he learned while studying and practicing it, and how he fashioned a career for himself in science. As later chapters will show, it was the skills and values (as opposed to theoretical knowledge) that Thomson acquired while doing science in the 1870s that permitted him to become a successful inventor of electric lighting systems.[3]

---

2 David A. Hounshell, "Edison and the Pure Science Ideal in 19th-Century America," *Science*, 207:612–17 (8 February 1980); W. Bernard Carlson, "Building Thomas Edison's Laboratory at West Orange, New Jersey: A Case Study in Using Craft Knowledge for Technological Invention, 1886–1888," *History of Technology*, 13 (1991).

3 My thinking on scientific career building has been shaped by the work of Charles Rosenberg: "Science and Social Values in Nineteenth-Century America: A Case in the Growth of Scientific Institutions," in *No Other Gods: On Science and American Cultural Thought* (Baltimore: Johns Hopkins University Press, 1976), p. 151; and "Science in American Society: A Generation of Historical Debate," *Isis*, 74:356–67 (September 1983), especially pp. 365–6.

Family background and early years

Elihu Thomson was born into a Scottish family of mechanics and artisans. Elihu's paternal grandfather, James Thomson, was a mechanic who worked in Glasgow, Paisley, Carlisle, and Manchester. James had 12 children, of whom Daniel (1829–1904), Elihu's father, was the youngest. Following his father's footsteps, Daniel became a mechanic. As mechanics, both James and Daniel specialized in the construction and installation of factory machinery, an occupation that required a general knowledge of existing technology and industrial practice.

On his mother's side, Elihu's family can be traced to his great-grandfather, James Tenant, a prosperous Huguenot shipowner who migrated to Scotland in the eighteenth century. He had three children, including a daughter, Nancy, who married a Scottish bootmaker, James Rhodes. Mary Ann (1828–1903), Elihu's mother, was one of the 10 Rhodes children raised in England. Mary Ann Rhodes married Daniel Thomson in Manchester, England, in 1850. Together, they settled in that industrial city, where Daniel was able to find work.[4]

Elihu was born in Manchester on 29 March 1853, the second of seven children. Whereas most of his brothers and sisters were auburn-haired and blue-eyed, Elihu had brown hair and gray eyes. He was given the distinctive biblical name of Elihu in honor of a paternal uncle. A blacksmith, that uncle was remembered as being so skilled that he could shape a piece of iron to the required dimensions without using a gauge or ruler.[5]

As a mechanic, Daniel Thomson was a member of the working-class elite, a group that comprised skilled craftsmen, artisans, and foremen. But even as an elite workingman he found it difficult to obtain steady work. Thus, when he found himself unemployed during an economic depression in Britain, he decided to migrate to America. After landing in New York in March 1858, Daniel took his family at once to Philadelphia. Most likely, he chose to settle there because he hoped to find work in the city's extensive iron and machine-tool industries. In addition, Philadelphia may have been appealing to a Scotsman because

---

4 "No. 1 Genealogical Memoranda as to Family," 1919, Notebook, TP. George B. Thomson, Elihu Thomson's grandson, provided additional family history: George B. Thomson to the author, 10 August 1982 and 18 December 1982.
5 Untitled, Autobiog. Papers, TP.

its textile mills had already attracted numerous Scottish and English workers.[6]

In Philadelphia, Daniel secured a position in the Southwark Foundry of Merrick & Sons. Employing over 350 men, Merrick & Sons was famous for its boilers, steam engines, machine tools, and sugar-refining equipment. The firm also operated a shipyard on the Delaware River, where it built many of the first steam-powered warships used by the U.S. Navy. At Merrick & Sons, Daniel first worked in the shipyard, but he later specialized in erecting sugar-refining equipment. To be close to his work, in late 1858 Daniel moved his family to the South-wark neighborhood in South Philadelphia. The family lived first at 920 Cross Street before purchasing a row house at 517 Pierce Street.[7]

Because of his work installing sugar-refining machinery, Daniel traveled frequently, and he spent parts of many years working in Cuba. Daniel's absences meant that the responsibility for raising the Thomson children fell upon their mother, Mary Ann. Later in life, Elihu seldom spoke of his father, perhaps because they had seen each other so little. Elihu's father taught him to read, but his only other positive recollection of his father was that he once was praised for running the household while his mother was away.[8]

In contrast to his father, Elihu's mother was a great influence in his life. Mary Ann was plainly a strong woman; over 20 years she gave birth to 11 children and endured the tragedy of losing four daughters as infants. Her strength and virtues made a lasting impression on Elihu. At an early age she taught him to work hard, having him sweep and scrub the front stoop of their row house. She had him help in the kitchen, where she taught him how to bake bread and pies. Beyond the kitchen, Mary Ann was interested in astronomy, and she showed her

6 "First Impressions of the Seas," Autobiog. Papers, TP.
7 "Early Days in Philadelphia," Autobiog. Papers, TP. For a description of the work done at the Southwark Foundry, see advertisement in *J. Franklin Inst.*, 95 (June 1873). See also J. Leander Bishop, *A History of American Manufactures*, 3 vols. (Philadelphia: Edward Young, 1868), Vol. 3, pp. 27–8; and Bruce Sinclair, *Philadelphia's Philosopher Mechanics: A History of the Franklin Institute, 1824–1865* (Baltimore: Johns Hopkins University Press, 1974), pp. 290–1. 920 Cross Street is the address from 1860 manuscript census schedule, PSHP. The Thomson family probably resided there from 1858 to 1863. In 1863, Mary Ann Thomson purchased 517 Pierce Street; see deed abstract for 517 Pierce Street, Department of Records, City of Philadelphia.
8 Clarissa Thomson, "Notes on Elihu Thomson's Early Life," Biographical Material, TP.

son stars, comets, and meteor showers in the evening sky. An Episcopalian, she sent Elihu to church regularly, even though he preferred to play in the fields on Sunday mornings. Most of all, however, his mother taught him perseverance and ambition. At various times during his career, Elihu was known to quote a verse he learned from her:

> All that other folks can do,
> Why, with patience, may not you;
> Always keep that point in view,
> And try again.[9]

Observing Philadelphia technology

As a boy, Thomson quickly became a keen observer of people and scenes, and he thoroughly explored the neighborhood of Southwark. In the 1860s, Southwark was a relatively new section of Philadelphia, built to accommodate an influx of immigrants. Although there were many Irish immigrants in Southwark, there also were native white American, Scottish, and German workers. Consisting of street after street of small row houses, the monotony of the neighborhood's architecture was broken only by small corner shops and an occasional factory. Yet because it was a new neighborhood, there was open space near Southwark. A map of Philadelphia from the 1860s shows that if Thomson walked only a few blocks south of his home on Pierce Street he would find open fields. As a youngster, Thomson delighted in exploring those fields, kindling an interest in the natural world.[10]

Interesting as the open fields were, Thomson was more strongly attracted to the technological world of factories, machines, and rail-

9 "Notes on ET's Early Life," "Philadelphia Days," "Philadelphia – Continued," and "Attitudes as to Religious Beliefs," Autobiog. Papers, TP. From 1851 to 1873, Mary Ann Thomson had a child nearly every two years; the daughters who died were Mary A. (1857–8), Annie Laura (1859–65), Annie Amelia (1864–5), and Aubrey B. (1868–74); see "No. 1 Genealogical Memoranda as to Family," Notebook, TP. For a discussion of how another mother influenced the career of an American inventor, see Gordon Bordewyk and Gregory Green, "Ford, His Mother, and Progress," *Michigan History,* 65:39–46 (September–October 1984).

10 For a general description of the physical features of Philadelphia in the 1860s, see Sam Bass Warner, Jr., *The Private City: Philadelphia in Three Periods of Its Growth* (Philadelphia: University of Pennsylvania Press, 1968), pp. 49–62. For the ethnic makeup of Southwark, see manuscript census schedules for 1860, 1870, and 1880, PSHP. See also "Early Days in Philadelphia," Autobiog. Papers, TP.

The cultivation of a scientific man

The cultivation of a scientific man

Table 1.1. *Major industries of Philadelphia, 1860*

Type of business	Number of establishments	Capital (millions)	Number of employees
Clothing	352	$ 4.37	14,387
Gas works	3	3.9	863
Cotton textiles	132	3.5	8,938
Leather	130	2.9	1,666
Iron products	65	2.6	2,734
Breweries	68	2.1	596
Book publishing	42	1.9	844
Chemicals	35	1.86	737
Shipbuilding	16	1.75	958
Machinery	63	1.72	1,983
Boots and shoes	701	1.7	8,424
Locomotives	2	1.6	1,255
Sugar refining	8	1.5	478
Bricks	44	1.26	1,965
Cured meats	23	1.14	238

Source: J. L. Bishop, *A History of American Manufacture*, 3 vols. (Philadelphia: Edward Young, 1868), Vol. 3, pp.14-17.

roads. For a boy curious about this industrial world, mid-nineteenth-century Philadelphia was a marvelous place to live. Because of capital from mercantile enterprises, coal and iron from northeastern Pennsylvania, and a transportation network of railroads and canals, Philadelphia had grown to be the second largest industrial center in America. In 1860, the city had a population of 565,000 and supported 6,200 manufacturing establishments. Philadelphia's industry employed 100,000 men and women, was capitalized at $73.3 million, and produced $135.9 million worth of goods. Rather than concentrating on a few products, Philadelphia's factories produced a wide range of goods (Table 1.1). Although clothing, cotton textiles, and leather goods were the largest industries, the city also had a significant number of plants producing iron products, machinery, and chemicals. By 1860, in certain areas, individual firms had achieved national and even international prominence: Baldwin locomotives were used by railroads worldwide, and William Sellers & Co. was known for its excellent machine tools.[11]

11 Thomas C. Cochran, *Frontiers of Change: Early Industrialism in America* (Oxford University Press, 1981); Bruce Laurie and Mark Schmitz, "Manufacture and Productivity: The Making of an Industrial Base, Philadelphia, 1850–1880," in Theodore Hershberg, ed., *Philadelphia: Work, Space, Family, and Group Experience in the Nineteenth Century* (Oxford University Press, 1981), pp. 43–92; Elizabeth M. Geffen, "Industrial Development and

Unlike other cities, where factories tended to be located in outlying districts, Philadelphia's factories were scattered throughout the city, mingling with both residential and commercial neighborhoods. For Thomson, that meant that his home on Pierce Street was surrounded by industrial sites. He was a frequent visitor to the foundry and shipyard where his father worked, and he probably also visited the stove works, glassworks, firebrick factory, and shot tower near his home. Somewhat farther away, but still accessible to a curious lad, were the Philadelphia gas works, the Navy Yard, and chemical plants. For a look at craft technology, Thomson could have visited any of the many small shops near Pierce Street; there he would have observed cigarmakers, butchers, and carpenters plying their trades (Figure 1.1).

In his autobiographical notes, Thomson recalled a variety of technological scenes. He described seeing a munitions factory explode during the Civil War, watching trains on Washington Street shuttle freight between the Delaware and Schuylkill rivers, and observing water and gas mains being laid in the streets. In visiting those different plants, shops, and construction sites, Thomson was able not only to see machines in operation but also to examine how they were constructed by skilled workmen. Technological progress was something young Elihu saw firsthand in his own neighborhood, and he was deeply impressed with how technology was altering the daily patterns of life. Influenced by what he saw, it is not surprising that for his high-school graduation address he chose to speak on "The Manufactures of Philadelphia."[12]

Social Crisis, 1841–1854," in Russell F. Weigley, ed., *Philadelphia: A 300-Year History* (New York: Norton, 1982), pp. 307–62; John H. White, Jr., *A History of the American Locomotive: Its Development, 1830–1880* (New York: Dover, 1979), pp. 27–8; and Philip Scranton, "Milling About: Family Firms and Urban Manufacturing in Textile Philadelphia, 1840–1865," *Journal of Urban History*, 10:259–94 (May 1984). Statistics are from Bishop, *A History of American Manufactures*, Vol. 3, p. 14.

12 ET to P. F. Brockett, 26 January 1933, CL; "Philadelphia–Continued," "Early Days in Philadelphia," "Philadelphia Days," Autobiog. Papers, TP; and "The Manufactures of Philadelphia," in Collected essays, TP. To determine what factories and technological sites were near ET's homes, see Ernest Hexamer and William Lochner, *Maps of the City of Philadelphia* (Philadelphia: Hexamer & Lochner, 1860), especially Vol. 7 (Philadelphia City Archives). For information on the shops and businesses in the Pierce Street area, I used a computer sorting of the 1870 business directory by grid square made available to me by the Philadelphia Social History Project.

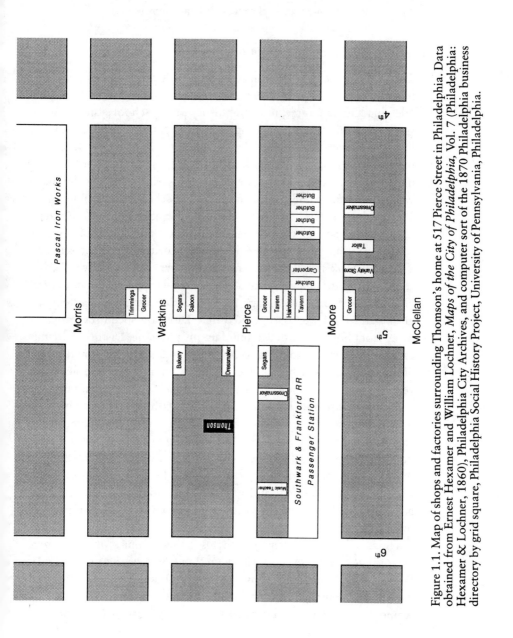

Figure 1.1. Map of shops and factories surrounding Thomson's home at 517 Pierce Street in Philadelphia. Data obtained from Ernest Hexamer and William Lochner, *Maps of the City of Philadelphia*, Vol. 7 (Philadelphia: Hexamer & Lochner, 1860), Philadelphia City Archives, and computer sort of the 1870 Philadelphia business directory by grid square, Philadelphia Social History Project, University of Pennsylvania, Philadelphia.

Education in and out of school

The urban context further shaped Thomson's childhood by providing him the opportunity to receive a public education. Since 1834, Philadelphia had had a free, noncompulsory public school system. Thomson's schooling began at age six, when his parents enrolled him in a local elementary school. Initially, he did not care much for the elderly women who taught in that school, but under the tutelage of his first male teacher, George Stuart, he began to excel. He did exceptionally well in arithmetic and completed grammar school by age nine.

For a bright pupil such as Thomson, the next step was to attend Central High School, the premier institution in the Philadelphia public school system. (This school will be described in the next section.) Thomson took the entrance examination when he was age 11, but could not matriculate because school regulations required Central High students to be at least age 13. Rather than continue to attend the grammar school, Stuart suggested that Thomson spend several years away from books in order to build up his physique. Disturbed by this proposal, Thomson told Stuart and his parents that he would rather die than do without books. He got his way, and over the next two years he embarked upon a remarkable period of self-education.[13]

During that period, his education took three forms: He read popular books about science, constructed scientific apparatus, and imitated the technical processes he saw around him. From reading, he not only obtained new knowledge about science but also absorbed something of the ideology and methodology of science. In constructing different devices and duplicating technical processes, Thomson developed manual skills and discovered the satisfaction of converting ideas into functioning devices.

Thomson's reading began with his father's copies of the *Imperial Journal of Art, Science, Mechanics and Engineering* (Figure 1.2). Published in Manchester, England, in 1840 and 1841, that journal was in the spirit of the mechanics-institute movement, which attempted to enlighten and control the working class through the pro-

13 On the development of public education in Philadelphia and elsewhere, see Warner, *The Private City*, pp. 111–23; and Michael B. Katz, *The Irony of Early School Reform: Educational Innovation in Mid-Nineteenth Century Massachusetts* (Cambridge, Mass.: Harvard University Press, 1969). See also "Early Days in Philadelphia," Autobiog. Papers, TP.

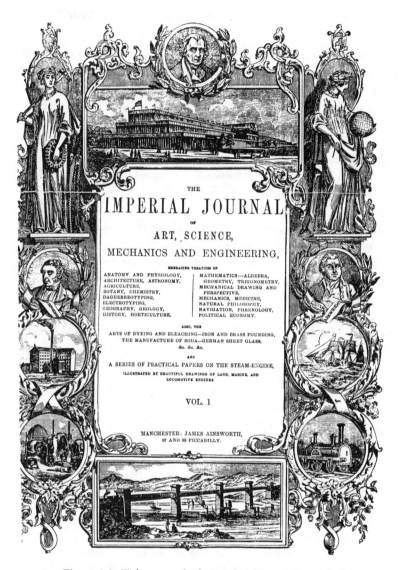

Figure 1.2. Title page of *The Imperial Journal of Art, Science, Mechanics and Engineering*, Vol. 1 (Manchester, 1840).

motion of science. In the Preface, the editors of the *Imperial Journal* explained that

> this work is principally intended to strengthen the intellect, elevate the moral character, and improve the social condition of the opera-

tive classes, by instructing them in the principles and practices of their several vocations.[14]

The periodical sought to accomplish those goals by surveying a wide range of topics in science and technology. Its articles covered the basic principles of anatomy, arithmetic, astronomy, chemistry, natural history, geology, natural philosophy, and medicine. Detailed descriptions were given concerning the manufacture of iron, coal mining, textile dyeing, and the construction of locomotives. There were illustrations of the telegraph, steam engines, and various mechanical inventions. Encyclopedic in scope, the *Imperial Journal* fascinated Thomson, and he spent many hours reading about the wonders of science and technology.[15]

Beyond its long descriptions and numerous illustrations, the *Imperial Journal* sought to impress its readers with the importance of the inductive method of science: Through observation and experimentation, anyone was capable of gathering facts. By applying reason to the gathered data, one was expected to deduce general principles, not only about the physical world but also about the structure and order of human society. The *Imperial Journal* stressed that by studying science and learning how to reason, one could improve oneself and advance socially. As it explained in its long-winded way,

> one of the many advantages to be derived from the study of general science, independent of its practical applications, is the amount of wholesome discipline which the mind undergoes in its investigations, and the influence which it exerts in the formation of the moral and intellectual character. By dint of application, the mind attains strength, the judgement is matured, and the individual acquires correct ideas of his own powers, and the best modes of applying them. Taught by habitual analysis of evidence rightly to esteem *facts*, and trained by a practical logic to the vigorous use of his reasoning faculties, he insensibly contracts an abstract love of truth, and renders the mental powers pliant and ready to bend to objects at once useful and sublime.... He may be deficient in many ornamental accomplishments, which it were desirable to possess; but there are

14 "Preface," *The Imperial Journal of Art, Science, Mechanics and Engineering* (Manchester, England), 1:iii (1840) (hereafter cited as *Imperial Journal*). For a discussion of the English mechanics-institute movement, see Steven Shapin and Barry Barnes, "Science, Nature, and Control: Interpreting Mechanics' Institutes," *Social Studies of Science*, 7:31–74 (1977).

15 "Continuation of Activities During Stay out of School," Autobiog. Papers, TP.

none of the honourable avocations of life in which such discipline of the mind will not be abundantly useful.[16]

The *Imperial Journal* reinforced the message of self-discipline by including biographies of famous scientists. In recounting the lives of Galileo, Francis Bacon, Benjamin Franklin, and others, the journal stressed how these men had used reason and self-control to contribute to human knowledge.

In all likelihood, Thomson read the *Imperial Journal* because he was interested in its factual content; intrigued by the technology he saw around him, he wished to know more. In reading the articles, however, he also must have absorbed the empirical methodology and ideology of self-discipline, because he later expressed similar ideas in his high-school writing and activities. Over time, Thomson integrated these values into his style as an inventor.

Of the many articles in the *Imperial Journal,* Thomson was particularly fascinated by those on photography. Disappointed that they did not go beyond the rudiments of this new art, he asked his mother for a book about photography. Unable to find a book on the subject, she instead presented him with *The Magician's Own Book.* At first, Thomson thought that this volume contained only instruction on legerdemain, card tricks, and numerical puzzles, but he soon discovered that its later chapters described hundreds of experiments in chemistry, electricity, optics, mechanics, and acoustics. Using household utensils and chemicals from the local drugstore, Thomson performed vivid chemical experiments, generated static electricity, and delighted in creating optical illusions. The experiments in *The Magician's Own Book* were aimed at demonstrating the spectacular: bright sparks, brilliant color changes, and remarkable transformations of ordinary substances. Although the book did not explain the principles behind the experiments (chemical reactions were discussed in terms of simple affinity), Thomson was not concerned; he was enthralled by the wonderful effects he could produce. If the *Imperial Journal* had exhorted him to observe and experiment, then *The Magician's Own Book* provided numerous experiments for him to try.[17]

16 "Preface" and "Introduction to the Study of Physical Sciences," *Imperial Journal,* 1:iii and 1:7–8.

17 *The Magician's Own Book or the Whole Art of Conjuring* (New York: Dick & Fitzgerald, 1857); "Continuation of Activities During Stay out of School," Autobiog. Papers, TP.

Figure 1.3. Wine-bottle electrostatic machine constructed by Thomson as a boy. From the collections of the Franklin Institute Science Museum, Philadelphia. Photo by the author.

From *The Magician's Own Book* Thomson first learned about electricity. Included in its pages were instructions for building Leyden jars, galvanic cells, an electrostatic machine, and an electromagnet. In terms of theory, there were only rules of thumb about obtaining static charges from rubbing silk and glass or amber and wool; there was no mention of positive or negative charge. Nonetheless, its coverage of the empirical aspects of electricity was remarkable for a popular book of that period. By constructing the apparatus and following the experiments, Thomson was introduced to many of the static and galvanic electrical effects commonly known in the 1860s.

Of the apparatus described in the book, Thomson was especially interested in the electrostatic machine. Following the instructions, he constructed such a machine from a wine bottle, a piece of silk, and some wood scraps. When he turned the handle, the glass bottle rubbed against the silk, creating a static charge that could be discharged as a spark or stored in a Leyden jar (Figure 1.3). The construction of this machine represented quite an accomplishment for a boy of age 11 or 12, because it required drilling a hole in the bottom of the wine bottle, as well as careful preparation of the amalgam, a metallic mixture used to improve the machine's generating qualities. With this machine, Thomson tried many tricks and experiments; *The Magician's Own Book* showed how to draw off sparks, make pith toys dance, create the "electric kiss," and cause hair to stand on end. In building and operating this machine, Thomson undoubtedly learned much about the vagaries of static electricity.[18]

In his autobiographical notes, Thomson recounted how his electrostatic machine had brought about an encounter with his father. His father had previously taken electric shocks for medical purposes, and he ridiculed his son's efforts at producing electricity with his homemade machine. Hurt by his father's disparaging remarks, Thomson set up a battery of Leyden jars for storing up electrical charge. He then cranked his machine hundreds of times, and on a crisp winter night he invited his father to take another shock. That shock was strong enough to cause his father to throw his arms back violently. The young boy laughed heartily about tricking his father in this way. Following the incident, Thomson's father apparently was cautious about criticizing his son's experiments.[19] In a larger sense, Thomson learned for the first time how he could use a technological artifact to redefine a social relationship.

Besides the electrostatic machine, Thomson built other devices during his time out of school. He constructed a microscope, a camera, galvanic cells, an electromagnet, and telegraph instruments. With the telegraph set, he showed both ingenuity and manual skill; unable to secure any insulated wire for his relay coils, he insulated copper wire by wrapping cotton thread around it. Thomson even ambitiously set up a small iron furnace in his backyard and tried to cast a piston cylinder for a toy steam engine. Such projects seem to have been typical for future inventors; both Elmer Sperry and Charles Brush constructed models and toys when they were boys. In doing so, Thomson and these other inventors acquired not only skill in using tools but also an ability to visualize and develop their ideas through the manipulation of objects.[20]

---

18 See *The Magician's Own Book*, pp. 120–46. For Brush building a similar machine, see Harry J. Eisenmann III, "Charles F. Brush: Pioneer Innovator in Electrical Technology" (unpublished Ph.D. thesis, Department of History, Case Institute of Technology, 1967), p. 13.

19 "Continuation of Activities During Stay out of School," Autobiog. Papers, TP.

20 "Continuation of Activities During Stay out of School" and "Interest in Optical Work," Autobiog. Papers, TP. " 'Electrical World' Portraits. – II. Elihu Thomson," *Electrical World*, 12:102 (1 September 1888); "Philadelphia

Science at Central High School

In two years of reading popular science books, performing experiments, and building apparatus, Thomson learned much about science and technology. He was impressed by their wonders and was exposed to the experimental method and an ideology of science as a means of self-discipline. He began to develop the manual skills necessary for translating abstract ideas into three-dimensional objects or machines. His self-education did have gaps, though; he had not yet come to see science as an organized body of knowledge or as a community of practitioners. His education had not covered many subjects, and it lacked thoroughness and orderliness. Thomson remedied those deficiencies by attending Central High School from 1866 to 1870.

Established in 1836, Central High School was one of the first public high schools in America. In its early years the school was greatly influenced by Alexander Dallas Bache, who established a curriculum combining science, business, and the classics. Known as the "people's college," Central High in the nineteenth century was attended by bright boys from the lower middle and working classes. By providing a broad education with some business skills, the school helped these youngsters move securely into the middle class as clerks, storekeepers, and professionals. For a select few, Central High provided the preparation for the university or medical school. For Thomson and his classmates, Central High was very much an avenue of upward mobility; along with Thomson, who became a successful inventor, his class included Robert E. Pattison, twice governor of Pennsylvania, Dewey Bates, a successful painter in England, and others who became prominent businessmen and lawyers in Philadelphia. For these young men, Central High was a way out of the working class, and they consequently took their education quite seriously. Associating with these young men at Central High undoubtedly stimulated in Thomson a desire to advance himself.[21]

Days," Autobiog. Papers, TP; "Iron Founding," *Imperial Journal,* 1:593–6 (1840). On Brush and Sperry doing the same, see Eisenmann, "Brush," pp. 12–17; and Thomas P. Hughes, *Elmer Sperry: Inventor and Engineer* (Baltimore: Johns Hopkins University Press, 1971), p. 5.

21 Franklin Spencer Edmunds, *History of the Central High School of Philadelphia* (Philadelphia: Lippincott, 1902) (hereafter cited as *History of CHS*); David F. Labaree, "The People's College: A Sociological Analysis of the Cen-

Figure 1.4. Thomson as a student at Central High School, circa 1866–70. From Thomson Papers, American Philosophical Society, Philadelphia.

During the years Thomson attended Central High School, the curriculum was well suited for helping ambitious boys become men capable of handling practical business affairs. Although the students studied Latin and German, they spent much more time taking courses in physics, calculus, chemistry, astronomy, and physiology. To develop business skills, they studied composition, bookkeeping, political economy, and drawing. There were no electives in the curriculum, and each student had to pass every course.[22]

Thomson entered Central High School in February 1866. The school was located in an imposing brick building at the corner of Broad and Green streets, and Thomson frequently walked three miles to and from school (Figures 1.4 and 1.5). His report cards show that he had an occasional poor term, but that he did very well in his last two years, standing generally in the top 10 of his class. Thomson was not particularly proficient in German or declamation, and he disliked Latin so much that he did just enough work to keep from failing. In a poem,

tral High School of Philadelphia, 1838–1939" (Ph.D. dissertation, Department of Sociology, University of Pennsylvania, 1983); and John Thomas Scharf and Thompson Wescott, *History of Philadelphia, 1609–1884,* 3 vols. (Philadelphia: L. H. Everts, 1884), Vol. III, pp. 1928–32. For details on Thomson's classmates, see "Seen and Heard in Many Places," Philadelphia *Times,* 29 April 1898, in Scrapbook, Notebooks, TP.

22 Edmunds, *History of CHS,* pp. 207–8.

Figure 1.5. Central High School. From M. King, *Philadelphia and Notable Philadelphians* (New York: 1901), p. 13.

he quipped that "Caesar and Virgil had their time / but now they claim a part of mine."[23]

Bored by the required languages, Thomson was enthusiastic about his science courses. In physiology, natural philosophy, and mathematics he took careful notes, often with detailed sketches. These notes reveal that he learned his science in an orderly way, with general principles followed by examples, facts, and experiments. His science classes involved a balance of theory and practice; a chemistry examination dating from just before Thomson's time at Central High had questions on the theories behind electricity and heat, the preparation of ethyl and acetal alcohol, and the history of the steam engine. The courses were also exhaustive; in anatomy, for instance, Thomson studied the entire human body, including bone structure, arrangements of muscles and digestive, nervous, and circulatory systems, and sexual

23 Nicholas H. Maguire to [Daniel Thomson], 13 February 1866, Scrapbook, Notebooks, TP; "The Period of the Civil War," Autobiog. Papers, TP; "Central High School Monthly Reports," 1866–70, CL, TP. Quotation is from "Lines by a Lover of Science," in "The Universal Journal: Being a Journal of Romance, Art, Science, and Literature Generally" (hereafter cited as "Universal Journal"), No. 3 (September 1868), Collected Essays, TP.

reproduction. The school possessed a well-equipped astronomical observatory, but Thomson was disappointed that the students were not permitted to use the telescopes as much as he would have liked. Given the range and thoroughness with which science was taught at Central High, Thomson received one of the better educations in science available in America in the 1860s.[24]

By far the most informative course that Thomson took was natural philosophy, with Edwin J. Houston. Appointed professor of physical geography and natural philosophy in 1867, Houston was a graduate of Central High and had spent a year studying abroad at the universities of Berlin and Heidelberg. He brought to his lectures an extensive knowledge of electricity and regularly illustrated them with elaborate apparatus. From Houston's lectures Thomson learned Ohm's law, Faraday's law of electrolysis, and the principles of induction. In class, Houston also explained how arc lights, the telegraph, and electric motors worked, giving Thomson a practical sense of how electricity could be employed. To supplement his lectures, Houston assigned problems from Benjamin Silliman's *Principles of Physics,* a college-level textbook, which Thomson found to be a complete and orderly catalog of physical phenomena. Excited by what he was learning, he wrote that "electricity seems destined at some future period to become applied to every manufacture and to every art. Lightning will be the future slave of man." Impressed by the content and orderliness of Houston's lectures, it is not surprising that Houston became one of his favorite teachers.[25]

Thomson's science courses inspired him to continue to experiment and construct apparatus. He acquired a small foot-powered lathe, tried his hand at glassblowing, and performed chemical experiments on a small scale. In the bathhouse behind his home, Thomson set up a small

24 See the following high-school notebooks in TP: "Anatomy and Physiology Lectures in Osteology by Prof. Holt D term," "Anatomy and Physiology by Prof. Holt C term," "Lectures in Anatomy and Physiology by Dr. Holt C-B term," "Lectures on Beverages A term, Sept. 1869," "Mathematics McClune E term," and "Mathematics McClune." See also Edmunds, *History of CHS,* p. 212; "History of the Forty-Ninth Graduating Class of the CHS of Philadelphia," CHS Archives, pp. 40–1; and "Universal Journal," Vol. 2, No. 1 (1869), Collected Essays, TP.

25 Edmunds, *History of CHS,* pp. 211, 331; "Professor Houston's Lectures A term," Notebook, TP; Benjamin Silliman, *Principles of Physics, or Natural Philosophy,* 2nd ed. (Philadelphia: Theodore Bliss, 1865). Quotation is from "Universal Journal," No. 10, Collected Essays, TP.

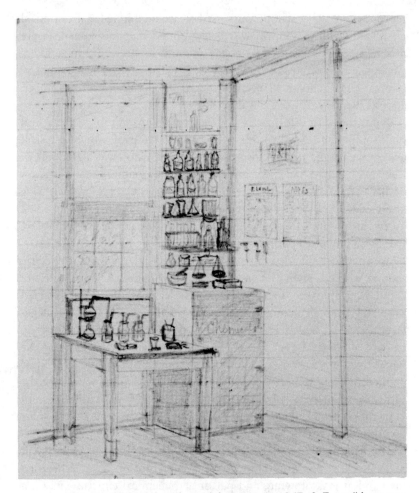

Figure 1.6. Thomson's home laboratory in 1867–8. From "Anatomy and Physiology Lectures in Osteology by Professor Holt" notebook, Thomson Papers, American Philosophical Society, Philadelphia.

laboratory, stocking it with chemicals purchased at the local drugstore (Figure 1.6). In his home laboratory he studied different phosphorous compounds and noticed that positive and negative sparks from a Leyden jar left different impressions on glass plates covered with wax, a discovery that he boldly claimed as original. Fascinated by chemistry, he visited a nearby chemical works to observe the production of acids,

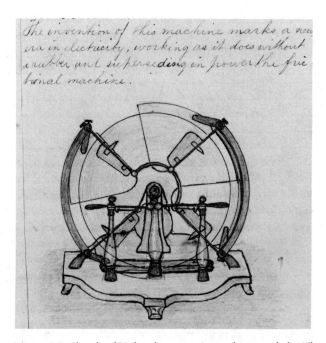

Figure 1.7. Sketch of Holtz electrostatic machine made by Thomson, circa 1868. From "Professor Houston's Lectures" notebook, Thomson Papers, American Philosophical Society, Philadelphia.

paints, and pigments.[26] Such observations and experiments added a tangible dimension to the chemistry he was learning in the classroom.

Deeply interested in electricity, Thomson visited the Franklin Institute in September 1866 to see a demonstration of a Holtz electrostatic machine. Recently developed in Europe, that machine produced a torrent of high-voltage sparks through induction between two revolving glass plates; compared with his homemade wine-bottle machine, the Holtz machine must have seemed marvelous to Thomson (Figure 1.7). After seeing a second Holtz machine in the showroom of James Queen & Co., a large instrument manufacturer, Thomson resolved to master the theory behind the machine and build one himself. In seeing apparatus such as the Holtz machine, Thomson was becoming aware

26 "Re. Central High School," Autobiog. Papers, TP; ET to P. Brockett, 26 January 1933, CL, TP; "Lectures on Beverages" and "Anatomy and Physiology Lectures in Osteology by Prof. Holt," Notebooks, TP.

that science was not simply an abstract, untouchable set of truths, but, more important, a set of concepts to be studied empirically.[27]

Thomson's enthusiasm for science spilled over into his other courses, especially composition. To make the routine chore of writing essays tolerable, Thomson frequently wrote on scientific subjects. In some essays he was factual and descriptive; he explained the physical properties of steam, how a microscope worked, and the uses of photography. In others he emphasized the importance of science for material progress. Not only had science uncovered the secrets of the stars, but, as Thomson observed, it had contributed directly to the development of major inventions, such as the steam engine, azo dyes, improvements in medicine, and the telegraph. He was especially impressed with chemistry:

> Chemistry now ranks as one of the most important of the sciences. The reason for its occupying such a position is perceived when we consider its manifold applications in the arts and manufactures. In proportion as advancement is made in it, so the wealth and prosperity of a nation, other things being equal, increase.[28]

Appreciative of scientific discoveries, Thomson readily saw scientists and inventors as heroes. Sprinkled throughout his compositions were references to the genius of James Watt, Benjamin Franklin, and Sir Humphrey Davy. Using intellect and reason, these men had contributed to the material progress of civilization, and he felt certain that they would be remembered by posterity. "When the names of the world's conquerors shall have passed from men's lips," he wrote, "the names of her philosophers will live, unfading even when 'the sun himself shall grow dim with age, and nature sink in years'."[29] Impressed, perhaps Thomson dreamed of becoming an immortal scientist or inventor.

In addition to writing about science in his essays, during his last two years in high school he produced a scientific journal. With his friend

27 "Continuation of Activities During Stay out of School," Autobiog. Papers, TP. See *J. Franklin Inst.*, 82:281–3 (October 1866), for the demonstration ET presumably attended.

28 "The Chemical Nature of Steam," "The Microscope," "The Photographic Art," "Alchemy," Collected Essays, TP. Quotation is from "Chemistry," Collected Essays, TP.

29 "Intellect," Collected Essays, TP. Quotation is from "The Triumphs of Science," Central High School *Monthly Portfolio* (October 1869), Collected Essays, TP.

Harry Willis, Thomson prepared in longhand "The Universal Journal: Being a Journal of Romance, Art, Science, and Literature Generally." Like other informal student publications at Central High, it probably circulated among Thomson's friends.[30] Inspired by the *Imperial Journal* and perhaps other scientific publications they had seen at school, Thomson and Willis tried to make the "Universal Journal" as scientific as possible. Thomson wrote articles on the microscope and a new theory of meteoric showers, and Willis prepared stories on geology. Much of the text was devoted to small fillers that ranged from reports of fossils to cures for rattlesnake bites to ideas for chemically preserving wood. One notable article was titled "Excitement and its effects on Life." Drawing on the Victorian theory of vital bodily energy he had learned in his physiology class, Thomson warned that "unnatural and unreasonable excitement is one of the deadliest foes to long life." Reflecting that one can live life either quickly or slowly and consume one's stock of vitality proportionately, he suggested that life was governed by the formula $D = V \times T$, with D being a constant, V the velocity of life, and T the length of life. Although somewhat overzealous in quantifying the amount of excitement in life, Thomson had learned the importance of expressing science relationships in mathematical terms.[31]

The "Universal Journal" also served as the publication for a scientific society created by Thomson and Willis. Out of the group of boys with whom they regularly walked to school, they organized the "Junior Scientific and Literary Society." Although they frequently went hunting for minerals, went swimming, or explored local points of interest, the members of the society also met to practice the speeches they were required to give at school. Gathering in the bathhouse behind Thomson's home on Pierce Street, the members at first rehearsed their declamations, but soon started hearing lectures by Thomson on chemistry and by Willis on geology. Thomson supplemented his lectures by demonstrations of chemical reactions and endeavored to present the principles behind the experiments. The soci-

---

30 Copies of the "Universal Journal" are in Collected Essays, TP. See also John Louis Haney, "The Philadelphia Period in the Life of Professor Elihu Thomson," *The Barnwell Bulletin* (of Central High School), 16(67):9–10 (February 1939). Quotation is from "Universal Journal," No. 12 (12 February 1869), Collected Essays, TP.

31 "Universal Journal," No. 9 (18 December 1868), Collected Essays, TP.

ety appears to have had a small chemistry laboratory, but the laboratory was dropped after complaints that Thomson was spending too much of the society's dues on chemicals.[32]

Not satisfied with meeting in a bathhouse, Thomson, Willis, and William H. Greene organized another scientific group in December 1869. Known as the "Scientific Microcosm," this society met monthly in the evening at Central High. The meetings were formal and quite ambitious; one to four papers were read, several scientific questions were discussed, and a reviewer summed up and reported on previous meetings. Thomson was a regular participant, speaking on "Ozone," "Artificial Heats," and "On Chemistry and Metallurgy of Iron." Active for nearly seven years, the Scientific Microcosm attracted the attention of the professors at Central High and other local scientists. Along with Houston, William H. Wahl of the Franklin Institute and Professors George Barker and Andrew J. Parker of the University of Pennsylvania attended meetings. To attract public interest for their winter lecture series, the society placed advertisements in the streetcars, and Thomson recalled that as many as 750 people attended meetings in the high-school auditorium. Through the Scientific Microcosm, Thomson learned much about the operation of a scientific organization, and he achieved some visibility in the local scientific community.[33]

It is certainly not remarkable for high-school students to form clubs and publish magazines, but why did Thomson and his young colleagues choose a scientific motif? They may have been influenced by the Franklin Institute and the American Philosophical Society, two prominent scientific bodies in Philadelphia. Perhaps Professor Houston played an important part; with his exposure to German university science and his strong ties to the Franklin Institute, he may have encouraged Thomson and the others in their scientific pursuits.

Although the inspiration is not clear, what is significant is that as a teenager Thomson related scientific knowledge to a social context.

32 "Re. Central High School," Autobiog. Papers, TP. For details of the meetings, see "Universal Journal," No. 4 (16 October 1868), No. 6 (13 November 1868), No. 9 (18 December 1868), and No. 11 (29 January 1869), Collected Essays, TP.

33 See "Re. Central High School," Autobiog. Papers, TP; Edmunds, *History of CHS*, pp. 215–19; and J. A. McManus to G. C. Dahl, 22 March 1933, Hall of History Collection. Notes to some of Thomson's talks can be found in "Notes in Astronomy, A term 1869," Notebook, TP.

Thomson was not satisfied simply to read about chemistry and physics, conduct experiments, and build apparatus; it became equally important for him to be involved with science as a community or social enterprise. By putting out a journal, organizing scientific clubs, and giving demonstrations, Thomson drew attention to himself and sought legitimation for his interests and abilities. Finding these early experiences with scientific groups congenial, Thomson subsequently concentrated on securing for himself a position in the scientific community of Philadelphia in the 1870s. But even more broadly, throughout his career Thomson sought validation for his work from scientific and professional societies. Perhaps because of these early experiences, Thomson in his mature years found that he preferred the approval of professional colleagues to financial gain or public celebrity as a reward for his inventions and discoveries. Identifying strongly with professional and scientific organizations, Thomson often shaped the content and style of his work so that it would bring him scientific recognition from those groups.

Thomson graduated from Central High School in February 1870, ranked fourth among the 18 students in his class. As part of the commencement exercises, Thomson spoke on "The Manufactures of Philadelphia," discussing the importance of both economic resources and science in maintaining Philadelphia's eminence as an industrial city. His central theme was that men of science and scientific institutions were as important to manufacturing as were labor and capital. "The sciences, without which there could be no progress in manufacturing industry," he remarked, "are fostered and nourished in her institutions, and a large number of her citizens have distinguished themselves in its many walks." With his sound education in science from Central High, perhaps Thomson envisioned himself as someday becoming one of Philadelphia's distinguished men of science.[34]

Changes in Thomson's family situation

Graduation from high school did not immediately bring Thomson the opportunity for social or professional advancement. Rather, at about that time his family situation changed for the worse. While installing

34 "Central High School Semi-Annual Commencement . . . 10 February 1870," program inserted in Faculty Minutes for 1870, CHS Archives; "The Manufactures of Philadelphia," Collected Essays, TP.

sugar equipment in Cuba, Thomson's father suffered a severe head injury, leaving him unable to work full-time. With no workmen's compensation, that accident was catastrophic for the still-growing Thomson family. Between 1868 and 1874 Mary Ann Thomson gave birth to three more children, one of whom died. Making matters even worse, another child, George, contracted a painful hip-joint disease in about 1868. To provide some money, the family rented out their Pierce Street home. From 1869 to 1872 the family lived in smaller quarters at 2136 Webster and 1707 South Sixth streets. Eventually, after securing steady work as a chemistry teacher at Central High, Thomson helped his mother purchase a more comfortable home at 2134 Fitzwater Street.[35]

These family misfortunes forced Thomson to curtail his education and begin working. During the last two years of high school he had worked nights as a clerk in the Western Union telegraph office, a job that he found boring and depressing. After graduating from Central High, Thomson might well have wanted to continue his education in science. At the University of Pennsylvania, Thomson could have studied chemistry or engineering in the new Department of Science, but he probably could not have afforded the annual tuition of $150. Another educational option would have been to join his friend William Greene in studying chemistry while earning a medical degree at Jefferson Medical College, but perhaps medicine held little appeal for him. Instead, Thomson responded to his family's needs by taking a job as a chemical analyst.[36]

Instability at home made Thomson all the more ambitious. The necessity to help support his brothers and sisters forced the young man

35 Mention of his father's accident is made by David O. Woodbury, *Beloved Scientist: Elihu Thomson, a Guiding Spirit of the Electrical Age* (New York: Whittlesey House, 1944; reprinted Cambridge, Mass.: Harvard University Press, 1960), p. 43. Data on the newborn children and George's condition are from "No. 1 Genealogical Memoranda as to Family," Notebook, TP. The renting of the Pierce Street house to a lithographer named David Partridge is from "Interest in Optical Work," Autobiog. Papers, TP. The additional addresses were obtained from the 1870 census and city directories from the period. Because deed abstracts do not show Mary Ann or Daniel Thomson owning either of these two properties, one must conclude that they were renting; see deed abstracts, Department of Records, City of Philadelphia.
36 Haney, "The Philadelphia Period," p. 11; ET, "The Pioneer Investigations on Dynamo Machines Fifty Years Ago," *J. Franklin Inst.*, 206:17–25 (July 1928); Thomas J. Misa, "The Changing Market for Chemical Knowledge: Applied Chemistry and Chemical Engineering in the Delaware Valley, 1851–1929," *History and Technology*, 2:245–68 (1985).

to forgo further education and to work hard, but he did not let that responsibility stand in the way of his dreams. The early lessons from his mother had taught him the importance of perseverance, and she had encouraged him to excel. Central High not only had provided him the skills needed to move into the middle class but also had inculcated the expectation of upward mobility. Perhaps feeling that his father was a failure for not being a better provider, he may have chosen to reject his father as a role model and redouble his efforts to make something of himself. There was no reason that he should accept the working class as his station in life; he was bright and talented, and opportunities abounded in Philadelphia.

But in what direction should he channel his ambitions? Science was the obvious answer. From an early age he had studied and admired science, absorbing facts and theories as well as ideology and an organizational motif. He was impressed by science's potential for promoting material progress, and he was impressed by the honors bestowed upon scientific heroes. Science represented order and control, making it especially appealing to a young man who lacked those things in the emotional world of his family. As he was finishing high school, Thomson was discovering the Philadelphia community of scientists who could recognize and reward him in ways that were no longer available through his family life. Thus, for these personal reasons, Thomson took seriously the scientific role he assumed over the next 10 years of his career.

Earning a living in science

Upon graduating from Central High School in 1870, Thomson sought work to help support his family. The first position that he found was with the Ironmasters' Laboratory of J. Blodgett Britton, a busy commercial chemical laboratory in Philadelphia. Organized in 1866 by the American Iron and Steel Association, that laboratory was intended to "encourage the development of workable bodies of iron ore and to inform producers of the quantity and quality of the metal they would yield." By providing chemical analyses of iron ore, coal, limestone, pig iron, and steel, the laboratory permitted ironmasters to improve and modify their smelting and refining processes, especially the new Bessemer steel process then being introduced. In supplying analyses for industry, the Ironmasters' Laboratory was one of many commercial laboratories that sprang up after the Civil War, and it helped promote an awareness of the importance of science for industry.[37]

At the Ironmasters' Laboratory, Thomson became an "embryo 'iron metallurgist'," performing routine analyses. His textbook knowledge of chemistry was enhanced by the firsthand experience of working in a busy laboratory. He also traveled throughout Pennsylvania, visiting different furnaces and mills to collect and test samples. Thomson remained at the laboratory for six months, learning much about how science could be applied to commercial problems and how a practical laboratory was organized.[38]

In September 1870, Thomson left the Ironmasters' Laboratory to accept the position of adjunct to the Department of Chemistry at Central High School. Dr. Isaac Norris, the professor of chemistry, selected Thomson to help supervise the chemistry laboratory. Although the annual salary was only $500 (in contrast, the school's janitor was paid $960), it may well have been an increase in pay for Thomson.[39] More important, Thomson saw the assistantship as an opportunity to advance his scientific career. Because of Central High's distinguished faculty and its extensive collection of scientific apparatus, Thomson accepted the assistantship hoping that it would allow him to become involved in Philadelphia scientific circles.

As the assistant in chemistry, Thomson quickly set to work expanding the laboratory. Central High had had a chemistry laboratory since its earliest days, and an assistant in chemistry to run the laboratory since 1868, but it had never been used for teaching. When Thomson started, the laboratory had consisted only of a basement storeroom

37 Howard R. Bartlett, "The Development of Industrial Research in the United States," in *Research – A Natural Resource. Part II: Industrial Research: Report of the National Research Council to the National Resources Planning Board* (Washington, D.C.: 1941), pp. 19–42, quotation on p. 27; Victor S. Clark, *History of Manufactures in the United States, 1860–1914* (Washington, D.C.: Carnegie Institution, 1928), p. 78; *Bulletin of the American Iron and Steel Association*, 1:326, 331 (12 June 1867), and 4:10–11 (15 September 1869).

38 ET to P. F. Brockett, 26 January 1913, CL, TP; "Testimony for Thomson," paper 129, Patent Interference No. 15,511, Pratt and Johns vs. Thomson (subject: composition for insulating material), NARS (hereafter cited as "Testimony for Thomson," Pat. Intf. 15,511).

39 G. I. Riche to ET, 13 September 1870, CL, TP; H. B. Hirsch, "Memorandum," Biographical Material, TP; *Fifty-second Annual Report of the Board of Public Education of the First School District of Pennsylvania . . . for 1870* (Philadelphia: 1871), p. 84 (hereafter cited as *Education Report for 1870*).

filled with bottles and demonstration apparatus. Within a short time, Thomson installed nine worktables, equipping each with a few test tubes and reagents. Under his direction, students performed a few elementary experiments to enhance their understanding of chemistry. The Board of Education supported Thomson's laboratory development by permitting the high school to spend $1,200 on scientific instruments in 1870. This laboratory is believed to have been the first teaching laboratory in an American high school; although that may not have been the case, Thomson's basement laboratory was certainly a reflection of the larger movement toward the establishment of laboratories in colleges and universities in the 1870s.[40]

The Board of Education evidently was pleased with Thomson's efforts to expand the laboratory; in their report for 1870 he was characterized as "a young man of great promise . . . giving entire satisfaction." However, Thomson was not pleased by his low salary; when offered a better salary to join the analytical laboratory of Thomas M. Drown in 1872, Thomson considered leaving. To retain him, the high school raised his salary to $575 and appointed him professor of chemistry in the Artisans' Night School in 1872. The evening high school of Philadelphia, the Artisans' Night School was attended by young workmen and was staffed primarily by professors from Central High. Because the night school attempted to impart practical knowledge appropriate for factory workers, Thomson taught a course "with special reference to the steam engine and chemistry."[41]

Teaching helped Thomson to expand his understanding of chemistry and to improve his skills in demonstrating science. In his lectures he emphasized the orderliness and methodology of science; years later, he explained that his teaching experience had convinced him that

> the aim of education, in science at least, should not be to store the mind with facts and theories but rather to inculcate principles and to teach the student how to think, and to show him the sources of such information as he may need.[42]

40 Edmunds, *History of CHS*, pp. 200–1, 211–12; *Education Report for 1870*, p. 28.
41 *Education Report for 1870*, p. 30; ET to P. F. Brockett, 26 January 1913, CL, TP; *Fifty-fourth Annual Report of the First School District of Pennsylvania . . . for 1872* (Philadelphia: 1872), p. 41; Edmunds, *History of CHS*, p. 224. As a professor in the Artisans' Night School, Thomson received a salary of $20 per week.
42 Edmunds, *History of CHS*, p. 212.

His lecture notes indicate how Thomson strove to fulfill this educational goal. During an introductory chemistry class, he spoke of science as the discovery of laws about nature, based on careful observation and experiment. In advanced lectures, Thomson taught his students to seek patterns. Rather than treat each chemical element as unique and separate, for instance, he suggested they view the elements as belonging to a system with laws and regularities; such a system, the periodic table, had recently been developed by Dmitri Mendeleev, but Thomson does not seem to have known about it during his teaching career. To help students remember the laws and patterns, Thomson supplemented his lectures with demonstrations; he showed his students the telephone, the phonograph, the incandescent light, and later his own dynamo and arc lights. These demonstrations, coupled with Thomson's enthusiasm for science, made him a popular teacher. Many students found him inspiring, and one, Edwin Wilbur Rice (later president of the General Electric Company), was motivated to set up his own home laboratory, where he constructed his own telescope and other devices.[43]

Thomson's effectiveness as a chemistry teacher was eventually recognized by his superiors at Central High. The school had the power to award master's degrees to graduates of at least five years' standing who had excelled in literary, scientific, or professional studies, and in 1875 they awarded an M.A. to Thomson. In the following year, Dr. Isaac Norris resigned his chair in chemistry, and the school elected Thomson as his replacement. As professor of chemistry and mechanics, Thomson now drew an annual salary of $2,100 and shared with Houston the prestige of teaching physical science at Central High. Throughout his life, Thomson was extraordinarily proud of the title "Professor," cherishing it more than all the numerous honorary degrees and awards he later received.[44]

As a professor at Central High, Thomson enjoyed a good salary, a respectable position in society, and colleagues with whom he could

43 "Chemistry Introduction," in "Notes on Astronomy," Notebook, TP; ET to P. F. Brockett, 26 January 1913, CL, TP; H. B. Hirsch, "Memorandum," Biographical Material, TP; E. W. Rice Jr., "Missionaries of Science," GE Rev., 32:355–61 (July 1929).

44 Haney, "The Philadelphia Period," p. 12; Minutes for meeting of 14 January 1875, Faculty Minutebook, 1872–97, CHS Archives, Philadelphia; Fifty-eighth Annual Report of the Board of Public Education of the First School District of Pennsylvania . . . for 1876 (Philadelphia: 1877), pp. 33, 113.

discourse on intellectual matters. Like other professors at Central High, he could have rested on his laurels for the remainder of his career, occasionally writing a paper or undertaking some experiment. Instead, Thomson used his position at Central High as a foundation for pursuing science in a variety of directions.

Experimenting in the attic

Like other academic chemists of the period, Thomson supplemented his teaching by applying chemistry to a variety of practical and technical problems. He used the commercial chemistry he had learned while working at the Ironmasters' Laboratory to perform an occasional analysis for a manufacturing firm or iron foundry. He was very interested in chemical technology, and his notebooks include calculations of the cost of producing sulfur dioxide using the lead-chamber process. Taking advantage of the widespread concern about ventilation, Thomson tested the level of carbon dioxide in classrooms throughout the city, perhaps for the Board of Education. In 1876, Thomson used his knowledge of chemistry to patent a centrifugal separator for processing milk, paint pigments, and other liquids. (This invention will be described in the next chapter.) Thomson's dedication to chemistry was so strong that after 1878 he listed himself in the Philadelphia city directory not as a teacher but as a chemist.[45]

Although chemistry was his main passion as a young professor, Thomson did not forget about electricity, a subject that had intrigued him as a boy. In his family's home he set up a workshop in the attic and equipped it with an old foot-powered lathe and hand tools. Working in that shop, he constructed not only laboratory apparatus but also telegraph instruments and electrostatic machines of his own design.[46] As early as 1873 Thomson built a small dynamo, which will be

45 Thomson discussed his early work in chemistry in "Testimony for Thomson," Pat. Intf. 15,511, pp. 36, 72. For his notes on sulfur dioxide, see "Notebook 1875–1876 First Made," TP. Data from the carbon dioxide tests are in "Phila Central High School in a/c with Newbold Bros . . . ," Notebook, TP. Thomson listed himself as a chemist in *Gopsill's Philadelphia City Directory for 1878* (Philadelphia: James Gopsill, 1878); and also in "List of Members of the Franklin Institute. January 1st, 1877," *J. Franklin Inst.*, 103 (January 1877).
46 " 'Electrical World' Portraits. – II. Elihu Thomson," *Electrical World*, 12:102 (1 September 1888). George Thomson, one of Elihu's grandsons, has a telegraph set estimated to have been made in 1873 and now on loan to the Boston Museum of Science.

Figure 1.8. Self-portrait of Thomson in his home laboratory and workshop. From Thomson Papers, American Philosophical Society, Philadelphia.

described in the next chapter. At this point in his career, Thomson was simply dabbling in electricity; it was just one of many interests. Only later, after 1877, did Thomson turn his full attention to electrical technology, finding it to be a congenial field where he could work on "scientific" problems while seeking status and intellectual fulfillment.

Supplementing his work in chemistry and electricity, Thomson pursued other interests in his attic workshop. He built a pipe organ, designing the pipes, reeds, bellows, and other parts himself. After seeing a large pipe organ with an electropneumatic key action at the Centennial Exhibition in Philadelphia, he added this feature to his home organ. In another corner of the attic he set up a darkroom, where he developed wet photographic plates and made prints. Thomson became a proficient photographer, taking pictures of landscapes and even a self-portrait in the pose of the studious man of science[47] (Figure 1.8).

47 Edmunds, History of CHS, pp. 212–13. The pipe organ is discussed in ET to P. F. Brockett, 26 January 1933, CL, TP. Sketches and notes for the organ are in "Lectures on Beverages" and Large Composition Notebooks, TP. For a description of an electropneumatic action that Thomson might have copied,

From photography, Thomson moved to optics. Since boyhood he had been fascinated by lenses, cameras, and magic lanterns and had wanted to learn how those devices were made. In 1874, while attending an exhibition at the Franklin Institute, he met William Gerhardt, a master optician. An elderly German, Gerhardt had a tiny shop at 817–18 Filbert Street, equipped only with an old foot lathe, a small workbench, and a coal stove. Despite his age and limited equipment, Thomson remembered that Gerhardt produced excellent lenses and optical instruments. Sensing Thomson's keen interest in learning, Gerhardt agreed to teach him some of the trade secrets of optical work. After a few preliminary lessons, he assigned Thomson the task of constructing a 10-element microscope objective. Thomson struggled with the task for three weeks and only reluctantly brought the finished objective to Gerhardt. The master examined it carefully and noted that the lenses were not fully polished, but praised the young man for undertaking such a demanding project.[48]

Gratified by that experience, Thomson went on to construct an entire microscope and to grind his own photographic lenses. Desiring a powerful reflecting telescope, he made his own 12-inch concave mirror by grinding two optical-glass blanks together. Because this technique was simpler and more economical than the method generally used by astronomers at the time, Thomson was able to publish an article on his new technique in 1878 in the *Journal of the Franklin Institute* and the *English Mechanic and World of Science*.[49]

Thomson later remarked that in learning optics as an informal apprentice, he realized for the first time that "it is the head guiding the

see "New Applications of Electricity to Organ Building," *Scientific American*, 34:177 (19 February 1876). In Unsorted Material, TP, there are photographic prints of scenes from Columbia, Pennsylvania, dated in Thomson's hand circa 1870.

48 "Interest in Optical Work," Autobiog. Papers, TP. Gerhardt's address is from *Gopsill's Philadelphia City Directory for 1872* (Philadelphia: James Gopsill, 1872). Thomson's calculations for his first microscope objective are on a folded sheet inserted in E. Loomis, *Table of Logarithms* . . . (1867), Notebooks, TP.

49 ET, "A New Method of Grinding Glass Specula," *J. Franklin Inst.*, 106:117–21 (August 1878); *English Mechanic and World of Science*, 27:593 (23 August 1878). Thomson's grinding technique was an improvement over Henry Draper's method in that he eliminated the need for precision iron tools to cut the shape of the mirror. Henry Draper, "On the Construction of a Silvered Glass Telescope, Fifteen and a Half Inches in Aperture and its Use in Celestial Photography," *Smithsonian Contributions to Knowledge*, 14 (1865). See also "My Interest in Astronomy," Autobiog. Papers, TP.

hand, and not so much a matter of fine tools as fine workmanship that gives results in this field." [50] Not only true for optics, Thomson applied this lesson throughout his career. As an inventor, his success was based on the intellectual and manual skills necessary for building, testing, and refining models of inventions. Though familiar with electrical theory, it was more the craft skills he acquired as a young man that permitted him to devise new and practical devices.

Despite his many chemical, electrical, photographic, and optical projects, one should not assume that Thomson was interested only in science and technology. In addition to building his own pipe organ, Thomson played the cornet. He and his friends attended plays and concerts. His notebooks reveal that he played chess and wrote poetry. In the summer of 1872 he went camping with his friend Greene in the Adirondacks. Because he could not afford to buy camping gear, Thomson used his ingenuity to fashion his own camp clothing, as well as ammunition for an antique gun to use on the trip. [51]

A high point in Thomson's pursuit of his varied interests came with his trip to Europe in the summer of 1878. Such a trip was extraordinarily ambitious for a young man from a working-class background. After probably having saved much of his teaching salary, Thomson spent nine weeks touring Europe, France, Switzerland, and Germany. Although he went primarily to see the electrical exhibits at the Paris Exposition, Thomson also spent time touring chemical plants in Manchester, visiting cathedrals and art museums, hiking in the Alps, and buying scientific instruments. In many ways, the trip was Thomson's "grand tour," a capstone to his broad and varied education. [52]

With his many interests, Thomson must have come across to his friends and colleagues as a studious, cultured, and yet ambitious young man. Although from a working-class background, he was striving to better himself, much like a character in a Horatio Alger story. Unlike the typical Alger character, who made his way by luck and pluck in the

50 "Interest in Optical Work," Autobiog. Papers, TP.
51 Thomson's cornet is in the Thomson Collection, Franklin Institute Science Museum, Philadelphia. In regard to attending plays, see "Fusel Oil as a Remedial Agent in Respiratory Disorder," Autobiog. Papers, TP. Thomson chronicled a trip to Lancaster to hear a concert in a poem titled "Cornet Quartette" (1872), in "Notes on Astronomy," Notebook, TP. Thomson described his camping trip in "First Visit to the Adirondacks in 1872," Autobiog. Papers, TP.
52 Untitled notebook on European trip (1878), Notebook, TP.

world of commerce or industry, though, Thomson had instead chosen science as his path upward.[53] To secure a regular income and middle-class respectability, he had become a scientific practitioner. However, still intellectually curious, Thomson engaged in a variety of activities, many of which were devoted to scientific research and publication. With each new activity he was responding to his thirst for knowledge, as well as seeking professional recognition. Eventually his research and his efforts at self-improvement were recognized by the Philadelphia scientific community and rewarded by election to the leading scientific societies. Let us consider next how Thomson became an aspiring researcher and how he participated in those scientific organizations.

Thomson as aspiring researcher

For Thomson, science was not only an occupation but also an intellectual challenge. While working as a chemical analyst, laboratory assistant, and professor, Thomson was not satisfied with merely performing his job; to satisfy his intellectual curiosity, he took up an array of research projects, and he struggled to orient his creative output in directions that would lead to scientific and professional recognition. He obtained that recognition by publishing articles, giving public lectures, and becoming a member of scientific societies.[54]

53 For a perceptive analysis of Horatio Alger's heroes, see James Oliver Robertson, *American Myth, American Reality* (New York: Hill & Wang, 1980), pp. 165–70.

54 To analyze Thomson's career as a scientist, Nathan Reingold's model of professionalization in nineteenth-century American science provides a useful framework. Seeking to avoid the whiggish pitfalls inherent in using a modern definition of professional science to describe past scientific endeavors, Reingold categorizes nineteenth-century scientists in three categories. "Cultivators" were the rank-and-file members of local scientific societies who attended lectures, collected mineralogical and biological specimens, and occasionally bought scientific instruments. Cultivators did not hold remunerative scientific jobs and generally did not publish scientific articles. Reingold calls those who did hold remunerative positions "practitioners." The number of practitioners expanded rapidly in the second half of the nineteenth century as certain scientific tasks were routinized and science was converted into a viable, upwardly mobile occupation. Although some practitioners performed research and occasionally published, the routine duties of teaching, administrative work, or performing standard chemical analyses limited their efforts. For new ideas and inspiration, the practitioners looked to the "researchers," who were the leaders of American science. Through their own investigations

Thomson's first research projects reflected more his boyish enthusiasm for science than any intellectual rigor. In 1870, for instance, he investigated the nature of hailstorms by observing storm clouds and cutting apart several hailstones. Inside he found concentric layers of snowy ice and clear ice that he concluded were created when the stones passed through different portions of the atmosphere. Thomson presented those opinions at a meeting of the Scientific Microcosm in June 1870. Impressed with how he correlated theory with data, the members of the Microcosm had his report printed. Illustrated with sketches by his friend Dewey Bates, this paper was Thomson's first scientific publication.[55]

From meteorology, Thomson moved to chemistry, performing experiments and making minor discoveries as he worked as the chemistry assistant at Central High. He investigated the anesthetic effect of nitrous oxide ("laughing gas") on a kitten and reported the results in the *Philadelphia Medical Times*. In 1871 and 1873 he published several brief research notes in the *Journal of the Franklin Institute*, which at that time carried reports of local Philadelphia research along with its main fare of engineering articles. To a certain extent, Thomson was still concentrating on the chemistry of the spectacular and brilliant that he had learned as a boy. Two of the reports describe novel ways of producing an explosive reaction, and a third gives directions for producing stalactites using a soda solution and sulfuric acid. Yet these reports did show how the young bomb-maker's knowledge of chemistry was growing. In explaining how crystals of potassium chlorate wrapped in tinfoil could be detonated, he remarked that it was not

and by their supervision of cultivators and practitioners, researchers directed science toward the problems they considered the most interesting. With these three categories, it is possible to interpret the wide variety of scientific activities in nineteenth-century America within a framework of different social relationships. See Nathan Reingold, "Definitions and Speculations: The Professionalization of Science in America in the Nineteenth Century," in A. Oleson and S. Brown, eds., *The Pursuit of Knowledge in the Early American Republic* (Baltimore: Johns Hopkins University Press, 1976), pp. 33–69. Using these categories, Thomson can thus be characterized as a practitioner, with aspirations toward research.

55 "Interest in Natural Phenomena," Autobiog. Papers, TP; Clarissa Thomson, "Notes on Elihu Thomson's Early Life" (25 January 1938), Biographical Material, TP; ET, *Report on the Hailstorm of May 8, 1870, as Read before the Scientific Microcosm* (Philadelphia: 1870), Collected Papers, TP.

generally known that metals such as tin could be oxidized in this manner.[56]

Although Thomson was capable of undertaking small research projects on his own, he soon realized that he did not know much about the accepted practices of scientific research and publication. Through his high-school education and independent reading, Thomson had absorbed factual scientific knowledge, but he was not familiar with the full range of contemporary experimental methods or with the preparation of detailed scientific articles. He simply did not know the quotidian professional practices of science. Although Thomson held a scientific post, his projects were allied with popular science rather than with the cutting-edge knowledge of the researcher. Yet, because of his desire for professional recognition, Thomson was dissatisfied with popular knowledge and instead wished to undertake original research.

Faced with the same problem of not knowing the professional practices of science, Thomson's friend William Greene chose to attend the Jefferson Medical College and then study organic chemistry with Charles Adolph Wurtz at the Sorbonne in Paris.[57] Because Thomson could not afford those educational options, he instead entered into an intellectual partnership with Houston, his former physics professor (Figure 1.9). Around 1871, Thomson and Houston appear to have agreed to work together on various scientific and technical schemes, pooling their skills and sharing in the publications and recognition. Houston brought to the partnership experience in performing electrical experiments, writing scientific articles, and making contacts through professional scientific organizations. In contrast, Thomson provided manual skills, fresh ideas, and a willingness to work hard. The skills and personalities of the two men were complementary, and

---

56 ET, "A Spontaneous Explosive," *J. Franklin Inst.*, 92:84 (August 1871); "A New Experiment," *J. Franklin Inst.*, 95:156 (March 1873); "Stalactitic Gelatinous Silica," *J. Franklin Inst.*, 95:157–8 (March 1873); "On the Inhalation of Nitrous Oxide, Nitrogen, Hydrogen, and Other Gases and Gaseous Mixtures," *Philadelphia Medical Times*, 15: 97–8 (15 November 1873). Thomson's notes for the kitten experiments are in "Lectures on Beverages," Notebook, TP.

57 Obituary for William H. Greene, *J. Franklin Inst.*, 186:387–93 (September 1918).

Figure 1.9. Edwin J. Houston. From the Portrait Collection, History of Science and Technology Department, National Museum of American History, Washington, D.C.

as a team, Thomson and Houston were able to accomplish much in science and technology.[58]

Working with Houston, Thomson learned how to knit together elements of the practitioner and researcher roles to form a viable scientific career. Along with being professor of physical geography and natural philosophy at Central High, Houston was the consummate practitioner, capitalizing on a variety of opportunities to do science in Philadelphia. He was an active member of both the Franklin Institute and the American Philosophical Society, serving on committees and

58 That Thomson and Houston were able to achieve more by working together will become apparent when we consider the development of their first arc lighting system in the next chapter. As an old man looking back, Thomson decided that Houston had taken too much credit for their joint efforts, and that feeling provided the basis for Woodbury's description of their relationship in *Beloved Scientist*, pp. 47–8, 93–7. According to Woodbury, their relationship was parasitic, with Houston taking advantage of Thomson. My characterization of the partnership of Thomson and Houston is based on inferences drawn from descriptions of the two men and from a general reading of Thomson's correspondence. It was not until about 1881, after Thomson had gone to New Britain, that the two men had a falling-out. At that time, it was over patent and royalty rights. Further details of the relationship between these two men are given in the next chapter. Woodbury based his analysis on Thomson's disparaging remarks in "Dynamo Work and Its Development," Autobiog. Papers, TP.

frequently reading short papers at their meetings. Later in his career, Houston taught physics at the Medico-Chirurgical College, did electrical engineering consulting work with Arthur E. Kennelly, and wrote scientific textbooks. Although the quality and content of Houston's work varied – he was capable of writing papers on the intricacies of geometrical chemistry as well as the peculiarities of waterfalls – he nonetheless received the professional rewards of honorary degrees, special titles, and membership in scientific societies for his scientific labors. Houston appears to have shrewdly utilized the ambiguity of scientific roles in the late nineteenth century. From Houston, Thomson learned how to shape a scientific career for himself in which he capitalized on opportunities for expanding his practitioner role while he received professional recognition for the various research projects he chose to pursue.[59]

Drawing on his professional contacts, Houston helped Thomson join the two key scientific societies of Philadelphia: the Franklin Institute and the American Philosophical Society. As a member of these organizations, Thomson secured not only professional recognition but also access to a variety of individuals and resources.

Thomson's most important institutional affiliation was that with the Franklin Institute in Philadelphia. Formed in 1824, the institute had been founded by businessmen and manufacturers who wished to acquire information about technical developments as well as promote industrial progress. Through its journal, exhibitions, schools, lecture series, and library, the institute gathered and diffused technical knowledge. Finding no reliable information on certain topics, the institute periodically formed committees to conduct research; as a result, institute members had contributed new data concerning the strength of materials, the design of waterwheels, and the causes of steam-boiler explosions. Although it suffered from a chronic shortage of funds and bouts of membership apathy, the many activities of the Franklin

59 For biographical information on Houston, see *Electrical Engineering*, 53:792 (May 1934); Edmunds, *History of CHS*, p. 331; and " Prof. Edwin J. Houston Dead" and ET, "In Memoriam – Prof. Edwin J. Houston," *Electrical World*, 63:522–3 (7 March 1914). For articles by Houston, see "Geometrical Chemistry – Remarkable Discovery by Professor Henry Wurtz," *Scientific American*, 34:361 (3 June 1876); "A Simple Phonoautograph," "On the Nature of White Light," and "A Sensitive Waterfall," *J. Franklin Inst.*, 64 (July–December 1872); and "The Artificial Production of Low Temperatures," *J. Franklin Inst.*, 67 (January 1874).

Figure 1.10. Library of the Franklin Institute. From "Official Catalogue of the International Electrical Exhibition" (Philadelphia: Burke
& McFetridge, 1884).

Institute made it the foremost technical society in nineteenth-century
America.[60]

Elected to the Franklin Institute in 1874, Thomson participated in
many of its activities. As a new member, he first served as a judge of
philosophical, optical, and mathematical instruments at the institute's
1874 industrial exhibition. In that capacity he evaluated burglar and
fire-alarm telegraphs, microscopes, and surveying instruments. He
undoubtedly attended many of the institute's meetings and heard
reports on the latest technical developments; in January 1874, for
example, he could have heard a report on the new Gramme dynamo,
recently imported from France. Thomson also made use of the institute's library, where he studied scientific and technical journals and
consulted the patent files (Figure 1.10). Both Thomson and Houston
took advantage of the *Journal of the Franklin Institute,* using it as their
primary vehicle for publicizing their research findings.[61]

60 Sinclair, *Philadelphia's Philosopher Mechanics.*
61 "Address by Elihu Thomson, Ph.D., Sc.D., on the Occasion of the Observance
    of the Centenary of the Founding of the Franklin Institute," *J. Franklin Inst.,*
    198:581–98 (November 1924), pp. 585, 589–90 (hereafter cited as "1924
    Address"). For reference to objects judged at the 1874 exhibition, see "Awards

The Franklin Institute also provided the opportunity for the young professor to gain proficiency in giving public lectures and demonstrations. Although considered by some members to be too young and inexperienced to lecture before the institute, Thomson's personal connections must have helped him secure a place in the lecture series; his old chemistry professor, Dr. Isaac Norris, was secretary of the institute, and Houston was a regular speaker. During the winter season of 1877, Thomson gave five lectures on electricity and eight on elementary chemistry. The following year, Thomson spoke on the correlation of forces, comparing mechanical forces with heat, electricity, and chemical changes. Finally, in 1879 he lectured on explosive compounds, mirrors and lenses, the spectroscope, electric lighting, and electrochemistry, a series that reflected all his interests.[62]

Along with the opportunity to lecture and publish, the Franklin Institute provided Thomson and Houston two additional opportunities that helped their subsequent research in electricity. First, by authorizing a series of tests on commercial dynamos and arc lights in 1877, the institute gave them a chance to study several commercial dynamos. As we shall see in the next chapter, Thomson and Houston learned from those tests much about the factors influencing the operation of a practical arc lighting system. Second, meetings of the institute provided Thomson and Houston a forum for exhibiting their inventions. During 1878 and 1879 they gave several demonstrations of their new electric lighting system that attracted investors to their work. With its resources and programs, the Franklin Institute gave Thomson and Houston an institutional setting congenial to both scientific research and technological innovation.[63]

of Premiums," *J. Franklin Inst.*, 98:102 (January 1875). "Gramme's Magneto-Electric Machine for Continuous Currents," *J. Franklin Inst.*, 97:55–62 (January 1874), provides a description of a demonstration that Thomson may have seen at the institute.

62 For doubts about ET's lecturing abilities, see ET, "1924 Address," p. 586. For a listing of the lectures given by Thomson between 1877 and 1879, see "Announcement of Lectures," *J. Franklin Inst.*, 102:297 (October 1876); "Lectures at the Franklin Institute," *J. Franklin Inst.*, 104:293 (November 1877); and "Lectures at the Franklin Institute," *J. Franklin Inst.*, 106:356 (November 1878). Sketchy notes for his lectures on the correlation of forces, on the spectroscope, and on electrochemistry can be found in "Notebook 1875–76 First Made," TP.

63 For Thomson's and Houston's work on dynamo testing, see "Report of the Committee on Dynamo-Electric Machines," *J. Franklin Inst.*, 105:289–303,

Thomson's other major institutional affiliation was with the American Philosophical Society. Founded by Benjamin Franklin in 1743, this society had long been a gathering place for the social and intellectual elite of Philadelphia. Although the society had promoted both science and technology during its early years, by the late nineteenth century its members were concentrating on pure scientific research. For instance, Houston, a member since 1873, reported to the Philosophical Society the findings from his experiments with a Crookes radiometer and the influence of heat radiation from the moon on the earth's atmosphere. Elected a member in 1876, Thomson was stimulated by the combination of social status and pursuit of "pure" science. Finding the small monthly meetings of the society a receptive audience, Thomson and Houston frequently reported their discoveries first at those gatherings, and then at the Franklin Institute and through publication. Although the society did not provide Thomson much technical support, it nonetheless influenced him by reinforcing and rewarding his desire for professional recognition and by allowing him to meet other Philadelphia men of science.[64]

An established man of science: the etheric force controversy

With his professorship and memberships in the Franklin Institute and the American Philosophical Society, Thomson had become an established member of the Philadelphia scientific community. Working as both practitioner and aspiring researcher, Thomson had created for himself a congenial career. Underlying his research and institutional affiliations was a growing familiarity with the reward system for research and publication. He also liked meeting and socializing with fellow practitioners and researchers, and he clearly had begun to absorb scientific values such as empiricism, objectivity, and idealism.

363–78 (May–June 1878). For a mention of demonstrations of their new arc lights and dynamos at institute meetings, see *J. Franklin Inst.*, 108:70 (January 1879), 108:142 (February 1879), and 78:432 (December 1879).
64 For ET's election to the American Philosophical Society (APS), see J. P. Leshy to ET, 21 April 1876, CL, TP. For Houston's scientific contributions to meetings, see minutes of meetings for 17 October 1873 and 16 June 1876, *Proceedings of American Philosophical Society* (hereafter cited as *Proc. APS*), 13:264 (1873), and 16:279 (1876–7). For demonstrations and reports of their research, see minutes of meetings for 3 April 1874 and 20 September 1878, *Proc. APS*, 14:108–10 (1874–5), and 18:2 (1878–80), respectively.

However, more than just acquiring that outlook, Thomson was also learning how the scientific community defined and verified new knowledge. In reading scientific journals, attending meetings, and talking with other Philadelphia scientists, Thomson obtained a sense of how observation, experiment, and publication were all parts of the process of scientific discovery. That Thomson had become acculturated to the scientific community is well illustrated by how he helped Houston dispute the nature of the "etheric force" with Thomas A. Edison in 1875 and 1876. In that controversy, the young professor not only made use of his knowledge of the intricacies of nineteenth-century electrical science but also demonstrated that he understood the unwritten rules of the scientific community.

In 1875, Thomas A. Edison was known primarily as an inventor of novel telegraph systems. In the preceding five years he had perfected a "stock ticker," experimented with a high-speed automatic telegraph, and devised a quadruplex system for transmitting four messages simultaneously over a single wire. Edison was pursuing yet another multiple message system in November 1875, an acoustic telegraph that used different tones to send several messages over the same wire, when he made what he considered to be a scientific discovery.[65]

Using an electromagnet with an armature – a piece of steel positioned horizontally across its iron core – Edison noticed that a strange spark jumped between the core and the steel whenever the current to the electromagnet was interrupted (Figure 1.11). He had seen similar sparks previously but had attributed them to induction. (An induced spark or current is produced when an interruption or variation of the current in a coil alters the strength of the coil's magnetic field.) Particularly impressed with the brightness of the spark, Edison chose to investigate it further. Much to his surprise, he found that the spark affected neither the gold leaves of an electroscope nor the needle of an astatic galvanometer. Indicating a lack of charge (positive or negative), this experiment suggested to Edison that the spark was nonelectric, and perhaps a new force. He found that when one end of a wire was

65 Reese V. Jenkins and Paul B. Israel, "Thomas A. Edison: Flamboyant Inventor," *IEEE Spectrum*, December 1984, pp. 74–9; Reese V. Jenkins and Keith A. Nier, "A Record for Invention: Thomas Edison and his Papers," *IEEE Transactions on Education*, E-27:191–6 (November 1984); and Reese V. Jenkins et al., eds., *The Papers of Thomas A. Edison. Vol. 1: The Making of an Inventor, February 1847–June 1873* (Baltimore: Johns Hopkins University Press, 1989).

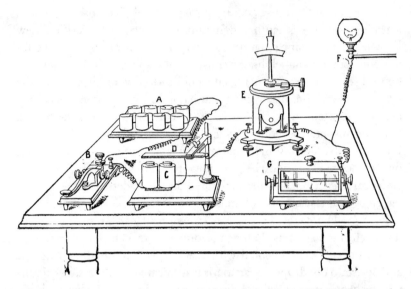

Figure 1.11. Edison's etheric force apparatus: (A) battery, (B) telegraph key used to interrupt current, (C) electromagnet, (D) steel armature, (E) astatic galvanometer, (F) gas fixture used to ground apparatus, (G) black box used to detect sparks. The spark was first seen jumping from the cores of the electromagnet (C) to the steel armature (D). From "The New Phase of Electric Force," *Scientific American,* 33:401 (25 December 1875).

connected to the steel armature, sparks could be drawn by touching the other end to gas pipes and other metallic objects. "This is simply wonderful," wrote Edison in his notebook, "and a good proof that the cause of the spark is a true unknown force." Without hesitation and with characteristic hyperbole, he announced to the newspapers that he had discovered a new force. Edison called the spark a manifestation of an "etheric force" and excitedly predicted that it could be used as a new means of communication.[66]

Thomson and Houston followed the reports of Edison's discovery in the newspapers and the *Scientific American.* Houston took a special

66 Matthew Josephson, *Edison: A Biography* (New York: McGraw-Hill, 1959), pp. 127–30. Edison's authorized biography contains long excerpts from his notes on the etheric force; see F. Dyer, T. C. Martin, and W. H. Meadowcroft, *Edison: His Life and Inventions,* 2 vols. (New York: Harper's, 1929), Vol. 2, pp. 855–60. The quotation is from a notebook entry dated 22 November 1875, p. 855. Several of the early newspaper articles from the New York *Tribune* were reprinted as "Edison's New Moonshine," *The Telegrapher,* 11:289 (4 December 1875).

Figure 1.12. Apparatus used by Thomson and Houston to study the etheric force in December 1875. On the left is the Ruhmkorff coil, with its secondary coil connected to a grounded pipe and to a large tin still mounted on a glass jar for insulation. The right-hand illustration shows Thomson's black-box detector with a large brass bell mounted on one terminal. From E. Thomson, "Wireless Transmission of Energy," *General Electric Review*, 18:316–26 (May 1915), p. 316.

interest in Edison's claims, because he had observed a similar phenomenon in 1871 while using a Ruhmkorff coil, a forerunner to the modern transformer. Consisting of two coils wound on a single iron core, the Ruhmkorff coil used an alternating current produced by a break-wheel to induce a high-voltage current in the secondary coil. In his experiments, Houston had connected the terminals of the primary coil to a battery, and the leads from the secondary coil to both a grounded gas pipe and a long wire. With this arrangement on the lecture table in his classroom, Houston found that sparks could be drawn from metallic objects scattered throughout the room. Houston found the sparks interesting, but in his published report he simply attributed them to induction.[67]

On reading Edison's claims for a new force, Houston repeated his experiments and published an article claiming priority for the discovery of the sparks. Thomson helped Houston with this project by devising better experimental apparatus. Rather than simply using a length of wire on one of the terminals of the secondary, Thomson replaced it with a large tin still from the chemistry laboratory; he insulated this conductor from its surroundings by putting it on top of a large glass jar. To detect the sparks, Thomson and Houston duplicated the "black box" used by Edison, with two adjustable pencil points inside, but they added a large brass ball to one terminal of the box to aid in detecting the sparks[68] (Figure 1.12).

67 EJH, "On a New Connection for the Induction Coil," *J. Franklin Inst.*, 91:417–19 (1871).
68 ET, "Wireless Transmission of Energy," *GE Rev.*, 18:316–26 (May 1915), p. 316.

Once the apparatus was operating, Thomson made the new observation that sparks could be drawn off metallic objects with a sharpened pencil point not only in Houston's classroom but throughout the high-school building. Flushed with the excitement of discovery, Thomson ran through the building, drawing sparks off doorknobs. Rushing up to the observatory on the roof, he found that sparks could even be drawn off metal objects in glass storage cabinets. Believing that he could have detected these sparks even a quarter of a mile away from the school, Thomson saw in the sparks the possibility of a new system of communications.[69]

Houston communicated these results to the *Journal of the Franklin Institute* in December 1875. In an article titled "Phenomena of Induction," he tried to discredit Edison's claims for an etheric force by explaining the sparks in terms of induction. Edison had based his claim for a new force on the fact that the spark failed to exhibit any sign of charge or polarity, a fundamental attribute of electricity. Houston responded that the absence of polarity in the spark could be explained by two instantaneous opposite currents canceling each other out. When the current was interrupted, there was an instantaneous outgoing current, followed immediately by an incoming induced current. Because it was well known that the induced current would be in a direction opposite to that of the interrupted current, the two currents would neutralize each other, giving the spark its apparent nonpolarity. Because of the extremely high velocity of electric currents, it was not surprising that no change could be observed in relatively slow acting electroscopes and galvanometers. Houston concluded that the sparks could be accounted for in terms of the existing principles of electrical science, making it unnecessary to resort to the hypothesis of a new

69 Although the article describing this experiment was authored by Houston, Thomson claimed in his later years that he suggested the experiment to Houston, that he set up the apparatus, and that the article embodied his ideas. See ET, "Additional Notes for my Secretary, Mr. J. A. McManus," 1 March 1935, Autobiog. Papers, TP. My interpretation is that Houston, having previously published an article on the sparks, wanted to assert his priority and that Thomson helped him devise better apparatus. Once the apparatus was in place, Thomson went beyond Houston and made new observations. See ET to A. B. Johnson, 29 January 1930, CL, TP. Monroe B. Snyder, "Professor Elihu Thomson's Early Experimental Discovery of the Maxwell Electro-Magnetic Waves," *GE Rev.*, 23:208 (March 1920); "Early Wireless Experiments," Autobiog. Papers, TP.

force.[70] From his previous training and experience in the scientific community, Houston knew that the rewards often went to those who sustained the existing corpus of theoretical knowledge, rather than those who tried to undermine it for personal gain.

Following Houston's report, other investigators reported that they had observed the sparks, and most agreed that they were best explained by induction. Edison replied to Houston's analysis with a letter to the *Scientific American*, asserting that Houston did not understand the properties of low-resistance electromagnets. Although the *Scientific American* sided with the induction explanation, the editors did give Edison the benefit of the doubt and asked men of science to continue to investigate the phenomenon.[71]

Thomson responded to that call by undertaking a second set of experiments with Houston. Their goal now was to demonstrate conclusively that the spark lacked polarity because it was caused by two opposite induced currents. For these experiments, Thomson used two identical electromagnets. One lead of each electromagnet was connected to the positive or negative pole of a battery, and the other leads were joined by a switch. Short wires connected the metal cores of each magnet to a pencil tip in the black-box detector (Figure 1.13). Employed individually, each electromagnet generated sparks visible in the black box. However, when used together, the coils produced opposite induced currents that canceled each other, and hence no spark was visible. For this neutralization, Thomson found that it was necessary to balance precisely both sides of the circuit, which he did by adding bits of sheet metal to the wires on one side of the circuit. Thomson realized later that in doing this he had been adjusting the capacitance of the

70 EJH, "Phenomena of Induction," *J. Franklin Inst.*, 101:59–63 (January 1876). That article received wide circulation because it was reprinted in *Scientific American Supplement*, 1(5):77–8 (29 January 1876), and *Telegraphic Journal and Electrical Review* (London), 4:61–2 (15 February 1876).

71 For other early claims to the discovery of etheric force sparks, see George Little, "Etheric Static Currents of Tension . . . ," *The Telegrapher*, 12:9 (8 January 1876); W. E. Sawyer, "The Etheric Force," *Scientific American*, 34:36 (15 January 1876); and Samuel H. Frisbee, "Increasing the Spark of the Induction Coil," *Scientific American Supplement*, 1(17):271 (22 April 1876). Discussion of the sparks as caused by induction can be found in Physical Student, "The New Force," *The Telegrapher*, 12:1 (1 January 1876); and Electron, "Mr. Edison's New Force," *Scientific American*, 34:69 (29 January 1876). Edison's reply to Houston is in *Scientific American*, 34:101 (12 February 1876). For the position taken by the editors, see "Mr. Edison's Electric Discovery," *Scientific American*, 34:12 (8 January 1876).

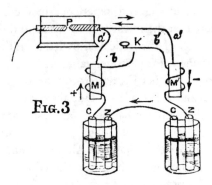

Figure 1.13. Apparatus used by Thomson and Houston to disprove the existence of the etheric force: (C, Z) battery, (M, M') electromagnets, (K) switch, (P) gap in black-box detector where spark was seen. From E. J. Houston and E. Thomson, "Electrical Phenomena," *J. Franklin Inst.*, 101:271–4 (April 1876), p. 273.

circuit, and consequently demonstrating the "tuning" principle of radio for the first time. At the time of the experiment, though, he did not recognize that principle, as he was far more interested in showing that the spark had a polarity, because two opposite induced currents failed to produce a spark.[72]

Thomson's ingenious experiment seems to have provided the necessary experimental proof that an etheric force did not exist. When coupled with tests conducted by the British physicist Silvanus P. Thompson, Thomson's experiment seems to have convinced the scientific community that the etheric force was nonexistent. Wishing to avoid further controversy, Edison busied himself in moving his laboratory from Newark to Menlo Park and said nothing more in print about the etheric force.[73]

72 EJH and ET, "Electrical Phenomena: The Alleged Etheric Force – Test Experiments as to Its Identity with Induced Electricity," *J. Franklin Inst.*, 101:270 (April 1876); reprinted in *Scientific American Supplement*, 1(21):326 (20 May 1876). For details of "tuning" the circuit, see ET to P. F. Brockett, 26 January 1933, CL, TP.
73 Charles Susskind, "Observations of Electromagnetic Waves Before Hertz," *Isis*, 55:32–42 (March 1964), especially p. 37; "Etheric Force," *Scientific American Supplement*, 1(26):405 (24 June 1876); "Edison About to Astonish the World Again – Stand From Under!" *The Telegrapher*, 12:185 (29 July 1876); William S. Pretzer, ed., *Working at Inventing: Thomas A. Edison and the Menlo Park Experience* (Dearborn: Henry Ford Museum and Greenfield Village, 1989).

More than simply ferreting out "the truth" about the etheric force, Thomson and Houston fared better than Edison in the controversy because they understood the unwritten rules of the scientific community regarding discovery and publication. First, they made sure that their results were not first carried in the newspapers, but in a professional journal. Because they had ready access to the *Journal of the Franklin Institute,* they published their results there initially, but within a short time their article was reprinted in the *Scientific American Supplement* and the *Chemical News.* Although Houston was just as anxious as Edison to secure priority for discovery of the sparks, he covered his desire in his December 1875 report by appealing to a professional audience rather than going public with the newspapers.

Second, in the structure of their argument, Houston and Thomson strove to relate the spark phenomenon to the existing body of electrical theory, rather than isolate the phenomenon because of its novelty. As they commented in one report, the "experiments were thought in accordance with the known laws of electricity and the results fully confirmed our expectations." Behind this strategy was an awareness that contributions supporting the existing body of knowledge were more likely to be rewarded than were discoveries that upset the accepted order of knowledge. Wishing to increase their respectability in the scientific community, Thomson and Houston took the conservative route and gained credit for their careful argument employing the accepted idea of induction. In contrast, Edison was painfully aware that he was an outsider to the scientific community and perhaps believed that he could gain entry into the community only by making the large claim of a new force.

Third, when it seemed necessary to devise a new experiment to counter Edison's claims, Thomson used his craft and experimental skills to devise a test that would satisfy the scientific community. Assuming that the spark, no matter how short-lived, had some polarity, he used the polarity of one spark to cancel out another. Thomson may very well have modeled his experiment on the well-known Wheatstone-bridge test, where an unknown resistance is measured by balancing it against a known resistance. In contrast to Thomson's experiment, Edison's subsequent experiments were far more complicated and inconclusive, showing that the spark could travel through insulated materials and over long telegraph wires. Based on a belief that the spark was novel, Edison's research strategy isolated the etheric force from the existing corpus of electrical science. Edison's efforts probably led scientists to conclude that he was confounding the issue, rather than helping to clarify and verify the existence of a new force. In that context, knowing that it was not necessary to address all of Edison's claims about the etheric force, Thomson gave the scientific community what it wanted – a simple test that disconfirmed the force in terms of existing knowledge. Utilizing his scientific education and experience, Thomson knew how to organize empirical data so as to satisfy other men of science.

Throughout the controversy, one can see not only what Thomson and Houston knew about electricity but also how they used their knowledge. Caught between the economic necessity of having to be schoolteachers and the intellectual idealism of the scientific researcher, the two men anxiously looked for opportunities to promote their own careers by contributing to the stock of knowledge. Because they oriented their work toward a scientific audience, the professors couched their self-promotion in terms of the scientific virtue of disinterested objectivity. As a result, they came across to some as experimenters dedicated to the pursuit of truth; in 1879, they were introduced in a British electrical journal as "two American men of science, who labour in a truly scientific spirit, and not, as is too common in their country, for mere gain."[74] One cannot help but think that the British writer was contrasting them with Edison.

To some of their professional colleagues, however, Thomson's and Houston's efforts at building their careers were not fully respectable. With the etheric force controversy and their invention of a carbon microphone (which is described in the next chapter), their claims of discovery came at the expense of denigrating the work of other scientists and inventors. It was from this perspective that George Barker, professor of physics at the University of Pennsylvania, advised his friend Edison not to display his latest telephone before the Franklin Institute. In May 1879, Barker wrote that

> I could not believe that a society which is controlled scientifically by Houston & Thomson, who have themselves said so many shameful things about you, and a society in whose meetings you have been held

74 "Curious Thermo-Motor," *Telegraphic Journal and Electrical Review*, 7:88 (1 March 1879).

up to ridicule & against whom I have had to defend you often, could
have the cheek to ask such a thing of you.[75]

To be sure, Barker was strongly prejudiced toward Edison (he is credited with first suggesting to Edison that he work on an electric light),
but Barker's remarks nonetheless suggest that not everyone in Philadelphia approved of Thomson and Houston's scientific style.

Although Barker may have been an enemy of Thomson, even he had
to concede that the young man was one of the scientific leaders of the
Franklin Institute. Clearly, by the late 1870s, Thomson had established
himself in the Philadelphia scientific community. Working as both a
practitioner and aspiring researcher, he had created for himself a comfortable career that responded to his needs and desires. Mixing employment, research, and institutional connections, the young man had
attained for himself some degree of security and status. Yet he was still
intellectually curious and in search of challenging problems. Rather
than resting content with his situation, Thomson utilized his professional scientific base to launch himself into the world of electrical
technology. How the young professor made use of his scientific background to build dynamos and arc lights is the topic of the next chapter.

75 George F. Barker to Thomas A. Edison, 16 May 1879, 1879 TAE General File,
    ENHS. I am indebted to John Deasey for bringing this letter to my attention.

2. Learning the craft of invention

By 1877, Thomson had become moderately successful in Philadelphia scientific circles. He was professor of chemistry at the prestigious Central High School, he had published half a dozen scientific articles, and he had challenged Edison's claim concerning the etheric force. An active member of both the Franklin Institute and the American Philosophical Society, Thomson was regularly giving lectures and presenting papers on chemistry and electricity. Given those activities, it would have seemed likely for Thomson to have spent the rest of his career pursuing chemistry in Philadelphia as a teacher and researcher, as did his associate Edwin Houston.

Within three years, however, Thomson radically altered the course of his career. Rather than pursue science exclusively, he became an inventor. Prior to 1877, electrical technology had been only one of Thomson's many interests; after 1877, he devoted nearly all his free time to studying it. With the assistance of Houston, Thomson designed an alternating-current system of arc lights that they demonstrated in December 1878. Though not entirely practical, this first system did attract the attention of several businessmen, who subsequently underwrote Thomson and Houston's research.

This chapter narrates how Thomson made the transition from professor to inventor, emphasizing how he learned the craft of invention. In particular, it investigates the several ways in which he acquired the skills and knowledge necessary for invention. After exploring how Thomson gained some of the craft knowledge needed for invention, we shall examine how Thomson applied those skills and ideas to his first arc lighting system. Significantly, that system reflected the values and attitudes he had acquired from practicing science in Philadelphia. Although one might assume that Thomson and Houston designed their first system for an audience of potential investors and businessmen, they instead created their system to impress their scientific peers at the Franklin Institute and the American Philosophical Society. Thus, that first system offers an opportunity to see how inventors construct technological artifacts in response to their own values and those of their audience. Moreover, this case suggests that the interaction between science and technology in late-nineteenth-century America was not simply a matter of reducing theory to practice, but also a transfer of skills, values, and attitudes.

Learning about dynamos and electricity, 1873–7

Along with his strong interest in chemistry, Thomson found time in the 1870s to investigate electrical science and technology. Not only was he aware of the major developments in the field, but he also frequently studied those developments by carefully examining new machines and building models. Because physicists had yet to articulate a comprehensive theory for what they called the "imponderable" forces of electricity, light, and heat, one of the few ways to learn about electricity was to study it firsthand by observation and model building.[1]

Thomson first studied electrostatic machines, which accumulated electrical charge, as opposed to generating current. From the wine-bottle machine of his youth Thomson graduated to the construction of Holtz electrostatic machines, which produced substantial amounts of charge by using large revolving glass plates. Using scraps of wood and tin cans, he built two of these machines, one in high school and another around 1877 (Figure 2.1). An advertising circular suggests that Thomson also may have helped his brother Fred sell these machines for demonstration purposes. In building the machines, Thomson observed that the amount of charge or output was limited by the speed at which the glass plates rotated; to overcome that limitation, he designed two new machines in which he substituted paraffin-covered cardboard cylinders for the glass plates; being lighter, the cardboard cylinders could be rotated faster and hence could generate more charge.[2]

1 Benjamin Silliman characterized electricity, light, and heat as "imponderable" forces in his textbook *Principles of Physics, or Natural Philosophy*, 2nd ed. (Philadelphia: Theodore Bliss, 1865). This was the textbook that Thomson studied as a student at Central High.

2 "Continuation of Activities During Stay out of School," Autobiog. Papers, TP. An electrostatic machine said to be built by Thomson in 1877 is on display in the Elihu Thomson Hall of Electrical Science, Boston Museum of Science; it is on loan from the MIT Museum, Cambridge, Massachusetts. For Frederick

Figure 2.1. Electrostatic machine built by Thomson, circa 1877. From the collections of the Boston Museum of Science. Photo by the author.

As he experimented with electrostatic machines, Thomson also learned about the first self-excited dynamos. Prior to the late 1860s, the only machines that used Faraday's principles of electromagnetic induction were magneto generators; with large banks of permanent magnets, those machines generated current by having an armature revolve through the magnetic field. Because the output of the magneto generators was limited by the strength of the magnetic field, experimenters soon replaced the permanent magnets with more powerful electromagnets. At first the electromagnets were excited by small separate magneto machines, but it was then discovered that generators could be designed so that they would produce enough current for output and for exciting the electromagnets. Because those machines were self-exciting or self-sustaining, they were termed "dynamic electromagnetic machines" or "dynamos." Thomson first saw a dynamo in the laboratory of Robert E. Rogers, the professor of physics at the University of Pennsylvania. Based on the designs of English instrument makers Henry Wilde and William Ladd, that dynamo was cranked by

Thomson's efforts at selling electrostatic machines, see "Electrical Machines and Electrical Apparatus . . . ," circa 1873–4, Miscellaneous Boxes, TP. See also ET, "Cylinder Holtz Machine," *J. Franklin Inst.*, 103:207–9 (March 1877); and *Telegraphic Journal and Electrical Review* (London), 5:126–7.

two men and produced enough current to keep a strip of platinum glowing red-hot.[3]

Thrilled by the Wilde-Ladd machine, Thomson fashioned his first dynamo between 1873 and 1875. A small model, this machine was carved out of wood, using iron only where necessary, such as for the cores of the field magnets (Figure 2.2). To simplify construction of the armature, he wound four coils around several wooden vanes, rather than struggle with the more common practice of winding a Gramme ring armature by passing the wire around and through a ring (Figure 2.3). Thomson initially thought that he had discovered that armature winding, but he soon learned that it had been invented by Werner Siemens in 1867 and was known as a drum-wound armature (Figure 2.4). A working device, that small dynamo was one of many models and experiments undertaken by Thomson during the 1870s in order to learn firsthand about electricity.[4]

Over the next two years, Thomson had opportunities to observe other dynamos in Philadelphia. At the Centennial Exhibition during the summer of 1876, Thomson studied the machines displayed by the Société des Machines Magneto-électriques Gramme of France. Designed by Zénobe T. Gramme, a Belgian working in Paris, those dynamos were among the first to be commercially feasible, because their unique ring armatures produced a strong, steady current. At the Centennial Exhibition, several Gramme dynamos were imaginatively arranged to illustrate the potential uses of electricity; while one dynamo powered an arc light, another was used to transmit energy to an electric motor and pump that ran a small waterfall. Perhaps inspired by that exhibit, Thomson and Houston arranged for Central

3 For information on the development of the dynamo, see W. James King, "The Development of Electrical Technology in the 19th Century. 3: The Early Arc Light and Generator," *United States National Museum Bulletin 228,* paper 30 (Washington, D.C.: Smithsonian Institution, 1962), pp. 333–407 (hereafter cited as King, "The Early Arc Light and Generator"); ET, "The Pioneer Investigations on Dynamo Machines Fifty Years Ago," *J. Franklin Inst.,* 206:17–25 (July 1928); ET to [J. W.] Hammond, 18 June 1927, Hall of History Collection.

4 See dynamo model, item 1467, Thomson Collection, Franklin Institute Science Museum, Philadelphia, and "Dynamo Work and Its Development," pp. 1–2, Autobiog. Papers, TP (hereafter cited as "Dynamo Work"). The surviving artifact is dated 1873, but Thomson's memoirs state that he built his first dynamo in 1875.

Figure 2.2. Model of a dynamo made by Thomson in 1873. From Thomson Collection, General Electric Hall of History, Schenectady.

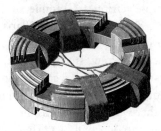

Figure 2.3. Ring armature for Brush dynamo. From A. R. von Urbanitzky, *Electricity in the Service of Man* (New York: 1886), p. 261.

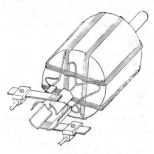

Figure 2.4. Drum armature for dynamo. From S. P. Thompson, *Dynamo-Electric Machinery,* 3rd ed. (London: 1888), p. 42.

High School to purchase a small Gramme machine in 1876, which they used for both lecture demonstrations and personal experiments. In addition to the Gramme dynamo, Thomson also must have seen a demonstration of a Wallace-Farmer dynamo at the Franklin Institute in February 1877. On loan from its builders, William Wallace and Moses Farmer of Ansonia, Connecticut, that dynamo was used for arc lighting as well as electroplating.[5]

After studying those machines and reading about others, Thomson's interest in the technology of electrical generation grew. In the fall of 1876 he built a second dynamo in his attic workshop. Larger than his first model, the second dynamo required about 0.5 horsepower, but it could run a small arc light. Using his foot lathe to power the machine, Thomson recalled that "by working very hard and perspiring a great deal I could keep the light going for about a minute or so." Thomson wanted to run his new machine during his January 1877 lectures on electricity at the Franklin Institute, but the institute's lecture hall lacked a steam engine to power it. As the proper scientist, he was not about to work up a sweat while at the podium, so instead Thomson used his dynamo as an electric motor. Like other dynamos of the period, this machine could also be employed as a motor by providing an electric current to its armature. To supply a current for the motor, Thomson set up a battery of chemical cells and thus was able to demonstrate in his lectures how galvanic (i.e., based on chemical reactions) electricity could be converted into dynamic (i.e., based on mechanical motion) electricity.[6]

With this second model, Thomson sought to understand and improve the operation of dynamos. He studied the performances of various armature designs by constructing at least two different armatures for his model. He began keeping a notebook in which he tried to classify existing dynamo designs and in which he periodically sketched his own modifications (Figure 2.5). Through such efforts Thomson was organizing his random observations and experiments into a mental model of how dynamos worked. As Michael E. Gorman and I have

5 ET, "Personal Recollections of the Development of the Electrical Industry," *Engineering Magazine*, pp. 563–72 (July 1905); *Fifty-eighth Annual Report of the Board of Public Education of the First School District of Pennsylvania ... for 1876* (Philadelphia: 1877), p. 34; "Proceedings of the Franklin Institute," *J. Franklin Inst.*, 73:151 (March 1879).
6 "Dynamo Work," p. 2; ET to Hammond, 18 June 1927, Hall of History Collection. Quotation is from ET, "Personal Recollections," p. 565.

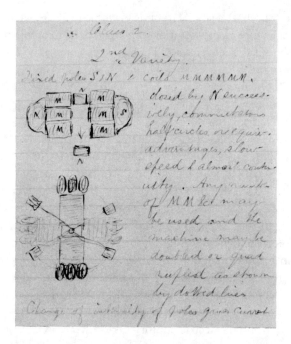

Figure 2.5. Page from Thomson's "Dynamo-Electric Machines" notebook, Thomson Papers, American Philosophical Society, Philadelphia.

suggested elsewhere, inventors frequently develop mental models of their inventions that are not theories but rather dynamic representations that they can "run" in their imaginations.[7] Inventors utilize mental models because the phenomena or forces that they are investigating often are poorly understood and frequently can be comprehended only by means of a specific physical example. Such was the case in the 1870s for dynamos, and the only way for Thomson to understand how such machines could convert mechanical motion into electricity was to observe them and construct his own mental model.

In formulating his mental model of how dynamos worked, Thomson became skeptical of the prevailing wisdom of armature design. Most electricians at that time thought that the only part of the armature coil that produced current was the part that cut the magnetic field horizon-

7 Michael E. Gorman and W. Bernard Carlson, "Interpreting Invention as a Cognitive Process: The Case of Alexander Graham Bell, Thomas Edison, and the Telephone," *Science, Technology, and Human Values*, 15:131–64 (Spring 1990), especially pp. 134–6.

tally; consequently, they tried to maximize the amount of "active" wire, and hence current output, by using long, narrow armatures.[8] On the basis of his own observations, Thomson decided that all parts of the armature coil produced current, making it preferable to have the various dimensions of the armature approximately the same. Thomson incorporated that preference into his mental model, and subsequently he used it to develop a series of improved dynamos.

Learning by doing: early inventions, 1875–8

Paralleling his growing fascination with dynamos, Thomson also experienced some of the special tasks related to invention. In working on several electrical and mechanical inventions, Thomson learned the details of getting models to work, the intricacies of filing patents, and the problems of defending one's inventions in print. Although only one of his early inventions had any commercial significance, these projects exposed Thomson to the range of challenges associated with bringing an idea out of the realm of the imagination and presenting it to the marketplace. In these early endeavors, Houston served as both mentor and partner to Thomson, and together they accomplished much more than they would have had they worked separately.

Thomson's first patented invention was a fastener for street-railway rails. He did not identify the need for such an invention, but rather produced it in response to a request from several businessmen. Working with Houston, he designed a self-locking tie plate that held the rail securely. In applying for a patent on their device in the fall of 1875, they divided the work by having Houston prepare the written specifications and handle the correspondence with the U.S. Patent Office, while Thomson constructed the model to be submitted. After some delay because of vague claims, Thomson and Houston received a patent for their invention in May 1876. Like many other inventions patented during that period, the device was never employed on a regular basis.[9]

8 One of Thomson's experimental armatures, a two-coil drum version, is item 162 in the Thomson Collection at the Franklin Institute Science Museum in Philadelphia. For his classification of dynamos, see "Dynamo-Electric Machines," 1876–85, Notebooks, TP. For a discussion of armature proportioning, see "Dynamo Work," p. 2.

9 ET and EJH, "Street Railway Fasteners," U.S. Patent No. 177,124 (filed 18 October 1875, granted 9 May 1875). See also Thomson's own comments on his patents, TP. For Houston's role in securing the patent, see the application file for this patent, NARS.

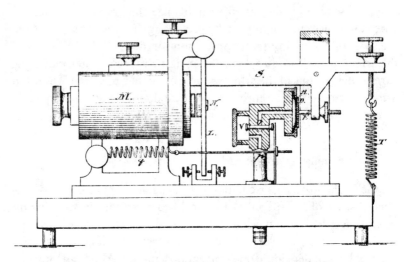

Figure 2.6. Thomson and Houston's pneumatic telegraph relay. From E. Thomson and E. J. Houston, "Improvement in Electrotelegraphic Apparatus," U.S. Patent No. 183,031 (10 October 1876).

At the same time that Thomson and Houston were working on the rail fastener, they were also perfecting a "pneumo-dynamic relay sounder" for telegraph applications. Intended as a replacement for the electromagnetic sounder commonly used to receive telegraph messages, this invention was a sensitive electromagnetic valve that released compressed air (Figure 2.6). By having compressed air do the work of the relay, Thomson and Houston believed that they had eliminated the need for cumbersome batteries at every telegraph station. In filing for the patent, Houston handled the paperwork, and again the patent examiners complained that the claims were not in good legal form; clearly Houston was learning the art of patenting by trial and error. Houston drew attention to this invention by demonstrating it at a meeting of the American Philosophical Society in October 1876. Although a few people in the telegraph industry showed some interest, the pneumatic relay did not meet any pressing need. Consequently, it too was laid aside.[10]

10 ET and EJH, "Improvement in Electrotelegraphic Apparatus," U.S. Patent No. 183,031 (filed 8 November 1875, granted 10 October 1876); see also Patent Comments, TP; and application file for this patent, NARS; [Meeting of 7 October 1876], *Proc. APS*, 16:286 (1876–7).

With their third invention, a centrifugal cream separator, Thomson and Houston achieved some success, having learned the importance of developing devices that would respond to existing marketing opportunities. Drawing on a few contacts in the Philadelphia business community, Thomson was also able to secure some financial support for this invention.

Thomson recalled that the initial idea for the invention came to him in 1876 while teaching his class at Central High School about centrifugal forces. To demonstrate those forces, he whirled around a vessel with liquid and sediment in it, probably to show that the liquid did not spill out even when the vessel was spinning horizontally. However, he was impressed at how quickly the centrifugal force separated the sediment from the liquid by pushing the sediment to the outside of the vessel. Realizing that such an idea could be used to separate liquids in his chemistry experiments, Thomson built a device with two swinging baskets, much like the small centrifuges occasionally used in laboratories today.[11]

Hoping to secure assistance and financial support, Thomson showed his device to several Philadelphia businessmen. His first contact was Thomas McCollin, a dealer in photographic supplies from whom he regularly purchased chemicals. McCollin found that the centrifuge could be used to concentrate photographic emulsions, and he encouraged Thomson to perfect the invention. Aware that a centrifugal device was already being used to refine sugar, Thomson next approached Henry G. Morris, a major manufacturer of sugar-refining equipment in South Philadelphia, for financial support in developing his centrifugal separator. Morris agreed to help with the development in return for one-third of any royalties received after the invention was patented and sold.[12]

---

11 ET, "The Centrifugal Creamer: From Laboratory to Factory and Farm," *Research Narrative No. 9*, 15 May 1921, Engineering Foundation (copy in Collected Essays, TP); see also Patent Comments, TP; and ET to Brockett, 26 January 1933, CL, TP.

12 Morris's interest in sugar refining was extensive; in *J. Franklin Inst.* for August 1871 he advertised that his Southwark Foundry could provide "Everything demanded in the erection and fitting-up of *references for working sugar and molasses.*" Thomson may have met Morris at the Franklin Institute, because they were both members. For the business arrangements with Morris, see EJH to ET, 3 February 1885, LB 3/86–9/86, between p. 10 and p. 11, TP.

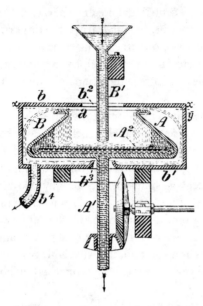

Figure 2.7. Thomson and Houston's centrifugal creamer, 1877. The cream was fed into the machine through the funnel in the top center, and spun around in the inner vessel (A); the lighter constituents were collected in the outer vessel (B). From E. Thomson and E. J. Houston, "Centrifugal Creamer," U.S. Patent No. 239,659 (5 April 1881).

By that time, Thomson had involved Houston in the invention. Together, they developed a separator suitable for several industrial applications, but increasingly they focused on a centrifugal machine for separating cream from milk. Abandoning the swinging-basket arrangement, they constructed a separator that could be fed liquid continuously. Ultimately they patented a device with a cone-shaped vessel revolving inside a larger tank (Figure 2.7). The liquid to be separated was introduced into the inner vessel through a pipe that ran down the vertical shaft of the machine. As the incoming liquid revolved around in the cone-shaped vessel, its lighter constituents (the skim milk) were pushed by the centrifugal force out of the cone-shaped vessel and into the outside tank. A small pump was then used to keep the liquids flowing by removing the lighter liquid from the outer compartment.[13]

13 ET and EJH, "Centrifugal Creamer," U.S. Patent No. 239,659 (filed 29 October 1877, granted 5 April 1881).

Securing a patent on the invention proved to be difficult. In April 1877 Houston filed the specifications and drawings; it was not until October that they submitted the model, perhaps suggesting that there were problems in getting the separator to work. Intending to patent a machine that could be used with a variety of liquids, Houston drew up the application so as to cover seven different versions. However, because the patent rules permitted a patent to have only one specific application, the patent examiner rejected the initial application and advised the inventors to seek the assistance of competent legal counsel. Rather than struggle further with the complexities of patent law, Thomson and Houston engaged J. Snowden Bell, a patent attorney who conveniently had his offices in the Franklin Institute's building. Bell shepherded the patent application through a preliminary interference and secured a patent on the separator in 1881.[14]

To exploit their invention, Thomson and Houston assigned the patent to Theodore Bergner, a Philadelphia mechanical engineer who in turn organized the Philadelphia Creamery Supply Company. Through that company, Bergner sold a number of separators, and he paid Thomson about $1,000 in royalties during the 1880s. In 1889, Bergner sold the patent to the DeLaval Company, the leading producer of cream separators. DeLaval purchased the patent in anticipation of controlling the manufacture of separators, but much to its chagrin, the company found that a separator based on the Thomson-Houston patent could not be made to work. As a result, the company was unable to use the patent to sue competitors for infringement. Such difficulties with the cream separator patent suggest that Thomson and Houston had not perfected their invention in the late 1870s and that they were still learning the art of invention.[15]

The lack of commercial interest that Thomson and Houston encountered in regard to their rail fastener and pneumatic relay and their difficulties in getting the cream separator to work undoubtedly were typical of the problems encountered by novice inventors in the 1870s. Such difficulties reveal that invention was not simply a matter of dreaming up new ideas, but an intensive craft that required the abilities

14 Application file for U.S. Patent No. 239,659, NARS.
15 For a record of the royalties Thomson received between 1885 and 1889, see "C.H.S. – courses Div. A & B Chemistry 1878," Notebook, TP. The later problems with the separator are outlined in R. H. Heep to John A. McManus (Thomson's personal secretary), 28 May 1937, Hall of History Collection.

to manifest new ideas in working devices and to present these ideas persuasively to patent officials and businessmen. Yet despite their setbacks, Thomson and Houston continued to invent.

Still another of their early efforts involved a microphone relay that was an improvement on the telephone. After Alexander Graham Bell announced his invention in 1876, Thomson and Houston built a telephone that they demonstrated for their classes. Like Edison and other experimenters, they noted that whereas Bell's magneto telephone could transmit sound, it was unable to amplify the signal, and they sought ways to overcome this problem. Thomson and Houston found a solution to the problem of amplification in David E. Hughes's carbon microphone. In May 1878, Hughes described how the resistance in carbon varied with slight changes in pressure. Hughes demonstrated this principle in a device he called a "microphone," which comprised a sharpened pencil rod resting loosely in the conical depressions in two carbon blocks. With his microphone, Hughes was able to amplify whispers, much to the amazement of scientists and laymen.[16]

On learning of Hughes's discovery, Thomson and Houston at once applied it to Bell's telephone. By fastening several small carbon microphones to the front of the vibrating diaphragm of the telephone, they found that the volume of the signal could be greatly enhanced (Figure 2.8). They observed further that the resistance of the carbon rods was greatest when they were perfectly vertical; to reduce the sensitivity of the device, it was necessary only to tilt the rods slightly. Considering this design to be a remarkable improvement on the telephone, Thomson and Houston presented it at a meeting of the American Philosophical Society and published a description in the Franklin Institute's Journal. To broadcast their claims to the scientific and technical community, they also published notices in Nature and the English Mechanic and World of Science.[17]

16 George B. Prescott, The Speaking Telephone, Electric Light, and Other Recent Electrical Inventions (New York: D. Appleton, 1879), p. 224; M. D. Fagen, ed., A History of Engineering and Sciences in the Bell System: The Early Years (1875–1925) (Bell Laboratories, 1975), pp. 66–7.

17 [Notes on 3 May 1878 meeting], Proc. APS, 17:720 (1877–8). Thomson and Houston also demonstrated their microphone before the Franklin Institute; EJH, "The Telephone Relay" (letter to editor), J. Franklin Inst., 106:206–7 (September 1878). For their articles, see EJH and ET, "The Microphone Relay," J. Franklin Inst., 106:60–3 (July 1878); reprinted in English Mechanic and World of Science, No. 696 (26 July 1878), p. 493. The two professors even went so far as to design one with 30 separate pairs of carbon rods in parallel; see ET to EJH, 18 August 1885, LB 5/83–8/85, p. 243, TP.

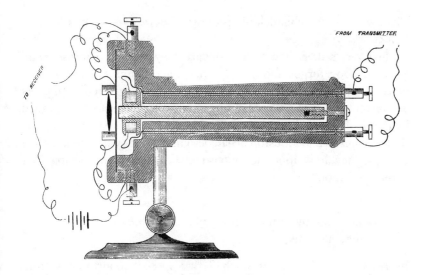

Figure 2.8. Thomson and Houston's carbon microphone attached to the front of Bell's telephone, 1878. From E. J. Houston and E. Thomson, "The Microphone Relay," *J. Franklin Inst.*, 106:60–3 (July 1878).

Their claim to priority in having applied the microphone to Bell's telephone was soon hotly contested by Edison. Since 1873, Edison had been experimenting with carbon in several telegraphic and telephonic inventions. As early as July 1877, he published a report of his experiments that described how he was using a small button of carbon fastened to the center of the telephone's diaphragm as a means for improving amplification. On the basis of that publication, Edison was already feuding with Hughes about the discovery of the basic principle behind the microphone, and so it was but a short reach for Edison to attack Thomson and Houston's claims. In letters to the *Chemical News,* Edison cited his previous work and rudely dismissed their invention, noting that "change of form and name appears to be an easy and favourite method now-a-days of making discoveries and inventions." Houston responded lamely by claiming that Edison had applied his carbon button only to the speaking telegraph, not to Bell's articulating telephone, but that was a rather specious distinction. Whereas they had been able to discredit Edison in the etheric force controversy, Thomson and Houston were forced to concede the carbon microphone to Edison, and they published nothing further about their device. By early 1878, Edison's carbon-button telephone was commercially feasible, whereas the Philadelphia professors' device was only a lecture-hall curiosity.[18]

However, rather than feeling thwarted by Edison, Thomson and Houston soon forgot about the carbon microphone as they became excited about another field of electrical technology: arc lighting. As Thomson learned about arc lighting in late 1877, he became intrigued by the challenges of building a commercially feasible system. In a short time, Thomson and Houston began designing their own system, and in doing so they drew upon the lessons they had learned in devising their earlier inventions.

Learning by testing: the Franklin Institute dynamo tests, 1877–8

In 1877 and 1878, Thomson had two special opportunities from which he obtained a detailed understanding of the state of the art in arc lighting. First, with Houston, Thomson served on a Franklin Institute committee for the testing of dynamos. While participating in these tests, Thomson examined the major arc lighting systems then available in America. Second, he added to this knowledge by traveling to Paris in 1878 to examine Continental arc lighting systems. From those two experiences, Thomson became convinced that he, too, could design a practical lighting system. Because of the tests and the trip, Thomson entered the arc-lighting field with a good overview of the technology, an advantage that proved essential for surviving in this new field.

Although arc lighting often is downplayed in favor of incandescent lighting, the former nonetheless played a central role in the history of electrical technology. Arc lamps preceded incandescent bulbs and helped define the contours of the electrical industry. Unlike the incan-

18 Francis Jehl, *Menlo Park Reminiscences* (Dearborn, Mich.: Edison Institute, 1936), Vol. 1, pp. 134–9; quotation is from Thomas A. Edison, "Telephone Relay" (letter to editor), *Chemical News*, 38:198 (18 October 1878); Thomas A. Edison, "Telephone Repeaters" (letter to editor), *Chemical News*, 38:45 (26 July 1878); EJH, "The Telephone Relay," *Chemical News*, 38:138–9 (13 September 1878); Reese V. Jenkins and Keith A. Nier, "A Record for Invention: Thomas Edison and His Papers," *IEEE Transactions on Education*, E-27:191–6 (November 1984); W. Bernard Carlson and Michael E. Gorman, "Thinking and Doing at Menlo Park: Edison's Development of the Telephone, 1876–1878," in W. E. Pretzer, ed., *Working at Inventing: Thomas A. Edison and the Menlo Park Experience* (Dearborn, Mich.: Henry Ford Museum and Greenfield Village, 1989), pp. 84–99.

Figure 2.9. Charles Brush. From Brush Papers, Special Collections Department, Case Western Reserve University Library, Cleveland.

descent lamp, which produces light by having a current heat a high-resistance filament to the point where it glows and gives off light, an arc lamp generates light when a voltage is applied across two carbon electrodes. If the voltage is sufficiently high and the carbons are close enough, then an arc jumps across the gap and creates a brilliant light. As the arc jumps the gap, it tends to oxidize and burn away the carbons; hence, it is necessary to provide some means of moving the carbons together, and they must eventually be replaced. The arc light was first demonstrated by Sir Humphrey Davy in 1808 using two charcoal electrodes and an enormous battery consisting of hundreds of electrochemical cells. During the next 60 years, numerous scientists and inventors devised various arrangements for controlling the electrodes, but their efforts were limited by the size and expense of batteries. It was not until Wilde and Ladd in England and Gramme in France developed practical dynamos in the 1870s that arc lighting could be exploited commercially.[19]

In the United States, the first arc lighting system was developed by Charles Brush of Cleveland (Figure 2.9). Like Thomson, Brush had studied chemistry, at the University of Michigan, and he worked for a

19 King, "The Early Arc Light and Generator."

time as an analytical chemist. From his youth he had been fascinated by electricity, and in 1876 he drew up plans for his first dynamo. To arrange for machining the parts for that dynamo, Brush approached his friend George W. Stockly, who was vice-president of the Telegraph Supply Company. Stockly not only ordered his company's machine shop to build Brush's first dynamo but also had Brush hired to develop his dynamo and other electrical devices. Over the next two years, Brush designed dynamos for electroplating and arc lighting, as well as a practical arc lamp.[20]

As Brush and the European inventors improved their designs for both arc lamps and dynamos, the Franklin Institute became interested in acquiring an arc lighting system. Over the course of the nineteenth century, the institute had developed a tradition of having expert committees conduct tests of new technology. Having already undertaken comparative tests on boilers, strengths of materials, and waterwheels, it is not surprising that the institute sponsored an examination of commercial dynamos in 1877 and 1878. The institute had recently installed a six-horsepower steam engine in its hall, and its governing board of managers wished to supplement that engine with a dynamo and arc light that could be used for experiments and demonstrations. In order to select a dynamo for purchase, the managers decided to hold a series of comparative trials. To compensate inventors for the cost of shipping their dynamos to the institute, the managers proposed to describe each machine in a published report, indicating how much light each dynamo produced, how much power it required, and the capability of each machine for prolonged operation. Implicitly, of course, the institute promised the winner of the competition the privilege of advertising that his machine had been judged superior by an objective panel of experts.[21]

20 There is no definitive biography of Thomson's arc-lighting rival, Charles Brush. Brush's papers are available in the Special Collections Department, University Libraries, Case Western Reserve University, Cleveland, and this collection was used by Harry J. Eisenmann III in preparing "Charles F. Brush: Pioneer Innovator in Electrical Technology" (unpublished Ph.D. dissertation, Department of History, Case Institute of Technology, 1967). For Brush's training and early work with the Telegraph Supply Company, consult the following items in the Brush Papers: "Charles F. Brush, M.E., Analytical & Consulting Chemist, ... Price List for 1871," box 20; Brush, "The Arc-Light," *Century Magazine* (May 1905), box 8; contracts between Brush and the Telegraph Supply Co., 7 June 1876 and 4 March 1877, box 20.

21 See Bruce Sinclair, *Philadelphia's Philosopher Mechanics: A History of the Franklin Institute, 1824–1865* (Baltimore: Johns Hopkins University Press,

The institute publicized the trials in newspapers, scientific periodicals, and its own journal; however, it also sent special requests to the leading manufacturers of electrical equipment in Europe and America.[22] Unfortunately, only two manufacturers, the Telegraph Supply Company and Wallace & Sons, chose to participate, with each supplying two different commercial dynamos. The institute partly offset that disappointment by having Professor Harvey W. Wiley of Purdue University (and later of USDA Pure Food and Drug Law fame) send a Gramme dynamo that had previously been displayed at the Philadelphia Centennial Exhibition.

To conduct the tests, the institute appointed a committee of nine men; as an indication of the importance of the undertaking, five members of the committee were managers of the institute. Already known for their electrical experiments, Thomson and Houston were invited to make the electrical measurements. Working through the fall of 1877 and the winter of 1878, the committee rigged a special dynamometer for measuring the power used by each of the five dynamos, and they conducted photometric tests to determine the amount of light each machine produced. In measuring the light put out by each generator, Thomas McCollin, the photographic dealer, assisted the committee by taking detailed photographs of the burning carbon electrodes.[23]

Thomson and Houston probably helped with those tasks, too, but on their own they tackled the problem of measuring the voltage, current, and resistance of the machines when operating. Lacking voltmeters and ammeters, they used a calorimeter and the traditional Wheatstone-bridge method. With cumbersome methods, Thomson and Houston were careful to duplicate the external resistance of the arc light, for experiments quickly revealed that such resistance affected the

1974); and "Franklin Institute," *J. Franklin Inst.*, 74:145–6 (September 1877). The institute's board of managers may have been inspired to undertake the tests because a similar set of trials was held in Britain in 1876–7 by Trinity House at the South Foreland Lighthouse; see J. N. Shoolbred, "On the Present State of Electric Lighting," *Engineering*, 26:362–5 (1 November 1878), especially p. 364.

22 For the dynamo tests, the Franklin Institute contacted the following: M. Breguet of Paris, manufacturers of the Gramme dynamo; Siemens Brothers of London; Condit, Hanson, & Van Winkle of Newark, New Jersey, producers of Edward Weston's machine; the Telegraph Supply Company of Cleveland, makers of Charles Brush's dynamo; and Wallace & Sons of Ansonia, Connecticut, makers of the Wallace-Farmer dynamo.

23 "Report of the Committee on Dynamo-Electric Machines" (Part I), *J. Franklin Inst.*, 105:289–303 (May 1878).

dynamo's internal resistance, current, and efficiency. Once they had secured reliable figures for the current and voltage output of each machine, they calculated the work performed and determined the efficiency of each machine by comparing the work with the amount of power used to run the machine. From a purely technical standpoint, Thomson and Houston found the Gramme dynamo to be the most efficient, followed by the large and small Brush machines (Table 2.1).

The investigating committee, however, recommended that the institute purchase the small Brush machine because it was "admirably adapted to the production of currents of widely varying electromotive force." Furthermore, the committee was impressed with the construction of the machine's commutator and its overall mechanical design, leading them to conclude that the Brush dynamo would be the easiest to maintain and repair. Following success in the competition, sales of the Brush arc lighting system increased rapidly. Because of the Franklin Institute tests, John Wanamaker chose Brush arc lights for his department store, and by December 1878 he had installed 28 such lights.[24]

Thomson and Houston came away from these tests with much firsthand knowledge about different dynamos. In particular, they learned about the complex relationships embodied in a dynamo. Although some of those relationships remained unarticulated and part of their mental model of how a dynamo worked, they expressed other relationships in several formal papers. One relationship that they discerned involved waste heat and eddy currents. In conducting tests with the calorimeter, Thomson and Houston were impressed with the amount of energy lost through the heating of the dynamos' armatures. They attributed this heat to "local action" or what is now known as eddy currents. Not knowing how to minimize those extra currents generated in the armature's core, Thomson and Houston could only

24 See EJH and ET, "The Investigations of the Sub-Committee on Electrical Measurements," Part II of the "Report of the Committee on Dynamo-Electric Machines," *J. Franklin Inst.*, 105:363–78 (June 1878); quotation on p. 376. For the purchase of a Brush machine by John Wanamaker, see Nicholas B. Wainwright, *History of the Philadelphia Electric Company, 1881–1961* (Philadelphia Electric Company, 1961), p. 13. Additional details concerning the tests are given in ET, "Electrical Measurements," 4 December 1912, Hall of History Collection.

Table 2.1. Effects of dynamo-electric machines in foot-pounds per minute.

NAME OF MACHINE.	Dynamometer reading, F. P. consumed.	Friction and resistance of air.	F. P. consumed, after deducting friction.	F. P. appearing in arc as heat.	F. P. appearing in whole circuit.	F. P. unaccounted for in the circuit.	Per cent. of power utilized in arc.	Per cent. of effect after deduct. friction.
A¹, Large Brush,	107606	17950	89656	33457	53646	36010	31	37½
A², Small Brush,	117700	12328	105372	26148	45448	59924	22	25
A², " "	124248	14976	109272	33543	58340	50932	27	31
B², Small Wallace,	97068	7800	89268	13780	37596	51672	14	15¾
B², " "	128544	11072	117472	15469	38862	78610	12	13
Gramme,	60992	4512	56480	23384	43448	13082	38	41

For conversion into Gramme-metres – – 1 foot-pound = 138 Gramme-metres, nearly.

Source: Edwin J. Houston and Elihu Thomson, "The Investigations of the Sub Committee on Electrical Measurements" Part II of the "Report of the Committee on Dynamo-Electric Machines," Journal of the Franklin Institute, 105:363–78 (June 1878), p. 375.

cite the problem and remark on the desirability of reducing that source of inefficiency.[25]

Similarly, in measuring the resistance of the arc light powered by each generator, Thomson and Houston proposed several laws linking arc resistance, current strength, and illuminating power. For instance, they noted that there was an inverse relationship between the resistance of the arc gap and the current in the circuit; they found that the resistance of the arc fell as the current increased. From this observation, Thomson and Houston concluded that economical subdivision of light was possible; as they argued in an 1879 paper based on the dynamo tests, if the current in an arc-light circuit was doubled, then the resistance of the arc was halved, rather than staying constant as some electrical scientists had thought. However, this relationship was based on the assumption that the gap between the electrodes of the arc was kept constant. Thus, for a practical lighting system with more than one arc lamp, it would be necessary to provide each lamp with a regulator for maintaining a fixed distance between the carbons. Although Brush had hit upon this idea through his own experiments and was the first to succeed in developing a simple self-regulating arc lamp, Thomson and Houston used their conclusions to follow up and rapidly improve upon Brush's work.[26] (The problem of subdivision will be discussed further in the next two sections.)

Equally significant were their observations about the internal and external resistances of a dynamo circuit. Previously, electrical scientists had assumed that the internal and external resistances should be equal, because that was the best arrangement for battery circuits. Thomson and Houston, however, observed that a dynamo worked most efficiently when the resistance of its load was greater than its own internal resistance. With a high internal resistance, a dynamo drew too much of its own current to excite itself, leaving little current available to run lights or do other outside work. Thomson and Houston soon put this realization to use in designing their first dynamos, and this principle proved to be important for the development of other successful lighting systems. For instance, once Edison had decided to develop a high-resistance incandescent lamp, he then knew that it would be necessary

25 EJH and ET, "The Investigations of the Sub-Committee on Electrical Measurements," p. 368.
26 ET and EJH, "The Electric Arc – Its Resistance and Illuminating Power," *J. Franklin Inst.*, 108:46–8 (July 1879).

to complement it with an efficient dynamo with a low internal resistance. Central to further improvements in dynamos, the principle of low internal resistance was perhaps the most important idea to come out of the Franklin Institute's dynamo tests.[27]

Learning by observing: the trip to Paris, 1878

Wishing to supplement what he had learned from the Franklin Institute tests, Thomson studied several arc lighting systems during his "grand tour" of Europe in the summer of 1878. Along with visiting castles and cathedrals, climbing in the Alps, and looking at art, Thomson visited the Universal Exposition in Paris. There he reviewed the chemical and telegraphic displays, as well as the exhibits of Gramme and Siemens dynamos. However, he was most excited by the large-scale demonstrations of lighting undertaken in the streets of the city to celebrate the exposition. Those demonstrations impressed him with the great possibilities of electric lighting and gave him several specific ideas about how to build a system of his own.[28]

To appreciate what Thomson saw in the streets of Paris, it is necessary first to outline the major "reverse salient" in the field of electric lighting in the late 1870s.[29] Contemporaries referred to the problem as

27 EJH and ET, "Circumstances Influencing the Efficiency of Dynamo-Electric Machines," *J. Franklin Inst.*, 77:106–10 (February 1879); this article appeared earlier in other journals: *Proc. APS*, 18:58 (December 1878); *Telegraphic Journal and Electrical Review*, 7:25–6 (15 January 1879). ET to E. W. Rice, 6 December 1916, CL, TP; "Address by Elihu Thomson, Ph.D., Sc.D., on the Occasion of the Observance of the Centenary of the Founding of the Franklin Institute," *J. Franklin Inst.*, 198:581–98 (November 1924), especially p. 592. For a discussion of Edison's dynamo work, see Robert Friedel and Paul B. Israel, *Edison's Electric Light: Biography of an Invention* (New Brunswick, N.J.: Rutgers University Press, 1986), p. 72.
28 See [European trip to 1878], Notebook, TP. For a general description of the scientific exhibits at the Paris Universal Exposition, see *Engineering*, 26:24–5 (12 July 1878).
29 In explaining problems or difficulties that occur in evolving technological systems, Thomas P. Hughes has used the term "reverse salient," which he describes as "that section of an advancing battle line, or military front, which is continuous with other sections of the front, but which has fallen behind or been bowed back. . . . This concept is preferable to 'disequilibrium' or 'bottleneck,' which some economists and economic historians use, because. . . . 'Disequilibrium' suggests a relatively straightforward abstraction of physical science, and 'bottleneck' is geometrically too symmetrical." See Thomas P. Hughes, *Networks of Power: Electrification in Western Society, 1880–1930* (Baltimore: Johns Hopkins University Press, 1983), p. 79.

the "subdivision of the electric light." By "subdivision" we do not mean that electrical scientists and inventors were concerned with the problem of replacing a large, powerful arc light with smaller lighting devices. Rather, they had found that it was not possible to operate several arc lamps in a simple series circuit, because each lamp drew a different amount of current and rendered the load unstable. Hence, the problem of subdivision was not one of getting smaller lamps, but rather the challenge of getting several lamps of any size to operate on a single circuit. Even with his sophisticated dynamo, Gramme was able to power only one light, and Brush addressed the problem by having each light on a separate circuit (Figure 2.10). Clearly, neither of these solutions to the problem of subdivision was particularly economical, and so electrical inventors were very much interested in new ways to arrange and control arc lights.[30]

It was on the streets of Paris that Thomson witnessed two new ways to subdivide and control the electric light. The lighting of the streets of Paris during the summer of 1878 was the outgrowth of four decades of work on electrical technology in France. Fascinated with the electric arc, Parisian instrument makers and scientists attempted in the 1840s to light the streets using batteries and charcoal electrodes; in the 1850s, they perfected a differential regulator for the arc lamp; in the 1870s, they organized the Société des Machines Magneto-électriques Gramme to manufacture Gramme's self-exciting generator. Building on that base, Paul Jablochkoff, a Russian military engineer working in Gramme's factory, devised an "electric candle" in 1878 that did not require a special regulator and yet provided a softer light than the existing powerful arc lamps. Jablochkoff's candle consisted of two carbon rods placed side by side in an insulating material. As the current passed through the carbons and completed the arc, the insulation melted away. With its simple design, this candle made possible large-scale electric illumination, and Jablochkoff demonstrated his invention by spectacularly lighting the Avenue de l'Opéra and the Place de

30 On the problem of subdivision as getting several electric lights to operate on a single series circuit, see John W. Urquhart, *Electric Light Fitting: A Handbook for Working Electrical Engineers* (London: Crosby, Lockwood & Son, 1890), pp. 89–90; Charles Brush, "The Brush Electric Light" (September 1879), Trade Catalog Collection, Franklin Institute Science Museum, Philadelphia; Jehl, *Menlo Park Reminiscences*, Vol. 1, pp. 197–9. For an example of how subdivision has been characterized as the desire to get smaller lights, see Hughes, *Networks of Power*, p. 31.

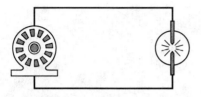

(a) Gramme generator with single light.

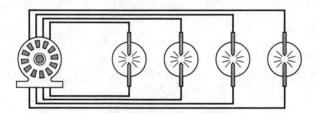

(b) Brush generator with four lights, each having its own commutator.

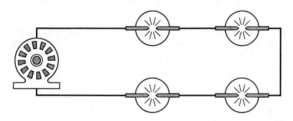

(c) Lontin generator with lights in series.

Figure 2.10. Circuit configurations of arc lighting systems available in 1878.

l'Opéra in 1878 with 62 candles powered by several Gramme genera-tors[31] (Figure 2.11).

Like other visitors to Paris that summer, Thomson was taken with the beauty of Jablochkoff's electric lights. More than that, he carefully studied the details of Jablochkoff's system. Thomson was fascinated

31 King, "The Early Arc Light and Generator," pp. 334–48; "Physical Sciences at the Paris Exhibition – No. II, III, IV. The Jablochkoff System of Electric Illumination," *Engineering,* 26:63–6, 125–7, 321–2 (26 July, 16 August, 18 October 1878).

Figure 2.11. Avenue de l'Opéra illuminated by Jablochkoff candles in 1878. From *La Lumière électrique*, 4:186 (10 August 1881). Neg. No. 46957-G, National Museum of American History, Washington, D.C.

with the system because it operated on alternating current, something he had not seen in the dynamo tests. Jablochkoff used alternating current in order to have the carbons burn evenly in the candle; had he used direct current, the positive carbon would have burned away twice as fast as the negative carbon. To supply alternating current, Jablochkoff employed a special generator designed by Gramme. Thomson examined this generator and after returning home provided the *Journal of the Franklin Institute* a sketch of the machine's armature winding.[32]

Thomson also noted the manner in which Jablochkoff rendered each light independent by using induction coils and thus solved the problem of subdivision. In this arrangement, Jablochkoff placed the primaries

32 See ET, "Personal Recollections," pp. 564–5. Thomson's sketch was used to illustrate "The Gramme Dynamo-Electric Machine For Producing Alternating Currents," *J. Franklin Inst.*, 106:181–5 (September 1878).

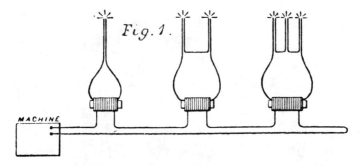

Figure 2.12. Circuit diagram showing how Jablochkoff used induction coils for the subdivision of his electric lights. Neg. No. 45393-K, National Museum of American History, Washington, D.C.

of the induction coils in series with his dynamo, while the secondaries of the coils were connected to one or more candles (Figures 2.12 and 2.13). Because his system employed alternating current, cycles in the current flowing from the generator through the primaries induced a current in the secondaries that powered the candles. The advantage to the arrangement was that current could continue to flow through the primaries of the induction coils and maintain the primary circuit even when one or more candles in the secondary circuits had burned out. Although it was an ingenious idea, Jablochkoff apparently could not perfect his induction coils and did not pursue the idea any further. Thomson, however, was rather taken with the idea and made use of it following his return to America in the fall of 1878.[33]

Besides Jablochkoff's system, Thomson came across another arc lighting system during his stay in Paris, that of Dieudonné François Lontin. Technically more sophisticated than Jablochkoff, Lontin had devised a complete system with an alternating-current generator and specially designed arc lights using a differential regulator. The regulator permitted a number of large arc lights to be strung from a single dynamo in series, thus doing away with the cumbersome and inefficient separate circuits used previously (Figure 2.10). Knowing that the

33 King, "The Early Arc Light and Generator," pp. 395–6; ET, "Testimony" (typescript), Interference No. 13,761 (on transformer distribution systems), p. 62, NARS (hereafter cited as ET, "Testimony," Intf. 13,761). Although there are no technical details available for Jablochkoff's induction coils, it would appear likely that they were very inefficient, because he probably wound both the primary and the secondary with the same number of turns.

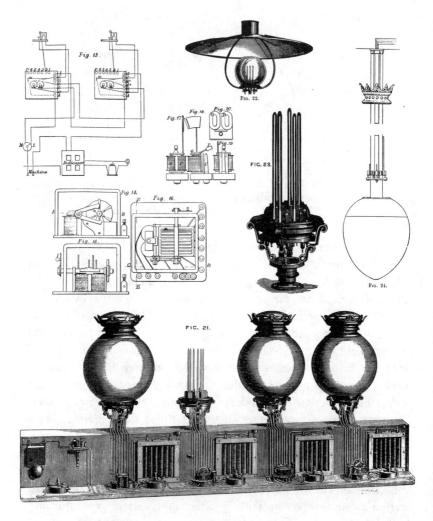

Figure 2.13. Components of the Jablochkoff system of electric lighting as applied in London in 1881. Neg. No. 45394-K, National Museum of American History, Washington, D.C.

Gramme dynamo could power only a single lamp, that the Brush machine handled only four lamps by having a separate circuit for each, and that Jablochkoff's candle and induction coil had limitations, Thomson was immediately impressed with the importance of

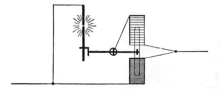

Figure 2.14. Diagram of differential regulator for arc light. The shunt electromagnet is the upper coil, and the series magnet is the lower one. From H. Schroeder, *History of Electric Light* (Washington, D.C.: Smithsonian Institution, 1923), p. 22.

Lontin's regulator as a means for economically operating several arc lights from one dynamo.[34]

The differential regulator was based on a principle that Thomson had observed in the course of the dynamo tests: the inverse relationship between the resistance of the arc and the current in the circuit. As the gap between the two carbons in an arc light increased, the resistance of the arc gap increased, and the current in the arc-lamp circuit decreased. In the differential regulator, this current change was used to move the carbons and shorten the arc gap. In this device, the current passed through two solenoids, one in series with the arc and the other in shunt with the arc (Figure 2.14). (A solenoid is a coil wrapped around a movable iron core. When the current in the coil changes, it induces a magnetic field that causes the core to move.) The shunt solenoid was wound with finer wire than the series solenoid, giving the shunt solenoid a lower resistance than the series solenoid. The solenoids were mechanically arranged so that the series solenoid pushed the carbons together, and the shunt solenoid pulled them apart. When the current was flowing, the series solenoid pulled the carbons apart and started the arc. As the carbons burned away and the arc gap lengthened, the resistance rose, thereby reducing the current flowing through the series solenoid and weakening its pull on the carbons. Because an electric current always takes the path of least resistance, current then flowed through the shunt solenoid, which had a lower resistance than the series solenoid. The diverted current energized the shunt solenoid, so that it pushed the carbons together again and

34 "Lontin's Dynamo-Electric Machines," *Engineering*, 25:49 (18 January 1878); ET, "Testimony," Intf. 13,761, p. 61.

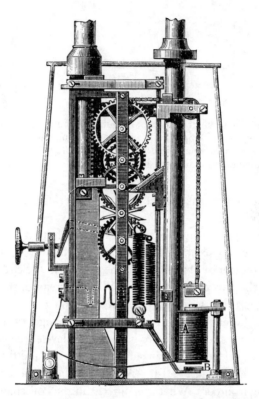

Figure 2.15. Lontin's differential regulator for arc lamps. From
E. Alglave and J. Boulard, *The Electric Light* (New York: 1884),
p. 73.

reestablished the arc gap at a particular distance. Thus, the differential
regulator not only adjusted the carbons but also kept the resistance of
the lamp constant; hence, it rendered the arc lamp a steady load that
could be powered by a dynamo.

The idea for a differential regulator for an arc lamp had first been
employed in 1856 by two Frenchmen, Joseph Lacassagne and Ro-
dolphe Thiers, in an impractical lamp that had one carbon floating on
a column of mercury whose height was controlled by the shunt and
series solenoids. In 1876, Lontin adopted their idea and replaced the
mercury column with a mechanical feed mechanism[35] (Figure 2.15).

35 Henry Schroeder, "History of Electric Light," *Smithsonian Institution Miscel-
    laneous Collections,* Publication 2717 (Washington, D.C.: Smithsonian Insti-
    tution, 1923), 76(1):22–4.

Figure 2.16. Arc lighting in the fast-freight room of the Paris depot of the Paris, Lyons, and Mediterranean Railroad, circa 1884. From E. Alglave and J. Boulard, *The Electric Light* (New York: 1884), p. 422.

His design proved to be practical, and Lontin installed a number of the lamps in a Parisian railway station in 1877 (Figure 2.16). While in Paris, Thomson visited this demonstration system and examined the lamps carefully. As he soon realized, the differential regulator kept the length of the arc and the resistance of each arc lamp steady, thereby making the lighting-circuit load stable enough to be run by a dynamo. With this desirable characteristic, Lontin's system completely convinced Thomson that arc lighting was commercially feasible, for he had no sooner returned to America in the fall of 1878 than he began designing his own system of arc lights.[36]

36 Although Thomson recalled that he saw the Lontin system in the Gare Saint Lazare, other sources suggest that the only Lontin railway installation in Paris was in the depot of the Paris, Lyons, and Mediterranean Railroad. See ET to J. R. McKee, 23 October 1913, CL, TP; and E. Alglave and J. Boulard, *The Electric Light: Its History, Production, and Applications,* trans. T. O. Sloane (New York: D. Appleton, 1884), pp. 73, 289, 421–2.

Subdividing the electric light by induction coils: Thomson and Houston's first lighting system, 1878−9

Thomson returned from Europe in August 1878 brimming with enthusiasm and ideas about electric lighting. Whereas prior to the trip he had been interested in chemistry, photography, and music, he returned with but a single passion: electric lighting. All other activities were pushed aside, and Thomson plunged into the challenges of building a lighting system. Not surprisingly, he approached the development of his new inventions with a methodology that reflected his previous training and work as a scientist. Oriented toward earning recognition from the scientific community for writing papers and making novel discoveries, it took time for Thomson to learn to think in terms of practical inventions that could be patented and marketed.[37]

Imbued with his new zeal, Thomson sought the assistance of Houston in planning a new system of lighting. Together, they reviewed what Thomson had seen in Paris and soon concluded that the reverse salient in the field was indeed the subdivision of the electric light. As they saw it, the challenge was to devise a system whereby a generator could power more than one electric light economically. Once a single generator could run more than one light, the commercial potential for electric lighting would be greatly increased. Whereas Edison attacked this reverse salient by developing his incandescent lamp, arc-light inventors in the 1870s successfully addressed subdivision by defining and solving two critical problems. First, they improved arc-lamp regulators so that each lamp independently controlled its own carbons. Second, they looked for ways to shunt the current around lamps that had burned out when a series circuit was used. Because Jablochkoff had effectively addressed these two problems with his electric candles and induction coils, Thomson and Houston chose initially to pattern their system after his.[38]

---

37 "Dynamo Work," pp. 3−4.
38 According to Hughes, once an inventor has identified a reverse salient (see footnote 29) in an evolving technological system, he or she then redefines the reverse salient as a critical problem that can be solved. Generally, one defines the critical problem in a way that allows one to use one's unique skills or knowledge. See Hughes, *Networks of Power*, pp. 79−85. For a discussion of the specific problems of subdividing and controlling arc lights, see Otto Mayr, *Feedback Mechanisms in the Historical Collections of the National Museum of History and Technology*, Smithsonian Studies in History and Technology, No. 12 (Washington, D.C.: Smithsonian Institution Press, 1971), p. 105.

From the outset, Thomson and Houston conceived of a system using induction coils to make each light function separately.[39] Induction coils, however, would mean that their system would employ alternating current and would require a new form of arc lamp; such changes would make their system radically different from the commercial arc systems then available in America, which used direct current. Neither Thomson nor Houston was especially concerned about that, for they believed that induction coils would eliminate the reverse salient of the subdivision of the electric light. Furthermore, they were already quite familiar with induction coils, as shown by their etheric force experiments. But perhaps most important, as scientists Thomson and Houston were interested in alternating current because it was at the cutting edge of science and technology. Unlike other inventors who were more closely attuned to the practical and economic factors influencing electric lighting, Thomson and Houston were willing to take chances in developing an alternating-current system, hoping that the novelty of such a system would attract recognition from the scientific community in the same manner as the discovery of a new phenomenon.

Having chosen to work with induction coils, Thomson and Houston conceptualized other features of their system. Rather than use Jablochkoff's candle, in September 1878 they designed a vibrating arc lamp (Figure 2.17). In this design, the lower carbon was vibrated by an electromagnet, while the upper carbon was partially free to fall vertically. With each fluctuation in the current, the magnet released the lower carbon, allowing it to touch the upper carbon and reignite the arc; because the lamp vibrated many times per second, the light appeared to be steady. As the lower carbon moved up and down, the upper carbon was free to move slowly downward, thus providing the feeding action necessary as the carbons burned away. Confident that their new lamp would allow them to place several lights on a series circuit, the two professors publicized their new system of electric lighting by discussing it before the American Philosophical Society and by publishing articles in the *Journal of the Franklin Institute.* Curiously, although Thomson and Houston must have understood the phenomenon of induction, they were hard-pressed to explain to their colleagues exactly how the induction coils contributed to the production of the electric light. In a report of their talk before the American Philosophical Society, their new system was described as one "in which

39 ET, "Testimony," Intf. 13,761, p. 4.

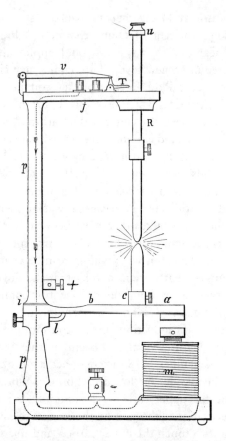

Figure 2.17. Thomson and Houston's vibrating arc lamp, October 1878. From E. Thomson and E. J. Houston, "A New Electric Lamp," *J. Franklin Inst.*, 106:252-3 (October 1878).

the sparks ('extra sparks') produced by interrupting feeble currents are utilized for the purpose of dividing the light."[40]

Having finished a design for a vibrating arc lamp, Thomson and Houston next drew up patent applications for a dynamo. Because they

40 ET and EJH, "A New System of Electric Lighting" and "A New Electric Lamp," *J. Franklin Inst.*, 106:251−3 (October 1878); quotation is from *Proc. APS*, 18:2 (1878−80). In addition to their vibrating lamp, Thomson and Houston experimented with other possible electric lights by passing a charge from a Ruhmkorff coil through glass tubes containing silica, carbonates of ammonia, and similar substances; see [Minutes of 4 October 1878 meeting], *Proc. APS*, 18:8 (1878−80).

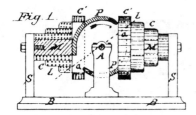

Figure 2.18. Thomson and Houston's design for extending the field magnets (P, P') over the dynamo armature, October 1878. From E. J. Houston and E. Thomson, "Dynamo-Electric Machines," U.S. Patent No. 219,157 (2 September 1879).

had yet to build and test a dynamo suited to their proposed system, their applications covered a wide range of ideas, suggesting that they were planning an experimental machine rather than a commercial machine. For instance, in an October 1878 application, they proposed that the dynamo armature have both drum and bobbin windings, a feature they never attempted in an actual machine.[41]

Their applications also indicate some of the basic building blocks or mechanical representations that Thomson used to design dynamos. As Michael E. Gorman and I have shown elsewhere, inventors frequently use familiar components in their designs, which we have termed "mechanical representations."[42] One example of Thomson and Houston's mechanical representations can be found in their October application for a dynamo patent. There they proposed that the cores of the magnetic field pieces would extend over the armature so that the armature would cut through as large a magnetic field as possible, thereby permitting it to generate more current; this idea recurs in subsequent dynamo designs (Figure 2.18). Similarly, in an application from November 1878, Thomson and Houston described a dynamo with four field cores and a drum-wound armature, and those two mechanical representations were repeated in all of their dynamo designs until 1880 (Figure 2.19). Still another recurring design element was that the professors planned to construct both their field and armature cores out of laminated sheet metal in order to dissipate the heat produced by eddy currents; whenever they later had the materials to

41 EJH and ET, "Dynamo Electric Machines," U.S. Patent No. 219,157 (filed 30 October 1878, granted 2 September 1879).
42 Gorman and Carlson, "Interpreting Invention as a Cognitive Process."

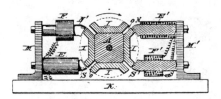

Figure 2.19. Illustration from Thomson and Houston's design for a dynamo with four field coils and a drum-wound armature, November 1878. The field coils are E, E', F, and F', and the drum windings would have fit in the spaces marked (I). From E. Thomson and E. J. Houston, "Dynamo-Electric Machine," U.S. Patent No. 232,910 (5 October 1880).

do so, they implemented that idea. Diffuse and unfocused, their applications show that Thomson and Houston were working with a variety of mechanical representations for dynamos and that they gradually selected certain ideas to be mainstays of their designs. Although other innovations were added to and subtracted from their dynamos, these mechanical representations permit us to discern continuity and order in the creative process.[43]

From patent applications for the dynamo, Thomson and Houston next turned to the induction coils for their system. At this point, they constructed an experimental model and began drawing up a patent application for it. The component consisted of two coils wound around an iron core and then enclosed by sheet metal (Figure 2.20). The professors obtained an inductive effect by winding the primary with coarse wire and the secondary with fine wire; if the ratio of the number of turns in the two coils had been sufficiently high, then this device would have produced a voltage step-down in the manner of a modern transformer. However, it is not clear that the device served that function. Instead, as they explained in a patent application of 5 November 1878, Thomson and Houston designed their induction coil to permit a large number of vibrating arc lamps to operate independently on a single circuit. Despite later claims that the device had functioned as a step-down voltage transformer, at that time Thomson and Houston had been concerned only with devising a novel means of

43 ET and EJH, "Dynamo Electric Machine," U.S. Patent No. 232,910 (filed 14 November 1878, granted 5 October 1880); ET and EJH, "Dynamo Electric Machine," U.S. Patent No. 296,569 (filed 30 November 1878, granted 8 April 1884).

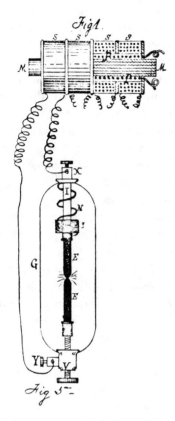

Figure 2.20. Sketch from Thomson and Houston's patent application of November 1878 showing their induction coil and vibrating arc lamp. From "Exhibit No. 1. Specification [for vibrating arc light and induction coil system]." Printed testimony for Thomson and Houston, Interference No. 13,761 (on transformer distribution system), Thomson Collection, General Electric Hall of History, Schenectady.

subdividing the electric light, and their induction coil apparently served this purpose quite well. Intent on earning the approbation of their professional colleagues for "the principle . . . which they think will solve the problem of producing small electric lights economically," Thomson and Houston displayed their induction coil before a gathering at the Franklin Institute in December 1878.[44]

44 See the following exhibits in "Testimony on behalf of Elihu Thomson and Edwin J. Houston . . . ," Interference No. 13,761 (on transformer distribution systems), Hall of History Collection (hereafter cited as Printed "Testimony,"

It was only after this demonstration that Thomson and Houston undertook the task of building the central component of their new lighting system: an alternating-current dynamo. Because Thomson did not pick up the castings for the dynamo until Christmas vacation had begun, it would appear that their teaching responsibilities at Central High School delayed the project; however, it seems equally likely that the professors may have preferred to theorize about the system prior to construction.[45] With patent applications filed and sketches made, Thomson and Houston had determined what kind of machine they wanted; it was to be larger than Thomson's 1876 dynamo and fitted with features that would permit experimentation.

Thomson and Houston incorporated a number of experimental features in their dynamo, suggesting that the machine was not for commercial sale, but rather was for exploring arc lighting generally (Figure 2.21). Following that strategy, Thomson attached both a commutator and slip rings for obtaining direct and alternating current from the machine. To investigate the best position for the brushes, he mounted them on an adjustable arm. In order to have the machine produce current at different voltages, Thomson wired the armature coils to a wooden connection board where adjustments could be made by inserting or removing screws. Thomson added these experimental features at the expense of using some traditional components; rather than worry about armature design, he used a two-coil drum-wound armature, and the arrangement of the four field coils may well have been borrowed from Edward Weston's dynamo. To study the machine's varied output,

Intf. 13,761): No. 1 (patent application for vibrating arc light system with induction coils), 5 November 1878, pp. 257–62; and No. 14 (receipt from Alfred F. Moore, 1 November 1878, for cotton magnet wire). Late in life, Thomson insisted that the induction coils were able to step down the voltage, but under cross examination in interference proceeding in the 1890s he was less certain; see "Dynamo Work," p. 6, and Printed "Testimony," Intf. 13,761, p. 34. Quotation is from "Proceedings of the Franklin Institute," *J. Franklin Inst.*, 77:70 (January 1879). In their December 1878 demonstration, Houston and Thomson planned to use the institute's Brush dynamo with a special commutator to provide alternating current to the induction coils, but they were unable to do so because of a broken wire in the dynamo; see ET to EJH, 24 September 1887, LB 3/87–4/88, pp. 487–8, TP; and "From Public Ledger, Philadelphia, Friday Dec. 20, 1878" (an exhibit in Printed "Testimony," Intf. 13,761, pp. 385–6).

45 Building the 1878 dynamo: Exhibit No. 16 (receipt from Eagle Iron Foundry, 26 December 1878, for three 230-pound castings), Printed "Testimony," Intf. 13,761, p. 321.

Figure 2.21. Dynamo designed by Thomson, fall 1878. Catalog No. 181,718, Division of Electricity, National Museum of American History, Washington, D.C. Photo by the author.

Thomson sketched and may even have built a crude instrument for measuring the continuity and strength of the current. In general, the machine served its purpose well, and the professors used it to study the generation and application of electricity for the next several years.[46]

Although Houston undoubtedly helped in the planning of the new machine, it fell to Thomson to build it. On his own, he made the wood patterns for parts, ordered the castings, and wound the coils. The surviving machine reveals that Thomson worked under the constraints of little money and few tools. Wherever possible, he used wood instead of cast iron, thus avoiding the cost of machining the parts. The field cores had to be made of iron, and Thomson's design made them all identical so that the foundry could use the same mold. To wind the

46 Thomson's 1878 dynamo is in the collection of Div. Elec., NMAH, Cat. No. 181,718. ET described this machine in "For the Lynn Works News," 4 February 1920, Collected Essays, TP; and in "Recent Developments in the Electrical Art," *J. Franklin Inst.*, 174:211–18 (August 1912). For an example of a four-field coil dynamo by Edward Weston, see Cat. No. 315,078, Div. Elec., NMAH. For Thomson's measuring instrument, see "Dynamo-Electric Machines," 1876–85, last page, Notebook, TP. Details of construction are given in ET, "Personal Recollections," p. 565.

Figure 2.22. Replica of the induction coils used by Thomson and Houston at the Franklin Institute, January 1879. From the collections of the Franklin Institute Science Museum, Philadelphia. Photo by the author.

coils, the young electrician relied on the foot lathe in his attic workshop. Yet despite these limitations, Thomson did incorporate at least one imaginative feature into the machine's construction; intent on avoiding eddy currents in the armature, he fashioned its core out of cast-iron disks strung on a wooden shaft.

The professors demonstrated their new dynamo at a meeting of the Franklin Institute on 15 January 1879. Determined to impress the audience, Thomson and Houston put the machine through its paces. To illustrate the transmission of power, they strung wires around the lecture hall and transmitted current from their dynamo to a Gramme machine, which ran as a motor. With their induction coils they operated several arc lamps independently. Not only did they run the lights in series, but also they arranged the primaries of the induction coils in parallel in an attempt to have each lamp draw less power (Figures 2.22 and 2.23). (They did not realize how important this circuit design would later be for the efficient use of alternating-current transformers.) Favorably taken with this novel demonstration, the members of the Franklin Institute rewarded Thomson by electing him to their governing board of managers.[47]

47 "Proceedings of the Franklin Institute," *J. Franklin Inst.*, 77:142 (February 1879); "From the Public Ledger, Philadelphia, Thursday, January 16, 1879, Under Heading – Local Affairs" (an exhibit in Printed "Testimony," Intf. 13,761, p. 387); ET to J. R. McKee, 23 October 1913, CL, TP.

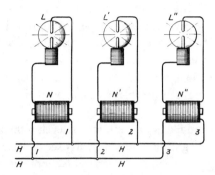

Figure 2.23. Diagram showing how Thomson and Houston connected induction coils or transformers (N, N', N″) in parallel with the
main circuit HH to render each arc lamp (L, L', L″) independent. This
diagram is based on drawings from their 13 January 1879 patent
application. From W. J. Foster, "Early Days in Alternator Design,"
General Electric Review, 23:80 (February 1920).

The demonstration had the important effect of bringing Thomson
and Houston to the attention of businessmen who were willing to
finance further development work in electric lighting. Through his
friend Thomas McCollin, the photographic dealer, Thomson was
introduced to George S. Garrett, a Quaker businessman and sales
agent for the Brush lighting system. As we shall see in the next chapter,
Garrett challenged Thomson and Houston to imitate Brush and design
a direct-current dynamo that could power four arc lamps on separate
circuits. Garrett and McCollin offered to underwrite the cost of building such a new dynamo in return for the privilege of manufacturing
and marketing it. Anxious to secure Garrett and McCollin's support,
Thomson and Houston agreed to undertake the project.[48]

In designing a new dynamo for Garrett and McCollin, Thomson and
Houston were obliged to give up their work on alternating current.
The Brush system that they were to duplicate was a direct-current
system employing a lamp that was far more practical than their vibrating model. However, they were not especially disappointed, because
their application for the use of induction coils had been rejected by the
U.S. Patent Office on the grounds of previous work by Charles G. Page
and S. A. Varley. Unable to afford a patent attorney to advise them
otherwise, Thomson and Houston decided that it was not possible to

48 "Dynamo Work," p. 7; ET, "Personal Recollections," pp. 565–6.

secure a broad patent on the use of induction coils for subdividing the electric light. Although they prepared another application in January 1879 that showed induction coils with their primaries in parallel (the circuit configuration later used in alternating-current distribution), they did not bother to file the application (Figure 2.23). Instead, they turned their attention to the new problem posed by their financial backers.[49]

In examining Thomson and Houston's efforts to develop their alternating-current system of arc lighting, one can clearly see their acquired craft knowledge regarding invention and electrical technology coming into play. Because of several years of building model dynamos and other devices, Thomson had the manual skills needed to plan and assemble an alternating-current generator, the vibrating arc lamp, and induction coils. Moreover, by observing and testing different dynamos, he had acquired a clear mental model of how such machines operated and how they could be improved. Specifically, Thomson began developing an intuitive understanding of how a dynamo combined mechanical, magnetic, and electrical forces. And finally, his experience with Houston in designing and filing patent applications for the railway tie fastener, the pneumatic telegraph sounder, and the cream separator had exposed him to the problems of presenting inventions to the key audiences of patent examiners and investors. All in all, Thomson learned about invention and electrical technology not from books or theories but from a variety of firsthand experiences. These experiences provided him the knowledge and skills that proved to be essential to his success as an inventor.

Although Thomson and Houston had acquired a foundation of craft knowledge about invention, their first arc lighting system also reveals

49 For rejection of their November 1878 patent application, see Exhibit No. 1 (specification for vibrating-arc light system with induction coils, 5 November 1878), Printed "Testimony," Intf. 13,761, pp. 263–7. For their January 1879 application, see Exhibit No. 2 (application for Improvements in Electric Lighting, 13 January 1879), Printed "Testimony," Intf. 13,761, pp. 273–9. Thomson later claimed that he did not pursue those applications in 1879 because they needed more developmental work and because he was unwilling to share those ideas with Houston. In 1885, however, when he did submit an application for a distribution system using transformers in parallel, Thomson advised his patent attorney that he had let the earlier application lapse because he believed that it was not possible to get a broad patent on the use of induction coils in parallel. See "Dynamo Work," pp. 6–7; ET to Henry C. Townsend, 23 October 1885, LB 83–11/85, pp. 249–50, TP.

that scientific values and attitudes informed their approach or method-ology. As good scientists, they theorized first and conducted experi-ments second. Recall that the professors started by writing a paper conceptualizing the system, then filed patents, and only finally built the machinery. In planning the components and drawing up the patent applications, they drew on the results of the Franklin Institute dynamo tests and idealized the characteristics of the components. For example, Thomson set as a design ideal the goal of enclosing the armature in the magnetic field, and he pursued that ideal in the construction of all his dynamos. Similarly, their scientific preferences appeared again when Thomson actually began to build the apparatus. Most notably, the 1878 dynamo was loaded with experimental features, so that they could explore all aspects of alternating current. Underlying their ten-dency toward the scientific, the ideal, and the experimental was a desire to garner recognition from the scientific community. Wherever possible, Thomson and Houston tailored their work so that they could secure recognition and reward from their colleagues at the Franklin Institute and the American Philosophical Society. It was for this reason that they published seven papers and gave three presentations on elec-tric lighting between September 1878 and January 1879.[50]

This is not to say that Thomson and Houston's scientific approach hampered their first efforts as inventors; on the contrary, a scientific background was a positive help. Clearly, they benefited by going through the exercise of deducing "laws" linking arc resistance, current strength, and illuminating power; such abstract statements permitted Thomson to evaluate the various lighting systems he saw. Likewise, although Thomson and Houston followed a theory-to-practice ap-proach because it appealed to their scientific colleagues, that strategy proved valuable, permitting them to conceptualize the system at the outset and to integrate abstract knowledge into their designs. In the same manner, years of experience in giving classroom demonstrations and performing experiments in the name of science ensured that they had the skills needed to get their apparatus to work and to convince audiences of the value of their discoveries. The point is that Thomson

50 In addition to the papers and demonstrations previously cited, see also ET and EJH, "On the Transmission of Power by Means of Electricity," "A Curious Thermo-Magnetic Motor," and "Induction Apparatus for Revised Currents," all in *J. Franklin Inst.*, 77:36–9, 39–40, and 40–1, respectively (January 1879).

and Houston's methodology was scientific in the sense that they utilized values and skills that they had learned in their scientific endeavors, and that preference informed the character of their first system.

More broadly, Thomson and Houston's first arc lighting system
suggests that the interaction of science and technology in the late
nineteenth century may have been as much the transfer of techniques
and norms as it was the application of theory to practice.[51] As we have
seen, the ideas that these two professors used came not from books or
formal theories but from firsthand observation and craft knowledge.
Nonetheless, their first system was scientific both because they designed it using their experience as practicing scientists and because they
wanted to please a scientific audience. This case suggests that historians of science and technology should be cautious in claiming that
modern technology became scientific in the late nineteenth century
because only the ideas of science could resolve the growing complexity
of technology. Instead, this early case suggests that science and technology became intertwined for a variety of social reasons.

In working on subsequent inventions, Thomson learned the importance of responding to commercial considerations, and over time he
reoriented his method of invention so that it would better reflect the
reward system of technology, which prized profitability and practicality over theoretical elegance and novelty. Thomson began learning
about the new values of profit and practicality with his second lighting
system, which will be discussed in the next chapter. Yet, as we shall see,
Thomson never completely shunned his preference for scientific values, and he reintroduced them periodically in his later work. Acquired
during his education and early career as a scientist and inventor, these
values informed the worldview that Thomson brought to the development of electric lighting.

51 Through much of his work, Edwin T. Layton has emphasized that the interac-
    tion of science and technology in the nineteenth century involved exactly this
    sort of transfer of values and techniques; see especially his "Mirror-Image
    Twins: The Communities of Science and Technology in 19th Century Amer-
    ica," *Technology and Culture*, 12:562–80 (October 1971); and "Millwrights
    and Engineers, Science, Social Roles, and the Evolution of the Turbine in
    America," in W. Krohn, E. T. Layton, and P. Weingart, eds., *The Dynamics of
    Science and Technology* ((*Sociology of the Sciences Yearbook*, Vol. 2) (Dor-
    drecht, Holland: D. Reidel, 1978), pp. 61–87.

3. The Philadelphia partnership, 1879–1880

Before 1880 electricity was sparingly used – the first central station for arc lighting had just been established in 1879. Its recognition as a source of energy for universal lighting, for propulsion, for power, and for heat – for all the large and vital uses it could be put to – was a matter of speculation, and not one of expectedly near realization. No one, even of the wildest imaginings, could have dreamed of the transformation so close to hand.

Scientific American (1915)[1]

In the winter of 1878–9, Thomson and Houston entered into an informal partnership with two businessmen: George S. Garrett and Thomas H. McCollin. As in many partnerships of that era, they drew up no written agreement, but they were nonetheless clear in their purpose: They intended to develop, manufacture, and market an arc lighting system. Working from Thomson and Houston's first dynamo, they would transform electric lighting from a laboratory curiosity to a commercial product.

This chapter tells the story of that partnership, narrating the efforts of the entrepreneurs and the inventors to perfect and sell their new technology. We begin with a discussion of general business conditions circa 1880, noting the circumstances favoring the introduction of electric lighting. A second purpose of this chapter will be to investigate how electric lighting was marketed in its early years. Looking at the efforts of Thomson and his backers, as well as those of Charles Brush and the Telegraph Supply Company of Cleveland, we shall see that it was not an obvious choice for inventors to promote electric lighting for use in central-station utilities. Rather, they initially chose to sell arc lighting as a capital good and only gradually developed the notion of a central station. Finally, a third purpose will be to consider Thomson's early method of invention. Drawing on his accumulated craft

---

1 "The Greatest Ten Years of Invention," *Scientific American,* 112:510 (5 June 1915).

knowledge about electric lighting, Thomson the novice inventor closely studied the work of his competitor Brush and then imitated those designs. Yet by the time he left Philadelphia in 1880, Thomson had developed his skills to the point that he was able to invent a dynamo regulator superior to Brush's design.

Business conditions and organizations, 1875–1900

To understand the experiences of Thomson, Houston, and their backers in developing electric lighting, it is necessary to review both the general conditions of the American economy and the trends in business organization in the last quarter of the nineteenth century. By doing so, we shall be able to appreciate the challenges they faced and comprehend why they made some of their decisions.

By all measures, the American economy in the late nineteenth century was dynamic and thriving. From 1869 to 1901 the gross national product (GNP) grew from $9.11 to 37.1 billion, while income per capita tripled.[2] That spectacular growth was based on three factors: population growth, improvements in transportation and communication, and exploitation of America's abundant natural resources.

Because of immigration from Europe and improving health conditions, the U.S. population grew steadily during that period. In 1870 the population of the United States was 40 million, and by 1900 it had nearly doubled to 76 million. Significantly, more Americans were living in cities; whereas in 1870 some 10% of the population lived in 14 cities of 100,000 or more inhabitants, by 1900 that percentage had doubled, and the number of cities of that size had nearly tripled. That population growth ensured an adequate supply of labor, and the growing urban concentration provided a large and ready market for food and consumer goods.[3]

Along with population growth came improvements in transportation and communications. Over the course of the nineteenth century, Americans built an extensive railroad network across the continent. From 1875 to 1900 that network grew from 75,000 to 200,000 miles

2 Elisha P. Douglass, *The Coming of Age of American Business: Three Centuries of Enterprise, 1600–1900* (Chapel Hill: University of North Carolina Press, 1971), p. 521.

3 Harold C. Passer, *The Electrical Manufacturers, 1875–1900: A Study in Competition, Entrepreneurship, Technical Change, and Economic Growth* (Cambridge, Mass.: Harvard University Press, 1953), pp. 4–5.

of track. Through a variety of technological and managerial innovations, American railroad leaders created not only the first large business organizations but also a cost-effective system; in the last quarter
of the century, freight rates fell from one cent per mile to one-half cent
per mile. Complementing the railroad were steady improvements in
communications through the creation of nationwide telegraph and
telephone systems.[4]

The railroads not only helped the growing population spread across
the American continent but also furthered the utilization of the na-
tion's natural resources. Blessed with huge forests, fertile farmland,
and rich deposits of coal, iron, and minerals, America possessed a
resource endowment that could readily be used to fuel the process of
industrialization. From 1880 to 1900, American businessmen eagerly
tapped those resources; one indication of their efforts is that the value
of mineral output tripled during those decades.[5]

Together, the growing population and the railroads helped create
national markets, and the rich flow of resources provided the raw
materials for a variety of goods and products. Eager to capitalize on
the new markets and resources, businessmen organized a host of firms,
both large and small. From 1870 to 1900 the number of business
establishments nearly tripled.[6]

Yet despite those promising conditions, it was not always easy for an
individual business to survive. The large number of firms and the scale
of the national markets stimulated intense competition that led to
generally falling prices through the last years of the century. According
to Louis Galambos and Joseph Pratt, most businessmen were "price-
takers," forced to accept the market conditions as they found them.
There also were two major depressions during that period: 1873–8
and 1893–7. Finally, often it was difficult to secure capital. Although
Wall Street had emerged by the 1860s as a financial center for the
railroads, it did not provide investment capital for manufacturing and
other enterprises until the 1890s. Banks did extend credit to businessmen, but did not generally offer loans for capital equipment or new

4 Passer, *The Electrical Manufacturers,* p. 4; Alfred D. Chandler, Jr., *The Visible Hand: The Managerial Revolution in American Business* (Cambridge,
   Mass.: Belknap Press of Harvard University, 1977), pp. 79–206.
5 Passer, *The Electrical Manufacturers,* p. 5.
6 Harold C. Livesay, "Lilliputians in Brobdingnag: Small Business in Late-
   Nineteenth-Century America," in Stuart W. Bruchey, ed., *Small Business in
   American Life* (New York: Columbia University Press, 1980), pp. 338–51.

factories. Consequently, most of the investment for new technology and enterprises in that period came from accumulated savings and reinvestment of profits.[7]

To survive in that rapidly growing but topsy-turvy world, businessmen pursued several different strategies. Unable to set prices and control markets, many manufacturers sought out new technological innovations to reduce costs, speed up production, and increase output. By means of new production machinery, more intensive use of energy, and better factory layout, businessmen achieved significant economies of speed. At the forefront of such changes were firms specializing in food processing, refining, distilling, and metalworking. Still other entrepreneurs tapped the potential of national markets by creating new distribution arrangements, including department stores, chain stores, and mail-order firms. As Alfred D. Chandler, Jr., has demonstrated, those strategies toward mass production and mass distribution led businessmen to create new business structures. In particular, they created the modern business enterprise, characterized by a staff of middle managers who coordinated the many tasks that were being undertaken by a single firm. Highly successful at organizing production and then shaping the public demand, the new class of managers vastly increased the productivity and wealth of American society.[8]

Although the large integrated firm came to play a prominent role in the American economy, the pursuit of economies of speed and the creation of managerial hierarchies were not the only ways to survive in the rapidly changing economy of the 1880s. Other businessmen succeeded by continuing the older tradition of the entrepreneurial firm. Characterized by having two or three partners who made all of the decisions, such firms were the most common form of business organization in nineteenth-century America. Their hallmark was their ability to adapt and innovate – be it in terms of marketing, technology, or organization. Often, such small firms survived by carving out niches for themselves in which they provided products or services suited to local markets or special needs. In other instances they prospered by drawing on close personal contacts with customers or by using trademarks

7 Louis Galambos and Joseph Pratt, *The Rise of the Corporate Commonwealth: United States Business and Public Policy in the 20th Century* (New York: Basic Books, 1988), pp. 19–24; Thomas R. Navin and Marian V. Sears, "The Rise of a Market for Industrial Securities, 1887–1902," *Business History Review*, 29:105–38 (June 1955).
8 Chandler, *The Visible Hand*, pp. 207–314.

to highlight their products. Frequently such firms employed technology effectively and skillfully because one or more of the partners had firsthand experience as a craftsman or inventor. Many, if not most, of those entrepreneurial firms failed, but they nonetheless contributed to the late-nineteenth-century economy considerable vitality and innovation.[9]

Both the modern business enterprise and the small entrepreneurial firm played important roles in shaping the American economy in the late nineteenth century. Whereas the big integrated firms achieved high levels of productivity by judicious use of technological and organizational innovations, the smaller entrepreneurial firms often were the sources of the new technology and techniques. As we shall see, that was especially true of the early electric-lighting industry; as entrepreneurial firms were the first to develop that technology, their first customers were the firms seeking to achieve high-volume production and distribution. Intent on using their capital equipment continuously, those firms purchased electric lighting to permit nighttime operations.

Garrett and McCollin: small businessmen, but sanguine risk-takers

It was thus a favorable business environment in which Thomson, Houston, Garrett, and McCollin began their partnership. After the recession of the mid-1870s, prosperity was gradually returning, and businessmen were willing to invest in new ventures. The close of the decade saw the formation of many new firms that sought to achieve economies of speed in production and distribution; in Philadelphia, these included the opening of John Wanamaker's Grand Depot and the expansion of metalworking firms such as the Baldwin Locomotive Works and the Cramp shipyards and larger factories for processing food and brewing beer.[10] Moreover, as per capita income rose and the populations of cities such as Philadelphia grew, there was an expand-

9 I have taken the concept of the entrepreneurial firm from Galambos and Pratt, *The Rise of the Corporate Commonwealth,* pp. 18–28. Also helpful is Livesay, "Lilliputians in Brobdingnag." For an example of how an entrepreneurial firm supported technological innovation, see George David Smith's discussion of the early years of the Pittsburgh Reduction Company, *From Monopoly to Competition: The Transformation of Alcoa, 1888–1986* (Cambridge University Press, 1988), pp. 23–42.

10 Nicholas B. Wainwright, *History of Philadelphia Electric, 1881–1961* (Philadelphia Electric Company, 1961), p. 3.

Figure 3.1. George S. Garrett. From J. W. Jordan, *Encyclopedia of Pennsylvania Biography* (New York: Lewis Historical Publishing Co., 1921), vol. 13, p. 252.

ing consumer group with surplus income that could be spent on illuminating streets and business establishments.

As established businessmen in Philadelphia, Thomas H. McCollin and George S. Garrett probably possessed an intuitive sense of those broad changes. McCollin was a large dealer in cameras and photographic supplies. Although his business was in the city, McCollin invested his earnings in real estate in nearby Delaware County; by the early 1880s, R. G. Dun & Co. estimated his personal worth at $20,000.[11] McCollin had become acquainted with Thomson, who regularly purchased chemicals and apparatus from McCollin. Sharing with Thomson a keen interest in scientific and technical affairs, McCollin became a close friend of the young professor and followed the progress of his early inventions, particularly the cream separator. A member of the Franklin Institute, McCollin also participated in the dynamo tests by taking photographs of the burning arc lights. Thus, McCollin knew Thomson well and undoubtedly was anxious to see his friend succeed in the new business of electrical invention.

McCollin introduced Thomson and Houston to his relative, George S. Garrett (Figure 3.1). Garrett was a Quaker banker and businessman who lived in Upper Darby, just outside Philadelphia. He was closely

11 On Thomas H. McCollin, see his entry in Pennsylvania Vol. 152, p. 87, R. G. Dun & Co. Collection.

affiliated with several suburban banks, serving as director of the First National Bank of Darby and the Media Title and Trust Company, as well as secretary of the Upper Darby Savings and Loan Association. In partnership with his cousin, Nathan Garrett, he undertook real-estate development, and during the 1870s they promoted a residential community called Garrettsford in the area now known as Drexel Hill. Consequently, Garrett held considerable real estate, worth $150,000. In addition to his business success, Garrett was highly regarded by his peers; according to one biographer,

> in business he was active and enterprising, keenly sagacious, diligent, adhering closely to upright, honorable principles which brought him abundant success. His name was a synonym for integrity, and in his community no man was held in higher respect. In his public life he was ever found on the side of progress and improvement. Many of the enterprises he assisted to develop are now strong and successful.[12]

Excited by the potential of electric lighting, Garrett became an agent for the Brush organization and purchased two Brush dynamos in 1879. Not surprisingly, he was in the audience when Thomson and Houston demonstrated their alternating-current (ac) dynamo and arc lights at the Franklin Institute in January 1879. Knowing that Brush had recently introduced a system in which a direct-current (dc) dynamo powered four arc lamps on separate circuits, Garrett asked Thomson and Houston if they could design a similar dynamo. Along with McCollin, he promised to underwrite the cost of building the new dynamo in return for the manufacturing and marketing rights.[13]

12 For information on George Garrett, see his entry in Pennsylvania Vol. 157, p. 71, R. G. Dun & Co. Collection. It is not clear how McCollin and Garrett were related; in "Dynamo Work and Its Development," Autobiog. Papers, TP, Thomson recalls that they were cousins, whereas in some untitled notes in the GE Hall of History Collection he stated that McCollin was Garrett's brother-in-law. On Garrett's real-estate activities, see Thomas Ray Smith, *Drexel Hill, 1875–1912: Life in Addingham and Garrettsford: America's Clandestine "Hollywood"* (Drexel Hill, Pa.: 1980), pp. 1–3. Quotation is from *Encyclopedia of Pennsylvania Biography* (New York: Lewis Historical Publishing Co., 1921), Vol. 13, pp. 252–4. I am grateful to Jeff Cohen for help in locating information about Garrett.

13 On Garrett's connection with Brush, see entries for Garrett, 30 March and 1 April 1879, "Statement of Shipments, 1878–1881," Charles F. Brush Papers, Special Collections, University Libraries, Case Western Reserve University, Cleveland. On Garrett and McCollin's proposal to Thomson and Houston, see ET, "Dynamo Work," p. 7; and ET, "Personal Recollections of the Development of the Electrical Industry," *Engineering Magazine* (July 1905), pp. 563–72.

It is significant that Garrett and McCollin showed no interest in promoting Thomson and Houston's ac system, but proposed a dc system patterned after that of Brush. In all likelihood, Garrett and McCollin made that decision because they wanted to capitalize on the marketing patterns being established by Brush and his backers at the Telegraph Supply Company of Cleveland. (Brush's marketing strategy is discussed later.) Because of its recent success in the Franklin Institute dynamo tests, the Brush system was selling well to individual firms, probably leading Garrett and McCollin to conclude that there was no need to undertake the cost of perfecting the complex ac system in order to enter the new field. If Thomson and Houston could come up with a "clone" of the Brush system, then they could begin turning a profit at once.

Surprised but delighted by Garrett's offer, Thomson and Houston agreed to design and build a four-light dc dynamo. In doing so, they were obliged to drop their work on an ac system. However, they may not have been especially disappointed, because, as noted in the preceding chapter, their patent applications for the ac system had recently been rejected. During the next few months, Thomson threw himself into his work, and Garrett responded by providing the capital, guidance, and contacts needed for building and testing the new machine.

The bakery dynamo and system

Though simple from a commercial standpoint, the challenge that Garrett and McCollin offered the professors was hardly a simple technical problem. They were to duplicate Brush's successful generator, but at the same time they were to produce a machine that would not infringe on his patented design (Figure 3.2). Specifically, the challenge for Thomson and Houston was to develop a machine that would provide four separate direct currents. Their solution to that technical challenge, the three-coil dynamo, was at once elegant and practical. Although Thomson later claimed (just as other inventors had) that the idea for three coils came to him in a flash, it appears instead that he gradually came upon the idea and that it took time to perfect it.[14]

14 For the "idea in a flash" story, see ET to J. W. Hammond, 18 June 1927, CL, TP; and ET, "Dynamo Work," pp. 7–8. For a description of how Thomson spent evenings gathering information and doing calculations, see ET, "Personal Recollections," pp. 565–6.

Figure 3.2. Brush's arc-lighting dynamo. From E. Alglave and J. Boulard, *The Electric Light* (New York: 1884), p. 280.

Thomson developed the three-coil dynamo as an improvement on Brush's generator. Prior to Brush, most dynamos had been built with closed-coil armatures, meaning that each coil of the armature was connected to the next coil, so that the armature was in effect one continuous circuit (Figure 3.3). The difficulty with that winding was that the current produced by the armature fluctuated, because the current had to overcome the resistance in the portions of the winding that were at any given moment not being magnetized and hence not producing current. Brush overcame that difficulty by cutting the non-producing coils out of the circuit. Using what was known as an open-coil winding, Brush joined coils on opposite sides of the armature ring together and then attached the remaining terminals to individual commutator pieces (Figures 2.3 and 3.4). By placing his brushes 90 degrees from the neutral line, Brush was thus able to draw current only from the coils that were producing the maximum amount of current; the other nonproducing coils were at that moment cut out of the circuit (Figure 3.5). The result of his open-coil design was that his generators produced a much steadier current that was well suited to powering arc lights.[15]

15 Silvanus P. Thompson, *Dynamo-Electric Machinery: A Manual for Students of Electrotechnics,* 3rd ed. (London: E. & F. N. Spon, 1888), pp. 229–34; Harry J. Eisenmann III, "Charles F. Brush: Pioneer Innovator in Electrical Technology" (Ph.D. dissertation, Department of History, Case Institute of Technology, 1967), pp. 31–54.

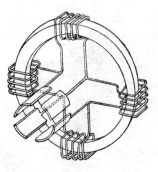

Figure 3.3. Closed-coil armature for a dynamo. From S. P. Thompson, *Dynamo-Electric Machinery*, 3rd ed. (London: 1888), p. 41.

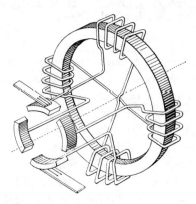

Figure 3.4. Open-coil armature for a dynamo. From S. P. Thompson, *Dynamo-Electric Machinery*, 3rd ed. (London: 1888), p. 222.

Thomson improved on Brush's design by reducing the number of armature coils from eight to three, by connecting three of the coils' ends together, and by using a three-piece commutator. With that arrangement, Thomson found that two of the coils functioned as if they were on opposite sides of an armature, generating a large current; in the meantime, the third nonproducing coil was cut out of the circuit. By using several large windings in an open-coil arrangement, he found that the dynamo generated a steady current with few fluctuations (Figure 3.6). Calling that his "commutator *par excellence*," Thomson wrote in January 1879 that the advantages of his three-coil design were "wonderful simplicity and perfect control, continuous current and if needed two distinct currents from only three coils on the armature." He probably was equally pleased that the three-coil design took advan-

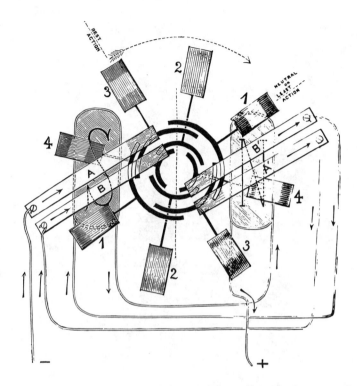

Figure 3.5. Wiring diagram for Brush's arc-lighting dynamo. The numbered coils are the ring windings on the armature, the strips A, A', B, and B' are the brushes, and the dark semicircles in the center are the commutator pieces. From S. P. Thompson, *Dynamo-Electric Machinery*, 3rd ed. (London: 1888), p. 231.

tage of the Brush open-coil arrangement without directly infringing on the patent covering the specific configuration of Brush's armature.[16]

In studying, copying, modifying, and ultimately improving Brush's armature, Thomson was employing an invention strategy, or "heuristic," that Brooke Hindle characterized as emulation.[17] "Emulation," wrote Hindle,

16 "Dynamo-Electric Machines," 1876–85, Notebook, TP.
17 There is an extensive literature in cognitive science on the concept of "heuristic." For a discussion of heuristics and invention, see Robert J. Weber and David N. Perkins, "How to Invent Artifacts and Ideas," *New Ideas in Psychology*, 7:49–72 (1989); and W. Bernard Carlson and Michael E. Gorman, "Understanding Invention as a Cognitive Process: The Case of Thomas Edison and Early Motion Pictures," *Social Studies of Science*, 30:387–430 (August 1990).

Figure 3.6. Thomson's notebook entry describing his three-coil armature winding in January 1878. From "Dynamo Electric Machines" notebook, Thomson Papers, American Philosophical Society, Philadelphia.

represented an effort to equal or surpass the work of others; it was more a striving for quality and recognition than a marketplace competition and seems to have emerged from the manner of instruction and improvement in the arts and crafts. There the striving was frequently spurred by contests and by constant measurement against the best models. The apprentice learned by copying the work of the master, but the journeyman had to go beyond copying. In order to become a master himself, he had to produce his own "masterpiece."[18]

Hindle emphasized that emulation involves both the means by which individuals learn craft knowledge and their additions to it through innovation. As mentioned previously, Thomson the apprentice inven-

18 Brooke Hindle, *Emulation and Invention* (New York: Norton, 1981), p. 13.

tor learned about electrical technology by observing, testing, and building models of dynamos. Through such practice he internalized the complex relationships among mechanical, magnetic, and electrical forces embodied in a dynamo, and that process gave him a mental model of how dynamos worked. Thomson then used that knowledge to penetrate the essence of Brush's armature design and produce his own satisfying alternative. Brush provided the "best model," and Thomson the journeyman inventor emulated it.

Having hit upon the idea of a three-coil armature, Thomson went forward in designing a new dynamo for Garrett and McCollin. Through February 1879 he made calculations and drew up plans for a full-size machine. In its basic appearance, the new machine looked much like the ac dynamo, except that it was larger and had a substantial iron frame. The abundant use of iron indicated not only that Thomson was building his machine with sufficient financial support but also that he was expecting to see the machine put into commercial use.[19]

When the plans were ready, Thomson took them to the Harrison Machine Works at 1710 Barker (now Ludlow) Street in Philadelphia (Figure 3.7). In all likelihood, either Garrett or McCollin had some contact with that shop and arranged for the dynamo to be built there. At Harrison's, workmen cast and machined the parts for the generator. Having never built an electrical machine before, they referred to the castings in familiar terms; hence, the armature became a "grate casting," the field pieces were "bases of heavy castings," and the commutator was marked "copper disk." Thomson considered the armature and field coils to be so important that he insisted on winding them himself. Along with some workmen, McCollin helped with the assembly, but Houston was conspicuously absent.[20]

The three-coil dynamo was ready by the end of March 1879 (Figure 3.8). Anxious to test it, Thomson had the workmen mount the machine on the bed of a large planer and connect it by belting to a 10-horsepower steam engine in the shop. Five arc lights were borrowed and strung up around the shop. Drawing all of the engine's power, the new generator was able to power the lights, but not without

19 Cat. No. 181,717, Div. Elec., NMAH.
20 John W. Gibboney to H. B. Prindle, 2 February 1891, LB 11/90–1/92, pp. 155–60, TP; ET, "Dynamo Work," p. 8; "Birthplace of the Thomson-Houston Electric Company," Lynn *Item* (souvenir edition 1892), Lynn HS.

Figure 3.7. Harrison Machine Works, where Thomson's 1879 bakery dynamo was assembled. From Thomson Papers, American Philosophical Society, Philadelphia.

disappointment. On the first night, the lights burned brilliantly for awhile, but then the ends of carbons became red, and the lights went out; not until the third or fourth night did Thomson eliminate the difficulty and get the whole system to work satisfactorily.[21]

Those early difficulties with the lights signaled to Thomson, Houston, and their backers that additional developmental work would be necessary. The dynamo needed to be thoroughly tested while running, which meant that they required access to a more powerful steam engine. Looking about the neighborhood of Harrison's machine shop, they found that D. B. Fuller's Aerated Biscuit Company at 10–16 South Eighteenth Street (around the corner from Harrison) possessed two engines, one delivering 25 horsepower, the other 10. A verbal agreement was quickly reached between the inventors and the owners

21 "Birthplace of the Thomson-Houston Electric Company"; ET, "Dynamo Work," pp. 8–9.

Figure 3.8. Dynamo built by Thomson and Houston in spring 1879 and used to light Fuller's bakery. Catalog No. 181,717, Neg. No. 9072, Division of Electricity, National Museum of American History, Washington, D.C.

of the bakery whereby the owners would furnish the power necessary for testing the dynamo and lamps in return for providing electric lighting to the bakery for several months.

It is not surprising that Fuller's bakery agreed to such a trial, for it was a large, modern operation using a new technique for raising the bread dough using carbonic gas instead of yeast. Dwight B. Fuller, the principal of the firm, was an inventor in his own right, having designed several laborsaving machines that sifted flour and prepared dough for baking. To take full advantage of those innovations, Fuller ran his bakery all night, making him a likely customer for electric lighting. Thomson and his backers hoped that Fuller would be impressed with the lighting system and would decide to purchase the system. They also attempted to ensure that the tests would attract other potential customers by strategically placing their dynamo in a corner window of the bakery, where it could be seen by all who passed by.[22]

Through the summer of 1879 the three-coil dynamo was run every evening. Being on vacation and free from teaching, Thomson devoted his full attention to eliminating defects from the dynamo and perfecting the other components of the lighting system. Because the ovens ran

22 For information on Dwight B. Fuller & Company, see *The Manufactories and Manufacturers of Pennsylvania in the Nineteenth Century* (Philadelphia: Galaxy Publishing, 1875), pp. 250–1. For the arrangements for testing the dynamo, see affidavit of EJH, 18 February 1883, Patent Interference No. 8,638, Weston vs. Houston and Thomson (subject: dynamo electric machines), NARS (hereafter cited as Intf. 8,638).

all night, the temperature in the bakery often climbed to 140°F; yet the young electrician was there, sweltering and "tenderly nursing" his dynamo. "We had to be there nights giving it close attention as many babies require," he recalled. "Sometimes we were up all night attending to this baby, and under conditions which were not altogether agreeable in mid-summer."[23]

Bearing with the heat, Thomson investigated first the lighting circuit, and therein we catch a glimpse of how he and Garrett worked together to match the design of the hardware to marketing considerations. Initially, Thomson wired the lights exactly as Brush had; for each lamp, he had a separate circuit connected to one commutator (as in Figure 2.10b). Although Garrett understood little about electricity, he did know that the lighting system would be more attractive to customers if the individual lamps could be made smaller and more numerous; consequently, he asked Thomson if the power of the lights could be halved, and their number doubled from four to eight. Anticipating that possibility, Thomson had made the armature coils double so that they could be connected in a manner that would double the voltage necessary for more lights. Using a screwdriver to change the coil connections, Thomson was able to increase the number of lamps to eight. Impressed, Garrett next asked Thomson if all the lights could be put on a single circuit in series, an arrangement that Brush had just introduced. To do that, Thomson connected the four commutators together in series, and Garrett borrowed eight Brush arc lamps. To their delight, they found that the three-coil machine produced a steady current of 10 amperes, which permitted all the lamps to operate. Convinced by that experiment of the feasibility of a series circuit, Thomson replaced the four commutators with a single large commutator. Working together, Garrett and Thomson were able to establish a dialogue whereby one raised questions about commercial practicality while the other supplied technical answers.[24]

Because they could not employ Brush lamps in their system without infringing on his patents, Thomson set out to devise his own improved arc lamp. Invented in 1878, Brush's basic lamp consisted of a regulating solenoid placed in series with the arc. Attached to the upper carbon electrode in the lamp, the solenoid kept that electrode in place by

23 ET, "Arc Lighting – Electric Welding," [*Proceedings of the*] *Thirteenth Convention of the National Electric Light Association* (1891), pp. 103–18; quotation on p. 111.
24 ET, "Personal Recollections," pp. 565–6; ET, "Dynamo Work," pp. 10–11.

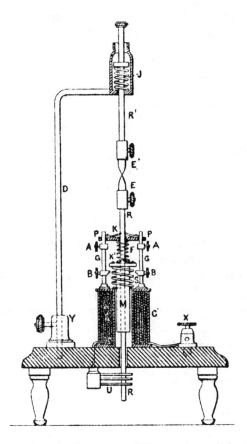

Figure 3.9. Thomson and Houston's arc light, January 1879. From E. J. Houston and E. Thomson, "Regulator for Electric-Lamps," U.S. Patent No. 220,287 (7 October 1879).

causing a washer to tilt and lock. When the carbons became too far apart (and the current in the lamp decreased), the solenoid was deenergized, thus releasing the upper carbon, which fell downward until the arc was reestablished. In a January 1879 patent application, Thomson and Houston simply inverted Brush's design by having an electromagnet pull the lower carbon down whenever current was passing through the arc. If the arc went out, strong springs would push the lower carbon upward to restart the lamp[25] (Figure 3.9). Here again Thomson

25 Otto Mayr, *Feedback Mechanisms in the Historical Collections of the National Museum of History and Technology,* Smithsonian Studies in History and Technology, No. 12 (Washington, D.C.: Smithsonian Institution Press,

employed the heuristic of emulation, but he did so rather poorly, because it did not lead to any substantial improvement over Brush's design.

Although the new lamp worked satisfactorily on the separate circuits first set up with the three-coil dynamo, Thomson and Garrett soon realized that it would not operate in the series circuit. The difficulty was that although each lamp could adjust itself, as one lamp did so it would vary the line current and cause all the other lamps to adjust themselves; soon all the lamps would be flickering, and the load on the dynamo would become unstable.[26] Consequently, while his dynamo was running in the bakery, Thomson experimented with his lamp design.

Beginning with the arc lamp that he and Houston had invented in January, Thomson added a shunt solenoid in parallel to the arc, similar to the one he had seen in Lontin's arc lamp in Paris. Because the series solenoid was energized whenever the arc was operating, it pulled the carbons apart and ignited the arc; in contrast, the shunt solenoid was energized only when the arc became too long, thus pushing the carbons together (Figure 3.10). Thus, by opposing each other, the two solenoids maintained a constant distance between the carbons and hence a steady arc. Although Brush had introduced a lamp very similar to that using a single solenoid wound with two coils, Thomson avoided infringement by using two separate solenoids in his lamp. Thomson tested his design extensively at the bakery and eliminated such mundane problems as keeping insects from crawling into the mechanism. Operation in the bakery showed that each lamp independently regulated its own arc gap, despite sudden changes in the current, making the design ideally suited to a series circuit. Because of that quality, Thomson and Garrett used the new lamp mechanism in their first installations.[27]

1971), pp. 107, 109; ET and EJH, "Regulators for Electric Lamps," U.S. Patent No. 220,287 (filed 23 January 1879, granted 7 October 1879).

26 John W. Urquhart, *Electric Light Fitting: A Handbook for Working Electrical Engineers* (London: Crosby, Lockwood & Son, 1890), pp. 89–90; Mayr, *Feedback Mechanisms*, pp. 119–20.

27 See EJH and ET, "Regulator for Electric Lamp," U.S. Patent No. 220,508 (filed 11 June 1879, granted 14 October 1879). For the patent model of this lamp, see Cat. No. 251,233, Div. Elec., NMAH. For Brush's differential or shunt lamp, see E. Alglave and J. Boulard, *The Electric Light: Its History, Production, and Applications* (New York: D. Appleton, 1884), pp. 82–4. For problems with insects in the lamp mechanism, see "The Thomson-Houston Electric Company," *Electricity*, 3:17–21 (27 July 1892).

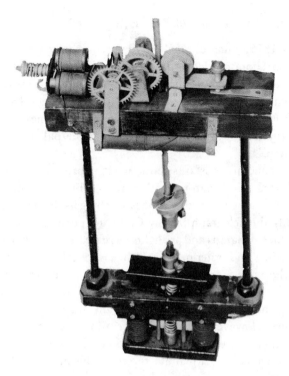

Figure 3.10. Thomson and Houston's arc light with differential regulator, 1879. The shunt electromagnet is on the top left, and the series magnet is visible at the bottom of the light. Catalog No. 251,233, Neg. 71886, Division of Electricity, National Museum of American History, Washington, D.C.

Patented in June 1879, the lamp continued to be refined; for instance, Thomson tried substituting a small electric motor for the shunt solenoid. He also worked on a double lamp with two pairs of carbons that would require less servicing because it would burn one pair and then the other. In 1880, Thomson reworked the design so that the two solenoids moved only the upper carbon, and that version became known as his drop-and-lift lamp. Over time, that design became standard for all of Thomson's arc lights.[28]

28 ET and EJH, "Regulators for Electric Lamps," U.S. Patent No. 223,646 (filed 24 November 1879, granted 20 January 1880); ET, "Electric Arc Lamp," U.S. Patent No. 261,790 (filed 17 December 1880, granted 25 July 1882); ET to J. J. Wright, 3 September 1885, LB 8/85–3/86, p. 12, TP.

Selling dynamos in Philadelphia, 1879–80

In September 1879, Fuller decided not to purchase the electric lighting system, and so Thomson, Houston, and their backers were obliged to move elsewhere. To permit Thomson to continue his experiments, Garrett rented several rooms at Thirteenth and Buttonwood streets, a few blocks from Central High School. Helping out in the new shop was Joseph J. Wright, the former chief engineer at the bakery, and one other workman.[29]

As Thomson and his assistants continued to improve the machinery, Garrett and McCollin began to market it. As a Brush agent, Garrett was familiar with how the competition was selling its dynamos and arc lights. Initially the Telegraph Supply Company pursued a marketing strategy in which dynamos and arc lights were treated as capital goods; like steam engines and other machines, they were sold outright to any customers who were interested. Such a strategy made sense because many of the first Brush dynamos were sold to metalworking firms for electroplating and hence were equivalent to any other piece of production machinery. However, because the operation of dynamos and the chemical processes of electroplating were poorly understood at the time, Brush often had to let manufacturers test his machines first and pay for them only if they performed adequately.[30]

The Telegraph Supply Company first sold Brush's arc-lighting dynamos on the basis of their novelty. One of Brush's first sales in 1878 was to a Cincinnati doctor who displayed a light on his balcony as a means of attracting patients. Likewise, John Wanamaker purchased Brush lamps to draw customers to his department store, and Brush lights were installed on the iron pier at Coney Island. Brush also

29 See entry for George S. Garrett, Pennsylvania Vol. 157, p. 71, R. G. Dun & Co. Collection; affidavit of John J. Wright, 13 February 1883, Intf. 8,638. For additional information on Wright and his career with the Toronto Electric Light Company, consult Christopher Armstrong and H. V. Nelles, *Monopoly's Moment: The Organization and Regulation of Canadian Utilities, 1830–1930* (Philadelphia: Temple University Press, 1986), pp. 75–6.

30 For an example of Brush's problems in selling electroplating dynamos, see his letters to Manning, Bowman & Co., 31 January and 27 February 1877, LB 1876–7, box 4, Brush Papers. Brush's rival, Edward Weston, encountered similar resistance from manufacturers and had to offer to send his machines on a trial basis as well; see Condit, Hanson & Van Winkle, "Catalogue of Nickel & Electro-Plating Material" (Newark, 1876), Wheeler Collection, WP 50:1, United Engineering Library, New York.

Table 3.1. *Brush arc-lighting installations, 1880*

Facility	Number of lights	Percentage of total
Textile mills	894	39.5
Iron and steel works, machine shops	313	13.8
Central stations[a]	282	12.5
Other factories	196	8.7
Parks, docks, and resorts	188	8.3
Large stores	179	7.9
Mines and smelting works	70	3.1
Hotels	54	2.4
Wholesale grocers	30	1.3
Circuses	28	1.2
Steamships	23	1.0
Colleges and churches	7	0.3
Totals	2264	100.0

[a]Includes systems in New York, San Francisco, Detroit, Grand Rapids, Wabash, Indiana, and Galesburg, Illinois.
Source: Anglo-American Brush Electric Light Corporation, Limited, *Testimonials and List of Employers*, circa 1880, Wheeler Collection, United Engineering Library, New York.

sold a few systems to circuses and hotels, and by 1880 those novelty sales accounted for approximately 20% of the total lights installed (Table 3.1).

Following those sales based on the novelty of the electric light, Brush and his associates next marketed their system to selected manufacturers. Notably, they found that arc lighting sold well to firms that were moving toward large-scale, high-speed production and would be at the forefront of the second industrial revolution. In particular, the Telegraph Supply Company concentrated on large metalworking and textile firms that had started nighttime operations in order to achieve economies of speed and offset the cost of their capital equipment.[31] In addition, it sold lights to smelting works, paper mills, refineries, and breweries. With all those customers, the company emphasized that arc lighting was better than gas lighting for illuminating large spaces and

31 For example, John Roach installed Edison incandescent lights in his large Philadelphia shipyard in late 1881 in order to have "longer workdays in the winter months and second shifts when the yard was busy." See Leonard Alexander Swann, Jr., *John Roach, Maritime Entrepreneur* (Annapolis, Md.: United States Naval Institute, 1965), p. 58. I am grateful to John K. Brown for bringing this example to my attention.

could cost as little as one-quarter of the cost of gas.[32] By 1880, manu-facturing customers were burning 1,473 Brush lights, or 65% of the total sold (Table 3.1).

Garrett imitated the Brush strategy of selling lights to large manu-facturing establishments. For their first order, Garrett arranged to sell the bakery machine, another eight-light dynamo, and one two-light machine to Gardiner's Continental Brewery in South Philadelphia for $2,500. That large brewery was a likely candidate for electric lighting because it was moving toward mechanized, large-batch production and nighttime operation; as early as 1872, it had achieved an annual output of 15,000 barrels. The ruggedness of Thomson's dynamos and lights was soon tested in that installation, as they survived a devastat-ing fire and in fact helped light up the scene as firemen put out the blaze.[33]

Although the bakery dynamo performed well at Gardiner's Brewery, Garrett and McCollin found it difficult to sell other machines to Philadelphia businessmen. During the summer of 1879 they had Har-rison's shop build a two-light machine, only to find that no one was willing to buy it, and they were forced to use it to light their own workshop. In the fall, Thomson designed a larger dynamo that was built in the foundry of I. P. Morris & Company. Garrett and Thomson apparently hoped that Morris would purchase the machine, but the firm declined, reporting that it did not do enough night work to warrant the installation of electric lights. Built completely of iron and well machined, that dynamo, too, sat in the shop. The only other Philadelphia installation came in 1880, when they operated the bakery dynamo for several months in Ullman's beer saloon at Ninth and Locust streets.[34] With that installation, Thomson and Garrett perhaps hoped to demonstrate that the novelty of Thomson-Houston lights could attract customers to an establishment.

32 Eisenmann, "Brush," pp. 69–72; "The Brush Electric Light" (September 1879), Trade Catalog Collection, Franklin Institute Science Museum, Phil-adelphia; Passer, The Electrical Manufacturers, pp. 16–17.

33 Gardiner's Brewery is described as James Smyth's brewery in Manufactories and Manufacturers of Pennsylvania, p. 55. See also G. S. Garrett to J. Gar-diner & Co., 6 September 1879, Intf. 8,638; and ET, "Personal Recollec-tions," pp. 566–7.

34 Affidavits of John J. Wright, 13 February 1882, and EJH, 17 February 1882, Intf. 8,638; The machine built by I. P. Morris is most likely Cat. No. 181,719, Div. Elec., NMAH.

In all likelihood, the problem with selling dynamos and arc lights involved both the marketing strategy and the design of the machines. In trying to sell electric lighting to Philadelphia businessmen and manufacturers, Garrett and McCollin quickly encountered the limitations of the Philadelphia market, as well as their own personal limitations. Although it was the second largest manufacturing center in the United States, Philadelphia did not have a significant number of large industrial establishments intent on achieving economies of speed by mechanizing all production steps; rather, its industry was characterized by numerous small firms that lacked steam or water power. In 1880, 86% of Philadelphia firms had 25 or fewer employees, and only one manufacturer in five had access to a steam engine. As a result, there were few large integrated plants that operated at night and required illumination.[35] Thus, while Brush was selling electric lights to large textile and metalworking firms, the Thomson-Garrett partnership sold no lights to such industries. On a personal level, although Garrett and McCollin had connections to the Philadelphia business community, their ties probably did not reach beyond the city, thus limiting the number of customers they could bring into contact with the Thomson-Houston system.[36]

More broadly, the problem was the conservative attitude of businessmen. Garrett and McCollin's potential customers probably gave little thought to the lighting of their establishments and paid little for what night lighting they had, using oil or gas. Unless they had an extraordinary volume of business, most (like I. P. Morris) did not operate at night. Why, then, should they invest several thousand dollars in an electric lighting system? Undoubtedly, Garrett and McCollin

---

35 The statistics for firm size and use of power are from Bruce Laurie and Mark Schmitz, "Manufacturing and Productivity: The Making of an Industrial Base, Philadelphia, 1850–1880," in T. Hershberg, ed., *Philadelphia: Work, Space, Family, and Group Experience in the Nineteenth Century* (Oxford University Press, 1981), pp. 43–92 (see Table 5). For a detailed discussion of small firms in the Philadelphia textile industry, see Philip Scranton, *Proprietary Capitalism: The Textile Manufacture at Philadelphia, 1800–1885* (Cambridge University Press, 1983).

36 That Garrett and McCollin's business contacts did not reach much beyond the Philadelphia region is suggested by the fact that in the early 1880s most of the systems they sold while operating the Thomson-Houston Electric Light Company of Philadelphia were in the immediate vicinity. See "The Thomson-Houston Electric Light Company [of Philadelphia]" (1885), p. 47, Trade Catalog Collection, Franklin Institute Science Museum, Philadelphia.

worked hard to overcome such prejudices; however, those were the difficulties faced by all promoters of electric lighting in the early 1880s, and they were overcome only by imaginative and aggressive campaigning.

Accompanying their marketing difficulties were the limitations of the Thomson-Houston system as it existed in the fall of 1879. The initial market for arc lighting was constrained by the fact that neither the Brush nor the Thomson-Houston dynamo could power more than eight lights. Until they could develop larger-capacity machines, the capital cost per light was too high for most firms. In response, Brush redesigned his dynamo so that it could power 16 lights. He also developed a double-arc light that could burn for 16 hours on two sets of carbons, and he improved the quality of carbons by plating them with copper.[37] Thomson was aware of Brush's innovations, but he was unable to make similar improvements in his system until he moved to New Britain, Connecticut, in 1880.

It may seem obvious that electric lighting could have been sold by building central stations for lighting streets and businesses, especially because gas companies were already providing such service. The first gas utility was organized in Baltimore in 1816, and by 1875 there were more than 400 gas companies in the United States. Although those companies demonstrated that there was a substantial market for lighting in the larger cities, the gas companies did not provide a model that the early arc-lighting inventors chose to imitate in terms of technical design or marketing strategy. Nowhere in the surviving papers of Thomson, Brush, or Charles Van Depoele does one find any comparison of arc lighting to gas lighting. In all likelihood, the differences in illuminating power of gas and arc lights discouraged any automatic comparison; whereas the typical gaslight gave off 10–15 candlepower, the first commercial arc lamps were rated at 2,000 candlepower. Moreover, a citywide gas system included a generating plant costing tens of thousands of dollars and servicing hundreds of lights; in contrast, the arc lighting systems of the late 1870s cost between $2,500 and $5,000 and powered only 4–16 lights. Because of such technical and economic differences, it did not make sense for arc-light inventors

37 Passer, *The Electrical Manufacturers,* pp. 17–18; Margaret Richardson, chap. 6, "A Race for a Practical Arc-Light," and chap. 7, "The Race for Practical Electric Dynamo," in draft biography of Charles Brush, box 25, Brush Papers.

to draw analogies between their product and gas lighting. Of course, Thomas Edison, unfamiliar with arc lighting, saw the potential of drawing an analogy between gas lighting and electric lighting, and he used that analogy to guide the development of his incandescent lighting system.[38]

However, prior to Edison, Brush and a few local entrepreneurs had begun to investigate a strategy of central stations in response to the peculiarities of their product. In particular, the power of their lights suggested that they should investigate street lighting. Brush was especially eager to capitalize on the potential of arc lighting for outdoor illumination, and in April 1879 he lit Monumental Park in Cleveland by placing 12 lights on several tall towers. Brush hoped that the city of Cleveland would purchase his system, making the sale simply another capital-goods transaction. Like the purchasers of electroplating dynamos, the Cleveland city fathers did not know how to evaluate the reliability of electric lighting; consequently, they insisted that the Telegraph Supply Company first install and operate the system before the city purchased it. Fortunately, Brush's system worked well, and the city subsequently used it to light the park and a few neighboring streets.[39] Although that installation sometimes is touted as the first central station for electric lighting, it was not a true central station in the sense of being a single power plant used to provide service to customers at a variety of locations. Instead, Brush's Monumental Park installation was simply a system sold to a city rather than to a factory or business.

The first central station was established not by an inventor but by local entrepreneurs. In June 1879, several businessmen in San Francisco organized the California Electric Light Company for the purpose

38 This assessment of the gas-lighting industry is based on Louis Stotz and Alexander Jamison, *History of the Gas Industry* (n.p., 1938); and Passer, *The Electrical Manufacturers*, pp. 195–7. In addition to the Thomson Papers and Brush Papers, I consulted the papers of Charles Van Depoele in Baker Library, Harvard University Graduate School of Business Administration, Boston. Van Depoele invented one of the first electric street-railway systems, as well as an arc lighting system in Detroit in the late 1870s. On Van Depoele's early career, consult William H. Lane, *A History of Electric Service in Detroit* (Detroit Bureau of Governmental Research, 1937), pp. 3–16.
39 "Contract for Lighting the Monumental Park with the Brush Electric Light," 10 March 1879, box 20, Miscellaneous Items, Brush Papers; Margaret Richardson, chap. 5, "Light in the Streets," draft biography of Brush; and Eisenmann, "Brush," pp. 73–5.

of promoting electric lighting. Initially they planned to use the obscure Titzell system, but within a few months they had secured the rights to sell and install the Brush system from Brush's territorial agent. During the first few years, most of the company's business came from selling Brush dynamos and lights for use in free-standing or isolated plants, but California Electric's managers also experimented with selling the service of lighting. In September 1879 they erected a small, makeshift power station housing a boiler, steam engine, and two dynamos. The dynamos powered 21 lamps, each of which was rented for $10 per week to nearby shops and hotels. Thus, California Electric was the first central-station electrical utility.[40]

Although California Electric began operating its central station in 1879, it is not clear when the central-station strategy proved to be commercially viable or how fast it spread. As the next chapter reveals, Brush and Thomson found it difficult to convince local businessmen to put up the capital for such companies, and the locals often had problems in securing the necessary municipal permits. It was not until Edison opened his Pearl Street station in 1882 that this marketing strategy became commonplace.[41]

In general, electric lighting systems in 1879 and 1880 were sold as capital equipment, much like steam engines or machine tools. The purchaser simply bought a dynamo, lights, and the necessary wire, connected them to his steam engine, and created his own isolated plant. From the standpoint of the inventors and entrepreneurs, that strategy made sense in that it drew on existing marketing patterns and consumer expectations. Overwhelmed by the challenges of just getting the technology to work, they hardly had time to devise radically new ways of selling the lights. At best, all they could do was to stake out a niche for their product, recognizing that businessmen who purchased

40 Charles M. Coleman, *P. G. and E. of California: The Centennial Story of the Pacific Gas and Electric Company, 1852–1952* (New York: McGraw-Hill, 1952), pp. 57–61.
41 On the lack of a central-station marketing strategy, see Eisenmann, "Brush," pp. 73–7; and Passer, *The Electrical Manufacturers,* pp. 17–18. As evidence of the continuing importance of isolated plants for the Brush organization, one should note that by April 1881 they had installed 2,720 lights in factories and business establishments and only 1,500 in central stations. See "The Brush Electric Light," *Scientific American* (20 April 1881). Edison's work on perfecting the central station as a marketing strategy is detailed by Thomas P. Hughes, *Networks of Power: Electrification in Western Society* (Baltimore: Johns Hopkins University Press, 1983), pp. 38–46.

lights did so either to attract customers or because their scale of operations warranted nighttime operation. For Thomson, in his partnership with Garrett and McCollin, or Brush with the Telegraph Supply
Company, that was all that could be done with their existing business
organizations. Yet, as we shall see, the inventors and entrepreneurs
dramatically altered that situation by modifying the technology, their
business organizations, and their marketing strategies.

Going beyond Brush: the automatic regulator

The dearth of sales gave Thomson time to put his technical affairs in
order and experiment. First, he and Houston prepared a patent application to cover the ideas embodied in the bakery dynamo. In October
1879 they filed an application for a dynamo with a three-coil armature
and an enclosed magnetic field.[42] Once that was done, Thomson
turned to a new problem arising from the use of arc lights in a series
circuit: What would happen if one or more lights burned out or were
switched off by a customer? Although a shunt switch could be added
to allow the current to bypass a nonfunctioning lamp, the loss of a
lamp would mean an increase in the line current and the consequent
danger of burning out the dynamo. Essentially a load problem, the
difficulty had to be eliminated if arc lighting was to be used in large
factories or central-station installations in which customers would
want to turn their lights on and off as they desired.

To cope with the problem, Brush had introduced a regulator that
switched in additional resistance to compensate for the extinguished
lights.[43] Such a regulator was wasteful, in that the dynamo continued
to generate the same amount of current even when the lights were off.
Furthermore, Brush's regulator could compensate for one or two
lights, but it was unable to protect the dynamo from major changes in
the load when all of the lights were extinguished.

Whereas Thomson's three-coil dynamo and arc light had been imitative of Brush, Thomson now responded with an automatic current
regulator surpassing Brush's design. In running the bakery dynamo, he

---

42 ET and EJH, "Dynamo-Electric Machine," U.S. Patent No. 223,557 (filed 4
October 1879, granted 13 January 1880).
43 For a description of Brush's regulator, see Thompson, *Dynamo-Electric
Machinery,* pp. 127–8. For a critique of that device, see "The American
Electric Co. . . . " (Catalog, November 1882), p. 18, Unsorted Material, TP;
and ET, "Evolution in Street Lighting," *GE Rev.,* 24:686–8 (August 1921).

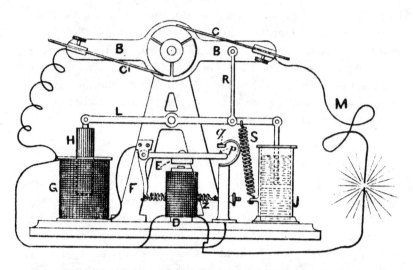

Figure 3.11. Thomson's 1879 current regulator: (G) electromagnet for moving brushes, (D) electromagnet for increasing sensitivity of regulator, (J) dashpot for dampening the motion of (L), the arm that moves brushes (C, C'). From E. Thomson and E. J. Houston, "Current Regulator for Dynamo Electric Machines," U.S. Patent No. 238,315 (1 March 1881).

had observed that the amount of current sent into the circuit varied with the position of the brushes. By shifting the brushes away from the point of maximum current, one could reduce the current in the system. Thomson took advantage of that observation by introducing a large electromagnet that automatically moved the brushes by means of a series of levers (Figure 3.11). Connected in series with arc lamps, the magnet was energized whenever the line current became too great, and it shifted the brushes to a new position where they picked up less current. In that way, Thomson's regulator permitted the dynamo to generate less current and hence draw less power from the steam engine. To increase the sensitivity of the regulator, Thomson added a second electromagnet that functioned as a relay. Detecting even slight changes in the line current, the second magnet closed a switch that allowed current to flow through the larger magnet and caused the brushes to shift. Though the intricacies of that feedback device were seldom understood by customers, they appreciated that the automatic current regulator permitted them to turn the lights on and off as convenience and necessity dictated. As a result, the automatic regulator became a major selling feature of the Thomson-Houston lighting system.[44]

In terms of Thomson's progress as an inventor, the automatic regulator was an important turning point. After development of that regulator, Thomson was no longer the apprentice emulating the master (Brush); he had surpassed his rival, demonstrating his ability to develop efficient and original electrical devices.

Spring 1880: a new dynamo and a new company

Undaunted by the lack of orders for his dynamos and arc lights, Thomson continued to invent through the fall and winter of 1879. In that work he was encouraged by Garrett and McCollin, who rented work space, provided tools, and purchased supplies. In all likelihood, Garrett and McCollin supported Thomson by drawing on their savings, not by borrowing money from a local bank.

In contrast to his appreciation of their support, Thomson was increasingly irritated by his technical partner, Houston. Although he had a good understanding of electrical phenomena, Houston apparently lacked manual skills. The older natural philosopher found it difficult to use tools and consequently often was absent during assembly of the machines. Many years later, Thomson accused Houston of unnecessarily demanding royalties from Garrett and McCollin and of never having contributed any original ideas to their partnership. Although there may have been some truth to those accusations, Houston did help with the patent work and the preparation of scientific

44 Thomson described the invention of his regulator in letters to J. W. Hammond, 18 June 1927, and to J. R. McKee, 23 October 1913, CL, TP. The regulator was covered by ET and EJH, "Automatic Adjuster for Commutator Brushes on Magneto Electric Machines," U.S. Patent No. 223,659 (filed 3 November 1879, granted 20 January 1880); and ET and EJH, "Current Regulator for Dynamo Electric Machines," U.S. Patent No. 238,315 (filed 26 June 1880, granted 1 March 1881). The patent model for Patent No. 223,659 is Cat. No. 181,725, Div. Elec., NMAH. For descriptions of how the regulator functioned, see "The Thomson-Houston Dynamo-Electric Machine," *Electrical World*, 5:123–4 (28 March 1885); Mayr, *Feedback Mechanisms*, p. 120; and Stuart Bennett, *A History of Control Engineering* (London: Peter Peregrinus, 1979), pp. 158–60. A rival inventor, Elmer A. Sperry, patented a similar regulator in 1882; see Thomas Parke Hughes, *Elmer Sperry: Inventor and Engineer* (Baltimore: Johns Hopkins University Press, 1971), pp. 16–23.

articles.[45] In all likelihood, what occurred in 1879 and 1880 was that Houston's talents became obsolete in terms of the development of the arc lighting system. As the work of perfecting the system came increasingly to depend on building and testing new devices, Houston's skills became less important, and Thomson's ability to visualize and fashion new devices came to the fore. In that context, Thomson began to feel that Houston was not contributing much to their technical partnership, and consequently the younger man began to work out new ideas on his own.

Thomson's disenchantment with Houston manifested itself most clearly in the design of an entirely new dynamo. Acting on his own, in May 1880 he filed a patent application covering a generator with a spherical armature enclosed within a cylindrical magnetic field. By having the magnetic-field circuit not only operate on each side of the armature but also travel through the cylindrical frame of the dynamo, Thomson ensured that the armature would cut through a maximum number of magnetic-field lines (Figure 3.12). With a spherical armature, he completely rejected the old belief of "active" versus "idle" wire, because all portions of the armature cut through the field.[46]

Integrating those two ideas, the new dynamo represented the culmination of Thomson's thinking about dynamo design, but it also suggests how production and aesthetic considerations were becoming part of his style. The design indicates that Thomson gave careful consideration to the problems of manufacture. Although the spherical armature would require the development of new winding techniques, the frame could be assembled from two large, round castings and 16 iron rods. Simple in form, the parts could be manufactured in quantity with a minimum of machining. Beyond its straightforward construction, the design also had geometrical elegance. In its earliest form the machine was sleek, with only the commutator breaking the clean lines of the cylinder and sphere. Such a design was unique in the early days of electrical technology and must have spoken to a machine aesthetic that

45 For Thomson's accusations against Houston, see ET, "Dynamo Work," pp. 11–14. Evidence of Houston's contributions to the technical partnership can be found in the application files in NARS for any of their joint patents.
46 ET, "Dynamo Electric Machine," U.S. Patent No. 233,047 (filed 4 May 1880, granted 5 October 1880); the model for that patent is Cat. No. 252,662, Div. Elec., NMAH. For evidence that Thomson handled that patent without Houston's help, see the patent's application file, NARS.

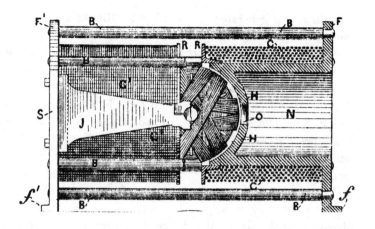

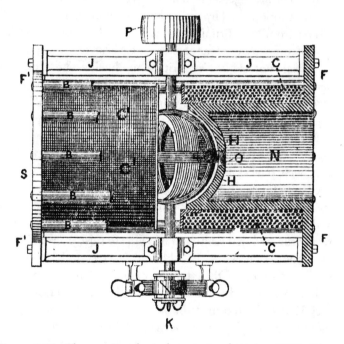

Figure 3.12. Thomson's spherical-armature dynamo, 1880. From E. Thomson, "Dynamo Electric Machine," U.S. Patent No. 233,047 (5 October 1880).

identified that generator as being highly efficient and the product of thoughtful planning.[47]

While in Philadelphia, Thomson appears to have designed two commercial versions of that dynamo. The first, whimsically known as "the Baby," could power a single arc light, but a second, larger version, the "Little Giant," could handle up to eight lights. Initially he did not intend to replace his older dynamo designs with those spherical machines, but instead planned them as additions to the product line he and Garrett were trying to market. Presumably, by having four different dynamo models to offer, they would be able to attract more customers by selling them precisely the machines they needed.[48]

Although Garrett helped Thomson in developing the spherical dynamo, the young inventor designed the new machine with a new set of business arrangements in mind. In the early months of 1880, Thomson was approached by Frederick H. Churchill, a scientifically minded lawyer from New Britain, Connecticut, who proposed that they form a new company for manufacturing electric lighting systems. By using his social contacts in New Britain and having Thomson and Houston demonstrate their lights, Churchill was able to raise capital and organize the American Electric Company. (Full details of how Churchill organized the company will be given in the next chapter.)

Rather than viewing the formation of American Electric as a threat, Garrett and McCollin saw it as an opportunity; the two businessmen may well have known that they did not have the "deep pockets" needed to finance new technology. They undoubtedly realized the limits of their ability to underwrite further work related to engineering and manufacturing the Thomson-Houston system, and they probably were delighted that Churchill was able to raise over $80,000 in capital to support that work. In addition, Garrett and McCollin probably knew the limits of their business contacts and marketing potential; although they had contacts in the Philadelphia business community, they lacked the resources or skills to go much beyond the city or its hinterland. Consequently, Garrett subscribed $6,000 to the new company, and in return he retained exclusive rights to sell the Thomson-Houston system in Pennsylvania, New Jersey, Delaware, and Mary-

47 This analysis of Thomson's spherical-armature dynamo is based on examination of Cat. No. 181,720 and 181,727, Div. Elec., NMAH.

48 "Notebook 1875–76 First Made," TP; based on the dimensions given, Cat. No. 181,727 (see footnote 47) is probably "the Baby" version.

land. Exercising that option, Garrett and McCollin organized the Thomson-Houston Electric Light Company of Philadelphia, which sold arc lighting systems in the early 1880s for use as isolated plants. As was the case for the Brush company, their sales were mostly to metalworking firms such as the Baldwin Locomotive Works and the Keystone Bridge Company. They also sold a large number of lights to the Baltimore & Ohio Railroad for use in freight yards and repair shops.[49]

Just as Garrett and McCollin were pleased with the formation of American Electric, so Thomson was excited by the prospect of manufacturing and marketing his inventions on a larger scale. In July 1880 he agreed to become the new company's chief engineer or electrician. As for Houston, he was interested in the new firm, but was unwilling to relocate to New Britain. Instead, he was retained as a consulting electrician in Philadelphia and was reimbursed in cash and stock for his share of the patents.[50]

In order to join American Electric in New Britain, Thomson resigned his professorship at Central High School in September 1880. Regretting his departure, the school's officials praised him in their annual report, noting that "his attainments in both physics and chemistry had given him an extended and growing reputation, and his inventive genius had displayed itself in many different directions." As a going-away gift, Thomson's students presented him an elaborate certificate that thanked him for being a "faithful teacher and a true friend." The only sour note at his departure came from Houston, who at Thomson's final faculty meeting congratulated him on securing "a position which would afford him a greater pecuniary reward." In making such a remark, Houston was referring to the fact that Thomson's annual salary was jumping from $1,925 to $2,500, but he probably was also criticizing Thomson for abandoning his career in science.[51] To Hous-

---

49 Garrett is listed as an investor in the American Electric Company in the "Articles of Association of the American Electric Company," 1 May 1880, HELCO. His selling territory is described in "Thomson-Houston Electric Light Company, Prospectus," circa 1882. Reference to lights sold to the Baltimore & Ohio Railroad can be found in "The Thomson-Houston Electric Light Company [of Philadelphia]," 1885, p. 47; both these items are in the Trade Catalog Collection, Franklin Institute Science Museum, Philadelphia. See also the entry for Thomson-Houston Electric Light Company, Pennsylvania Vol. 158, p. 153, R. G. Dun & Co. Collection.

50 ET, "Dynamo Work," pp. 17–18.

51 Sixty-Second Annual Report of the Board of Public Education of the First School District of Pennsylvania . . . for 1880 (Philadelphia: 1881), pp. 48–9;

ton, it may have been difficult to see how Thomson would be able to continue a search for nature's secrets while he was busy manufacturing electric lighting systems. Although the new position at American Electric Company would be challenging, the young man seemed to be giving up on the scientific life-style and values that the older man had taught him.

That Thomson left Central High is not particularly surprising; faculty members often resigned to take positions in business or education. Significantly, Thomson left just as the school entered into a difficult period in which the faculty lost much of its autonomy to the growing bureaucratic power of the city's Board of Education. One visible sign of the declining power of the Central High faculty was that the annual salary for individual professors fell from $2,178 in 1876 to $1,925 in 1879. With an exciting alternative career at hand, Thomson may have decided it was time to move.[52]

Yet still it is puzzling why Thomson abandoned his career as a local scientist, to which he had aspired since his student days. Why would he work so hard publishing scientific articles and obtaining membership in the Franklin Institute and the American Philosophical Society, only then to shift his interest to the electric-lighting business? Thomson probably made that career choice partly because there were few opportunities for him to move upward in local scientific circles. Along with 20–30 other chemists in the city, he was competing for a small handful of desirable teaching and research positions at the University of Pennsylvania, the Jefferson Medical College, and perhaps one or two other institutions.[53] Without a university degree, it is likely that he would have found it difficult to secure one of those positions, despite his publications and affiliations. Only 27 years old, he was still young and

the certificate from the students is in the oversize file, TP. Houston's remarks are from entry for 9 September 1880, Faculty Minutebook 1872–97, CHS Archives.

52 Franklin Spencer Edmunds, *History of the Central High School of Philadelphia* (Philadelphia: Lippincott, 1902), p. 205. On the decline of the school beginning in the 1880s, see David F. Labaree, *The Making of an American High School: The Credentials Market and the Central High School of Philadelphia, 1838–1939* (New Haven, Conn.: Yale University Press, 1988), pp. 115–33; faculty salaries are also from Labaree, Table 5.1, pp. 101–3.

53 In the "List of Members of the Franklin Institute, January 1st 1877," *J. Franklin Inst.*, Thomson is one of 34 chemists listed. An occupational sorting done by the Philadelphia Social History Project using 1880 census data listed 20 chemists and 39 laboratory workers.

quite ambitious. Why should he settle for being a high-school teacher, as Houston had? Finding that he liked to design and build things and that businessmen were willing to support him, Thomson embraced the role of the professional inventor.

Assessing the partnership

Through his partnership with Garrett and McCollin, Thomson secured the support necessary for transforming his arc-lighting inventions from scientific curiosities to a practical, commercial system. When he began working with those two businessmen in 1879, his inventions were crude and barely worked in the lecture hall; by the time he said good-bye in September 1880, he had a system with an efficient generator, a patented lamp design, and a novel regulator. One need only compare Thomson's complicated wood-frame dynamo of 1878 (Figure 2.21) with his sleek, all-metal, spherical dynamo of 1880 (Figure 3.12) to see how much he benefited from Garrett and McCollin's support.

In helping Thomson transform his inventions, Garrett and McCollin functioned as classic entrepreneurs. They identified the opportunity for innovation and brought together the resources needed to capitalize on the opportunity. Garrett and McCollin provided access to a machine shop, rented workrooms, hired assistants, and advanced money for the project. On occasion they even provided some muscle power, as when McCollin helped with the assembly of the bakery dynamo. Fortunately for Thomson, those two men had the contacts and skills needed to identify and coordinate the vital resources.

Garrett not only bankrolled the project but also played a crucial role in helping Thomson shape the design of his technology. By providing information about how Brush had designed and marketed his arc lights, Garrett helped Thomson focus his efforts on key problems. Through Garrett's guidance, Thomson developed a dc generator rather than an ac generator, used a single commutator and series circuit instead of the cumbersome four-commutator arrangement, and strove to increase the number of lights powered by a single dynamo. Garrett probably also encouraged Thomson to develop a lamp distinctly different from that of Brush and supported the young inventor's efforts with the automatic regulator. All of those improvements helped Thomson to prepare his arc-lighting inventions for commercial sale.

Garrett and McCollin further assisted Thomson by taking up the marketing function. Drawing on their contacts in the local business community, they found a few customers for Thomson's dynamos and lights. Like the Brush organization, they sold a few systems on the basis of novelty, but then sought out firms that were moving to nighttime operations to achieve economies of speed. Unfortunately, Philadelphia manufacturers were slow to purchase the new technology, because the scale of their operations did not warrant it and because the costs of installing an entire system may have been too high. Stymied by the conservative attitude of potential customers, Garrett and McCollin were unable to help Thomson market his technology further. Instead, it fell to Thomson's future business associates to address the challenge of developing a new marketing strategy.

The partnership of Garrett, McCollin, Thomson, and Houston was clearly a shoestring operation. Although they left no records of how much they spent to develop Thomson's inventions, the R. G. Dun & Co. credit investigator reported in October 1881 that Garrett had invested $20,000 in the business. That they accomplished what they did with so few resources stands in marked contrast to Thomas Edison's efforts to develop the incandescent light at the same time. Drawing on his contacts with Western Union and Wall Street, in November 1878 Edison was able to establish the Edison Electric Light Company, with capital of $300,000. Among Edison's backers were William H. Vanderbilt, Hamilton McKay Twombly, and Tracy R. Edson; compared with those rich and powerful men from Wall Street, Garrett and McCollin were indeed small businessmen. Within a year, Edison spent $50,000 in conducting experiments, hiring new staff, and enlarging his Menlo Park laboratory with a new machine shop and office-library building. Although that spending resulted in a new incandescent lamp, it does seem profligate compared with Thomson working at Harrison's machine shop or in rented rooms with one or two assistants. With those larger resources, Edison did produce a revolutionary technology (the incandescent lamp), whereas Thomson and Houston were engaged in incrementally improving an existing technology (arc lighting), and hence smaller resources probably were appropriate. Nonetheless, that difference should not prevent us from wondering which of the two development projects was more typical of the 1880s (or even today) and thus more instructive about the challenges of perfecting a new technology.[54]

Despite what Thomson achieved with Garrett and McCollin, there still was much to be done. They had not been successful in selling electric lighting; new, aggressive marketing strategies needed to be developed. Garrett and McCollin had hardly begun to take up the problems of manufacturing dynamos and arc lights, and they may have realized that they lacked the capital to do so. Furthermore, they probably lacked the contacts and skills needed to raise capital by organizing a joint-stock company. Fortuitously, just as the Philadelphia partnership encountered those difficulties, Frederick H. Churchill of New Britain appeared on the scene. He was able to overcome those limitations and help Thomson advance his system of electric lighting. Let us turn next to Churchill and the American Electric Company of New Britain.

54 Entry for Thomson-Houston Electric Light Company, Pennsylvania Vol. 158, p. 153, R. G. Dun & Co. Collection; Robert Friedel and Paul Israel, *Edison's Electric Light: Biography of an Invention* (New Brunswick, N.J.: Rutgers University Press, 1986), pp. 19, 22; Hughes, *Networks of Power,* p. 25.

4. Frustration in New Britain, 1880–1883

> It required as you may well believe, a considerable amount of courage to start an enterprise of this kind, not knowing what market there might be for electrical apparatus. It required that we, as it were, should prejudge the future. But it seemed as if an era was opening in which electricity should have a great part – at least so it seemed to me – and shortly afterwards a company was organized to begin operations, in New Britain, Conn., and it was called the American Electric Company.
>
> Elihu Thomson (1905)[1]

In September 1880, Elihu Thomson left Philadelphia for New Britain, Connecticut, with enthusiasm and anticipation. During the preceding two years he had devoted himself to the study of arc lighting, and now a group of businessmen had organized the American Electric Company to manufacture the lighting system he and Houston had designed. With their help, he would be able to see his inventions put into production, and he would have the chance to compete head-on with Charles Brush, the leading arc-light inventor in America. In New Britain, Thomson threw himself into his work, supervising the manufacture of electrical equipment and devising improvements for his lights and dynamos.

While in New Britain, Thomson learned much about the business of invention. Watching Frederick H. Churchill, a lawyer who enthusiastically believed in the future of electric lighting, the young inventor learned about financing and organizing a technology-oriented firm. As the new company's chief electrician, he confronted and solved myriad problems in development and production; the challenges included equipping the factory, training workmen, finding suitable materials, and redesigning his inventions for manufacture. Thomson also strove to adapt his system to new marketing opportunities. That meant

---

1 ET, "Personal Recollections of the Development of the Electrical Industry," *Engineering Magazine* (June 1905), pp. 563–7; quotation on p. 567.

adding accessories to his dynamo, and because it became desirable to sell installations with a large number of lights, Thomson began to think increasingly in terms of systems. New Britain was very much a "school of experience" for Thomson, and one purpose of this chapter will be to explore how he acquired the skills needed to take an invention from preliminary design to production model.

Yet, as Thomson soon learned, it is not enough to produce a technically sound system; one must also be able to market it. Consequently, a second theme is to examine the difficulties of cultivating a market for a new invention. In regard to electric lighting, it has often been assumed that the marketing problem was quickly solved in the early 1880s by Thomas Edison, with the development of the central-station strategy.[2] Although Edison may have been guided by that marketing strategy in building his incandescent lighting system, this chapter will suggest that the central-station idea was not an obvious or immediately profitable marketing strategy. In the case of Thomson and American Electric, we shall see that they only gradually took up that strategy, and they failed in their initial effort at promoting a central station. Although they eventually succeeded in selling equipment for arc-lighting central stations, their experience illustrates the difficulties of identifying and implementing a new marketing strategy.

Despite his hard work and initial enthusiasm, by 1882 Thomson was ready to leave the firm. As he gradually realized, the New Britain businessmen had invested in the firm for limited and immediate reasons and were not interested in the aggressive development of new products or marketing strategies. When the opportunity came to sell their stock in the company in April 1882, the major stockholders eagerly took the immediate profit, rather than wait for the company to develop fully. In order to explain why the New Britain investors chose to abandon Thomson, a third theme of this chapter will be to consider how Thomson came to take the long-term view of profits through continual innovation, whereas his backers saw electric lighting as a speculative investment.[3]

2 Thomas P. Hughes, *Networks of Power: Electrification in Western Society, 1880–1930* (Baltimore: Johns Hopkins University Press, 1983), pp. 34, 39–42; Harold Passer, *The Electrical Manufacturers, 1875–1900: A Study in Competition, Entrepreneurship, Technical Change, and Economic Growth* (Cambridge, Mass.: Harvard University Press, 1953), pp. 118–23.

3 Most accounts of Thomson's experience are based on his recollections written 40 years later. His most detailed description of his years in New Britain is

Financing high technology: the formation of the American Electric Company

Although his abilities as an inventor blossomed in the late 1870s, it took Thomson longer to master the ways of the business world. Just as he had looked to Houston to teach him the rules and rituals of the scientific community, so he had turned to George Garrett and Thomas McCollin to help him learn about manufacturing and marketing new machinery. To move beyond that informal partnership and reach a larger market, Thomson came to realize that it would be necessary to secure more capital, perhaps by means of a joint-stock company. By chance, Thomson met a gentleman with the skills needed to generate interest and investment in a new enterprise: Frederick H. Churchill of New Britain, Connecticut.

With his enthusiasm for electric lighting and his social contacts, Churchill was well suited for the role of technology entrepreneur. Born in 1848, he was the son of a successful jewelry manufacturer in New Britain. His father sent him to the local public high school and then to Yale College, where he studied science at the Sheffield Scientific School. As a career, Churchill chose the law and attended the Harvard Law School. He returned to New Britain in 1875 and established a local practice, drawing on his family's prominence and his appointment as clerk of the City Court to attract clients[4] (Figure 4.1).

Like Thomson, Churchill became fascinated with electrical technology in the late 1870s. On his own, he began to study the potential uses of the new force by reading scientific journals and experimenting with electrical machines. In 1878 he, too, journeyed to the Paris Universal Exposition to see the electric lights. Shortly after that, Churchill was introduced through a college friend to Thomson and Houston.[5] Excited by their new system of arc lights, Churchill sought to secure a

"Dynamo Work and Its Development," Autobiog. Papers, TP. See also David O. Woodbury, *Beloved Scientist: Elihu Thomson, a Guiding Spirit of the Electrical Age* (New York: Whittlesey House, 1944; reprinted Cambridge, Mass.: Harvard University Press, 1960), pp. 120–30.

4 Yale College Library, *Obituary Record of Yale College Deceased . . .* (New Haven, Conn.: Yale University, 1920), p. 54; A. J. Sloper to J. W. Hammond, 2 October 1930, item J871–3, Hammond File.

5 Churchill's electric machines and scientific journals are listed in "Estate of Frederick H. Churchill. Inventory" (hereafter cited as "Churchill Estate Inventory"), 20 April 1881, Berlin Probate District Court Records, New Britain, Connecticut, Vol. 24, pp. 348–52; I am grateful to Barbara Hubbard of the New Britain Public Library for locating this document for me. See also

Figure 4.1. Frederick H. Churchill, organizer of American Electric. From W. R. Cutter et al., eds., *Genealogical and Family History of the State of Connecticut* (New York: Lewis History Publishing Co., n.d.).

share in the new enterprise. Because Garrett and McCollin had already arranged with the two professors to manufacture their new system, Churchill initially offered them assistance in securing foreign patents. In May 1879, Churchill, Thomson, and Houston agreed to apply for patents in Canada, Great Britain, and France covering their best dynamo and arc lamp. In return for a 50% interest in those patents, Churchill paid the application fees and the cost of the models. Under that agreement they filed for one French and three British patents.[6]

Not satisfied with a share of the foreign patents, Churchill continued to negotiate with Thomson and Houston for greater involvement. In January 1880 he offered to create a joint-stock company in Connecticut to manufacture and sell their system.[7] That prospect excited Thom-

W. T. Sloper, *The Life and Times of Andrew Jackson Sloper* (New Britain: by the author, 1949), pp. 284–6.

6 Agreement among EJH, ET, and F. H. Churchill, 14 May 1879, Hall of History Collection. The number of patents filed under that agreement is taken from "Churchill Estate Inventory."

7 Reference to an agreement dated 16 January 1880 to form a joint-stock company in Connecticut is made in "Estate of Frederick H. Churchill. Return

son, as it was an opportunity to expand the business beyond the Philadelphia area. He and Garrett had not been particularly successful in
selling arc lighting in Philadelphia, but perhaps more capital, a new
location, and Churchill's business skills could overcome the marketing
difficulties.[8]

In New Britain, Churchill promptly began to stimulate interest in an
electric-lighting company among the business elite. A town of 20,000
in 1880, New Britain was known as the "hardware city," where
entrepreneurs Frederick T. Stanley, Philip and Cornelius B. Erwin, and
Henry E. Russell had organized some of the largest plants in America
for the manufacture of hardware, tools, and metal fittings. Those men
built up their businesses through shrewd use of new technology; as
early as 1830, Frederick T. Stanley employed a steam engine to power
his bolt-cutting machines. After the Civil War, the Stanley Works surpassed its competitors by introducing special-purpose tools for making
hinges and by developing cold-rolling techniques. In addition, the
hardware manufacturers were familiar with electrical technology; in
1878 the Stanley Works, P. & F. Corbin, and Russell & Erwin were
using dynamos manufactured by Edward Weston to electroplate
hinges with nickel. Perhaps on the basis of positive experiences with
electroplating, two more firms, Stanley Rule & Level and Plume &
Atwood, installed Brush lighting systems in their factories.[9]

of Sale of Choses in Action," 8 June 1887, Berlin Probate District Court
Records, New Britain, Connecticut, Vol. 24, pp. 45–6.

8 Garrett invested in American Electric but created a new company; see
"Articles of Association of the American Electric Company" (hereafter cited
as "Articles of Association"), 1 May 1880, HELCO Collection. Garrett's
selling territory is described in "Thomson-Houston Electric Light Company.
Prospectus," circa 1882, Trade Catalog Collection, Franklin Institute Science
Museum, Philadelphia. Additional information about this firm can be found
in the entry for Thomson-Houston Electric Light Co., Pennsylvania Vol. 158,
p. 285, R. G. Dun & Co. Collection.

9 Concerning the history of New Britain as a hardware manufacturing center,
see David N. Camp, History of New Britain, with Sketches of Farmington and
Berlin, Connecticut. 1640–1889 (New Britain: William B. Thomson, 1889);
Hartford Section, American Society of Mechanical Engineers, Connecticut:
The Industrial Incubator (New York: ASME, 1981), pp. 47–53; Robert Keith
Leavitt, Foundation for the Future: History of the Stanley Works (New
Britain: by the author, 1951); Marcus White, New Britain: The Center of
Hardware Manufacture (New Britain: 1903); and Donald W. Davis, The
Stanley Works: A 125 Year Beginning (New York: Newcomen Society, 1969).
References to Weston and Brush dynamos in New Britain can be found in
"Weston Dynamo-Electric Machine Co." (circular, London, January 1878);

Churchill approached the business leaders of New Britain through the Saturday Night Club, a group that he had helped organize in 1875. Consisting of the city's elite, the club met monthly to hear lectures and enjoy intellectual discussion. Churchill introduced that group to the marvels of electricity by speaking at the February 1880 meeting on "The Development and Utilization of Heavy Currents of Electricity." At the next meeting, Churchill presented Thomson and Houston and arranged for a demonstration of their arc lighting system to follow the meeting.[10]

That demonstration was held downtown in a vacant building previously used by a manufacturer of fruit baskets. With the help of Joseph Wright (the shop engineer from Fuller's bakery), Thomson operated a dynamo similar to the one tested at the bakery the previous summer (see Figure 3.8). Eight arc lamps were placed throughout the building, and visitors were shown how the automatic current regulator allowed the lamps to be turned on and off without having to adjust the dynamo. As a further attraction, Thomson demonstrated the transmission of power by using one dynamo to power another dynamo as a motor. Placed in an outbuilding some distance from the main dynamo, the motor ran a circular saw, which cut wood. The demonstration went well, although Wright was forced to burn many of the old wooden basket-making machines in order to maintain pressure in the old steam engine powering the dynamo.[11]

At the demonstration, Churchill distributed a pamphlet announcing the formation of an electrical manufacturing company. In that prospectus, Churchill praised Thomson and Houston's work on the Franklin Institute dynamo tests, described their scientific accomplishments, and listed their patents. Claiming that "the patents already issued comprise a complete electric light system," Churchill offered them as the basis for forming a joint-stock company. Lest investors feel

and Anglo-American Brush Electric Light Corporation, Limited, "Testimonial and List of Employers," 1880, p. 16; both in Wheeler Collection, United Engineering Library, New York, WP 52:16 and 136:14, respectively.

10 Dr. John C. White, "A History of the New Britain Saturday Night Club" (unpublished manuscript, 1975); "Minutes of Saturday Night Club, 1875–1883," pp. 121, 124, 126; both in NBPL.

11 ET, "Some of the Early Work at New Britain, Conn., U.S.A.," *Proceedings of the AIEE*, 28(Pt. 1):9–11 (February 1909); ET, "Arc Lighting – Electric Welding," in *Proceedings of the Thirteenth Convention of National Electric Light Association* (1891), pp. 103–18.

that they were buying shares in an unknown venture, Churchill invited local businessmen to form a committee to evaluate the patents. With that kind of committee, Churchill probably knew that he could generate confidence in the new undertaking.[12]

Churchill supplemented his brochure by arranging for an article to be published in the New Britain *Observer* entitled "A New Industry. The Manufacture of Electric Light Machinery in this City." After describing the demonstration in the basket shop, the newspaper story emphasized that the arc light was more practical and more reliable than the incandescent lamp. The arc light on display was not an "Edisonian light" but a "Voltaic arc which is no experiment as it has been demonstrated beyond doubt, both in this country and Europe that it is both a scientific, practical, and commercial success."[13] With such remarks, Churchill was striving to convince investors that arc lighting was a safe investment and that its commercial introduction would shortly yield handsome profits. "Such an industry," he promised in the prospectus, "would have within it a capacity for expansion and growth such as is furnished by but few business opportunities that to-day present themselves to the business world."[14]

Churchill's enthusiasm for the electric light was contagious. As he had suggested, a committee was promptly formed to evaluate Thomson and Houston's patents; it probably was no coincidence that all the committee members belonged to the Saturday Night Club. That committee prepared and printed two glowing reports on the Thomson-Houston system. In their second report, from April 1880, the committee members described another demonstration at the basket shop during which Thomson operated his new spherical-armature dynamo (see Figure 3.12):

> Although possessing only the size and proportions commonly adopted in . . . two-light machines hitherto in use, this new generator showed an ability to generate electricity of such quantity and intensity as we have never known of being equalled in any generator of its

12 F. H. Churchill, "A Statement Relative to the Proposed Organization of an Electric Light Company Based Upon the Patents of Professors Edwin J. Houston and Elihu Thomson, of Philadelphia, Pa.," 27 March 1880 (Hartford: privately printed, 1880), in Unsorted Material, TP.

13 "A New Industry. The Manufacture of Electric Light Machinery in this City," New Britain *Observer*, 30 March 1880, NBPL.

14 Churchill, "Statement Relative to the Proposed Organization."

size and weight. Its performance as applied to electric lighting was surprising.[15]

The committee was impressed that the new dynamo used less copper wire and would be simpler to construct than most other dynamos. Those design characteristics meant that the dynamo could be sold at lower cost, thus making a lighting system employing that machine more competitive. Echoing Churchill's remarks, the committee concluded that a company manufacturing such a fine dynamo was certain to succeed.

Having thoroughly laid the groundwork for the new enterprise, Churchill opened the subscription list for investors at the New Britain National Bank on 1 May 1880. The new company was initially capitalized at $87,500. To entice investors, additional demonstrations were given at the basket shop, displaying Thomson's dynamos capable of lighting one, two, four, or eight lamps. One of those evening demonstrations was followed by a "lunch" for the guests, reminiscent of the party given by Edison for the borough aldermen when he was trying to secure permission to dig up the streets of Manhattan for his electrical mains. Through Cornelius B. Erwin, president of the bank and a leading hardware manufacturer, businessmen not only from New Britain but also from nearby Hartford, Meriden, and Waterbury were persuaded to take shares in the new enterprise. With all that promotion, the stock sold quickly, and by the middle of June 1880, Churchill and the investors were ready to organize the company.[16]

The stockholders of the new enterprise met on 12 June 1880 and named the firm the American Electric Company. In the charter, the stockholders claimed not only that their company would manufacture and sell electrical machinery but also that it might furnish electricity to consumers. To oversee the company, the stockholders elected as directors both Churchill and Thomson, as well as several of the leading hardware manufacturers in New Britain. Such men were highly qualified to supervise a new firm; as one indication of their business acu-

15 Quotation is from William Parker et al., "Second Report of Committee of Investigation Relative to the New Electric Generator of Prof. Elihu Thomson," 27 April 1880; see also William Parker et al., "First Report of Committee of Investigation," 13 April 1880; both are in Historical File, General Electric Company, Schenectady, New York.
16 "Articles of Association"; A. J. Sloper to J. W. Hammond, 2 October 1930, Hammond File; articles in New Britain Observer, 27 April, 18 May, and 15 June 1880.

men, the capital values of their firm ranged from $200,000 to $1,000,000 (Table 4.1). All of the directors invested in the new firm, showing that they, too, expected the electric-lighting business to be highly remunerative. As officers, William Parker, secretary of the Stanley Works, was elected president, and Churchill was selected to be secretary, treasurer, and manager.[17]

In order to secure the rights to Thomson and Houston's patents, the stockholders voted to increase the capitalization of the company from $87,500 to $125,000. That new stock issue was assigned to Thomson and Houston, and it made them owners of 30% of the firm. The inventors also received $6,000 cash for their patents. Under a contract signed on 9 July 1880, Thomson was hired as resident electrician for two years at an annual salary of $2,500. Houston, who chose to remain in Philadelphia, was retained for one year as consulting electrician, with a salary of $700. In addition, under that contract, American Electric promised to proceed with "all reasonable diligence" in developing and manufacturing Thomson and Houston's inventions and acknowledged that failure to do so would result in the patents reverting to the inventors.[18]

The rapid organization of American Electric was largely due to Churchill's ability to generate interest for the new electrical technology among his friends and business associates. Churchill's efforts on behalf of Thomson remind one of how Grosvenor Lowrey assisted Edison in securing capital from the financiers of Wall Street and Western Union officials. Yet, without slighting Churchill's promotional abilities, one may inquire as to why the hardware manufacturers of New Britain chose to involve themselves with the development of a new technology. What did they see in electric lighting that made it an appealing investment?

Although the New Britain hardware manufacturers left behind no documentary evidence to explain their investment in American Electric,

17 "The American Electric Company. Certificate of Organization" (hereafter cited as "AEC Certificate of Organization"), 12 June 1880, HELCO Collection; New Britain Herald, 12 June 1880, NBPL.

18 "AEC Certificate of Organization"; "Certificate of increase of stock," 22 July 1880, HELCO Collection; "American Electric Company," New Britain Observer, 27 July 1880, NBPL; "C-Contract" (signed by EJH, ET, and F. H. Churchill), 21 April 1880, Hall of History Collection; agreement between ET and EJH and the American Electric Company, 9 July 1880, CL, TP (hereafter cited as "AEC Contract," July 1880).

Table 4.1. *Directors of the American Electric Company, 1880*

Name	Title	Firm and product	Capital value of firm	Amount invested in A.E.C.
Cornelius B. Erwin	President	Russell & Erwin Mfg. Co. (hardware)	$1,000,000	$5,000
Henry Stanley	President	Stanley Works (hardware); Stanley Rule & Level (hand tools); American Hosiery Co. (underwear)	300,000 300,000	5,000
J. Andrew Pickett	President	Landers, Frary & Clark (cutlery) Union Mfg. Co. (iron foundry)	500,000 200,000	3,000
D. S. Plume	President?	Plume & Atwood of Waterbury (brass goods)		2,500
Austin C. Dunham	President	Willimantic Linen Co. of Hartford (textiles)		1,000
Edward H. Davison	Superintendent	American Hosiery Co.; New Britain Knitting Co.		1,000
William Parker	Secretary President	Stanley Works		1,000
Frederick H. Churchill	Manager	American Electric Co.		6,000
Elihu Thomson	Electrician	American Electric Co.		

Sources: New Britain *Herald* 19 June 1880; "Articles of Association of American Electric Company," June 1880, HELCO Collection, Connecticut Historical Society, Hartford; *New Britain Directory, 1882-3* (New Britain: Price, Lee & Co., 1882).

one can infer several reasons for their actions. First and foremost, they probably considered electric lighting to be a desirable speculative investment. Through the newspapers they undoubtedly had learned that the Brush Electric Light Company of Cleveland was doing a brisk business and that financiers in New York were scrambling to buy stock in Edison's incandescent-lighting companies[19] (see Table 4.3 for prices of Edison stock a few years later, in 1883). Just as investors in the 1980s were "bullish" on biotechnology, so investors in the early 1880s were excited by the potential of electric lighting and readily invested in the field. Given the general excitement over electric lighting, the New Britain hardware manufacturers probably believed that their investment in a new electrical manufacturing company would appreciate rapidly.

Aside from speculation, a second probable reason that the hardware manufacturers chose to invest in Thomson's arc lighting system was related to local conditions. Although it had grown steadily through most of the nineteenth century, New Britain's hardware industry had suffered from periodic fluctuations in the market. As one instance, the Stanley Works, maker of hinges, bolts, and locks, enjoyed rapid expansion during the Civil War, but found itself overextended during the financial panic of 1873 and the ensuing depression. From 1876 to 1878 the firm declared no dividends, and a portion of its factory space went unused. Because a new industry such as electrical manufacturing could utilize that excess plant capacity, managers of the Stanley Works found it especially appealing. Thus, when American Electric set up its plant in the fall of 1880, it was in an old Stanley building that had been vacant since 1871.[20]

More than simply renting an empty building, though, the hardware manufacturers were interested in offsetting the fluctuations in the hardware business by diversifying the industrial base of their community. Prior to 1880, they had moved into the production of underwear and socks by organizing the American Hosiery Company and the New Britain Knitting Company. In 1882, many of the same men who had

19 Passer, *The Electrical Manufacturers*, pp. 20, 86–8.
20 Leavitt, *Foundation for the Future*, pp. 20, 37–8; Matthew Roth, *Connecticut: An Inventory of Historic Engineering and Industrial Sites* (Washington, D.C.: Society for Industrial Archaeology, 1981), pp. 70–1; "Stanley Works Growth Reviewed," Hartford *Times*, 14 September 1927, item J782, Hammond File; entry for Stanley Works, Connecticut Vol. 22, p. 1,061, R. G. Dun & Co. Collection.

invested in American Electric helped to create a firm for manufacturing sewing machines, and they encouraged the Stanley Works to begin manufacturing tacks.[21] The strategy behind those new ventures was that diversification might guarantee profits in the event of future slow-downs in the primary business of the community. That risk-minimizing strategy must have made good sense to the hardware manufacturers, but, as we shall see, it did not lead them to make a substantial commitment to solving the technical and marketing problems associated with electric lighting.

Setting up shop and getting down to work

When Thomson arrived in New Britain in September 1880, the directors of the company had already rented the old Stanley Works building at Lake and High streets (Figure 4.2). On the first floor, Thomson and his associates installed a machine shop for constructing dynamos and lamps. On the second floor, they placed offices, the lamp-testing room, and a private workshop that Thomson called his "Model Room." In the middle of the building was an old 25-horsepower steam engine that was used to power the machine tools and test the dynamos before shipping.[22]

Through the fall of 1880, Thomson busied himself with the tasks related to manufacturing. He ordered machine tools and hired workmen. Because the workmen were unfamiliar with the new techniques involved in electrical manufacture, Thomson taught them how to wind armature and field coils and to make rudimentary electrical measurements. He also designed dynamos in several sizes, prepared working drawings, and made wooden patterns from which the metal parts could be fashioned. Finally, Thomson devoted considerable time to business and marketing matters. Although Parker was knowledgeable about general business affairs, he knew little about electric lighting;

21 For the American Hosiery Company and New Britain Knitting Mills, see *New Britain Directory. 1880–81* (New Britain: Price, Lee & Company, 1880); for the sewing machine company, see New Britain *Herald,* 1 August 1882; for tack manufacturing, see Leavitt, *Foundation for the Future,* pp. 44–6.
22 Leavitt, *Foundation for the Future,* pp. 43–4; "Schenectady Works News," 4 August 1922, Unsorted Material, TP; J. I. Mitchell, "Reminiscences of Lynn," GE Pittsfield Works *Current News,* 2(4) (December 1914), item I53, Hammond File.

Figure 4.2. Building used by American Electric in New Britain. From Local History Room, New Britain Public Library.

consequently, Thomson had to help him integrate technical consider-ations into their business decisions.[23]

Assisting Thomson was one of his former students, Edwin Wilbur Rice, Jr. On graduating from Central High in 1880, Rice had consid-ered attending Yale College, but then chose to join his former professor at New Britain, believing that he would learn more about electricity from Thomson than in college. Hired as Thomson's assistant, Rice was paid $30 per month. Rice helped Thomson by keeping records and sketches of new inventions, supervising the machine-shop work, and testing dynamos and lamps. On occasion he served as the company's first "test man," installing new lighting systems and troubleshooting when customers were unable to get their systems to run. In performing

23 "AEC Contract," July 1880; "Extracts (or summaries of testimony in patent infringement suit of General Electric Co. vs. Butler Company) . . . ," item J457–9, Hammond File.

those different activities, Rice served as an intermediary between the Model Room and the factory floor, helping to get new inventions into production.[24]

From the outset at American Electric, Thomson and Rice encountered difficulties in designing and manufacturing electrical equipment, yet they overcame such obstacles by imagination and effort. The speed of their old steam engine varied erratically, making it difficult to test dynamos. In response, Thomson invented a special transmission dynamometer for measuring the power consumed by dynamos.[25] Besides a dynamometer, Thomson built other electrical measuring instruments. Curious as it may seem, inventors in the early 1880s constructed dynamos and lamps without being able to measure voltage, current, or power; instead, they depended on a "feel" for the phenomena as they designed equipment. Yet because of his scientific background, Thomson preferred to supplement his qualitative sense of electricity with quantitative measurements. Shortly after coming to New Britain, Thomson secured an expensive Western Union tangent galvanometer that he rewired with coarse wire so that it could measure the strong currents found in arc-lighting circuits. Because the galvanometer could indicate only current, Thomson fashioned his own Wheatstone bridge and resistance coils to use with the galvanometer for measuring current strength, resistance, and voltage. All of that cumbersome apparatus was necessary to check the resistances of coils in the arc lamps and to test the outputs of the dynamos. Dependent on a sensitive galvanometer, such apparatus could be easily disturbed; much to

24 "Supt. E. W. Rice, Jr.," Lynn *Item* (1892 souvenir edition), Lynn HS; J. R. McKee and W. S. Andrews, *Historical Notes: General Electric Company* (New York: privately printed, 1930), p. 45; ET, "Testimony" (typescript), Interference No. 13,761 (on transformer distribution systems), NARS (hereafter cited as ET, "Testimony," Intf. 13,761).

25 Styled after a friction dynamometer used for steam engines, Thomson's version offset the variability of the engine's speed by using weights to balance the tension on either side of the pulley belt connecting the engine with the dynamo. By employing his automatic regulator to keep the current output of the dynamo constant, Thomson used the dynamometer to measure the efficiency of each dynamo produced by the factory and to improve on his design. See ET, "A Simple Transmission Dynamometer," *J. Franklin Inst.*, 111:117–20 (February 1881); E. W. Rice, Jr., "Reminiscences of Early Arc Lighting Apparatus," *GE Rev.*, 12:158–62 (April 1909), especially p. 161 (hereafter cited as "Arc Reminiscences").

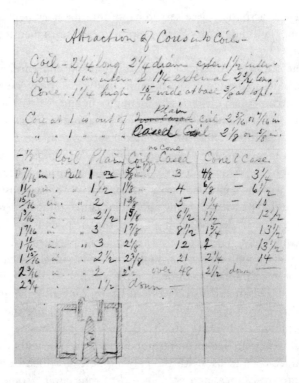

Figure 4.3. Thomson's notes on cores for automatic regulator magnet, circa 1880–1. From "Notebook 1875–1876 First Made,"
Thomson Papers, American Philosophical Society, Philadelphia.

Thomson's displeasure, trains passing by the factory often upset measurements.[26]

Despite those limitations, Thomson used his rudimentary apparatus
to hone his understanding of how his dynamos and lamps worked. As
an example, he developed a good grasp of the magnetic-saturation
curve for electromagnetic coils. Drawing on his scientific training and
experience with the Franklin Institute tests, Thomson improved the
solenoid coil in his automatic regulator (Figure 3.11) by measuring and
plotting the magnetic responses of various coils (Figures 4.3 and 4.4).
In particular, he found that if the end of the solenoid's core was made
cone-shaped, and the coil was placed in an iron case, the coil would

26 ET, "Electrical Measurements," 4 December 1912, Hall of History Collection; ET, "A Retrospect," *GE Rev.*, 10:259–64 (1907–8), especially p. 263.

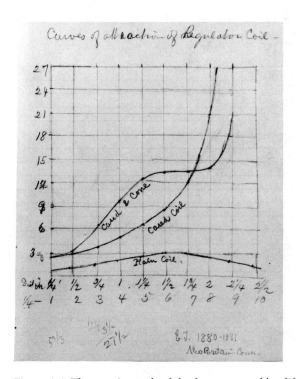

Figure 4.4. Thomson's graph of the forces exerted by different cores used in automatic regulator magnet, circa 1880–1. Vertical coordinates are in ounces; horizontal coordinates are the diameter of the core. From "Notebook 1875–1876 First Made," Thomson Papers, American Philosophical Society, Philadelphia.

pull more smoothly on the brush lever arm, thus preventing the lights from flickering when the brushes were adjusted[27] (Figure 4.5).

Other obstacles were presented by the materials needed to construct electrical equipment. As Thomson soon realized, Churchill was reluctant to order large quantities of the wire, castings, and hardware

27 Sketches and calculations for that work can be found in "Notebook 1875–1876 First Made," TP (hereafter cited as "First Notebook"). See also Rice, "Arc Reminiscences," p. 161; ET, "Electro-Magnetic Device," U.S. Patent No. 250,175 (filed 9 February 1881, granted 29 November 1881); Karen Belmore, "The Inventor-Entrepreneur: Elihu Thomson and the Dynamo" (master's thesis, Department of History and Sociology of Science, University of Pennsylvania, 1980), pp. 75, 78. Thomson also used that improved solenoid in an arc-light design; see ET, "Electric Lamp," U.S. Patent No. 250,463 (filed 2 March 1881, granted 6 December 1881).

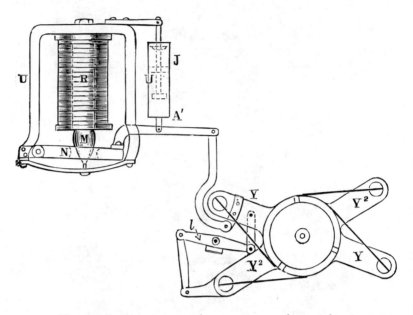

Figure 4.5. Automatic regulator magnet and gear, showing cone-shaped solenoid core: (M) solenoid core, (R) magnet coil, (Y, Y²) adjustable brush holders. From S. P. Thompson, *Dynamo-Electric Machinery,* 3rd ed. (London: 1888), p. 244.

needed to build dynamos and lamps, but even worse, he tended to purchase inferior supplies. Good insulated wire was especially difficult to find. Whereas bare copper wire could be used to connect the arc lamps to the dynamo, insulated wire was essential for the coils in the lamp mechanisms and the dynamos. In Philadelphia, Thomson had purchased cotton-covered copper wire from a manufacturer of ladies' bonnets, but in New Britain the company obtained wire from Plume & Atwood of Waterbury, a manufacturer of brass sheet, tubing, and wire. D. S. Plume, one of the principals in the firm, had invested in American Electric and paid for his stock by supplying the company with wire. Unfortunately, Plume & Atwood lacked the facilities to produce continuously drawn copper wire; instead, they made it by cutting copper sheets into thin strips, drawing the strips through a die, and then brazing or soldering the ends together. The result of that process was a spool of wire with dozens of joints, each of which had slivers breaking through the insulation. When that wire was used to wind an electrical coil, the slivers caused short circuits, rendering the coil useless.

To overcome the problem, Thomson had his workmen check by hand the hundreds of feet of wire needed for each coil. Because the diameter of the wire produced by that process also varied greatly, the resistance of a spool of the wire could not be calculated beforehand; as a result, coils that had to have precise resistances (such as the shunt coil in the lamp mechanism) had to be carefully wound and measured.[28]

Although the manufacturing problems occupied much of his attention through 1880 and 1881, Thomson still found time to sketch and test new inventions. Anxious to have the new firm succeed, the young electrician oriented his efforts at invention around three criteria. First, just as he had done in Philadelphia, he continued to develop inventions that would not infringe Brush's patents. During the early 1880s, Brush held patents covering the broad principles of the open-coil dynamo, the differential arc-light mechanism, and the bypass shunt. Although those patents eventually were interpreted in narrow terms by the U.S. Patent Office, Thomson protected his system by devising variations that did not appear to use those principles directly.[29]

Second, whereas such variations could easily become complex, Thomson offset that tendency by striving for simple, even elegant, designs. He seems to have preferred such designs for reasons of intellectual and aesthetic satisfaction, but more important, simple inventions were demanded by the market. As Rice later emphasized, rugged and reliable designs were essential because their "machines were not to be operated by experts, for electricity was so new that operating men with even a slight knowledge of electricity were rare."[30] If the company was to sell lighting systems, the machines had to be simple, reliable, and easy to repair.

Third, Thomson was forced to come up with simple designs that would require a minimum amount of machining. Having only a few small lathes and planers in the factory, he had to plan his dynamos carefully so that the metal parts could be easily made.[31] Though a

28 ET, "A Retrospect," p. 260; ET, "The Story of Electric Welding," Autobiog. Papers, TP; Rice, "Arc Reminiscences," p. 161; for information on Plume & Atwood, see William G. Lathrop, *The Brass Industry in the United States* (Mount Carmel, Conn.: by the author, 1926), p. 69.

29 Rice, "Arc Reminiscences," p. 158.

30 E. W. Rice, "Pioneer Days of a Great American Industry," *Magazine of Business,* 54:233–6, 298, 299 (September 1928).

31 "The Thomson-Houston Electric Company," *Electricity,* 3:17–21 (27 July 1892).

handicap, that constraint reinforced Thomson's efforts to keep his inventions simple.

In letting those criteria guide his efforts, Thomson was learning two important aspects of the craft of invention. First, because such criteria represented practical considerations, they suggest that Thomson was coming to understand how an invention must fit into a larger technical and business context. As obvious as it sounds, not all inventions can be manufactured and marketed, and often substantial skill and effort are required to make an invention commercially feasible. Of course, as we shall see shortly, the technical and business context can be altered and reinvented, but the important point here is that an inventor must learn how to make his or her inventions correspond to their environment. Second, although external criteria can be seen as constraints on creativity, an inventor can use them to help define problems. Rather than working on all aspects of electric lighting and trying all sorts of solutions, Thomson was forced by those criteria to concentrate his efforts on key parts of his lighting system. Thus, a key skill for an inventor is an ability to convert apparent obstacles into positive and useful guidelines.

Guided by those criteria, Thomson focused his attention on improving two components of his arc lighting system: the lamp mechanism and the automatic current regulator. Rather than invent entirely new components, Thomson strove to perfect or refine his existing devices so that they would perform better in the system. For instance, in his arc lamp, Thomson was using a "drop-and-lift" mechanism (see Figure 3.10), but he found that it caused the light to "wink." In that lamp, the series solenoid tended to keep the carbons apart, and the shunt solenoid tended to push them together, but the series solenoid short-circuited whenever the shunt solenoid fed the carbons. With the shunt solenoid not operating, the carbons fell together, and the light was temporarily extinguished, causing an annoying wink. To eliminate the problem, Thomson sought to modify the mechanical movement that fed the carbons; he tried various arrangements with racks and pinions, ratchets, clutches, and pneumatic cylinders. Out of that search, Thomson wanted to find a mechanism that not only would prevent the wink but also would avoid conflict with the Brush lamp patents and would be simple to manufacture. Eventually he settled on using a "walking beam" that was activated on either end by shunt or series magnets (Figure 4.6). If one side of the beam was pulled, that moved the car-

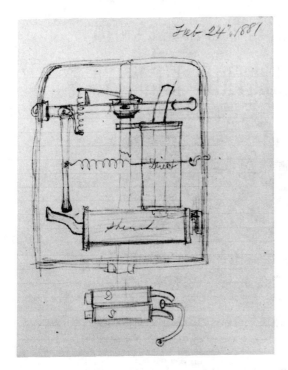

Figure 4.6. Sketch by Thomson of arc light using "walking beam" to feed carbon, February 1881. The "beam" is the horizontal bar near the top of the mechanism. It is pulled on the left side by the shunt magnet by means of the vertical arm, while the right side is pulled by the series or "direct" magnet. The carbon is fastened to the center of the beam. From "Notebook 1875–1876 First Made," Thomson Papers, American Philosophical Society, Philadelphia.

bons apart; if the other side was pulled, that moved the carbons together. To that basic configuration Thomson added several features: a dashpot to smooth the motion of the walking beam, an automatic shunt or cutout that permitted the current to bypass a nonoperating lamp in the series circuit, and various safety mechanisms to prevent the carbons from jamming. Known as the "D lamp," American Electric manufactured that lamp exclusively; it was superseded by a new version only after Thomson moved to Lynn in 1883.[32]

32 See E. W. Rice, Jr., [Address at MIT dinner], 29 April 1914, item J68–96, Hammond File; Rice, "Arc Reminiscences," p. 158; ET, "Development of Arc Lighting," *Electrical World,* 80:542–4 (9 September 1922). Sketches for this lamp can be found in "First Notebook."

THE AMERICAN ELECTRIC COMPANY,

Proprietors of the Thomson-Houston System of

ELECTRIC LIGHTING.

MANUFACTURERS OF THE

THOMSON-HOUSTON

Dynamo - Electric Machine,

Electric Lamps, Current Regulators,

And Electro-Plating Apparatus.

Unrivalled for Simplicity, Economy, and Efficiency.

MANUFACTORY AND PRINCIPAL OFFICE:
Nos. 25 and 27 Lake St., New Britain, Conn.

Figure 4.7. Advertisement showing Thomson's spherical-armature dynamo without the automatic regulator, 1882. In comparison with other spherical-armature dynamos, this machine is longer and more narrow. From *New Britain Directory, 1882–83* (New Britain: Price, Lee & Co., 1882), p. 225.

By far the most important component in Thomson's arc lighting system was the automatic current regulator, because it gave his system greater stability than any other available system. Shortly after going to New Britain, however, he tried to eliminate that component by proportioning the field coils and armature of his spherical-armature dynamo in such a way that the generated current would not increase in response to a drop in the resistance of the external lighting circuit (Figure 4.7). For such a dynamo, if one plots the voltage against current, one gets a characteristic curve that turns sharply downward after peaking; appropriately, such a curve is known in electrical engineering parlance

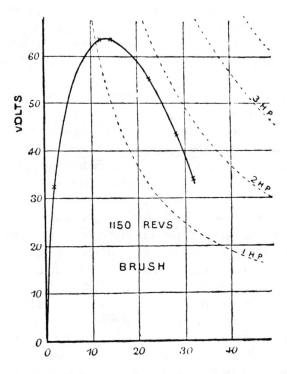

Figure 4.8. Example of drooping characteristic curve, derived for single-light Brush dynamo with open-coil armature. From S. P. Thompson, *Dynamo-Electric Machinery*, 3rd ed. (London: 1888), p. 379.

as a "drooping" characteristic curve (Figure 4.8). That feature was desirable because it would let the dynamo remain stable even as the lights were turned off. Normally, as lights were removed from the circuit, the overall external resistance dropped, causing the line current to increase. If it was designed with a drooping characteristic, the dynamo would not be affected by that change. Although the specially proportioned dynamo was able to power 16 lights without a current regulator, Thomson found that it did so only with a current of 15 amperes, which tended to burn out the dynamo windings. To overcome that unsatisfactory situation, he introduced a supersensitive lamp into the circuit that responded quickly to minor current variations with comparatively large changes in the arc length. Acting as a regulator, that special lamp allowed the spherical-armature dynamo to operate safely at 10 amperes. Because initially it appeared that that would be the only way to run the 16-light dynamo, Thomson contemplated enclosing a supersensitive lamp in an iron box and including it as the regulator for the dynamo.[33]

As he experimented with using a supersensitive lamp to regulate the dynamo, Thomson also investigated other methods of regulation. Rather than reduce the current output by shifting only the brushes, he observed in October 1880 that it was possible to enhance the effect by also switching an extra resistance into the circuit that would reduce the strength of the dynamo field coils (Figure 4.9). Thomson undoubtedly got the idea for switching in additional resistance from Brush's regulator, which operated exclusively on that principle. The advantage of Thomson's combination regulator was that it reduced sparking between the brushes and commutator; although it was novel, Thomson chose not to employ that regulator, and he did not bother to file a patent application for it until 1882. His reluctance to patent that regulator was due in part to the fact that Brush had already patented a similar device. In 1884, however, when it became clear that a regulator combining both brush movement and a resistance shunt might work well with all dynamos, Thomson and Rice pushed through another patent application covering it. In particular, because a combination regulator would work well on Brush's dynamo, they filed that patent as an offensive move. As a result, the Thomson-Houston Electric Company effectively blocked the Brush company from adding an improved regulator to its system, which greatly harmed Brush's position in the market.[34]

While still in New Britain, Thomson came to consider both the supersensitive lamp and the combination regulator to be inefficient and unnecessarily complex. Consequently, he adapted his original regulator to the larger spherical dynamos by reverting back to the proportions he had previously used for the field coils and armature. To

---

33 ET, "Conditions Affecting Stability in Electric Lighting Circuits," *Proceedings of AIEE*, 28:1–22 (January 1909); Rice, "Arc Reminiscences," p. 162.

34 "Evidence for Thomson and Rice," paper 23, Patent Interference No. 9,965, Thomson and Rice vs. Sheehy (subject: regulator for dynamo machines), RG-241, NARS (hereafter cited as "Testimony," Intf. 9,965); ET and E. W. Rice, "Regulator for Dynamo Electric Machines," U.S. Patent No. 339,079 (filed 22 January 1884, granted 30 March 1886); see also ET's comments on this patent, TP.

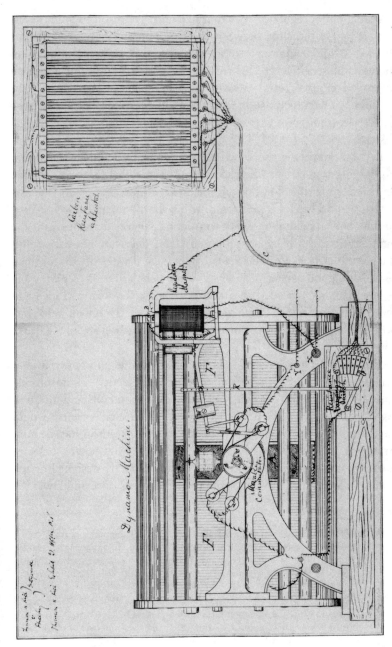

Figure 4.9. Drawing, probably by Thomson, showing combination regulator, circa 1881–3. In addition to adjusting the field strength by shifting the brushes on the commutator, the regulator magnet also switched a variable resistance into the circuit with the field coils. Exhibit G, Patent Interference No. 9965, Record Group 241, National Archives and Records Service.

coordinate that regulator with that dynamo, Thomson found it necessary to angle the slots between the commutator pieces so that the brushes would maintain contact while they were being shifted. To increase the sensitivity of his old-style regulator, in 1882 he added an improved control relay to switch in the solenoid that moved the brushes.[35] Overall, those modifications of the regulator reveal how he was learning about coordinating the components in an electrical system.

Beyond improving those two key components, Thomson enhanced his lighting system by adding accessories. Through 1880 and 1881, he designed apparatus for raising and lowering arc lamps so that the carbons could be changed, a lamp with a short arc gap for low-ceiling rooms, and a switchboard for connecting several dynamos into the lighting circuit.[36] He also proposed that American Electric manufacture the carbons for their arc lights, because it was difficult for them to procure good carbons. Thomson even went so far as to plan some of the machinery needed to produce carbons. Reluctant to invest in more equipment, the directors refused to let Thomson add carbons to the product line and instead purchased carbons from the Brush company.[37]

Manufacturing arc-light carbons was not the only project that Thomson was unable to pursue at American Electric. Thomson discussed with Rice the possibility of using induction coils and alternating current to distribute power to electric lights; such a system would have been an improvement over the ac system Thomson had demonstrated in 1878. Whereas Rice wondered about the power losses in such a system, Thomson maintained that a properly designed induction coil could efficiently transmit power as well as raise and lower the

35 ET, "Conditions Affecting Stability," p. 9; ET, "Commutators for Dynamo Electric Machines," U.S. Patent No. 242,488 (filed 10 January 1881, granted 7 June 1881); ET, "Electric Current Regulator," U.S. Patent No. 271,948 (filed 26 June 1882, granted 6 February 1883); Woodbury, *Beloved Scientist,* pp. 165–6.
36 ET, "Electric Lamp," U.S. Patent No. 256,605 (filed 20 June 1881, granted 18 April 1882); ET, "System of Electric Distribution," U.S. Patent No. 255,824 (filed 8 June 1881, granted 4 April 1882). Sketches and lists of other accessories can be found in "First Notebook."
37 ET, "Thomson-Houston demand of American Electric Co. for Reversion of Patents by them under Agreement of July 9th 1880," circa July 1882 (hereafter cited as "List of Complaints," July 1882), LB 82–99, pp. 90–106, TP.

voltage.[38] Although too busy with his day-to-day work of manufacturing arc lights to investigate an ac system, he probably was not concerned with it, as the sizes of their electric lighting systems had not increased to a point that losses due to dc transmission would have warranted changing over to alternating current.

Similarly, Thomson considered various schemes to distribute power to several electric motors on a single circuit, using either alternating or direct current.[39] In addition, he sketched ideas for an electroplating dynamo, an improved carbon microphone for the telephone, an electropneumatic system for igniting gaslights, and a gas-alcohol motor, but the demands of the factory and the company's limited resources prevented him from pursuing any of those ideas.[40] Instead, his creative energies were kept focused on innovations for his arc lighting system, and for over a year Thomson seemed content with the challenge of perfecting his system.

Working at the factory and planning new inventions kept Thomson and Rice quite busy. By November 1880 the local newspaper was reporting that lights often burned in the electric works until 9:30 in the evening. Some nights Thomson, Rice, and the workmen broke from their labors for a "midnight lunch." On one occasion, one of the men brought cooked oysters, and because he had forgotten to bring any butter in which to dip them, it was proposed that they use white paraffin instead. The chief electrician, however, objected to using the paraffin and jokingly complained that the "candlepower" flavor would be unpleasant. In general, Thomson and Rice appear to have had good rapport with the workers, perhaps as a result of having trained them in the electrical art. At least one, Charles A. Cooley, was sufficiently involved in designing parts of the arc lighting system that he received two patents. Other employees, such as W. O. Wakefield, the chief draftsman, and Clarence McNary, Thomson's personal machinist, liked working for Thomson and moved with him from New Britain to Lynn, Massachusetts, in 1883.[41]

38 ET, "Testimony," Intf. 13,761, p. 8.
39 ET, "Notes on the Properties of Dynamo-Electric Machines," *J. Franklin Inst.*, 112:427–9 (December 1881); ET, "Electric Power Distributing System," U.S. Patent No. 294,095 (filed 23 May 1883, granted 26 February 1884); ET, "Early Work at New Britain," p. 10.
40 Thomson sketched these miscellaneous inventions in "First Notebook."
41 New Britain *Herald*, 20 November 1880; "The Thomson-Houston Electric Company," pp. 20–1. Charles Cooley's patents are listed in James Shepard, *New Britain Patents and Patentees* (New Britain: by the author, 1901).

The evolution of the central-station marketing strategy

While Thomson was adding innovations to his arc lighting system in 1880 and 1881, his business managers were using the same marketing strategy that had been used in Philadelphia. Considering arc-lighting equipment to be a capital good, Parker and Churchill approached various firms that they considered to be likely candidates for artificial lighting, firms that could afford to purchase an isolated system consisting of a dynamo and lights. A typical sale was that to the Hartford Paper Company in Poquonock, Connecticut, where arc lights were installed in December 1880, permitting the workers to detect coloring matter creeping into the white paper pulp and allowing the mill to run all night.[42] During the first nine months of operation, American Electric sold six systems (Table 4.2). Initially, its informal sales effort kept the factory busy, but it soon became clear that for the firm to expand, a better sales network and a new marketing strategy were needed.

Unfortunately, Churchill was not capable of improving upon the marketing plan. Shortly after Thomson had set up his Model Room, Churchill decided that he, too, wanted to invent, and he had a room in the factory where he worked on a dynamo regulator. Perhaps distracted by his inventive efforts, Churchill overextended himself in a speculative real-estate deal related to his law practice. As a result, when the directors of American Electric called for a second payment of 20% on the stock, Churchill found himself short of cash and unable to pay his share. Being of "slender constitution and nervous temperament," he tried frantically to borrow money from the local bank, but failing that, he went into his father's barn and shot himself to death. His suicide shocked Thomson and the other members of the firm, and they passed a memorial resolution attributing his unfortunate death to the "new and most perplexing business" of electric lighting.[43]

To replace Churchill as manager, the directors selected Joseph John Skinner. Like Churchill, Skinner was a graduate of the Sheffield Scien-

42 "Electric Light in a Paper Mill," New Britain Observer, 7 December 1880.
43 Churchill's business activities and efforts at invention are described in A. J. Sloper to J. W. Hammond, 2 October 1930, item J871-3, Hammond File; and ET, "List of Complaints," July 1882. For the call on the stock, see New Britain Herald, 11 December 1880. Quotations are from In Memoriam. Frederick H. Churchill (New Britain: n.d.), NBPL, pp. 13, 19. A slightly different version of Churchill's suicide is given by Sloper, The Life and Times of Andrew Jackson Sloper, pp. 287–8.

tific School at Yale and had received a Ph.D. degree in 1876 for his work in physics, chemistry, and mathematics. Prior to coming to American Electric, he had taught mathematics at Yale and published a report on the 1879 transit of Mercury. Given his academic background, Skinner may not have seemed a likely candidate to be an imaginative and hardworking business manager, but over the next two years he helped the company sell at least 20 systems (Table 4.2). Skinner traveled on behalf of the company, even to Springfield, Illinois, where he made a sale. The new business manager selected Gerald W. Hart, another Sheffield man already employed by American Electric, to serve as the company's regular salesman. Brief newspaper reports indicate that in 1881 and 1882 Hart traveled to Manchester, New Hampshire, Boston, and Kansas City to promote and install Thomson-Houston arc lights.[44] Through the combined efforts of Skinner and Hart, the firm continued to receive orders for equipment, but not as many as Thomson would have liked.

Gradually, it became clear to Thomson and Skinner that there was only a limited market for free-standing, isolated arc lighting systems. Although many manufacturers and retailers were interested in electric lighting, only a few could afford to install a complete system with the required steam engine. To reach more customers, it was necessary to revise the marketing strategy, and like Edison and Brush, Thomson and Skinner chose to move in the direction of the central station. With the central-station strategy, consumers were sold the service of electric lighting by a utility firm that constructed and maintained the generating equipment in a conveniently located power station. By spreading the cost of the lighting system among many consumers, that strategy reduced the cost per light, thus permitting the rapid diffusion of electric-lighting technology. To take advantage of the new strategy, however, it was necessary to work out the organizational details of the utility firm and design larger dynamos capable of delivering more power. Solutions to those problems took several years; although the

---

44 For biographical information on J. J. Skinner, see Yale College Library, *Obituary Record of Yale College Deceased* . . . (New Haven, Conn.: Yale University, 1920), pp. 1518–20. For his work with American Electric, see New Britain *Herald*, 23 April and 16 July 1881. For biographical data on G. W. Hart, see his obituary in New Britain *Herald*, 10 March 1931, and *Record of Yale Class, 1878* (New Haven: 1903), p. 9, Manuscripts and Archives, Yale University Library, New Haven. For Hart's traveling, see New Britain *Herald*, 13 August and 15 October 1881.

Table 4.2. *Installations of lighting systems by American Electric Company, 1880-2[a]*

Date[b]	Firm and location	Type of business[c]	Description of system[c]
July 1880	Wentworth House, New Hampshire	Hotel	?
December 1880	Hartford Paper Co., Poquonock, CT	Paper mill	?
December 1880	P. & F. Corbin, New Britain	Hardware manufacturer	4 lights
January 1881	Russell & Erwin, New Britain	Hardware manufacturer	1 light
January 1881	Aur Silk Factory, Tariffville, CT	Textile mill	2 10-light dynamos
January 1881	Charles Parker Co., Meriden, CT	Foundry	2 dynamos
May 1881	Opera House, New Britain	Theater	2 lights?
June 1881	Allyn House, Hartford	Hotel	?
June 1881	American Theater	Theater	1 light
June 1881	A.L. Ide, Springfield, IL	Foundry	10 lights
August 1881	E.S. Wheeler, New Haven	?	?
August 1881	Amoskeag Works	Textile mill	?
August 1881	Mechanics' Institute, Boston	Exhibition	1-light, 6-light, an 12-light dynamos
September 1881	Waterbury Brass Co., Waterbury, CT	Metal work	5 lights
October 1881	Blackinton Mills, West Adams, MA	?	12 lights
November 1881	Holyoke, MA	?	6-light dynamo
November 1881	Russell & Erwin, New Britain	Hardware manufacturer	30 lights
November 1881	Charles Parker Co., Meriden	Foundry	12-light dynamo
December 1881	Hartford	Stores	6 small systems installed in stores for demonstration
December 1881	Meriden, CT	Possible street lighting	?
January 1882	F. H. Allis & Co., New Britain	Clothing store	?

Table 4.2. *(continued)*

Date[b]	Firm and location	Type of business[c]	Description of system[c]
January 1882	A. S. Thomas, Meriden, CT	Store	4
January 1882	P. & F. Corbin, New Britain	Hardware manufacturer	12-light dynamo
April 1882	E. H. Goff, Boston	Central station contractor	6-light dynamo
May 1882	Kawsmouth Elec. Co., Kansas City, MO	Central station for street and store lighting	110 lights, 6-10 dynamos?
May 1882	Lynn Elec. Lighting Co.	Central station for store lighting	26-light dynamo
July 1882	Farist Steel Co., Bridgeport, CT	?	?
September 1882	Corrugated Metal Co., East Berlin, CT	Metalwork	?

[a]This table may not be a complete list of all systems installed by American Electric. It includes only systems for which references have been found. It also does not include systems installed by the Thomson-Houston Electric Light Company of Philadelphia. Between 1880 and 1882 this firm installed at least 15 systems. See "The American Electric Co. Proprietors of the Thomson-Houston Electric Lighting System" (trade catalog, circa 1882), Unsorted Material, Thomson Papers; New Britain *Herald*, 23 April 1881; and "Thomson-Houston Electric Light Company. Prospectus," Trade Catalog Collection, Franklin Institute.

[b]Dates prior to January 1882 are dates when the New Britain *Herald* reported equipment shipped from the factory. Dates after 1882 are more approximate because they are from testimonial letters published in "The American Electric Co. . . ." *op. cit.*

[c]Question mark in these columns indicates no information available.

Sources: Articles in the New Britain *Herald*, 1880-1882; "The American Electric Co. Proprietors of the Thomson-Houston Electric Lighting System" (trade catalog, circa 1882), Unsorted Material, Thomson Papers; Glenn Weaver, *History of the Hartford Electric Light Company* (Hartford: 1969); H. L. Ide to J. W. Bishop, 12 April 1935, Thomson Collection, GE Hall of History, Schenectady.

California Electric Light Company established the first central station in 1879, that strategy did not become prevalent until Edison opened his Pearl Street station in 1882. In the intervening years, both the Weston Electric Light Company and the United States Electric Lighting Company opened small central stations in Newark and New York, neither of which was particularly successful.[45]

45 For the California Electric Light Company, see John W. Hammond, *Men and Volts: The Story of General Electric* (Philadelphia: Lippincott, 1941), p. 29; and Passer, *The Electrical Manufacturers,* p. 19. U.S. Electric's early station in

Like their competitors, Skinner and Thomson struggled to implement the central-station strategy. As a first attempt, Thomson proposed in November 1881 that American Electric establish a power station in nearby Hartford. The firm was able to undertake such an enterprise because its charter had broadly claimed the right to sell both electrical equipment and power. They probably chose Hartford for the project because it had a larger downtown area than New Britain. In a preliminary survey, they found 40 retailers along Asylum and Main streets interested in having electric lights in their shops. Having heard that the leading department stores in New York and Philadelphia had lights, those shopowners hoped that the new technology would attract customers. To supply those stores, American Electric erected a small building at the Hartford Steam Heating Company on Pearl Street. There they installed a dynamo and engine that was powered by steam from the Hartford Steam Heating Company.[46]

With customers and a power station, it remained only to connect the two together. But rather than being a simple technical connection, Skinner and Thomson soon discovered that it was much more a political connection. To obtain permission "to erect such poles as may be necessary for the placing of wires to be used for lighting streets, buildings, etc., by electricity," American Electric petitioned the Hartford Common Council in November 1881, which in turn passed the firm's request to the Board of Street Commissioners. After considering the matter briefly, the commissioners recommended that the Common Council deny the request. In response, the owners of the leading Main Street stores presented another petition to the Common Council on behalf of American Electric, but again the request was denied by the street commissioners. To reinforce the message being sent from the city government to American Electric, in December 1881 the Hartford Board of Fire Underwriters passed an unusually stringent code for electrical installations.

New York City is mentioned in "The Early Days of Electric Lighting," *Electrical Review*, 38:77 (12 January 1901); the Weston plant is described in David O. Woodbury, *A Measure for Greatness: A Short Biography of Edward Weston* (New York: McGraw-Hill, 1949), pp. 138–42. Edison's work on perfecting the central station as a marketing strategy is detailed by Hughes, *Networks of Power*, pp. 38–46.

46 "Electric Light in Hartford," New Britain *Herald*, 3 December 1881; Glenn Weaver, *The Hartford Electric Light Company* (Hartford: 1969), p. 14.

Why did the Hartford city fathers strongly oppose the establishment of a central station by American Electric? Although Skinner and Thomson may not have realized it at the time, they were blocked in their efforts because Mayor Morgan G. Bulkeley and other leading Hartford citizens had already secured a charter for the Hartford Electric Light Company. While he was in office, the mayor was unable to use that charter to sell electric lighting without raising the question of conflict of interest; nonetheless, he was hardly about to permit another firm to usurp the monopoly he had secured from the state legislature.[47] Because several American Electric stockholders were prominent Hartford businessmen, and even became officers of Hartford Electric, it might seem that those men could have arranged a favorable situation for American Electric. However, they chose not to do so, perhaps because they were not especially interested in seeing American Electric expand into the central-station business. American Electric, as they saw it, was a limited manufacturing operation in New Britain and should not be involved in the affairs of Hartford.

Skinner and Thomson seem to have lacked the skills of persuasion and politicking that would have been necessary to gain entry for a utility company. They could see the opportunity for a central station selling lighting to stores, but they lacked the knowledge needed to smooth away the local political obstacles. As a consolation, though, they did arrange for a demonstration of electric lighting in Hartford's shopping district during the Christmas season. On the evening of 21 December 1881, isolated systems were installed, and single arc lamps were hung in front of six stores. The lights attracted a large crowd of shoppers, who were delighted by the brilliance and "naturalness" of the light.[48]

To implement a new marketing strategy, not only would it be necessary to solve the political and organizational difficulties, but also they would have to match their technology to the newly developing market niche. Consequently, as the melodrama of the Hartford station was being played out, Thomson gave careful thought to how well suited his system was for use in a central station. To be employed successfully in

47 Weaver, *The Hartford Electric Light Company*, pp. 14–17.
48 Weaver, *The Hartford Electric Light Company*, p. 16. The New Britain *Herald*, 10 December 1881, reported cryptically that American Electric was lighting a portion of Meriden.

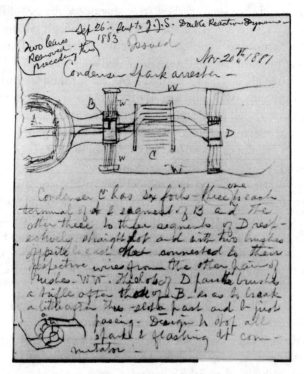

Figure 4.10. Sketch by Thomson of spark arrester using two commutators and a capacitor, November 1881. From "Notebook 1875–1876 First Made," Thomson Papers, American Philosophical Society, Philadelphia.

a central station, an arc lighting system would have to provide a large number of lights at a low cost. One way to achieve that would be to design dynamos that could power more lights. When Thomson had arrived in New Britain, his largest machine had been an eight-lighter, but by November 1881 he was producing machines with a capacity of 16–20 lights. In building the larger generators, however, Thomson encountered a serious difficulty: In delivering the 700–1,000 volts needed to power more than 16 lights, the commutator tended to spark badly and even arc over. In building dynamos of similar capacity, Brush had sidestepped that difficulty by using two commutators and two armature windings, each rated at 8 or 10 lights. Initially, Thomson tried to eliminate the sparking problem by placing a capacitor as a shunt between the commutator pieces (Figure 4.10). Although that arrangement worked, he found that the capacitor was not suited for "rough and tumble use." Such a solution was not congruent with Thomson's style of invention. As Rice later recalled,

> Professor Thomson was not satisfied with any easy or half-way solution of a difficulty; difficulties merely increased his determination to overcome them. He was also determined that the solution should be simple and inexpensive.[49]

In place of the capacitors, Thomson next tried to eliminate the arcing by using two commutators, as Brush had done. Although that solution also worked, it created another problem: The automatic regulator could not properly adjust two sets of brushes. Because the regulator was one of the major selling features of his system, he continued to search for a spark arrester that would be compatible with the regulator. Eventually Thomson hit upon the idea of using a blast of air to insulate the commutator. If the air was kept circulating, it was difficult for the high potential to ionize the air around the commutator, the ionization being the cause of the sparks. To test that idea, Thomson and Rice each took a short brass tube and blew on either side of the commutator. Finding that the jet of air effectively prevented sparks, Thomson went on to construct an air-blast device consisting of a small blower fan placed on the armature shaft, behind the commutator, that supplied an air blast to two nozzles positioned just in front of the brushes (Figure 4.11). Besides eliminating sparking, the air blast also simplified dynamo maintenance, because the commutator could then be completely oiled; in contrast to the situation with the Brush machine, which had to be carefully lubricated, even if an inexperienced workman poured oil all over the commutator, Thomson's dynamo would still operate. With the air blast, Thomson was able to increase the capacity of his spherical-armature dynamo, and by the mid-1880s he had designed machines that could power 75 lights.[50] By developing

49 See Rice, "Arc Reminiscences," p. 159; and ET, "Conditions Affecting Stability," p. 8. Although he never used it extensively, Thomson did file a patent for using a capacitor to extinguish commutator sparks; see his "Dynamo Electric Machine," U.S. Patent No. 269,605 (filed 18 September 1882, granted 26 December 1882). Quotations are from Rice, Address at MIT Dinner, items J75, J77, Hammond File.

50 See Rice, Address at MIT Dinner, items J75–6; ET to J. R. McKee, 23 October 1913, CL, TP; ET, "Means for Preventing Flashing between Electric Conductors," U.S. Patent No. 265,936 (filed 16 February 1882, granted 10 October 1882); ET, "Air Blast Attachment for Commutators of Dynamo Electric Machines," U.S. Patent No. 273,406 (filed 22 November 1882,

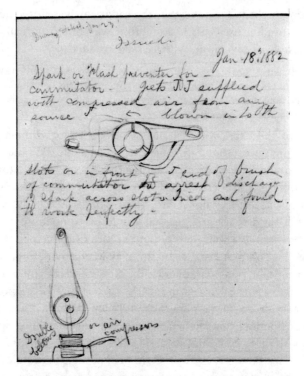

Figure 4.11. Sketch by Thomson of air-blast device for preventing commutator sparking, January 1882. From "Notebook 1875–1876 First Made," Thomson Papers, American Philosophical Society, Philadelphia.

the air blast, Thomson ensured that his dynamo would be suited for use in a central station.

Within a few months of Thomson's development of the air blast, American Electric sold its first central station to the Kawsmouth Electric Company of Kansas City, Missouri. In December 1881, a group of businessmen in that city had secured a local ordinance permitting them "to establish, construct, and maintain an Electric Works . . . for illuminating and heating purposes and for furnishing motive power."[51] As electric-lighting operations had been undertaken in other cities, both

granted 6 March 1883). The model for the latter patent is Cat. No. 308,603, Div. Elec., NMAH.

51 Ordinance 21,706 of Kansas City, 3 December 1881, Office of the City Clerk, Kansas City, Missouri. I am grateful to Mark Rose for providing me this document.

for profit and to show that those cities were modern and prosperous, so the motives were likely the same in Kansas City. The Kansas City investors were convinced by Gerald Hart, American Electric's traveling salesman, to buy Thomson-Houston lights in April 1882. Considered by his customers to be "a thorough electrician" and "a courteous gentleman," Hart must have been highly persuasive, for he initially sold the Kawsmouth Electric Company four dynamos and 40 lights, followed by a second order in May for six more machines and 66 more lights. The lights were used to illuminate both business establishments and streets. To ensure that his customers were pleased with their new lights, Hart supervised installation and remained in Kansas City until the system was fully operational. Kawsmouth Electric apparently was happy with the Thomson-Houston system, for over the next year it installed 100 lights.[52]

Thomson and the managers of American Electric must have been amazed by the Kawsmouth Electric orders, for the number of lights in those two purchases nearly equaled the number of lights sold by the firm in all of 1881 (Table 4.2). The good news from Kansas City was quickly followed by another central-station sale, in Lynn, Massachusetts.

In that city, Silas A. Barton, the owner of a stationery store, decided to enhance his business by securing electric lighting for the neighborhood surrounding his store. Barton convinced Henry A. Pevear, a manufacturer of morocco leather, that electric lighting was a promising business enterprise, and together they began to investigate the available systems. One of the first systems they saw, in the spring of 1882, was the Thomson-Houston system on Tremont Street in Boston. Consisting of six lights and a dynamo, that installation was being used by Edward H. Goff to attract investors for a possible central station in Boston. After viewing the lights in Boston, Barton and Pevear journeyed to New Britain, where they placed an order for 26 lights. On returning to Lynn, Barton and Pevear persuaded their friends to help establish a utility company. On 26 April 1882, a combination of

52 See New Britain *Herald,* 25 April, 16 May, and 16 June 1882. Quotations are from New Britain *Herald,* 11 October 1882. Details for the first lighting circuits are from an article in Kansas City *Star,* 25 March 1928, in Newspaper Clipping File, Missouri Valley Room, Kansas City Public Library. Mark Rose also kindly provided me this item. The number of lights subsequently installed is taken from "Exhibit. The Following List of Thomson-Houston Plants . . . ," circa 1888, Notebooks, TP.

Barton's fellow merchants on Market Street and Pevear's colleagues in the shoe and leather business chartered the Lynn Electric Lighting Company. Capitalized at $25,000, the firm installed its dynamos at 166 Market Street and hung lights in front of the shops of the merchants subscribing to its service. Like the Kansas City station, the Lynn utility grew steadily, and by October 1883 it was supplying 90 lights.[53] More important, however, the success of the Lynn Electric Lighting Company impressed Barton, Pevear, and other Lynn businessmen with the potential of electric lighting as a profit-making enterprise. As we shall see, when offered the opportunity to invest further in the new field, they acted quickly.

For American Electric, the sale of equipment to those two central stations was a clear indication of the future market. To some extent the firm was simply lucky that local entrepreneurs took the initiative in raising the necessary capital and securing permission from municipal authorities; other electric-lighting manufacturers, such as Edison and Brush, often found themselves closely involved with the local details of constructing central stations. Along with Skinner and Hart, Thomson was impressed by the new marketing opportunity, and he facilitated the firm's movement into that market by providing the air-blast device needed for larger dynamos. However, before American Electric could solidify its position in the new market, the firm was disrupted by a disagreement between Thomson and the major stockholders.

53 S. A. Barton was an ambitious and hardworking shopkeeper; in August 1878 he was described as follows: "His means are supposed to be small but he is said to be a wide awake fellow of good char[acter] & habits & states that he does not want to ask credit." See Massachusetts Vol. 25, p. 207, R. G. Dun & Co. Collection. For Barton and Pevear working together, see J. A. McManus, "Some Lynn Electrical History Involving the Lynn Electric Lighting Company, Predecessor of the Lynn Gas & Electric Company" (typescript), Hall of History Collection. For information on Goff, see Harold C. Passer, "E. H. Goff: An Entrepreneur Who Failed," *Explorations in Entrepreneurial History*, 1:17–25 (May 1949), especially p. 17; several pages of loose notes in Thomson's hand, Hall of History Collection; and "The American Electric and Illuminating Company" (a prospectus), January 1883, Electricity Boxes, Warshaw Collection of Business Americana, National Museum of American History, Washington, D.C. On the organization of the lighting company, see J. A. McManus, "History of the General Electric Co.," 27 May 1925, Hall of History Collection, p. 28; and Sampson, Davenport & Co., *The Lynn Directory, 1882* (Lynn, Mass.: George C. Herbert, 1882). For information on the lighting of the G.A.R. building, see entries for 1 and 8 June 1882, "Records of Meetings," Vol. 4 (1882–4), G.A.R. Post No. 5, Lynn, Massachusetts. The number of lights subsequently installed is taken from "Exhibit. The Following List of Thomson-Houston Plants . . . ," circa 1888, Notebooks, TP.

The selling of American Electric

Although Thomson had improved his lighting system and had the satisfaction of seeing a few systems sold, he became increasingly disappointed with the management of American Electric. In marketing the system, the directors had not gone to much effort. As shown by their indifference to the fate of the Hartford station, they were not especially interested in pursuing the central-station strategy. Even though the Stanley Works maintained a sales office in New York, the directors of American Electric had not bothered to open any such offices to promote Thomson's system.[54] Prospective customers had to call at the New Britain factory, often finding that it was closed, with Skinner and Hart away on sales trips. Thomson met with some of those customers, but he resented having to do so; as he saw it, his responsibility was to solve production and design problems.

In addressing production and design matters, Thomson encountered other disappointments. In manufacturing dynamos and lights, he was handicapped by the failure of the managers to maintain an adequate inventory of wire and castings, by having only a few machine tools available, and by difficulties in training workers. Not only did the firm refuse to let him produce lamp carbons, but also he found that he was unable to make certain parts interchangeable because the rate of production was kept too low. (Interchangeability of parts such as commutators was highly desirable, because they had to be replaced often in early dynamos.) Similarly, his efforts at invention had been hampered by the lack of a desk and files for his notes and sketches, the absence of a draftsman, and the shortage of electrical measuring instruments. Although he coped with those inconveniences, Thomson gradually concluded that the directors of American Electric were indifferent toward product development. He had received no encouragement to pursue his electroplating dynamo and some of his arc-lamp designs. In regard to his regulator, Thomson was disturbed that whereas the firm showed little interest in his efforts to improve that component, the directors were willing to permit Churchill to work on his own regulator in the factory. In general, Thomson was anxious to produce the best possible lighting system, and he was troubled by the indifference or ignorance of the directors in technical matters.[55]

54 Leavitt, *Foundation for the Future,* pp. 61–2.
55 ET, "List of Complaints," July 1882.

By all indications, it was not a lack of technical expertise or available capital that prevented the New Britain businessmen from aggressively developing the American Electric Company. Given that they had improved their hardware manufacturing techniques during the 1870s to meet the competition, they seem to have appreciated the potential of technological change. Likewise, the success of their businesses suggests that they may have had the capital needed to improve American Electric. Rather, there probably were several reasons that the directors and stockholders of American Electric were not interested in innovation and marketing issues. From the start, they had viewed the firm as a means to diversify the local industrial base of New Britain. Although an electrical-equipment plant was desirable, it was not absolutely essential to the well-being of the town, and consequently the businessmen did not devote much money, time, or effort to improving the firm. Furthermore, the local businessmen had invested in the firm not so much for the long-term benefits but because they anticipated short-term profits from the stock appreciating rapidly. Because they saw electric lighting as a speculative venture, they probably regarded investment in capital equipment or new innovations as tending to reduce their anticipated short-term profits.

But perhaps the most significant reason that the hardware manufacturers did not fully back American Electric was that they were unable to develop the business organization needed to exploit a novel marketing strategy. Throughout the nineteenth century, those manufacturers had not developed a sales force, but instead sold their products through a network of wholesalers. Until the twentieth century, the sales organization of the Stanley Works consisted of a showroom in New York City and three men who covered different regions of the United States. According to one historian of the industry, that organization was appropriate "since [the] competition was still a long way behind The Stanley Works in quality and price."[56] In contrast, as Thomson, Skinner, and Hart realized, the competitors in electric lighting were much better organized and, moreover, were willing to get involved in the promotion of central stations. Accustomed simply to

56 For a discussion of the marketing practices in the nineteenth-century hardware industry, see Glenn Porter and Harold C. Livesay, *Merchants and Manufacturers: Studies in the Changing Structure of Nineteenth-Century Marketing* (Baltimore: Johns Hopkins University Press, 1971), pp. 221–3. Quotation is from Leavitt, *Foundation for the Future*, p. 62.

selling hardware outright through a few agents, the New Britain manufacturers probably found the entire business of central-station promotion puzzling, if not incomprehensible. Nothing in their experience
had prepared them to think through an entirely new marketing strategy. Consequently, the business elite of New Britain may have expected Thomson simply to put his existing system into production and
may have been disturbed when he wanted them to help him pursue the
central-station strategy.

In contrast to his backers, Thomson was deeply committed to the
commercial success of his arc lighting system. Determined to perfect
his inventions and see them put into use, he took the long-term view
and could not comprehend why his backers did not share his enthusiasm.[57] As it became clear that the management of American Electric
viewed innovation differently than did he, Thomson began to contem-
plate taking control of the firm. That was feasible, because he and
Houston owned one-third of the company's stock, but to do so he
would need a financial partner who could buy additional shares in the
company. Probably through Houston, Thomson came into contact
with Charles R. Flint, who was willing to help him gain control of
American Electric.[58]

Flint was a principal in the New York firm of W. R. Grace and
Company, which specialized in shipping and trading in South America.
Always interested in new business ventures, Flint was attracted to the
electric-lighting field, and in 1879 he purchased stock in the United
States Electric Lighting Company. That firm had been organized to
exploit the incandescent-lighting patents of Hiram Maxim, William
Sawyer, and Albon Man. Soon named a vice-president of U.S. Electric,
Flint embarked on a campaign to improve the commercial position of
the company. While he helped the firm establish a central station for
incandescent lighting in New York in 1880, he also decided that the
firm should have an arc lighting system to complement its incandescent
lights. Flint first tried to buy the rights to the Brush system, but failing
that, he acquired controlling interest in the Weston Electric Light Com-

57 For another example of an inventor taking the long-term perspective, see W.
Bernard Carlson, "Edison in the Mountains: The Magnetic Ore Separation
Venture, 1879–1900," *History of Technology*, 8:37–59 (1983).

58 That Houston introduced Thomson to Flint is inferred from the fact that
Houston handled many details of the financial arrangements between Flint
and Thomson. See EJH to ET, 2 June 1881, and EJH to C. R. Flint, 6 October
1881, Hall of History Collection.

pany of Newark, New Jersey. Anxious to gain control of another arc lighting system, he readily entered into negotiations with Thomson and Houston.[59]

With Flint's help, Thomson and Houston signed an agreement with W. R. Grace and U.S. Electric in April 1881. Together, they created a trust in which Thomson and Houston deposited 1,250 shares of American Electric stock and W. R. Grace deposited $12,000. The money was to be used to purchase additional shares in American Electric until the trust held a controlling interest in the company. Once the trust had taken over American Electric, Thomson hoped that new directors would be elected who would support his efforts at innovation and development of new markets for his system.[60]

Through 1881, the trust apparently tried to buy stock in American Electric, but it did not acquire many shares. In the meantime, Flint had larger plans for the electrical industry. Like other businessmen of the period, he recognized that it could be highly profitable to consolidate firms within an industry into a single integrated and efficient corporation. Having organized the Export Lumber Company in 1878 out of a number of small firms in the lumber industry, Flint attempted to do the same in the electrical field. In early 1882 he brought together Brush, Edison, Weston, Thomson, and Houston for a meeting in his office. Flint proposed to create a consolidated electrical company, but no agreement could be reached. He later blamed the failure of that meet-

59 For information on Flint, see Charles R. Flint, *Memories of an Active Life* (New York: Putnam, 1923), especially pp. 288–94; and Lawrence A. Clayton, *Grace: W. R. Grace & Co., The Formative Years, 1850–1930* (Ottawa, Ill.: Jameson Books, 1985), pp. 71–2. Details about the organization and early operation of U.S. Electric can be found in R. Carlyle Buley, *The Equitable Life Assurance Society of the United States, 1859–1964*, 2 vols. (New York: Appleton-Century-Crofts, 1967), Vol. 1, pp. 231–8. According to one source, Thomson approached U.S. Electric after learning that one American Electric stockholder had quietly purchased a majority of the shares and sold them to the Brush Electric Light Company. Flint then tried to buy the remaining shares of American Electric in order to secure a "bargaining chip" for use in future negotiations with the Brush interests. See William J. Clark, "The Early Days of the General Electric Company," item L6290–350, Hammond File, especially L6329–30.
60 See ET, "Power of Attorney," 20 January 1882, and "Collateral Agreement," May 1881; the syndicate also agreed to finance Thomson and Houston's efforts to secure foreign patents; see "Memorandum of Agreement," 6 October 1881; all three legal documents are in the Hall of History Collection. See also C. R. Flint to ET, 17 March 1882, CL, TP.

ing on the fact that he was perceived not as a neutral negotiator but as a representative of U.S. Electric. More likely, Thomson, Edison, and Brush perceived a large market for electric lighting and saw no advantage in a merger at that time. Despite his failure with the electrical industry, Flint retained his belief in consolidation and went on to create the United States Rubber Company and other trusts in the 1890s.[61]

As Thomson and Flint were seeking to gain control of American Electric by quietly purchasing stock, so the major stockholders in New Britain were looking to sell their shares at the highest possible price. As they were approached by several interested parties, the asking price for their stock climbed, reaching the inflated value of perhaps $105 per share.[62] At that price, the Flint-Thomson trust probably was not able to purchase many shares with the funds it had available. Consequently, most of the stock fell into other hands. In early 1882, Thomson blocked one takeover attempt by refusing to sign a new contract that lacked the clause promising to promote all of his inventions with "reasonable diligence." Although that maneuver scared off the potential purchaser, the major New Britain stockholders soon found another buyer for their stock.[63] In April 1882, they sold between 2,400 and 4,000 shares to George W. Stockly, president of the Brush Electric Light Company.[64]

It is not clear why Stockly purchased controlling interest in American Electric. Although several historians have assumed that Stockly

---

61 See James Burnley, *Millionaires and Kings of Enterprise* (Philadelphia: Lippincott, 1901), pp. 151–2; and Flint, *Memories*, pp. 295–6. Although Passer estimates that the meeting took place in 1883, I would argue that it occurred in 1882, because it would have been facilitated by the agreements between Flint and Thomson, and those agreements were declared void in January 1883. See Passer, *The Electrical Manufacturers*, pp. 51–2; and addenda dated 26 January 1883 on ET, "Power of Attorney," 20 January 1882, Hall of History Collection.

62 As early as 16 April 1881, the New Britain *Herald* reported that all of the stockholders had been approached with offers for their stock, but few had sold their holdings. By 27 January 1882, the *Herald* was reporting that bids for the stock ran as high as $105 per share.

63 See J. A. McManus, "Memorandum," 9 January 1906, Hall of History Collection. Curiously, Thomson said almost nothing in his recollections about his negotiations with U.S. Electric. In the 1906 memorandum, Thomson claimed that he refused to sign because he had heard that the directors of American Electric considered him to be a "pushover," and he wanted to prove them wrong.

64 "The Electric Company," New Britain *Herald,* 21 April 1882.

wanted to eliminate Thomson as a competitor, his subsequent actions were contradictory to that goal. It is possible that Stockly hoped to acquire Thomson's services as an inventor, or perhaps he was seeking a plant to supplement Brush Electric's main factory in Cleveland. He may even have purchased the stock with the intention of selling it again and taking a profit on the speculation. Whatever his reasons, Stockly did not regard the tiny American Electric Company as a threat or Thomson as an enemy.[65]

Initially, Thomson was not sure how to interpret the selling of American Electric to Stockly. In speaking with a newspaper reporter on 21 April 1882, Thomson would not reveal his opinion concerning Stockly's action, other than to note the obvious that whoever held controlling interest could elect his own board of directors and run the firm as he chose. He was concerned about the rights of minority stockholders (such as himself) who had not sold out to Stockly, but he said only that subsequent events would show what effect the sale would have on their holdings.[66]

Five weeks later, Thomson was genuinely angry about the sale. What moved him from uncertainty to anger was the first evidence of the success of the central-station marketing strategy. Until the end of April 1882, the firm had not sold any equipment for central-station lighting, but then in quick succession came the large orders from Kansas City and Lynn. More than just showing him that there was a market for central-station lighting, those orders convinced Thomson that the management of American Electric clearly was either unable or unwilling to pursue that market aggressively. They simply had no commitment to addressing the long-term challenges of electric lighting or to supporting innovation. In fact, he was beginning to think that the New Britain businessmen might be taking advantage of him in order to serve their own needs to support and diversify the local hardware

---

65 Both Woodbury and Passer seem to have been guided by Thomson's own recollections (written between 20 and 40 years later), in which he claimed that Stockly intended to force him out of the electrical industry. See, in particular, ET, "Dynamo Work and its Development," Autobiog. Papers, TP; Woodbury, *Beloved Scientist*, p. 137; and Passer, *The Electrical Manufacturers*, p. 26. That Stockly was supportive and friendly toward Thomson is revealed in their correspondence during the summer of 1882 (cited later in detail). In one letter, Stockly did hint that he purchased American Electric with the intention to sell it again at a profit; see G. W. Stockly to ET, 10 July 1882, CL, TP.

66 "The Electric Company," New Britain *Herald*, 21 April 1882.

industry. In writing to warn Stockly that the stockholders might be lying to him about the condition of the firm, Thomson openly attacked his backers:

> All my efforts have been given to the working of the system in the best sense and I cannot afford to allow a system which I believe is without parallel to be crushed out of existence by a continuance of the business policy of the past two years; . . . a policy which reached its culmination in an attempt to lead us, if not entrap us, to make the electric business a bolster for a weakly hinge factory here, and failing in which now throws off its responsibility upon shoulders other than its own.[67]

Having come to that conclusion, Thomson decided to separate himself from American Electric and seek a new situation in which he could develop lighting equipment for central stations.

Although Flint and Skinner counseled caution, Thomson chose to pursue "the most definite and direct course."[68] To him, the easiest path to disengagement was to invoke again the "reasonable diligence" clause in his contract. Arguing that the firm had failed to promote his inventions adequately, in May 1882 Thomson (along with Houston) tendered his shares in the firm and demanded that the firm relinquish the rights to his patents. Because surrender of the patents to Thomson would ruin their deal with Stockly, the directors (some of whom must have been the major stockholders who sold out) refused to accede to Thomson's demand. Through June and July he repeated his demand, each time expanding his list of grievances against the company, but to no avail.[69] Thomson then turned to Flint and asked for assistance in taking legal action against the management for return of the patents. Flint did not help Thomson initiate any suits, in part because they were unable to agree on who would control the patents won in court. Unsuccessful in securing the return of his patents, Thomson refused to renew his contract with American Electric and resigned in July 1882.[70]

67 ET to G. W. Stockly, 31 May 1882, CL, TP.
68 Quotation is from ET to G. W. Stockly, 20 June 1882, LB 82–99, TP. See also C. R. Flint to ET, 31 May 1882, CL, TP.
69 ET and EJH to the American Electric Company, 27 May 1882, Hall of History Collection; W. Parker to ET and EJH, 22 June 1882, CL, TP; ET, "List of Complaints," July 1882; ET to W. Parker, 8, 18, and 29 July 1882, LB 82–99, pp. 79–81, 82, and 109–10, respectively, TP; ET and EJH to W. Parker, 22 July 1882, CL, TP.
70 ET to C. R. Flint, 17 June and 18 and 24 July 1882, LB 82–99, pp. 62, 84, and 86, TP; ET, "Testimony," Intf. 13,761, p. 8.

Free of the company, Thomson pursued several different alternatives. Because he would need some sort of income, Thomson first sought to secure patents for his system in Europe and Canada, which he in turn tried to sell to investors. Previously, Churchill had been responsible for securing foreign patents for Thomson and Houston, but he had not made much progress before his death; at best, he had filed for one patent in France, two in Britain, and several in Canada. After settling with Churchill's estate, Thomson retained the English law firm of Haseltine, Lake, and Company to apply for patents in not only France and Britain but also Belgium, Germany, Austria, Spain, and Italy.[71] Because some of the patents covered inventions that he had developed jointly with Houston, Thomson made arrangements with his former partner that permitted him to negotiate the sale of their joint patents. Being both cautious and acquisitive, Houston was reluctant to sign over his rights completely to Thomson, which made it difficult for Thomson to market their foreign patents as an investment.[72] Nonetheless, Thomson approached a number of investors during the summer of 1882, and he eventually sold partial rights to his European patents to Silas A. Barton of Lynn. In return for a share of Thomson's patents, Barton agreed to create a trust fund of $10,000 that was to be used for building new electrical apparatus and for demonstrating it at industrial exhibitions in several European countries.[73]

With his Canadian patents, Thomson pursued a different course. In Canada, he perceived a new market for electric lighting, particularly because Brush had yet to file for any patents there. However, under Canadian patent law it was necessary not only to hold Canadian patents for one's inventions but also to begin manufacturing the inventions in Canada within one or two years of securing the patents. Consequently, Thomson had to seek capital to pay for the patent fees and for establishing a Canadian company. Working through a Canadian businessman, C. B. Cushing, during the summer of 1882 Thomson filed for patents to cover his entire lighting system. Unfortunately, be-

71 ET to F. Hungerford, 1 June 1882; ET to Haseltine, Lake & Co., 22 June, 2 July, and 7 August 1882; ET to R. R. Hazard, 24 July 1882; all in LB 82–99, pp. 99, 67, 78, 113, and 85, TP.
72 ET to EJH, 15 and 20 (24?) June 1882; ET to S. D. Schuyler, 16 June 1882; all in LB 82–99, pp. 60–1, 65, and 71–2, TP.
73 ET to S. D. Schuyler and ET to S. A. Barton, both 23 June 1882, LB 82–99, pp. 66–7 and 68–70, TP; [Contract among ET, EJH, and S. A. Barton], circa 1882, Hall of History Collection.

cause he may have had difficulty in getting the models required by Canadian patent law made in time, Thomson was able to secure only four patents. After extensive negotiation, Thomson and Cushing agreed to create a firm to exploit those patents, and in November 1882 the Thomson-Houston Electric Light Company of Canada was chartered in Montreal. Thomson may have contemplated joining the firm, but instead he arranged for his brother Frederick to serve as the company's chief electrician.[74]

Although the sale of his European and Canadian patents may have yielded some immediate income, Thomson still was anxious to secure a position for himself. Unlike Thomas Edison and Elmer Sperry, who liked being independent inventors, with different backers for each project, Thomson did not enjoy looking for new financial backers. He clearly preferred the security of having a single company support his work as an inventor. Indeed, the tension of having to make business arrangements during the summer of 1882 made him physically ill. Consequently, as he wrote to investors offering his foreign patents for sale, he frequently asked if they might be interested in hiring him. He wrote as follows in several letters:

> Do you think that you shall organize to work in the United States as proposed? If so what are you disposed to offer for my services should you need them? If I go into anything of the kind I go in to beat Brush if possible, and after the turn our affairs have taken here, it seems the best thing to do. I undertook to beat Brush some years ago, and after having got as far as we did, it seems hard to begin the struggle all over again; but I believe it can be done in a short time with energetic work.[75]

74 ET to C. B. Cushing, 20 and 29 June, 25 July, 7 and 14 August 1882; ET to EJH, 31 October and (?) November 1882; all in LB 82–99, pp. 63–4, 73–5, 88, 112, 117, 125–6, and 127–8, TP; "The Thompson [sic] and Houston Electric Light Company of Canada," *Electrical Review*, 3:5 (27 September 1883). It is not clear what became of this firm, because in 1884 Montreal businessmen created another firm, the Royal Electric Company, to manufacture Thomson-Houston equipment in Canada. See Christopher Armstrong and H. V. Nelles, *Monopoly's Moment: The Organization and Regulation of Canadian Utilities, 1830–1930* (Philadelphia: Temple University Press, 1986), pp. 76–7.

75 For Edison's and Sperry's experiences, see Matthew Josephson, *Edison: A Biography* (New York: McGraw-Hill, 1959); and Thomas P. Hughes, *Elmer Sperry: Inventor and Engineer* (Baltimore: Johns Hopkins University Press, 1971), pp. 63–4. Thomson mentioned not feeling well in a letter to G. W. Stockly, 22 July 1882, LB 82–99, between pp. 70 and 71, TP. Quotation is from ET to S. D. Schuyler and ET to S. A. Barton, both 23 June 1882, LB 82–99, pp. 66–7 and 68–70, TP.

In spite of his desire to surpass Brush, Thomson's need for a position was sufficiently great that he turned to Stockly, president of the Brush company, for help. Initially, Stockly had hoped that Thomson would continue to work at the New Britain factory, but after meeting with Thomson several times, he became convinced that it would not be possible "to arrange matters pleasantly" for him there. Subsequently, Stockly may have tried to secure employment for Thomson with another firm. Failing that, Stockly agreed to let Thomson locate a new group of backers and buy back control of American Electric. In agreeing to relinquish his control of American Electric, it would appear that Stockly did not regard Thomson as a threat; perhaps he believed that the market for arc lighting was vast and that there was no need to vanquish the competition. "I have only the kindest feelings toward you personally," wrote the president of the Brush company to the rival electrician in July 1882, "and would prefer to see it [the American Electric Company] in your hands or the hands of your associates."[76] Because he already had other parties interested in purchasing his stock in American Electric, Stockly stipulated that Thomson and his future associates match what others were offering.

As Thomson later recalled, it required "a most strenuous effort and expenditure of time and money" to convince Stockly to permit him to buy back the stock. For the next five months, Thomson was in constant search of investors, traveling to New York, Boston, and other cities to meet with potential backers. Sick and nervous from the endless negotiations, he very much missed working on his inventions.

Finally, Barton, the Lynn entrepreneur, offered to buy the company.[77] To underwrite the purchase of the American Electric stock, Barton organized a group of shoe manufacturers who became known as the "Lynn syndicate." (Further information about that group of investors will be given in the next chapter.) In October 1882, several members of the syndicate met in Charles A. Coffin's office to reorganize the company. As officers of the firm, they elected Henry A. Pevear president, Coffin vice-president, and Barton general manager. Pevear

---

76 See G. W. Stockly to ET, 2 June and 10, 14, 17, and 31 July 1882, CL, TP; ET to G. W. Stockly, 22 July 1882, LB 82–99, between pp. 70 and 71, TP. Quotations are from G. W. Stockly to ET, 22 June and 10 July 1882, CL, TP.

77 Quotation is from "Brief in Behalf of Thomson," Patent Interference No. 12,763, Moses vs. Thomson (subject: electric welding, RG-241), NARS, p. 27. See also ET, "Testimony," Intf. 9,965, p. 9; ET, "Personal Recollections," p. 568; and Hammond, *Men and Volts*, pp. 52–3.

negotiated a new contract with Thomson that was signed on 1 November 1882. In that contract, Thomson agreed to serve as the company's electrician for the next five years, with an increase in salary to $3,000. Thomson insisted that the contract include a "reasonable diligence" clause permitting him to recover his patents after he had worked with the company for three years. He also protected himself by excluding a number of inventions from the contract; he was free to develop and sell on his own an electroplating dynamo, an electromotive exchanger (possibly a transformer), a system of power transmission, and an underground wire system.[78] By keeping those inventions for himself, Thomson was trying to avoid being as dependent on the Lynn syndicate as he had been on his New Britain backers.

The last days in New Britain, 1882–3

Although Thomson retained some inventions as a safeguard against mismanagement by the Lynn syndicate, the actions of his new backers soon proved that he had little to fear. Unlike the New Britain businessmen, the shoe manufacturers of Lynn took an immediate and active interest in the electric-lighting enterprise. Shortly after purchasing control of the firm, they decided to move the factory from New Britain to Lynn. To do so, however, it was necessary to obtain a revised corporate charter from the Connecticut legislature. In April 1883 a new charter was approved, allowing the company to relocate and to be renamed the Thomson-Houston Electric Company. In addition, the firm was permitted to increase its capital stock up to a million dollars; that the Lynn syndicate requested such a figure suggests that they wanted the firm to grow rapidly and to be on a par with other firms in the industry[79] (Table 4.3). However, because they probably wanted to avoid further reducing the value of individual shares, they increased the firm's capitalization only to $250,000 in 1883.

As the Lynn businessmen attended to those corporate matters, they also made arrangements to resume production. In Lynn, construction

---

78 For the date of the meeting, see item J811, Hammond File; [contract between ET and the American Electric Company, signed by H. A. Pevear], 1 November 1882, CL, TP.

79 "[An Act] Incorporating the Thomson-Houston Electric Company, Approved 17 April 1883," in *Special Acts and Resolves of the State of Connecticut* (Hartford: 1885), Vol. 9, pp. 791–3.

Table 4.3. *Capitalization and stock values of various electric lighting companies, April 1883*

Firm	Capital	Share (par value)	Highest price	Current price
American Electric Co.	$ 500,000[a]	$ 50	$ 35	$ 4.75
Edison Electric Light Co.	300,000	100	5,000	150
Edison Illuminating Co.[b]	1,000,000	100	125	40
Edison Isolated Lighting Co.	500,000	100	240	140
Edison Electric Light Co. of Europe	2,000,000	100	165	40
United States Electric Lighting Co.	1,500,000	100	300	130
United States Illuminating Co.	500,000	?	?	103
Brush Electric Light Co. of Cleveland	3,000,000	100	110	110
Brush Illuminating Co. of New York	1,000,000	100	15	100
Fuller Electric Co.	870,000	100	32	30
Brush-Swan Electric Light Co.	600,000	100	150	105

[a]All other sources indicated that as of April 1883, American Electric was still capitalized at $125,0000. It is not clear why this figure is higher.
[b]All firms with the word "illuminating" in their titles are utility companies employing central stations.
Source: "The Electric Light Companies," *Electrical Review,* 2:10–11 (5 April 1883).

of a new factory was begun in the spring of 1883, and the company occupied its new plant the following fall. In the meantime, to continue to fill orders for dynamos and lights, the Lynn backers installed more equipment in the old factory in New Britain and expanded the work force from 40 to 100 men. James F. Meech was hired to superintend the factory and reorganize production. Rather than have work scattered through the building, Meech established separate departments for assembling arc lamps, winding dynamos, and machining regulators. Meech's efforts were reinforced by sound business practices; for the first time, the firm paid its workers weekly rather than monthly. Similarly, the credit reporter from R. G. Dun & Co. noted that the new management settled its accounts within 30 days, an improvement over the previous management, which had paid its bills whenever convenient.[80] In improving the business operations at the New Britain factory, Pevear and the other Lynn backers undoubtedly were drawing on their experience in running shoe factories.

More than just getting the factory running again and the bills paid, the Lynn syndicate took a special interest in marketing the system. The new management actively embraced the strategy of selling arc-lighting equipment for central stations. They hired other salesmen, who joined Hart in traveling throughout New England and the Midwest promoting the system. Arrangements were made with Edward H. Goff of the American Electric Illuminating Company, who agreed to install Thomson-Houston equipment exclusively in the central stations he was promoting. Advertisements were regularly taken out in electrical trade journals. To supplement their advertisements, both Goff and the Lynn businessmen probably persuaded those journals to run articles about the Thomson-Houston system. To obtain further publicity, Charles A. Coffin, a young and energetic shoe manufacturer known for his salesmanship, suggested that the firm enter its system in a series of competitive tests being held at the 1883 Cincinnati Industrial Exhibition. Much as in the Franklin Institute dynamo tests of 1878, Thomson took his dynamo and arc lights to the exhibition and won the gold medal, beating out Brush, Edison, and Weston. Elated at their success, the

---

80 J. I. Mitchell, "Reminiscences of Lynn," GE Pittsfield Works *Current News,* Vol. 2, No. 4 (December 1914), item 153, Hammond File; New Britain *Herald,* 5 January 1883; entry for Thomson-Houston Electric Company, Vol. 89, Massachusetts, Suffolk County, Boston, p. 158, R. G. Dun & Co. Collection.

THE THOMSON-HOUSTON ELECTRIC COMPANY,

PROPRIETORS OF THE

Thomson-Houston System of Electric Lighting

The Company has just been awarded the *First Prize* at the competitive tests at the great *Industrial Exposition in Cincinnati*, for the

BEST SYSTEM OF ELECTRIC ARC LIGHTING and the
BEST ELECTRIC ARC LAMP.

This company is prepared to furnish on application the

ONLY AUTOMATIC SELF-REGULATING SYSTEM OF ELECTRIC ARC LIGHTING

in the market, and the only system provided with Thomson's Patent AIR BLAST to pre vent flashing.

More than enough can be

SAVED IN THE COST OF POWER, ATTENDANCE AND REPAIRS,

compared with any other system, to cover the interest on the whole first cost of plant. The Thomson-Houston dynamos can be operated by comparatively cheap help, and if located near the engine, the engineer can, without assistance, take entire charge of two or more dynamos. The lamps require *less attention* than those of any other system.

THE PERFECT AUTOMATIC REGULATION OF THE CURRENT

permits turning on or off any number of lights at will, consuming power only in propor tion to the number of lights burned. The system affords the

GREATEST POSSIBLE SAFETY

in all respects, and in every desirable quality of arc lighting it has

NO EQUAL IN THE MARKET.

Send for illustrated pamphlet, terms, &c., to

THOMSON-HOUSTON ELECTRIC CO., No. 131 Devonshire Street, Boston.

Figure 4.12. Advertisement for Thomson-Houston Electric Company in *Electrical Review*, 2:3 (11 October 1883).

Lynn managers celebrated by taking out a half-page advertisement in *Electrical Review*[81] (Figure 4.12).

As a result of those efforts, the New Britain factory soon was working at full capacity, and Thomson-Houston lights were burning in Boston, Fall River, Hartford, Utica, and Peoria. By October 1883, the firm had sold over 1,600 arc lights to central stations, a sizable number when one recalls that up until 1882, American Electric had installed a total of perhaps 400 lights. Impressed with the technical features of the system and the rapid growth of the company, *Electrical Review* noted that "the Thomson-Houston electric light is rapidly coming to front

81 "Annual Report . . . of the American Electric and Illuminating Company . . . May 24, 1884," MIT Archives; "American Electric and Illuminating Company of Boston," *Electrical Review*, 2:3 (7 June 1883); "The Thomson-Houston Electric Lighting System," *Electrical Review*, 2:1–3 (14 June 1883); see also *Electrical Review*, 2:7 (17 May 1883), and 2:4 (26 July 1883); ET to CAC, 27 June 1883, LB 5/83–8/85, pp. 9–15, TP; "Report . . . of the Eleventh Cincinnati Industrial Exposition . . . 1883" (Cincinnati: n.d.), pp. 202–40, in the library of the National Museum of American History, Washington, D.C.; "Tests of Electric-Light Systems at the Cincinnati Exposition," *Science*, 3:174–86 (15 February 1884).

and [we] will doubtless see this excellent system among the leading competitors for public favor in the near future."[82]

For Thomson, those signs of commercial success in 1883 must have been gratifying. Equally, he was pleased that the Lynn syndicate shared his interest in innovation. Overwhelmed with the task of supervising production and worried about the takeover by Stockly, Thomson filed for only a few patents in 1881 and 1882. Perhaps his most important invention during the hectic days of 1882 was a double-carbon arc lamp that could burn all night without attention.[83] Because Brush had already introduced a double lamp for his system, Thomson was anxious to have one as well.

With the Lynn syndicate in charge, Thomson not only followed up on some of his old ideas but also struck out in a new direction. After spending several months filing patent applications for safety shunt switches for his lights and an unsuccessful experimental dynamo, Thomson began to develop a smaller electric light, at the suggestion of the Lynn syndicate.[84] Undoubtedly hearing reports of the public acclaim over the opening of Edison's incandescent-light central station at Pearl Street in New York, the Lynn businessmen sensed that there was a market for lamps smaller than Thomson's arc lights. Even though the first incandescent lamps were nearly 10 times less efficient than arc lights, Barton and the others guessed that there would be a significant demand for incandescent lamps because they could be employed in offices and shops. Consequently, they encouraged Thomson to develop either a small arc light or an incandescent lamp. Accordingly, in 1882 and 1883 he filed for two patents for incandescent lamps. In working on such a lamp, Thomson was remaining competitive with Brush, who added incandescent lights to his product line in April 1883. Hoping to enter that market as quickly as possible,

82 "Exhibit. The Following List of Thomson-Houston Plants . . . ," circa 1888, Notebooks, TP. Quotation is from *Electrical Review*, 2:4 (26 July 1883).
83 ET, "Electric Arc Lamp," U.S. Patent No. 272,920 (filed 23 August 1882, granted 27 February 1883).
84 Among the patents Thomson filed in late 1882 and early 1883 were the following: "Electric Arc Lamp," U.S. Patent No. 274,413 (filed 28 December 1882, granted 20 March 1883); "Safety Self-Closing Shunt Switch for Electric Light Circuits," U.S. Patents No. 275,289 and 275,290 (filed 17 January 1883, granted 3 April 1883); "Safety Device for Electric Arc Lamps," U.S. Patent No. 289,580 (filed 6 March 1883, granted 4 December 1883); and "Dynamo Electric Machine," U.S. Patent No. 294,094 (filed 21 May 1883, granted 26 February 1884).

in June 1883 Barton wrote to a British electrical inventor, William Crookes, hoping to secure the American rights to his incandescent lighting system. Barton could not come to terms with Crookes, and instead the company purchased the incandescent-lamp patents of William Sawyer and Albon Man. In the meantime, Thomson proceeded to design a dynamo and the other components of an incandescent lighting system. Although Thomson did not finish his system until late 1884, well after he had moved from New Britain to Lynn, what is significant is that the Lynn backers identified that new market in mid-1883 and chose to pursue it.[85]

With the encouragement of the new management, Thomson developed several other new devices in 1883. Because one group of potential customers for arc lights comprised steamboat operators, Thomson designed a special focusing lamp for use as a headlight. He also resumed his work on enlarging the capacity of his dynamo; by the time he left New Britain, his dynamo could power 30 arc lights at 1,350 volts. To maintain such a high voltage, it was necessary to develop better insulation between the armature coils, and for that purpose Thomson fashioned an insulating material by using alternating layers of pasted mica and paper.[86]

With the larger dynamos came longer lighting circuits, and the Lynn businessmen grew concerned that those circuits might be struck by lightning, damaging the dynamos and interrupting service. Wishing to minimize the danger, they asked Thomson to design a lightning

85 "Depositions of Witnesses," May 1888, Patent Interference No. 12,570, Thomson vs. Edison and Ott vs. Lemp and Wightman (subject: incandescent lamps), NARS. The estimate of power consumed by arc lights versus incandescent lights is from E. W. Rice, "Pioneer Developments Within the General Electric Company," *Proceedings of AIEE*, 28:19–29 (March 1909), especially p. 20. ET, "Incandescent Electric Lamp," U.S. Patent No. 335,158 (filed 28 December 1882, granted 2 February 1886); "Incandescent Electric Lamp," U.S. Patent No. 335,160 (filed 15 March 1883, granted 2 February 1886). For additional notes and sketches of Thomson's incandescent system, see "Incandescent Dynamo," 31 July 1883 (loose sheet), Hall of History Collection; and entry for 14 September 1883, "First Notebook," TP; "The Brush Storage System," *Electrical Review*, 2:3–4 (26 April 1883); W. A. Crookes to S. A. Barton, 25 June 1883, CL, TP; Passer, *The Electrical Manufacturers*, p. 145.
86 ET to S. A. Barton, 10 July 1883, LB 5/83–8/85, p. 19, TP; ET, "Focusing Electric Arc Lamp," U.S. Patent No. 302,961 (filed 5 October 1883, granted 5 August 1884); Hammond, *Men and Volts*, pp. 69–70; ET, "Early Work at New Britain," p. 10.

arrester. Finding that the arresters used on telegraph lines would not work on high-voltage arc circuits, Thomson invented a new magnetic blowout arrester. In his version, the current of a lightning bolt would be unable to enter the lighting circuit, because the path it would follow would lead to a gap located at right angles to the poles of a strong permanent magnet. Under normal circumstances a powerful current could easily jump that gap, but the magnetic field would prevent the current from jumping the gap. Thomson probably got the idea for his lightning arrester from an 1872 article published by Houston that discussed how a horseshoe magnet could be used to extinguish an arc light.[87]

The Lynn syndicate did much to restore Thomson's confidence and enthusiasm, and in his last year in New Britain (November 1882 to November 1883) he filed for nearly as many patents as in the preceding two years.[88] Unlike their New Britain predecessors, the Lynn backers were willing to risk innovation and take a long-term view toward developing new products and markets. They attended to financial, production, and marketing matters, and they also assisted him by suggesting new inventions. Just as Garrett had helped Thomson plan his inventions in Philadelphia, the Lynn businessmen assisted him in moving toward incandescent lighting and in selecting accessories for his system. Thomson greatly benefited from interacting with businessmen such as Barton and Coffin, and it became a characteristic of his style as an inventor. Once he moved to Lynn, Thomson regularly discussed with the managers of the firm the links between his inventions and the available markets.

With his business affairs in capable hands, Thomson devoted more attention to his personal life. Although he had grown accustomed to living as a bachelor in a boardinghouse, at age 26 he was becoming interested in marriage. Along with Rice and another assistant, Fitch Seymour, Thomson began calling on the daughters of several socially

---

87 See E. W. Rice, "Pioneer Developments," p. 27. The earliest sketch showing the magnetic blowout idea is dated 21 November 1882 and depicts a device for preventing sparks between the sections of a commutator on a dynamo; see "Magnetic Spark Controller," 21 November 1882, in Sketch File (under dynamos), TP. The first patent embodying that idea is ET, "Electric Commutator or Switch," U.S. Patent No. 283,167 (filed 23 April 1883, granted 14 August 1883). See also EJH, "Extinguishing Electric Light by Approaching a Magnet," *J. Franklin Inst.*, 93:299 (1872).

88 From September 1880 to October 1882 Thomson filed 21 patents, whereas from November 1882 to November 1883 he submitted 19 patents.

prominent families in New Britain. Among the families Thomson met were the Pecks, cousins to the Stanleys, and well connected to the elite of the hardware business. At the head of the family was Charles Peck, who was secretary of P. & F. Corbin and a stockholder in American Electric. Given his modest working-class background and his desire to improve himself, Thomson was impressed with the gentility and security of the Peck family. Within a short time, he hired one Peck son, Edward, as his office boy, and he began to court one of the daughters, Mary Louise. Finding her affectionate, modest, and sensitive, Thomson soon fell in love with Mary Louise. After a year of courtship, they were married in May 1884. Though information relating to their marriage is scant, Mary Louise provided Elihu a stable and warm home life, and she did her best to supplement his busy professional life with some social amenities. One surviving letter from 1885 reveals that Mary Louise struggled to adapt to her husband's hectic schedule, that she closely followed his legal and patenting problems, and that she worried about his health.[89]

In November 1883, Thomson and Rice packed up the last of the machine tools in New Britain, and together with a few workmen they set out for Lynn. Awaiting them was a spacious new building and a group of backers anxious to promote electric lighting. Evidently, the émigrés were pleased by what they found, and as the New Britain *Herald* noted,

> the New Britain people who went to Lynn with the Electric Light company are much pleased with the city, and they also say that they have a very comfortable and convenient factory, and better adapted for their business than the one occupied here.[90]

The lessons of American Electric

In the final analysis, the American Electric Company failed because Thomson and his New Britain backers approached the electric-lighting

89 See D. O. Woodbury to Carolyn Peck Boardman, 25 October 1942, Unsorted Material, TP. For information on the Peck family, see William R. Cutter et al., eds., *Genealogical and Family History of the State of Connecticut* (New York: Lewis History Publishing Co., n.d.), Vol. 4, pp. 2032–4. Announcements from the wedding are in Scrapbook, Notebooks, TP. One of the few documents describing Thomson's married life is [M. L. Thomson] to Mother, 15 March 1885, CL, TP.

90 Quotation is from New Britain *Herald*, 10 November 1883. See also New Britain *Herald*, 26 December 1882.

business with two different business-technological mind-sets. Determined to beat Brush, Thomson was committed to perfecting his arc lighting system. His perspective was long-term; given sufficient time and resources, he was confident that his system would triumph. In contrast, his backers took a short-term view of electric lighting; they invested in anticipation of a rapid appreciation of their stock. Viewing electric lighting as a secondary investment designed to protect their primary business in hardware manufacture, the businessmen of New Britain did not devote much attention to production, innovation, or marketing.[91]

Although clearly there were specific factors informing the antagonistic relationship between Thomson and his backers, one also wonders if there may have been a general tension between investors and inventors. In an industrial economy, there generally is a high demand for capital, and investors often choose to place their money in safe, short-term enterprises with a reasonable yield. Innovation, in contrast, often involves a long-term investment, made risky by unsolved design and marketing problems. Inventors must regularly seek capital to solve such problems, but in doing so must account for the risk involved. Do investors and inventors frequently find themselves opposed like this? How do they resolve their differences in regard to expectations for profits? As will be shown in the next chapter, the tension between long- and short-term outlooks was partly addressed in the Thomson-Houston Electric Company by Thomson's ability to integrate organizational goals with his own personal and technical goals.

But where did Thomson acquire his ability to match his values and needs with those of the firm, thus reducing the tension between management and himself? He developed that ability during his three years in New Britain; there he learned how to handle himself within the business world, and he came to understand his own needs and preferences. Working for American Electric, he learned to adjust his efforts at invention to accommodate the problems of limited supplies and equipment and to use such constraints to focus his creativity. He acquired a sense of how to develop those inventions that were needed in the marketplace. In the case of the central-station strategy, for instance, he created his air-blast device in order to enlarge the capacity

91 In analyzing the business-technological mind-sets of Thomson and his New Britain backers, I am drawing on the work of Reese V. Jenkins, especially his book *Images and Enterprise: Technology and the American Photography Industry, 1839 to 1925* (Baltimore: Johns Hopkins University Press, 1975).

of his dynamo. More important, however, Thomson came to realize that although his primary desire was to invent, he would have to negotiate and even fight with his supporters and associates in order to do so. To be able to invent, Thomson was willing to enter the complex world of business negotiations with Flint, argue with the management over the ownership of his patents, and search on his own for new investors. He soon discovered, however, that he intensely disliked the stress of business negotiations and that he preferred to work within a firm, rather than being an independent inventor. Consequently, when Barton and the Lynn shoe manufacturers offered to support his inventions, Thomson chose to join them and to shape his efforts at invention to suit their perceptions and goals.

Thomson's struggle in New Britain was a story of acquiring self-knowledge. It was there that he identified his goals and ideals, but more significantly, he learned how to balance his goals and desires with those of a group or organization. Implicitly, he came to understand the irony that his creative freedom was best protected by learning to work within an organization. As we shall see in the next two chapters, it was his ability to internalize that irony that permitted him to be productive within the context of the Thomson-Houston Electric Company, and that context was the reason that many of his inventions proved to be commercial successes.

5. Success in Lynn: the Thomson-Houston Electric Company, 1883–1892

In contrast to the failure of the American Electric Company of New Britain, the Thomson-Houston Electric Company of Lynn was a phenomenal success. From 1883 to 1892 Thomson helped that new firm expand by developing a variety of new products, including both direct-current (dc) and alternating-current (ac) incandescent lighting systems, ac motors, street railways, and electric meters. Those inventions constituted a strong technical base that, when coupled with the marketing, financial, and production expertise possessed by other members of the firm, allowed Thomson-Houston to compete with the electrical manufacturing companies organized by Charles Brush, Thomas Edison, and George Westinghouse. By all measures, Thomson-Houston enjoyed remarkable growth; from 1883 to 1892 its capitalization grew from $125,000 to $15 million, the number of employees jumped from 45 to nearly 3,500, and annual profits increased from $93,000 to $1.5 million (Table 5.1).

Not only were the late 1880s good for the company, they also were the best years in Thomson's career as an inventor. Measured in terms of patent applications, his years with Thomson-Houston were his most productive (Figure 5.1). Whereas from 1880 to 1885 he had averaged 21 patent applications annually, during the next five years he doubled his average. In part, Thomson was able to file for so many patents because the firm supplied him the necessary personnel and resources, which he organized into a workshop called the Model Room. There Thomson perfected a method of invention that brought together his skills in analyzing problems, visualizing and sketching solutions, and building models so that he could produce new products quickly and dependably. Yet Thomson's talents reached beyond the Model Room. In order to put his designs into production, he negotiated with managers and engineers, integrated his inventions with marketing strategy, and, when necessary, redefined his role within the firm. Although such organizational skills seldom are attributed to inven-

Table 5.1. *Growth of the Thomson-Houston Electric Company, 1883-92*

Year	Employees	Capital stock	Sales	Profits			Accumulated surplus
				Total	Dividends[a]	Retained	
1883	45	$ 125,000	$ 426,988			$ 93,697	$ 110,935
1884	145	125,000	700,470			96,187	207,112
1885	160	125,000	983,986			106,687	313,809
1886	335	125,000	1,405,042			123,006	426,813
1887	571	500,000	2,335,595			313,597	750,412
1888	888	1,000,000	4,435,902			660,829	1,411,241
1889	1,225	7,500,000	8,222,789			1,309,175	1,685,516
1890	2,328	10,500,000	10,217,662	$ 4,591,884	$ 254,766	4,337,118	6,022,534
1891	2,422	10,500,000	10,304,580	2,760,780	1,236,366	1,524,414	7,546,948
1892	3,492						

[a] There are no dividend figures available for 1883 to 1889. However, the *Annual Report* for 1891 suggests that the company paid only $240,000 in dividends during these years.

Source: *Annual Reports of the Thomson-Houston Electric Company*, 1890 and 1891; employee figures are from H. C. Passer, *The Electrical Manufacturers* (Cambridge, Mass.: Harvard University Press, 1953), Table 1, p. 30.

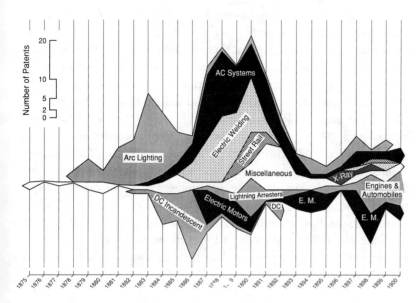

Figure 5.1. Chart showing Thomson's U.S. patent applications by year and category, 1875–1900.

tors, they clearly were essential to Thomson's accomplishments at Thomson-Houston.

Thomson and the Thomson-Houston Company were successful in the electric-lighting field because they integrated technology, marketing strategy, and business organization. As discussed in earlier chapters, in Philadelphia Thomson developed the hardware for arc lighting, but he and his backers were unable to complement it with a marketing strategy. In New Britain, Thomson identified the central station as the key to a marketing strategy, but his backers were unwilling to create the business organization needed to implement that strategy. But in Lynn, Thomson, Charles Coffin, and other managers brought those three components together, and as a result Thomson-Houston quickly became the leading electrical manufacturing firm.

This chapter investigates how Thomson-Houston linked marketing strategy, business organization, and technological innovation. Because the growth of the firm was driven by Coffin's understanding and implementation of the central-station strategy, we begin with a discussion of Coffin's background and how he shaped Thomson-Houston's strategy of selling equipment to utilities. The second section examines how the firm was organized along functional lines in response to the marketing strategy.[1] I shall describe the functional groups within the firm, emphasizing how each group acquired its own distinctive business-technological mind-set. To clarify Thomson's position in the firm and his mind-set, I shall also outline the method of invention he employed during those years. The third section is an investigation of how the strategy and the structure of the firm informed Thomson's efforts from 1885 to 1890 to develop an ac incandescent lighting system. Like the ac lighting system introduced by the Westinghouse Company, Thomson's ac system was significant because it provided the technical foundation for the development of a "universal" ac system of lighting and power in the 1890s.[2] But beyond the historical significance of that invention, this episode allows us to see that product innovation was not a smooth and orderly process within Thomson-Houston, but rather a process shaped by the interactions of groups within the firm.

Charles A. Coffin and the triumph of the central-station marketing strategy

In describing the state of the electrical industry in the 1880s, Frederick P. Fish, chief counsel for Thomson-Houston and General Electric, recalled that

> the business was new and presented problems which were substantially without precedent and which required new methods. People generally did not at all appreciate the need or value of electricity. They had to be educated to its use. . . . Suitable manufacturing methods as well as adequate ways of distributing the manufactured product had to be devised. . . . Customers did not exist; they had to be created.[3]

1 In making this "strategy informs structure" argument, I have been influenced by the work of Alfred D. Chandler, Jr. In particular, see his *Strategy and Structure: Chapters in the History of American Industrial Enterprise* (Cambridge, Mass.: MIT Press, 1962).

2 For the evolution of the "universal" ac system, see Thomas P. Hughes, *Networks of Power: Electrification in Western Society, 1880–1930* (Baltimore: Johns Hopkins University Press, 1983), pp. 106–39.

3 Quotation is from Frederick P. Fish, "[Charles A. Coffin:] Pre-eminently Successful as Organizer and Executive," Hammond File, J710–15; quotation on J711. For a similar statement that central-station customers had to be invented, see Sidney Alexander Mitchell, *S. Z. Mitchell and the Electrical Industry* (New York: Farrar, Straus & Cudahy, 1960), p. 47.

Figure 5.2. Charles A. Coffin. Courtesy of the General Electric Company, Schenectady.

The customers that had to be created were the central-station utility firms. As Thomson and his backers in Philadelphia and New Britain had learned, there was a limited market for selling free-standing, isolated stations. There were not many manufacturers and large retailers who had a need for artificial illumination and also had the capital required to purchase a steam engine, dynamo, and lights. Instead, it soon became clear that a different marketing arrangement would be necessary to sell electric lighting equipment; what was needed was a strategy that would reduce the cost of each light to the consumer by spreading out the capital costs of the steam engine, generator, and distribution network. The marketing arrangement that answered those requirements was the development of central stations. Although pioneered by local businessmen in San Francisco and Kansas City, that strategy was soon promoted and refined by leading electrical inventors and entrepreneurs such as Edison. However, foremost in the perfection of the central-station strategy was the vice-president of Thomson-Houston: Charles A. Coffin (Figure 5.2).

At first glance, it may seem surprising that Coffin became a leader in the electrical industry, for there was no study of science or electricity in his background as a shoe manufacturer. Yet it was the general lessons that Coffin had learned in the rapidly changing shoe industry that permitted him to succeed with the central-station marketing strategy.

Born in Fairfield, Maine, in 1844, Coffin was educated at Bloomfield Academy in Maine. At the age of 18 he came to Lynn and learned the shoe business by serving as a clerk in the factory owned by his uncle, Charles F. Coffin, and Micajah P. Clough. A center of shoe manufacturing since colonial times, Lynn must have been especially exciting to an ambitious young man in the 1860s because its industry was just beginning to mechanize and reach out to regional and national markets. With the introduction of the McKay stitcher and Matzeliger lasting machine, the Lynn shoe industry moved rapidly from having craftsmen working in central shops to having a small number of steam-powered plants employing semiskilled workers. With the new machines, output soared, but the prosperity of each firm depended on the careful coordination of production and the maintenance of an extensive distribution network.[4]

Coffin played a prominent part in those broad changes in the Lynn shoe industry. Early on, he showed "marked ability and originality in introducing new patterns and styles in men's shoes," and he was put in charge of designing the firm's product line. The elder Coffin and Clough made him a partner in 1866, even though the younger Coffin was unable to contribute any capital for several years. By 1870, the R. G. Dun & Co. credit reporter was impressed with the partnership's annual sales, and the firm soon became one of the largest shoe manufacturers in Lynn.[5]

4 For biographical details on Charles A. Coffin, see his obituary in *Lynn Historical Society Register*, 26(Pt. 1):32–3 (1934); and Charles E. Wilson, *Charles A. Coffin (1844–1926): Pioneer Genius of General Electric Company* (New York: Newcomen Society, 1946). On the development of the shoe industry in Lynn, see William H. Mulligan, Jr., "Mechanization and Work in the American Shoe Industry: Lynn, Massachusetts, 1852–1883," *Journal of Economic History*, 41:59–63 (March 1981); and Blanche Evans Hazard, *The Organization of the Boot and Shoe Industry in Massachusetts before 1875* (Cambridge, Mass.: Harvard University Press, 1921; reprinted New York: Augustus M. Kelley, 1969).
5 Quotation is from Micajah P. Clough, "Charles A. Coffin: A Reminiscence," Hammond File, J729–31. See also the entry for Micajah C. Pratt, 19 May 1870, Massachusetts Vol. 24, p. 165, R. G. Dun & Co. Collection.

Figure 5.3. Undated photograph of Charles A. Coffin & Co., shoe manufacturers. From Scrapbook 1, Thomson Collection, Lynn Historical Society.

The steady expansion of the firm Coffin & Clough was largely due to Coffin's marketing savvy. Considered by a later colleague to have been "a genius in merchandizing," Coffin thrived on the challenge of salesmanship, and it became "his master function, the work that he loved and in which he was never excelled."[6] Not satisfied with simply running the business in Lynn, Coffin frequently traveled and was among the first to sell Lynn shoes in Midwestern cities. To attract wholesalers and jobbers, who came to Lynn to order shoes, Coffin built a new factory in 1873 that was closer to the railroad station than any of the other shoe factories; in that way, visiting businessmen saw his merchandise first and often placed orders with him before they met any other shoemakers. Coffin's firm was also among the first to open a showroom in Boston for wholesale buyers. His efforts helped the firm establish an extensive sales network, and by 1873 the firm was worth $200,000. In 1876, Coffin and Clough reorganized the firm under the new name of Charles A. Coffin & Co. (Figure 5.3).

6 Jesse R. Lovejoy, "Personal and intimate recollections of Charles A. Coffin," Hammond File, L4392−411; quotation on L4404−5.

Working in the shoe industry, Coffin learned how markets could be continually refined and expanded. At the same time, he came to appreciate the importance of new machinery in manufacturing large quantities of shoes. According to his partner Clough, Coffin took a great interest in Gordon McKay's stitcher, and he advised other inventors of shoemaking machinery. Although Coffin chose not to finance the invention of any machinery, he was always willing to buy machinery for his factory once it was perfected.[7]

Coffin's experience in the expanding shoe industry of the 1870s taught him two important concepts that he carried over to electrical manufacturing. First, he learned how to create and sustain a large market for his product. Second, he discovered that technology was not a static component, but rather a dynamic component, of business strategy. By securing the latest and best shoemaking machinery, he could drive down costs and respond to the large demand of national markets. Technology was not a "given," but rather a means for capturing new markets. Coffin's use of insights from the shoe industry stand in marked contrast to the viewpoint of the New Britain hardware manufacturers; rather than attempting to see how marketing and technology could be combined effectively, the New Britain men were complacent regarding their existing distribution system of wholesale showrooms, and they saw no reason to support Thomson's efforts to improve his arc lighting system. Clearly, experiences in different industries played a role in determining who would be the creators of "big business" in the late nineteenth century.

Coffin first became involved with electric lighting through the Lynn syndicate. The syndicate was a group of businessmen who pooled their resources and invested in a variety of enterprises. By far their most important investment was the purchase of the American Electric Company, which they renamed the Thomson-Houston Electric Company and brought to Lynn in 1883. With the exception of Silas Barton, who was a shopkeeper, the syndicate consisted of self-made men from Lynn's shoe and leather industry; along with Coffin, it included Benjamin F. Spinney and John N. Smith, who manufactured women's shoes, and Henry A. Pevear, who owned the largest morocco tannery in Massachusetts. At the outset, the syndicate exercised firm control over the affairs of the Thomson-Houston Company. All of the mem-

7 Clough, "Charles A. Coffin."

bers of the syndicate sat on the board of directors; Pevear served as president, Coffin as vice-president and treasurer, and Barton as general manager.[8]

Initially, Coffin was reluctant to become deeply involved with the affairs of the Thomson-Houston Company, but also he was becoming bored with the shoe business. Once he realized that "there was a waiting market, one bound for swift and vast expansion," Coffin threw himself fully into the challenge of developing the electric-lighting business.[9]

The key to that potential market was, of course, the central station. Rather than sell equipment for isolated plants, Coffin had the Thomson-Houston Company concentrate on promoting central stations. He explained in the company's annual report for 1891:

> While some electric manufacturing companies have confined their operations to ... "Isolated" business ... which is of inferior value and importance, nearly ninety per cent of the business of your company has been in the sale of its apparatus to corporations organized to furnish light and power from central lighting and power stations. The business of these corporations is profitable and constantly increasing, and the orders received from them for increased plant and for renewal apparatus and supplies are secured with comparatively little solicitation or expense, and are chiefly for cash.[10]

Coffin perceived that the central-station strategy was promising because it permitted the development of a substantial market for electric lighting. By offering an extensive product line of different-size dynamos, one could provide the equipment needed to supply electric lighting to nearly every town and city. Furthermore, by selling machinery for both arc and incandescent lighting, it was possible to encourage utilities to add machines to expand their business to include lighting

8 For biographical information on Joseph N. Smith, Henry A. Pevear, and Benjamin F. Spinney, see their obituaries in *Lynn Historical Society Register*, 1913 (p. 169), 1914 (pp. 59–62), and 1928–31 (p. 77). See also the entry for H. A. Pevear & Son, Boston-Suffolk Massachusetts Vol. 89, p. 158, R. G. Dun & Co. Collection. For officers of T-H in 1884, see scrapbook 1, Lynn HS.

9 "Condensed notes of M. P. Clough ... ," and "Preliminary notes on recollections of Frederick P. Fish ... ," Hammond File, J722–7. Quotation is from "Achiever to Whom Fame Was Penalty," *Wall Street Journal*, 13 August 1926, Hammond File, J720–1.

10 *Annual Statement of the Thomson-Houston Electric Company*, 2 February 1891 (hereafter cited as *T-H Annual Statement*, 1891), Historical File, General Electric Company, Schenectady, New York.

for streets, shops, and homes. From the standpoint of the manufacturer of electrical equipment, central stations were ideal customers in
that they provided a ready demand for the product that was free of the
risky business of convincing consumers to install lights in their businesses and homes. In that sense, the central-station strategy was similar
to the manner in which Henry Ford externalized the risk of marketing
his Model T by developing a network of franchised dealers who were
required to purchase a certain quota of cars.[11]

However, to tap the vast potential market for central stations, often
it was necessary to help create local utility firms. As discussed in regard
to the Kansas City and Hartford stations in Chapter 4, the establishment of utilities was a complex process, often involving local politics,
mobilization of capital, and solutions to installation problems unique
to a particular city. Initially the Thomson-Houston Company preferred to avoid such local difficulties, and it gave Edward H. Goff and
the American Electric and Illuminating Company the exclusive right to
install its equipment in central stations. Rather than attempt to persuade a group of local investors to form a utility company, Goff would
create his own utility firm, install equipment, find customers for lighting, and then sell the successful utility to other investors. To reduce his
construction costs, Goff made special arrangements with the Jarvis
Engineering Company of Boston, which specialized in erecting electrical plants. Following that plan, in 1883 and 1884 Goff constructed
at least 16 central stations, most of which were in New England[12]
(Figure 5.4).

The advantage of the arrangement between Thomson-Houston and
American Electric and Illuminating was that the latter assumed the

11 Alfred D. Chandler, Jr., *The Visible Hand: The Managerial Revolution in
American Business* (Cambridge, Mass.: Belknap Press of Harvard University,
1977), pp. 359, 457.
12 *Annual Report of . . . the American Electric and Illuminating Company . . .
May 24, 1884*, MIT Archives; "American Electric and Illuminating Company
of Boston," *Electrical Review*, 2:3 (7 June 1883); "Economical Electric Light
Plants," *Electrical Review*, 4:3 (28 February 1884); "The Finest Arc-Light
Station in the Country," *Electrical World*, 3:101–3 (29 March 1884); Harold
C. Passer, "Edward H. Goff: An Entrepreneur Who Failed," *Explorations in
Entrepreneurial History*, 1:17–25 (May 1949); "Exhibit. The Following List
of Thomson-Houston Plants . . . ," circa 1888, Notebooks, TP (hereafter, this
pamphlet is cited as "List of T-H Plants"). During the 1880s, Sidney Z.
Mitchell (later of the Electric Bond and Share Company) ran a similar utility-
construction firm in the Pacific Northwest; see Mitchell, *S. Z. Mitchell*,
pp. 43–53.

Figure 5.4. Main dynamo room at Merchants' Electric Light and Power Company in Boston, 1884. This plant was constructed by E. H. Goff and the American Electric and Illuminating Company. From "The Finest Arc-Light Station in the Country," *Electrical World,* 33:101 (29 March 1884).

risks of organizing new utilities and stimulating consumer demand for lighting. In return, Goff's company was permitted to add a substantial markup to the price of Thomson-Houston equipment. By 1885, however, Coffin concluded that there was no need to have American Electric and Illuminating absorb a large portion of the profits through its markup and that Thomson-Houston could promote central stations on its own. Had he not extended the sales network of C. A. Coffin & Co. by traveling to cities on his own? Consequently, Coffin expanded the sales staff and established district sales offices in several major cities. In addition to selling equipment, salesmen were trained to help secure local capital, obtain the necessary franchise from the municipal government, and help organize the operating company. To follow the salesmen, an "expert" or construction engineer was sent from the Lynn factory to install the electrical machinery. With that sales staff in place, the number of central stations using Thomson-

Houston arc lights grew rapidly; whereas there were 44 companies using their equipment in July 1884, two years later there were 133[13] (Table 5.2).

One of the most serious challenges faced by many fledgling utility companies was raising sufficient capital to pay for equipment. According to one estimate, utilities in the 1880s had to invest between four and eight dollars in plant and equipment for each dollar of sales.[14] In response, Coffin had Thomson-Houston accept securities as partial payment. Whereas the Edison organization accepted stock shares in payment for equipment and patent licenses, Coffin was more conservative and accepted only utility bonds. That policy assured Thomson-Houston an immediate return on its investment in local central stations, because the bonds represented loans against a mortgage; although stock shares conveyed ownership and control, there was no guarantee that they would pay any dividends.[15] Coffin then converted the local utility bonds into capital by organizing a series of trust funds that sold bonds representing local utility securities to Thomson-Houston stockholders. Using that financial innovation, Coffin prevented utility securities (some of which were of little value) from accumulating in the company's treasury, while at the same time generating $2.6 million in capital. Drawing on the success of the trust series, Coffin had Thomson-Houston establish the United Electric Securities Company in 1890 to specialize in the remarketing of utility securities. Through those financial arrangements, Coffin helped local utilities purchase Thomson-Houston products and thus ensured that the market for central-station equipment would continue to expand through the 1880s and 1890s.[16]

13 For information on how Coffin organized the sales staff, see "Further recollection of T. A. McLoughlin . . . District office organization," 18 June 1925, Hammond File, L1028–9. The number of arc stations installed is from "List of T-H Plants."

14 Mitchell, *S. Z. Mitchell*, p. 45.

15 Forrest McDonald discussed the importance of accepting bonds instead of stocks in *Let There Be Light: The Electric Utility Industry in Wisconsin, 1881–1955* (Madison, Wisc.: American History Research Center, 1957), p. 21; and McDonald, *Insull* (University of Chicago Press, 1962), p. 43.

16 M. F. Westover, "History of the T-H Trusts, Series A, B, C and D," January 1916, Hammond File, J767; Harold C. Passer, *The Electrical Manufacturers, 1875–1900: A Study in Competition, Entrepreneurship, Technical Change, and Economic Growth* (Cambridge, Mass.: Harvard University Press, 1953), p. 29; Hughes, *Networks of Power*, p. 395.

Table 5.2. *Spread of Thomson-Houston lighting and street railway systems, 1883-92*

Year	Arc lighting		DC incandescent[a]		AC incandescent[b]		Street railways[c]		
	Number of companies	Lamps	Number of companies	Lamps	Number of companies	Lamps	Number of companies	Cars	Miles of track
1883[d]	5	365							
1884	31	2,478							
1885	59	5,867							
1886	100	13,227							
1887	171	21,840	29	11,275					
1888	303	39,936	78	59,330	23	11,100			
1889	419	51,621	200[f]	120,380			30[f]	200[f]	
1890	587	68,203	400[f]	281,555			92	701	420
1891	755[e,f]	87,131		616,355			145	1,532	1,160
1892	873[e]	100,293		806,500			204	2,769	2,364

[a]First introduced in 1886.
[b]First introduced in 1887.
[c]First introduced in 1888.
[d]As of 1 January.
[e]These totals include both arc and incandescent lighting stations. Approximately 500 companies operated both arc and incandescent systems.
[f]There is a discrepancy in the sources as to how many companies were using Thomson-Houston equipment in 1891. Whereas the *Annual Report* gives 755, Thomson-Houston also published a list claiming 666 central stations; see Table 5.3.

Sources: Annual Reports of the Thomson-Houston Electric Company, 1888-1891; *Exhibit: The Following List of Thomson-Houston Plants* (1888), Thomson Papers, American Philosophical Society, Philadelphia.

Coffin used the income from the trust series and surplus profits to strengthen the firm. First, he plowed those funds back into the firm and enlarged the Lynn factory; as will be discussed later, the factory grew rapidly, with a new building added each year between 1884 and 1891.

Second, Coffin used those funds to buy up smaller rival firms. Between 1888 and 1891, Thomson-Houston spent approximately $4 million to acquire seven electrical companies. Several of those companies, including Brush Electric, Fort Wayne, Schuyler, Excelsior, and Indianapolis Jenney, were competitors in arc lighting; others, such as Van Depoele Electric Manufacturing and Bentley-Knight Electric Railway, were purchased for their railway and motor patents. Several of the arc-lighting firms had encountered various problems in manufacturing and marketing their systems, but Coffin hastened their decline by having Fish and the other Thomson-Houston lawyers vigorously prosecute them for infringement of Thomson's patent for a dynamo regulator. It does not appear that Coffin undertook the merger campaign to acquire additional production capacity, because most of the purchased factories were closed. Instead, Coffin eliminated those rivals to increase Thomson-Houston's market share and secure control of key patents, such as Brush's double-carbon arc lamp. Still another important benefit of the merger campaign was that it brought a number of additional inventors into the Thomson-Houston organization, and they were soon designing products and filing for patents for the company.[17]

As Thomson-Houston was successful in selling arc lighting to central stations, Coffin was encouraging the company to move into new product areas (Table 5.2). With the business organization in place to market, finance, and install arc-lighting stations, it was an easy and logical step to have the same salesmen and engineers sell and service other electrical products. As early as 1883, Barton and Coffin asked Thomson to develop an incandescent lighting system, and the company began installing incandescent plants in 1885. Similarly, Coffin took an interest in selling dc motors that could be installed on arc-lighting circuits, in building ac stations, and in entering the field of electric street railways. Anxious to expand and diversify their customer loads, utilities readily purchased such new products. Hence, the manufacturer was taking advantage of economies of scope, and the utilities were capitalizing on economies of scale.

17 Passer, *The Electrical Manufacturers*, pp. 52–6.

In general, Coffin favored product innovation. Just as he had been quite willing to use new manufacturing machines in his shoe factory because they permitted him to produce enough shoes to reach new markets, so Coffin supported the development of new electrical products. With new products such as motors and ac lighting, he believed that he could better serve existing markets, as well as expand into new areas. As Thomson recalled, Coffin frequently visited the Lynn factory to see the latest inventions, and he invariably asked, "How soon can you have that done?" or "How long will it take to do that?"[18] As long as innovations facilitated market development (which they generally did), Coffin was an ardent supporter of Thomson's efforts. Thus, along with the development of central stations, Coffin helped establish product innovation as a key component of Thomson-Houston's overall strategy.

Diversifying into new product areas permitted Thomson-Houston to penetrate a large national market. Unlike the Edison organization, which had only one product or system suitable for one application, Thomson-Houston had several systems aimed at several different customers. Whereas the Edison company could offer only dc incandescent lighting suitable for businesses in densely populated urban districts, Thomson-Houston sold arc systems for street lighting, dc incandescent for cities, ac incandescent for smaller towns, and street-railway networks. In order to match the technology as closely as possible with each application, Thomson and Coffin chose to design and market each product as a separate system. Consequently, Thomson-Houston engineers erected a unique central station for each application.[19]

The Thomson-Houston approach of different systems for different applications was notable in that it was the opposite of Edison's vision of a single dc central station providing electricity for lights, motors, and other applications. Even though Edison's notion of a "universal" network became widespread in the early twentieth century (with ac, of course), that should not obscure the fact that the Edison organization encountered difficulty in selling its system in the late 1880s. That was largely because there were only a few cities with sufficient population

18 ET, "He Invented Methods of Business," in "Charles A. Coffin Mourned by Industry," *Electrical World*, 88:186–91 (24 July 1926); quotation on p. 189.
19 The full Thomson-Houston product line is described in "The Thomson-Houston Electric Company" (general catalog), 1 December 1890, Lynn HS (hereafter, this document is referred to as "Thomson-Houston General Catalog," 1890).

Table 5.3. *Electric-lighting central stations, 1891*

Thomson-Houston	666[a]	Excelsior	25
Westinghouse	323	Sperry	24
Edison	202	National	16
Brush	199	Remington	4
Ft. Wayne	144	Eickemeyer	2
American	67	Hawkeye	2
Western Electric	53	Standard	1
United States	51	Hochhausen	1
Schuyler	49	Beard	1
Heisler	49	Knowles	1
Waterhouse	41	Mayo	1
Ball	31	Keith	1
Van Depoele	31		

[a]Presumably includes stations using arc, dc incandescent, and ac incandescent.
Source: "Electric Light and Electric Railway Statistics," *Electrical World*, 17:110 (14 February 1891).

density to offset the high cost of the Edison system's large copper mains. After an initial flurry of interest in the Edison system, it became clear that the technology would have to be adapted to the utilities and the different services they were trying to provide.[20] If the market for electric lighting and power was to grow, it would be necessary for the technology to be tailored to the specific applications. It was in providing that second stage of development that the Thomson-Houston Company made a substantial contribution to the expansion of the electrical industry. Because of Coffin's ability to master the marketing strategy for central stations and Thomson's ability to design new systems for a range of applications, Thomson-Houston emerged as the leader in the central-station field. By 1891, Thomson-Houston had installed 666 stations, whereas Westinghouse could report only 323, and Edison 202 (Table 5.3).

The functional structure of Thomson-Houston

In order to implement the central-station marketing strategy, Thomson-Houston organized itself along functional lines. Just as American railroad companies in the 1850s had organized departments to carry out

20 For an example of how the Edison Company characterized its system as "universal," see "A Warning from the Edison Electric Light Co.," circa 1888, Electricity, box E5, Warshaw Collection of Business Americana, National Museum of American History, Smithsonian Institution, Washington, D.C.

the key tasks of operating trains, repairing rolling stock, and maintaining the roadbed, Thomson-Houston organized groups that handled the key jobs of designing, manufacturing, marketing, and financing electrical equipment.[21] Significantly, the firm organized those activities because they were the functions that had to be performed in order to sell electrical equipment for use in central stations. Had Coffin, Thomson, and other managers conceptualized either their marketing strategy or their technology in other ways, then they would have created a different business organization.

Although it is possible to draw an organizational chart for Thomson-Houston in the 1880s, it is important not to place too much emphasis on the hierarchical relationships depicted (Figure 5.5). For example, whereas the Lynn syndicate dominated the board of directors, and two syndicate members, Henry Pevear and Silas Barton, served as president and general manager, respectively, Vice-President Coffin was effectively the chief executive officer. Furthermore, whereas the organizational chart shows that Coffin was nominally in charge of both E. W. Rice, the superintendent of the Lynn plant, and Thomson, in practice he negotiated with them, rather than giving them orders.

Those peculiarities suggest that it might be useful to think of the Thomson-Houston organization not only as a set of formal departments but also as a coalition of groups. Although there are several intellectual frameworks that can provide insight into how a business organization operates, this interpretation seems to work best for understanding Thomson-Houston in that period of rapid growth.[22]

21 On the development of functional management by American railroads, see Chandler, *The Visible Hand*, pp. 81–121.

22 Like all organizations, the Thomson-Houston Electric Company can be conceptualized in various ways. If one were a vulgar Marxist, one could describe the firm as consisting of management and labor, emphasizing that management was a monolithic entity with the single-minded goal of securing profits. Within that framework one might expect to find that managers often exploited an inventor's creativity in the name of profit; such an outcome was what Thorstein Veblen predicted in his study of engineers and what Matthew Josephson concluded about Thomas Edison in his dealings with the robber barons of Wall Street. For a discussion of Veblen, see Edwin T. Layton, Jr., "Engineers in Revolt," in E. T. Layton, ed., *Technology and Social Change in America* (New York: Harper & Row, 1973), pp. 147–56. See also Matthew Josephson, *Edison: A Biography* (New York: McGraw-Hill, 1959), pp. 103–27. From another perspective, one could examine the firm as a vertical hierarchy, with decisions being made by the president at the top and then

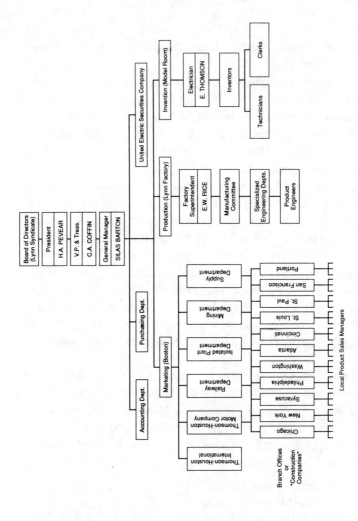

Figure 5.5. Organization of Thomson-Houston Electric Company, 1883–92. Sources: annual reports of Thomson-Houston Electric Company, 1888–91; various documents in Hammond File, General Electric Company, Schenectady.

Because this interpretation will permit us to see how Thomson-Houston implemented its marketing strategy and developed new technology, let me describe it explicitly.

Within any business firm there are different aggregates of individuals promoting their own interests and, at times, seeking to control the organization. Each of these aggregates may be called an "interest group," and within the firm they may be differentiated on the basis of their leaders, their functions, or, most important, their business-technological mindsets. Each group may articulate ideas about how new technology should be used to capture particular markets or perform certain production steps and hence ensure the growth and prosperity of the firm. The central point here is that groups within the firm may possess very different ideas about how the firm should operate. For the firm to make a decision about a technological innovation, a marketing program, or anything else, several of the interest groups must negotiate and compromise portions of their mind-sets and then direct other groups to implement the plan on which they agree. Generally, when the resources and rewards available to different intrafirm groups are ample, they find it easy to negotiate and implement decisions. Similarly, groups work well together when they feel that their positions within the firm are respected by the other groups. However, should a group perceive that its position in the organization is being challenged or that it may lose access to resources and rewards, then cooperation may give way to conflict and disorder.[23]

implemented by individuals in lower bureaucratic echelons. In this model, sometimes known as the heroic or entrepreneurial theory, often the firm is simply seen as an extension of the entrepreneur, owner, or chief executive officer. Typical of this approach are the histories of the Westinghouse Company depicting George Westinghouse as "masterminding," but not actually designing, early ac machinery. For a discussion of Joseph Schumpeter's conception of the heroic theory, see Jon Elster, *Explaining Technical Change: A Case Study in the Philosophy of Science* (Cambridge University Press, 1983), pp. 112–30.

23 This model of the business firm is drawn from several different sources. First, it is based on the "social construction of technology" model developed by Wiebe Bijker and Trevor Pinch. These two sociologists have suggested that technological artifacts are defined and shaped through the interactions of social groups. For a discussion of their model, see their essay, "The Social Construction of Facts and Artifacts: Or How the Sociology of Science and the Sociology of Technology Might Benefit Each Other," in W. Bijker, T. P. Hughes, and T. Pinch, eds., *The Social Construction of Technological Systems: New Directions in the Sociology and History of Technology* (Cam-

222   Innovation as a social process: Elihu Thomson

For Thomson-Houston, three interest groups appeared in response to the central-station strategy. Each performed a key function, and each was headed by a strong individual who ensured that the function was performed properly. While Coffin handled marketing and finance at the Boston office, E. W. Rice supervised manufacturing and engineering at the Lynn plant, and Thomson concentrated on invention and design in his Model Room. As each of those men pursued his function, each developed a mind-set that reflected his role in the firm and how he thought the firm should operate. Because the interaction of

bridge, Mass.: MIT Press, 1987), pp. 17–50. Although I am impressed with Bijker and Pinch's model, I am troubled that it fails to locate social groups in a larger framework of relationships; without understanding the positions of the groups relative to each other, it is impossible to comprehend how they will use and shape technology.

To offset this problem, and for guidance as to how to view how groups may act within the framework of an organization, I am drawing on the behavioral model of the firm developed by Richard Cyert and James G. March in the 1960s. Their model was a deliberate rejection of the belief that firms make rational decisions based exclusively on economic considerations. Instead, they asserted that firms come to decisions by "satisficing," that is, by negotiating and compromising the needs and goals of different groups. See their book, *A Behavioral Model of the Firm* (Englewood Cliffs, N.J.: Prentice-Hall, 1963). For an application of their model, see Leonard H. Lynn, *How Japan Innovates: A Comparison with the U.S. in the Case of Oxygen Steelmaking* (Boulder, Colo.: Westview Press, 1982).

Whereas Cyert and March's model implied that each group has a particular viewpoint, they said little about how and why each group chooses to articulate different goals, needs, and perceptions. Consequently, a third idea informing this chapter's view of the firm is Reese V. Jenkins's concept of the business-technological mind-set. In his study of the photographic industry, Jenkins observed that major changes took place in the industry when entrepreneurs succeeded in matching new technology with new marketing techniques, thus creating what he called a business-technological mind-set. See his book, *Images and Enterprise: Technology and the American Photographic Industry, 1839 to 1925* (Baltimore: Johns Hopkins University Press, 1975). Whereas Jenkins attributed different mind-sets to individual firms within the photographic industry, in this chapter I shall be arguing that different groups within the firm may possess different business-technological mind-sets.

Lastly, this approach to the firm has been shaped by George Wise's study of the formation of the General Electric Research Laboratory. In "A New Role for Professional Scientists in Industry: Industrial Research at General Electric, 1900–1916," *Technology and Culture*, 21:408–29 (1980), Wise demonstrated that the laboratory flourished at General Electric because its first directors succeeded in integrating the professional aspirations of research scientists with the commercial needs of the company. Like Wise, I shall suggest that progress occurs in the firm when the leaders of groups strive for cooperation rather than overtly challenge each other.

those mind-sets influenced how Thomson-Houston pursued product innovation, let us examine each group and its mind-set.

Selling dynamos: Coffin and the marketing group

As might have been expected, the central-station strategy led Coffin to establish a distinctive group around the functions of marketing and finance. That group was centered in the company's business office in Boston and thus was both physically and intellectually separate from the groups located at the factory in Lynn. Coffin himself generally worked in that office, aided by four or five sales managers. Each of the managers was assigned to a product area, such as arc lighting, incandescent lighting, or street railways, and they worked with the Lynn factory to coordinate production with sales. Given that the company sold each product as a separate system, it made sense to have a manager for each; notably, that was quite different than the Edison organization, which at that time had seven sales managers at its headquarters, each of whom was assigned a selling territory in the United States. To assist Coffin and the sales managers, the Boston office also had a staff of bookkeepers and clerks who handled the details of advertising, sales transactions, and the trust series.[24]

Beyond the Boston headquarters, Coffin established district sales offices in major cities. It appears that each of those district offices promoted Thomson-Houston products in the city and the surrounding region and handled the local details of each sale and installation. Because the district offices permitted the company to reach into new territory, Coffin carefully selected his district managers; for example, Coffin had Silas Barton move from being general manager to being the manager of the first of those offices, established in Chicago in 1885.[25]

24 "Methods of C. A. Coffin in building a commercial organization. Story told by J. R. McKee," 20 April 1927; and "Recollections of: C. B. Davis, J. P. Felton and C. B. Burleigh, all of Boston office," 29 May to 1 June 1925; both in Hammond File, J757–8 and J194–8; Harold C. Passer, "Development of Large-Scale Organization: Electrical Manufacturing Around 1900," *Journal of Economic History,* 12:378–95 (Fall 1952), especially p. 382.

25 By 1890, Thomson-Houston had district offices in Chicago, New York, Atlanta, Washington, San Francisco, Kansas City, Saint Paul, Cincinnati, and Philadelphia; see "Thomson-Houston General Catalog," 1890. See also A. L. Rohrer to J. A. McManus, 4 July 1945, Hall of History Collection; and "Further recollection of T. A. McLoughlin . . . District office organization," 18 June 1925, Hammond File, L1028–9.

Not content with a national market, Coffin pursued foreign markets through a separate firm, the Thomson-Houston International Company. Organized in 1885 by the Lynn syndicate, that company sold electric lighting systems worldwide, and it was especially successful in South America and Europe. In Europe, the company established a small central office in Brussels in 1886, but it was moved to Hamburg in 1888. From that office, James F. Meech (formerly the Lynn plant superintendent) worked with two or three other engineers who both promoted and installed electrical systems. Their strategy was to convince an established engineering firm in each country to become a partner in building central stations; in doing so, Thomson-Houston International had the foreign firm handle the local problems of raising capital, satisfying government requirements, and hiring workers. Eventually, the more successful of those foreign partners became subsidiaries; for instance, the British engineering firm of Laing, Wharton, & Down became British Thomson-Houston in 1894. In general, Thomson-Houston International did well in Britain, France, and Italy, but it was less successful in Germany, where it encountered strong competition from Siemens & Halske, Schuckert, and the Hungarian firm of Ganz & Co.[26]

Finally, below the managers in the Boston headquarters, the district offices, and the international office were the salesmen or "drummers." Traveling to towns and cities, they were the men who sold electric lighting equipment to the organizers and operators of the new utility companies. Like the managers, many of the salesmen were personally recruited by Coffin from the shoe and leather industry. Often those salesmen knew as little about electricity as did Coffin himself. However, Coffin believed that what the sales staff needed was not technical expertise (which could be provided by the factory's "experts" or engineers) but rather intelligence, enthusiasm, and commercial savvy.[27]

Guided by Coffin, the salesmen, managers, and clerks built up an effective sales organization. Because sales often depended on special arrangements, such as accepting utility bonds as partial payment, the marketing group naturally assumed the financial functions of the firm.

26 ET to EJH, 14 August 1885, LB 5/83–8/85, pp. 231–2, TP; "Memorandum [on the T-H International Company] Prepared by Mr. A. L. Rohrer – January 15, 1943," Hall of History Collection.
27 John W. Hammond, *Men and Volts: The Story of General Electric* (Philadelphia: Lippincott, 1941), pp. 90–1.

Closest to the central-station customers, that group frequently pushed for innovations that helped match the technology to customer needs. Furthermore, because they saw firsthand that the lack of a particular product often led to business being lost to rival manufacturers, they frequently pressed Thomson to rush new inventions into production. In sum, Coffin and his group had a market-oriented mind-set: Respond to the market quickly, give the people the products they want, and, if necessary, devise the means whereby customers can finance their purchases. In general, they favored product innovation only if it promised to help them increase market share.

Manufacturing dynamos: E. W. Rice and the engineering group at the Lynn factory

In implementing the central-station strategy, the marketing and finance group contributed much to the rapid growth of the Thomson-Houston Company. But marketing and finance are not the only functions that a machine-building firm must perform; to be successful, it must also address a host of manufacturing and engineering problems. Frequently it is not easy to transfer a new invention from the laboratory to the factory floor. Often the invention must be redesigned in order to simplify manufacture. Occasionally it may require new materials and production methods. At Thomson-Houston, for instance, Thomson and the other engineers were obliged to find better insulating materials, as well as devise faster ways to wind the coils used in dynamos, transformers, and arc lights. Once any invention goes into production, raw materials must be kept in stock, machine tools installed and maintained, and workers hired, trained, and paid regularly. As the volume of production grows, the layout of the plant and the work flow must be carefully planned, and cost accounting is needed to prevent waste and confusion. Naturally, if new inventions are introduced or existing products are modified, then the entire factory process may have to be revised and reestablished.

Because neither Coffin nor the Lynn syndicate was familiar with the intricacies of electrical manufacture, they willingly delegated responsibility for the company's factory in Lynn to Edwin Wilbur Rice, Jr. (Figure 5.6). In New Britain, he had served as Thomson's assistant, helping out with the drafting, building models, and winding armatures. Working with Thomson, Rice learned not only the craft of

Figure 5.6. Edwin Wilbur Rice, Jr. From Scrapbook 4, Thomson Collection, Lynn Historical Society.

electrical invention but also how to convert Thomson's inventions from experimental models to manufactured products. On coming to Lynn, he was put in charge of assistants in the Model Room or Experimental Department, but in February 1885 he was promoted to factory superintendent when James Meech went to Europe to head up Thomson-Houston International.[28]

As factory superintendent, Rice was responsible for all the work done at the Lynn factory. Referred to by the workmen as the "Lights," that factory was initially run in much the same way as the New Britain plant. Various rooms or departments were equipped for machining dynamo parts, assembling lamp mechanisms, and testing dynamos (Figures 5.7–5.9). As long as the firm's product line consisted only of

28 "Career of the New President," *Electrical World*, 61:1345–6 (21 June 1913); testimony of E. W. Rice, in "Testimony for Thomson in Rebuttal," Patent Interference No. 9,421, Thomson vs. Joseph Olmsted (subject: cutout apparatus for electric lamps), NARS, pp. 16–17.

Figure 5.7. First Thomson-Houston factory in Lynn, 1884. From Scrapbook 1, Thomson Collection, Lynn Historical Society.

Figure 5.8. Winding room in Lynn factory, 1885. From *Electrical World*, 6:83 (29 August 1885).

Figure 5.9. Dynamo-testing room in Lynn factory, 1885. From *Electrical World,* 6:83 (29 August 1885).

dynamos, arc lights, and regulators, Rice probably supervised operations by watching and participating in the work on the factory floor; there was no need for specialization or formal procedures. Wherever possible, Rice sought to improve production by rearranging the machine tools, introducing better assembly techniques, and designing special-purpose machinery. As a typical factory superintendent, Rice strove to lower manufacturing costs, thus permitting the firm to cut prices or expand its profit margin.[29]

Changing circumstances, however, soon forced Rice and the factory crew to modify their routine. As the company's salesmen sold more arc lighting systems, production had to be expanded. By November 1886,

29 "The Thomson-Houston Factory, Lynn, Mass.," *Electrical World,* 6:83 (29 August 1885); "Testimony for Thomson," paper 48, Patent Interference No. 15,876, Thomson vs. Dyer (subject: insulating materials), NARS, p. 28 (hereafter cited as "Testimony for Thomson," Intf. 15,876); "Misgivings as to Business ... ," Lynn *Item,* 24 October 1933, Lynn HS; "Electric Light Machinery. Sept. 1883. Completion of the Factory at West Lynn ... ," Hall of History Collection.

Figure 5.10. Thomson-Houston factory in Lynn, 1891. From Scrapbook 1, Thomson Collection, Lynn Historical Society.

for example, the company had so many orders that Thomson estimated that the factory had a backlog of 2,000 lights. In response to the growing demand, Thomson-Houston constructed at least one new factory building every year from 1883 to 1892 (Figure 5.10). Each new building had to be planned, equipped, and operating in a short time. During the same years, the work force jumped from 45 to 3,500 men. At the same time that demand was increasing, the company was also introducing new products; from 1885 to 1892, the Lynn factory turned out incandescent lamps, transformers, motors, meters, and trolley cars. To be competitive with Brush, Edison, and Westinghouse, Thomson-Houston offered those products in a variety of sizes and continually strove to improve them.[30]

To cope with the growing volume of production and the complexities of an expanding product line, Rice gradually created his own functional staff (Figure 5.11). To equip and maintain the factories, Rice selected Isaac F. Baker, an Englishman who had formerly installed incandescent stations for U.S. Electric, to serve as mechanical superin-

30 ET to Edward F. Peck, 13 November 1886, LB 9/86–3/87, pp. 88–9, TP; *T-H Annual Statement*, 1891.

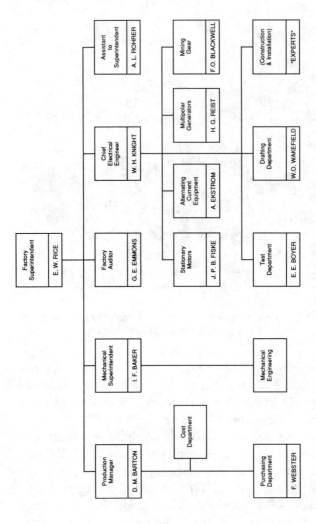

Figure 5.11. Manufacturing and engineering staff at Thomson-Houston factory in Lynn, circa 1890. Source: A. C. Shaw, " 'Thomson-Houston'; or Among the Dynamo Builders of Lynn," *Electrical Engineer*, 13:647–61 (29 June 1892), and various documents in Hammond File, General Electric Company, Schenectady.

tendent. Daniel M. Barton, brother of Silas Barton, monitored the flow of work through the factory and ordered supplies. Making up the weekly payroll, which typically was over $40,000, was George E. Emmons. Emmons had roomed with Rice in New Britain and had worked briefly as American Electric's bookkeeper.[31]

As the number of products manufactured in Lynn grew, Rice hired more engineers, and he organized them so as to cover the major product areas. Again, that arrangement reflected the fact that the company sold different products for different applications. Walter H. Knight, a pioneer in electric traction, served as chief engineer. It appears that the product engineers were self-educated, but many of the engineers on the staff below them were college graduates. By 1887, Thomson-Houston was regularly hiring young men from MIT's Electrical Engineering Department and Cornell's Sibley College of Engineering. To become familiar with the company's products, newly hired engineers worked first in the Testing Department, where dynamos, motors, and lamps were run and inspected. Some novice engineers also served as "experts," who were sent out to install electrical plants. Through his staff of engineers, Rice was able to monitor the work flow, improve manufacturing procedures, and design products.[32]

Whereas that staff provided advice and information, in 1890 Rice organized a Factory Committee to make decisions about operations. Consisting of D. M. Barton, Baker, and Emmons, the committee met at least once a week to handle employee problems, discuss new prod-

31 A. C. Shaw, " 'Thomson-Houston'; or Among the Dynamo Builders of Lynn," *Electrical Engineer*, 13:647–61 (29 June 1892), especially pp. 655–6; [memoir of Hermann Lemp], 2 July 1938, Biographical Material, TP (hereafter cited as Lemp Memoir); for information on I. F. Baker, see his testimony in "Testimony for Elihu Thomson," paper 129, Patent Interference No. 15,511, Pratt and Johns vs. Thomson (subject: composition for insulating material), NARS (hereafter cited as "Testimony," Intf. 15,511); for biographical information on G. E. Emmons, see his recollections, Hammond File, L13–19.

32 Shaw, "Dynamo Builders of Lynn," p. 658; ET to Theodore H. Seyfert, 23 September 1887, LB 3/87–4/88, pp. 489–90, TP; E. E. Boyer, "Observations on Historical Notes . . . ," Hall of History Collection; C. B. Burleigh to J. W. Hammond, 20 June 1925, Hammond File; George Wise, " 'On Test': Postgraduate Training of Engineers at General Electric, 1892–1961," *IEEE Transactions on Education*, E-22:171–7 (November 1979); and Robert Rosenberg, "Test Men, Experts, Brother Engineers, and Members of the Fraternity: Whence the Early Electrical Work Force?" *IEEE Transactions on Education*, E-27:203–10 (November 1984).

ucts, set production targets, and "exercise a general control over the foremen."[33] Thus, Rice and the Factory Committee exerted final control over all aspects of the factory, and the managerial and engineering staff primarily played an advisory role in day-to-day operations.

In running the Lynn factory, Rice and his staff of engineers and managers developed their own mind-set. Deeply involved in the details of manufacturing, their basic premise was that they should help the firm earn money by reducing production costs. Wherever possible, they strove to modify products so that they would be simpler to manufacture and install. The group also supported procedures that permitted greater control over the flow of work through the factory; D. M. Barton was quite proud of his system of wallboards, in which plugs were inserted to track the construction of large machines on the factory floor. Rice and the production managers also instituted a system of work orders that allowed them to assign workers to specific projects and at the same time monitor costs.[34]

As to product innovation, however, Rice and the engineers were cautious. Although some innovations were necessary for the firm to remain competitive, Rice and his staff soon learned that other changes upset the factory routine.[35] Their tendency to approach product changes skeptically was exacerbated by the fact that the factory was continually expanding in order to meet demand. Consequently, even though Rice had worked closely with Thomson in inventing new products, Rice's group was not always supportive of Thomson's efforts to improve his inventions. There was a limit to the confusion and change they could tolerate and still get the product out the door.

Designing dynamos: Thomson and the Model Room

Although Rice and the manufacturing group may have had mixed feelings about innovation, it was nonetheless essential to the well-being of the Thomson-Houston Company. Throughout the 1880s the firm generally supported product innovation. First, Coffin and the marketing group favored innovation because they saw it as a means to reach

33 Shaw, "Dynamo Builders of Lynn," p. 657.
34 Shaw, "Dynamo Builders of Lynn," pp. 655–6; "Testimony," Intf. 15,511, pp. 121–3; samples of the work orders can be found scattered throughout GE Transfiles, TP.
35 ET to F. P. Fish, 1 October 1889, LB 4/89–1/90, pp. 502–4, TP.

Figure 5.12. Thomson in the late 1880s. From Thomson Papers, American Philosophical Society, Philadelphia.

new customers and to acquire a larger share of the central-station market. Second, innovation was necessary for survival in a highly competitive industry. By the mid-1880s there were nearly 50 arc-light manufacturers, all competing for a portion of the evolving market (Table 5.3). Whereas creative financing arrangements and price cutting were two tactics that could be used to sell more equipment, customers also responded favorably to manufacturers with high-quality products. As Harold Passer has observed, electric lighting was a capital good whose purchasers had to make complex calculations concerning both original investment and operating costs; consequently, they frequently chose equipment on the basis of its efficiency and reliability, rather than simply its price.[36] In this situation, Thomson-Houston sought additional improvements and accessories that would accentuate those characteristics in their lighting systems. Third, but hardly the least important, the firm pursued innovation because of Thomson's presence. A key member of the firm, Thomson considered invention and development his personal domain, and he actively encouraged the company to make full use of his expertise (Figure 5.12).

Unlike Edison, who took an active part in the management of the companies manufacturing and marketing his inventions, Thomson

36 Passer, *The Electrical Manufacturers*, pp. 43–5.

concentrated on invention and engineering. Having developed a distaste for business matters in New Britain, he was content to leave the problems of raising capital and selling lights to Coffin and the Boston office. Although he sat for several years on the company's board of directors, Thomson eventually resigned because he felt that he contributed little to the financial planning undertaken by the board. "I have as little as possible to do with the business of the Company," Thomson explained in 1888, "my work being in the line of development of apparatus and the production of new inventions." He pursued his creative interests while serving as the company's electrician, a position that paid a yearly salary of $3,500. Initially, Thomson received stock in return for assigning his patents to the company, but when he renegotiated his contract in 1887 he chose to forgo his stock option and instead receive an annual salary of $8,000.[37]

In place of playing a prominent role in the day-to-day management of Thomson-Houston, Thomson created a niche for himself in the Experimental Department or Model Room of the Lynn factory (Figure 5.13). Although his work area could have been called a laboratory, Thomson referred to it as his Model Room, because the primary work performed there was the construction of models for testing and patenting. The Model Room was equipped with machine tools, electrical instruments, and a special switchboard for supplying electricity at various current strengths and voltages. In addition, the Model Room had its own supply room, patent library, and offices for Thomson and his assistants. Although adjacent to the factory floor, the Model Room was "off-limits" to employees and visitors, in order to prevent industrial espionage.[38]

37 On Thomson's preference for not being involved with business matters, see ET to H. B. Rand, 28 December 1888, LB 4/88–4/89, p. 586, TP. On his contractual arrangements with Thomson-Houston, see ET to CAC, 29 February 1884, LB 5/83–8/85, pp. 58–9; agreement between ET and Thomson-Houston Electric Company, 20 April 1887, CL; ET to T-H Electric Company, 29 April 1887, LB 82–99, pp. 217–18; all in TP. One questionable anecdotal source suggests that Coffin forced Thomson to relinquish his claim to additional stock shares, presumably to keep Thomson from becoming a majority stockholder. See Arthur Pound and Samuel Taylor Moore, eds., *More They Told Barron: Conversations and Revelations of an American Pepys in Wall Street* (New York: Harper & Brothers, 1931), p. 39.

38 Shaw, "Dynamo Builders of Lynn," pp. 653, 656; "Testimony," Intf. 15,511, p. 53; "Recollections of A. L. Rohrer," Hammond File, J217–23, especially J221; ET to CAC, 12 April 1887, LB 3/87–4/88, pp. 37–8, TP.

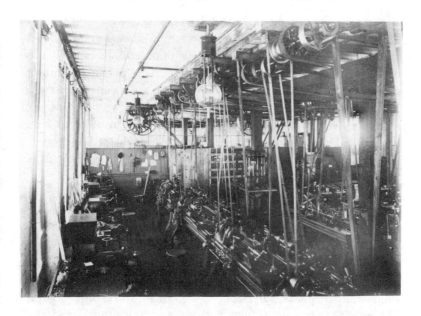

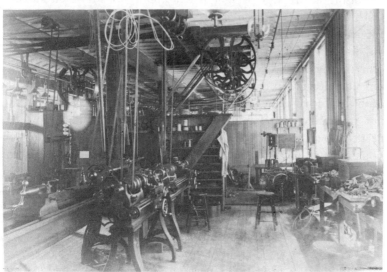

Figure 5.13. Two views of the Model Room in Factory B of the Lynn works of the Thomson-Houston Electric Company, late 1880s. From the Thomson Collection, General Electric Hall of History, Schenectady.

Assisting Thomson in the Model Room initially were skilled machinists and clerks (Figure 5.14). The machinists were responsible for constructing models of Thomson's inventions, and the clerks handled correspondence and the paperwork related to patents. Thomson's clerks apparently followed with great interest the technical work in the Model Room; for instance, it was J. W. Gibboney, Thomson's personal secretary, who suggested using jeweled bearings in order to reduce friction and hence the current necessary to drive the earliest recording wattmeter. Supplementing the machinists and clerks were a draftsman and one or two office boys.

Although Thomson preferred to work with only his skilled workmen, after 1888 he was joined in the Model Room by several other inventors who came to Thomson-Houston as a result of Coffin's merger campaign. Whereas Charles Van Depoele appears to have worked independently on electric motors and streetcars, Merle J. Wightman and Hermann Lemp worked on projects under Thomson's direction. Unlike the machinists, Van Depoele, Wightman, and Lemp shared with Thomson the privilege of filing patent applications for their ideas.[39]

Although there were variations in how Thomson worked on different inventions, one can detect a general pattern or methodology guiding his work in the Model Room. Unlike Edison, Elmer Sperry, and other independent inventors, Thomson did not have to spend much time identifying fertile areas in which to invent; most frequently, the problems to which he responded were identified by Coffin, who saw new marketing opportunities, or by Rice and the manufacturing engineers, who sometimes turned to Thomson for help in solving production problems. On occasion, Thomson did work on projects of his own choosing, either to satisfy his own curiosity or to develop his ideas so that he could publish an article. Some of those independent projects, such as his early transformers and electric welding, became major

39 See the following letters, in TP: ET to S. A. Barton, 19 February 1885, LB 5/85–8/85, p. 130; ET to H. C. Townsend, 6 September 1886, LB 3/86–9/86, pp. 243–4; ET to James J. Wood, LB 4/88–4/89, pp. 557–8; ET to CAC, 1 November 1888, LB 4/88–4/89, pp. 431–3; ET to J. P. Caveling, 6 September 1890, LB 1/90–11/90, p. 841. See also "Recollections of L. T. Robinson," Hammond File, L1109–14; Lemp Memoir; and "Testimony in Chief and Rebuttal on Behalf of Thomson," paper 94, Patent Interference No. 12,332, Edison vs. Thomson (subject: incandescent-lamp cutout), NARS, pp. 19–29. On Henry C. Townsend, see his obituary in *Journal of the Patent Office Society*, 18:788 (November 1936).

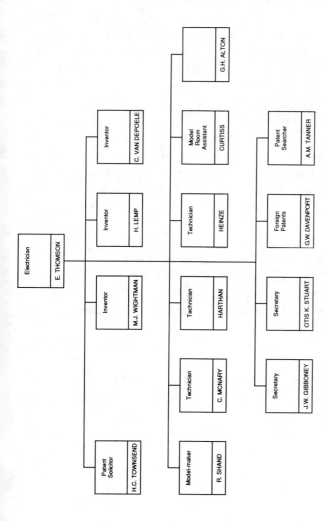

Figure 5.14. Organization of research and development at Thomson-Houston in 1888. Source: Various letters in the Thomson Papers, American Philosophical Society, Philadelphia.

inventions, but even then Thomson needed the assistance of others in planning how to market and manufacture those products.[40]

Once a problem area had been identified, Thomson began by making sketches of possible solutions. Although he kept notebooks when he first began inventing, by the mid-1880s he preferred to sketch his ideas on loose sheets of paper. They could then be sorted and shuffled so that he could study his ideas in different combinations. When Thomson was not using a particular set of sketches, they were filed by topic and date. If he considered a sketch to be significant, it was dated and witnessed, in anticipation that it might be needed as evidence in a patent case.[41]

During his preliminary stage of sketching, Thomson did not undertake any special search of technical or scientific literature to learn what others had done in the area. Such a search was not necessary, because Thomson regularly read the *Patent Gazette,* as well as all of the electrical journals published in America, Britain, and France.[42] Moreover, Thomson probably did not need to carry out literature searches, because the fields in which he concentrated – arc lighting, incandescent lighting, and ac apparatus – were relatively narrow fields with which he was thoroughly familiar.

After making several sketches of an invention, Thomson next had his machinists construct working models. The inventor then experimented, tested, and refined those models. A skilled machinist in his own right, Thomson frequently modified models himself. As a project progressed, the models became larger and more complex; presumably, his strategy was to have each successive model come closer to approx-

40 In seeking patterns in Thomson's work as an inventor, I am explicitly drawing on the approach taken by Thomas P. Hughes in *Elmer Sperry: Inventor and Engineer* (Baltimore: Johns Hopkins University Press, 1971), especially p. 65. For examples of problem areas identified for Thomson, see ET to G. Cutter, 7 October 1885, LB 8/85–3/86, pp. 76–80; ET to T-H Electric Co., 11 August 1886, LB 3/86–9/86, pp. 211–12; ET to W. J. Johnston, LB 9/86–3/87, pp. 48–9; and ET to H. C. Townsend, 23 October 1885, LB 1/83–11/85, pp. 249–250; all in TP.

41 "Testimony in Behalf of Thomson," paper 5, Patent Interference No. 12,841, A. G. Waterhouse vs. Thomson (subject: dynamo-electric machine), NARS, pp. 9, 10, 35. Part of Thomson's sketch file has been preserved in the form of tracings in the Thomson Papers at the American Philosophical Society.

42 ET to W. W. Munroe, 19 February 1885, LB 5/83–8/85, p. 129; and J. W. Gibboney to T-H Electric Co., 20 September 1889, LB 4/89–1/90, p. 48; both in TP.

imating the actual conditions under which the invention would have to operate if it were to be commercially feasible. Like the sketches, the models were saved in a special storeroom or vault for future reference and use as patent evidence.[43]

For Thomson, working with three-dimensional models was the essence of invention; with models, he could visualize and comprehend the complex relationships between electrical and mechanical forces embodied in his inventions. As one reads his correspondence, one comes away with a sense that he saw letter writing and patent work as unfortunate diversions from the excitement of working directly with his models. From an early age, Thomson had learned about science and technology not so much by reading but by building and manipulating devices. In his middle years as an inventor, he took that skill, refined it, and used it to develop a remarkable number of electrical inventions. Although Thomson could appreciate the theoretical explanations of electricity put forward by Michael Faraday, Lord Kelvin, and John Hopkinson, he did not move from theory or principle to application or invention. Rather, his talent as an inventor was fundamentally an ability to comprehend ideas such as the induction of alternating currents using the visual techniques of sketching and model building.[44]

In working with his models, Thomson chose to develop entire electrical systems, rather than simply components. In all likelihood, Thomson acquired that preference as a result of the patent situation and marketing conditions in the arc-lighting industry. Because it appeared in the early 1880s that Brush might well control several key patents for arc lighting, the only way to compete with him was to develop a system that would employ components that would not infringe and yet would work well together. Similarly, the systems approach undoubtedly was

43 See "Recollections of Charles H. Morey . . . ," Hammond File, J781; ET to T-H Electric Co., 11 August 1886, LB 3/86–9/86, pp. 211–12, TP; and "Testimony for Thomson," Intf. 15,876, p. 59. In his approach to model building, Thomson's methodology was typical of an inventor working in the development stage of Hughes's model of innovation; see Thomas P. Hughes, "The Development Phase of Technological Change," *Technology and Culture*, 17:423–31 (July 1976).

44 ET to George Cutter, 12 May 1888, LB 4/88–4/89, pp. 26–7; ET to Prof. R. R. Thretfall, 15 April 1889, and ET to G. M. Phelps, 26 April 1889, LB 4/89–1/90, pp. 30–1 and 110; ET to Charles R. Cross, 12 December 1890, LB 11/90–3/92, p. 34; all in TP; ET and Merle J. Wightman, "Phenomena of Magnetic Propagation," *Electrical World*, 12:220–1 (27 October 1888).

a response to customers wanting simplicity, reliability, and efficiency; to bring out those characteristics in electric lighting equipment, it was best to focus on making components work well together. Beyond those external factors, Thomson probably built whole systems because, like Edison and Sperry, he enjoyed having intellectual control over a project; thinking systematically, he could thoroughly shape an invention to suit his ideas. Thomson best expressed his preference for systems when he refused to enter his arc system in tests held in conjunction with the Franklin Institute's International Electrical Exhibition in 1884. He wanted to have nothing to do with those tests, because they focused exclusively on the efficiency of the dynamo, and as he put it, "the dynamo is not the system, nor the regulator, nor the lamp, nor the lines & switches, but the whole entity must be compared with another entity, under conditions which represent real, out & out commercial usage."[45]

Thomson conceptualized most of his inventions at Lynn as systems. For example, whereas initially he responded in 1884 to Coffin and Barton's request for an incandescent-lighting product by designing, with Rice, a distributor box that permitted incandescent lamps to be used on arc-lighting circuits, he insisted on replacing that device with an entire dc incandescent lighting system. For that system, Thomson redesigned his arc-lighting dynamo so that it operated at a constant voltage; he then fashioned a new regulator and drew up plans for the lighting circuits. Similarly, when he turned to ac lighting in 1885, he planned an entire system.[46]

The issue of patenting played a central role in Thomson's method of invention, and he often considered a variety of patent strategies: Should he file patent applications for the principle behind the invention or for the invention's specific configuration? Should he attempt to obtain a broad patent covering an entire system, or would the system

---

45 Quotation is from ET to Barton, 1 November 1884, LB 5/83–8/85, pp. 95–6, TP; see also ET to Frederick Thomson, 19 January 1886, LB 8/85–3/86, pp. 236–7, TP. On Edison and Sperry as systems builders, see Hughes, *Networks of Power*, pp. 20–3; and Hughes, *Sperry*.

46 For a description of Thomson's dc incandescent lighting system, see ET to G. Cutter, 10 February 1886, and ET to S. A. Barton, 22 January 1886, LB 8/85–3/86, pp. 279–84 and 242–50, TP. For the distributor, see "Thomson-Rice Individual Distributors" (sales brochure), MIT Archives. See also sketches and descriptions of lighting circuits (10–16 November 1885), LB 8/85–3/86, pp. 145–58, TP.

be best protected by numerous patents covering the components and accessories? Should he file for patents offensively, blocking other inventors from developing new devices that would improve their systems? (Recall his strategy with Brush and the combination regulator.) And what about patents in foreign countries? Should different applications be filed in each country so as to take advantage of variations in patent laws? Because of the competitive nature of the electrical industry, Thomson gave careful thought to such questions; if possible, he wanted to secure for the company broad patent coverage. In making decisions about patent strategy, Thomson frequently consulted with Coffin, his patent attorney Henry C. Townsend, and Frederick P. Fish. In addition, he closely studied the *Patent Gazette* and the electrical journals, trying to discern the patterns behind what his rivals were patenting.[47]

Thomson thought about patent strategy at different stages of the invention process. If he perceived that the patent situation was uncertain or that someone might get ahead of him with an invention, then he would file for patents while still sketching out his ideas. At other times, anticipating that the best patent coverage would be for specific design configurations, Thomson would begin drawing up specifications while working with the experimental models. Finally, if the marketing group was anxious to begin selling a new product (as it was in 1885 with the incandescent lighting system), then Thomson might postpone the preparation of patent applications until after the invention was put into production.[48]

Once the patenting process was under way, Thomson would turn an invention over to the engineering and drafting groups, which would decide how to manufacture it. They would make up formal blueprints and specifications to be used by workmen in constructing and installing the new product. In his first years in Lynn, Thomson took an

47 ET to CAC, 2 February 1885, LB 5/83–8/85, p. 121; ET to S. A. Barton, 8/85–3/86, pp. 206–9; ET to T-H International Electric Company, 10 September 1886, LB 3/86–9/86, pp. 259–60; ET to F. P. Fish, 2 September 1887, and ET to CAC, 6 April 1887, LB 3/87–4/88, pp. 407–13 and 22; ET to H. C. Townsend, 15 August 1888, and ET to CAC, 11 December 1888, LB 4/88–4/89, pp. 224–5 and 547–50; ET to Fish, 3 May 1889, and ET to S. C. Peck, 5 September 1889, LB 4/89–1/90, pp. 139–40 and 433–4, TP.

48 "Testimony for Thomson," Intf. 15,511, p. 24; ET to CAC, 8 May 1888, LB 4/88–4/89, p. 17; J. W. Gibboney to Bentley and Knight, 6 June 1890, LB 1/90–11/90, p. 597; ET to H. C. Townsend, 16 March 1886, LB 3/86–2/89, p. 92; all in TP.

active part in the conversion of his inventions into manufactured products; by doing so, he could be certain that the final product would meet his high standards of quality. He also could receive a certain amount of feedback information about his inventions that he could use to refine his designs. However, as the company moved into new product areas, such as alternating current and electric streetcars, Thomson was forced to devote nearly all of his time to invention, and he was unable to keep track of his inventions after they left the Model Room.[49] For the most part, Thomson accepted that situation, because he seems to have derived much satisfaction from perfecting his ideas at the model stage.

Besides invention and development, Thomson performed additional functions in the Model Room. When he was not working with models, much of Thomson's attention was given over to the details of patenting. As he described his work to Fish,

> I feel my position of being looked to by the management of the Company for the progress of various kinds of work, and for protecting the interests of the Company by patenting new devices and modifications of devices which otherwise would fall into other people's hands.[50]

One way that Thomson protected the interests of the firm was to defend his patents when they were placed in interference by the U.S. Patent Office. If an invention described in a patent application was similar to another invention covered in someone else's patent or application, then the Patent Office would initiate interference proceedings to determine who first invented the particular device. In the case of an interference, Thomson prepared statements and testimony detailing when and how an invention was created. By the late 1880s, because he had filed so many applications, Thomson found himself engulfed by interferences and was forced to respond only to the most important.

49 ET to Barton, 4 July 1884 and 20 August 1884, LB 5/83–8/85, pp. 68–71 and 76–9, TP; E. W. Rice to ET, 17 June 1889, CL, TP; "Testimony for Thomson," paper 56, Patent Interference No. 12,570, Thomson vs. Edison and Ott vs. Lemp and Wightman (subject: incandescent lamps), NARS, pp. 54–5.

50 Quotation is from ET to F. P. Fish, 29 December 1887, LB 3/87–4/88, pp. 733–5, TP. On Thomson having too many interference cases, see "Testimony for Thomson," Intf. 15,511, pp. 24–7. For information about the process of patent interference, see P. J. Federico, "Evolution of Patent Office Appeals," *Journal of the Patent Office Society*, 22:838–64, 920–49 (November–December 1940).

A second type of patent work that consumed much of Thomson's time involved infringement cases. If a competitor manufactured a product that an inventor believed to be a duplicate of his patented invention, then the inventor could initiate legal proceedings to stop the competitor's manufacture of the item. Several of the early electrical manufacturers periodically used infringement proceedings as a tactic to eliminate competition. For example, in reading the electrical trade journals, Thomson discovered a lamp patent by Clarence Ball that infringed on his design, and he did not hesitate to recommend to management that if the Ball company did not cease manufacture, then Thomson-Houston should take the necessary steps "to frighten their [i.e., the Ball company's] customers into not purchasing them." Further, if one of the patents owned by a firm was interpreted broadly by the Patent Office and the federal courts, then the firm could force its competitors out of business or require them to pay royalties for using that patent. Probably the most important infringement litigation in the early electrical industry was initiated in the late 1880s by the Edison organization to prevent rivals from manufacturing incandescent light bulbs.[51]

Emulating the Edison company's aggressive litigation strategy, Thomson-Houston decided in January 1887 to sue all manufacturers whose arc-lighting dynamo regulators infringed on Thomson's design. For Thomson, that decision meant that if he won the case, he would be recognized as the inventor of the moving-brush regulator, but it would require that he spend much time and energy in locating evidence, giving testimony, and building special models of both his regulator and those of his competitors. Although Thomson's success in that case helped weaken the Brush company's market position and thus led to the takeover of Brush by Thomson-Houston, the work involved in prosecuting the case kept Thomson away from invention and development.[52]

51 For the incandescent-lamp infringement case, see Hammond, *Men and Volts*, pp. 180–7. For Thomson advising the firm on possible infringements, see ET to T-H Electric Company, 28 November 1885, LB 8/85–3/86, p. 176, TP; and ET to CAC, 28 December 1888, LB 4/88–4/89, pp. 587–8, TP. Quotation is from ET to S. A. Barton, 27 March 1885, LB 5/83–8/85, p. 139, TP.

52 ET to F. P. Fish, 27 November 1886; ET to CAC, 25 January 1887; [notice of infringement], 26 January 1887, LB 9/86–3/87, pp. 107–9, 297–8, and 308, TP; ET to F. P. Fish, 21 November 1888, LB 4/88–4/89, p. 485, TP; Passer, *The Electrical Manufacturers*, p. 43.

244   Innovation as a social process: Elihu Thomson

In addition to attending to his own patents, Thomson evaluated patents offered for sale to the firm by outside inventors. Like other electrical firms, Thomson-Houston periodically purchased patents to supplement Thomson's work and to prevent valuable patents from falling into the hands of competitors. Often such patents could be purchased for only a few hundred dollars, which probably was far less than it would have cost to undertake the same research within the company. Deeply involved in formulating patent strategy, and knowledgeable about the current state of electrical technology, Thomson conscientiously studied the many patents forwarded to him by Barton and Coffin; as he explained in 1887, "I think, as electrician of the Company and one of its directors, that any purchase or arrangement for assignments of patents and inventions should include my judgement upon those inventions."[53] From 1884 to 1889, Thomson reviewed patents for storage batteries, motors, and incandescent lamps, all product areas that interested the Boston office as potential markets. Among the patents that he studied were several offered in 1888 by Nikola Tesla, the inventor who helped Westinghouse develop the first polyphase system of electrical distribution; Thomson considered Tesla's patents to be of such little value that they were not worth the required fees. In many cases Thomson advised against purchasing outside patents, finding them inferior to his own work.[54] However, he also may have rejected outside patents because he perceived them as a threat to his control of innovation within the company.

53 Quotation is from ET to CAC, 23 July 1887, LB 3/87–4/88, pp. 265–6, TP. For an example of another electrical firm relying on outside patents as its source of innovation, see Leonard S. Reich, "Industrial Research and the Pursuit of Corporate Security: The Early Years of Bell Labs," *Business History Review*, 54:504–29 (Winter 1980), especially pp. 508–9. See also ET to S. A. Barton, 29 December 1884, and ET to F. P. Fish, 2 April 1885, LB 5/83–8/85, pp. 107–8 and 144; ET to F. P. Fish, 24 October 1888, and ET to Prof. Geyer, 3 December 1888, LB 4/88–4/89, pp. 396 and 517–18; and ET to Herbert L. Harding, 1 April 1890, LB 1/90–11/90, pp. 354–5; all in TP.

54 Thomson's general attitude toward evaluating outside patents is summed up in the following quotation: "I hope that you will understand that I am not at all prejudiced in this matter, but that I look at the value of the patents through the substance which is in them, it being my general object to advise the purchase of any patent which is liable to strengthen us in any way." From ET to CAC, 1 November 1888, LB 4/88–4/89, pp. 425–6, TP. See also ET to Barton, 13 November 1884, LB 5/83–8/85, pp. 102–5; ET to CAC, 16 November 1885 and 19 January 1886, LB 8/85–3/86, pp. 159–60 and 230–3; ET to CAC, 5 May 1888, 13 November 1888, and 15 April 1889, LB 4/88–4/89, pp. 9, 463–5, and 991; ET to CAC, 9 November 1889, and ET to L. F. Smith, 25 October 1889, LB 4/89–1/90, pp. 686 and 607; all in TP.

Beyond advising the company on buying patents, Thomson further provided Coffin and other managers with advice on all sorts of technical matters. As the firm prepared to enter the incandescent-lighting market in 1884, Thomson offered his opinions about the strength of Edison's lamp patents, the advantages of his system compared with Edison's, and how Thomson-Houston should manufacture bulbs. He took a special interest in advising the firm about safety. For example, he became especially annoyed when workmen wired too many incandescent bulbs to his distributor box, thus raising the voltage and causing fires. At other times, he advised Thomson-Houston International on selling equipment in Europe, showing that he understood not only the intricacies of foreign patent laws but also how social and cultural differences required different marketing strategies. When managers needed help in deciding whether or not to enter the business of electrifying lighthouses or to light the Eiffel Tower, they turned to Thomson.[55] Just as Coffin and others helped Thomson recognize potential markets that needed inventions, so the inventor assisted the managers in comprehending the technical side of the business. Such advisory work distracted him from invention, but Thomson was willing to do it because it enhanced his status as the major technical authority in the firm.

Inventing new products, planning patent strategy, coping with patent litigation, evaluating outside patents, and giving advice kept Thomson and the Model Room staff busy. In fact, Thomson soon reported to Coffin that the Model Room was overworked. In 1884 and 1885, various inventions relating to the incandescent lighting system were delayed because he lacked skilled workmen, machine tools, or simply enough time to do all the necessary work. However, Thomson felt that he and the Model Room were especially overwhelmed during the regulator infringement suit. He wrote to Coffin in February 1888:

> My time, as you know, has been so broken up and rendered almost useless for other work by the amount of attention required in the regulator suit. So also have our model room facilities been strained to

55 ET to CAC, 8 March 1886, LB 3/86−2/89, pp. 1−5; ET to Barton, 13 and 20 August 1884, LB 5/83−8/85, pp. 73−5 and 76−9; ET to H. C. Townsend, 24 April 1885, LB 5/83−8/85, pp. 115−23; ET, "Remarks on the Townsend Report on Incandescent Lamps," 27 April 1885, and ET to T-H International Elec. Co., 28 July 1885, LB 5/83−8/85, pp. 157−64 and 210−11; ET to CAC, 3 November 1885, LB 8/85−3/86, pp. 125−7; ET to T-H International Co., 18 January 1887, LB 9/86−3/87, pp. 270−2; ET to CAC, 21 January 1885; ET to James Meech, 8 August 1888, LB 4/88−4/89, pp. 199−202; all in TP.

get out the necessary arrangements and try experiments in connection with the same, while I myself have been unable to follow the
work in the model room as closely as I could desire. We have on hand
now the development of arc light machines, the development of
alternating [current] apparatus and machines, the meter, motors,
railway motors and appliances, and I am of the opinion that much of
the work in each of these fields could be better done could one devote
the necessary time to stick to it until it was completed.[56]

In response to such complaints, Coffin periodically suggested that
Thomson expand the Model Room by hiring more assistants and
installing more machinery. In addition, Thomson regularly received
applications from inventors seeking employment with the company.
Although he had more work than he could handle, Thomson stead-
fastly refused to expand the Model Room or hire other inventors. If he
was so busy, why would he not want to enlarge his operation?

There are two probable reasons that Thomson took that position.
First, Thomson regarded the Model Room as his personal domain.[57]
It was his laboratory, and he wanted to run it in the manner that
best suited him. Because he could personally supervise only five or six
machinists, that was the limit on the size of the facility. Perhaps
recalling Churchill's suicide in New Britain, he was especially distressed by the prospect of other inventors, because he feared that
rivalry and "jealous feelings" would be counterproductive to invention. Indicative that the Model Room was Thomson's personal laboratory was that Rice was reluctant to interfere with its operation, even
though nominally it was part of the Lynn factory. For instance, only
when Thomson left for a long summer vacation in 1889 did Rice
investigate why the Model Room was encountering delays in securing patents, and he tried to remedy the situation by sending some
applications to lawyers other than Townsend.[58] In general, Thomson

56 Quotation is from ET to CAC, 21 February 1888, LB 3/87–4/88, pp. 867–9,
TP; see also ET to F. P. Fish, 12 July 1886, LB 3/86–9/86, pp. 177–8; ET to
F. P. Fish, 29 December 1887, LB 3/87–4/88, pp. 733–5; and ET to CAC, 8
August 1888, LB 4/88–4/89, p. 204; all in TP.

57 In the course of the regulator infringement case, Thomson made a remark that
suggests that he saw the Model Room as his personal domain; when asked to
make an extra model, he responded: "I have been away so much that the
model room here has practically slipped away from my control, and it would
only be possible to build that model by stopping all other work and giving the
matter my every day personal attention." From ET to F. P. Fish, 29 December
1887, LB 3/87–4/88, pp. 733–5, TP.

58 For Thomson's refusal to permit other inventors to work in his Model Room,
see ET to CAC, 18 June 1885, LB 5/83–8/85, pp. 6–8; ET to Edward E.

was highly protective of his Model Room, and he discouraged others from interfering with its operation. He had created a facility and staff that permitted him to invent on a regular basis, and he was reluctant to modify his operation to suit the whims of the marketing and manufacturing groups.

A second factor that explains the Model Room being overworked and understaffed is that such a situation gave Thomson a high degree of control over the direction of technological innovation within the firm. More than once, Thomson used the argument that his staff and workroom were overburdened as a tactic to discourage the company from introducing certain products. For instance, from 1884 to 1888 Coffin repeatedly asked Thomson to develop an electric motor that could be used on arc-lighting circuits. Initially, Thomson declined, arguing that motors constituted an irregular load that the arc dynamo's regulator could not control. When that technical argument failed to deter Coffin, however, Thomson simply informed him that the Model Room was too busy to work on motors. As long as Thomson's Model Room was the primary source of innovation for the firm, he was able to use that argument to limit the firm to development and manufacture of electrical equipment that would correspond to his business-technological mind-set.[59]

And what was Thomson's business-technological mind-set? How did he expect his inventions to contribute to the well-being of the company? Working with the Model Room staff, Thomson believed in building the best possible product. Seldom was he content with

Colby, 4 February 1886, LB 8/85–3/86, p. 261; ET to H. Haug, 22 May 1887, LB 82–99, p. 227; ET to CAC, 11 November 1887, LB 3/87–4/88, pp. 631–5; ET to C. J. Golmark, 25 July 1888, LB 4/88–4/89, p. 176; ET to CAC, 17 October 1889, LB 4/89–1/90, pp. 572–3; all in TP. For Rice's efforts to modify the processing of patent applications, see Rice to CAC, 5 June 1889, LB 4/89–1/90, p. 200, TP.

59 On Thomson's unwillingness to install motors on dc arc circuits, see ET to F. J. Sprague, 23 August 1884, LB 5/83–8/85, pp. 82–3; ET to CAC, 27 June 1888, LB 4/88–4/89, pp. 101–3; and ET to CAC, 21 February 1888, LB 3/87–4/88, pp. 867–9; all in TP. Thomson used the same tactic to control the design of meters and special arc lamps, to avoid having to make models for court cases, and to refuse to make demonstration apparatus; see ET to Geo. Cutter, 6 April 1886, ET to CAC, 28 June 1886, ET to T-H Electric Co., 23 August 1886, LB 3/86–9/86, pp. 33–5, 159–60, and 227–8; ET to CAC, 17 December 1889, LB 4/89–1/90, pp. 848–9; J. W. Gibboney to Ernst Thurnauer, 8 April 1890, and ET to C. R. Dean, 14 May 1890, LB 1/90–11/90, pp. 365 and 533; all in TP.

any halfhearted measures that responded only to the immediate opportunities of the marketplace. Rather, as he wrote in 1889,

> we admit, freely, the possibility of improvement in every possible direction. We are not contented to say that we have reached any ultimatum, but would be only too glad to work out results in new channels. In fact, we are doing that as far as our facilities permit.[60]

Thomson chose to design high-quality products because he found them personally and intellectually satisfying. He enjoyed finding elegant and efficient solutions to solve technical problems. Moreover, by being dedicated to regular improvement of the firm's products, Thomson ensured that he and the Model Room would have a continuing role to play in the company.

But beyond those reasons, Thomson was confident that the best product would, in the long run, capture the largest share of the market. Seeing that his arc lighting system sold well because it was efficient and reliable, the inventor strove to maximize similar characteristics in his other inventions. In 1890, Thomson phrased the importance of quality in capturing markets in the following way:

> In the development of any business it is attention to petty details of construction and designing which in the end tells ... yet there is an immense amount of it to be done, and I feel always that there is so much of it that we can not cover our points too quickly.[61]

What is significant about Thomson's outlook is that it was not shared by all groups within Thomson-Houston. As suggested earlier, the marketing and manufacturing teams had their own distinctive mind-sets regarding how the firm should operate. In particular, the various groups had quite different expectations regarding the role that product innovation should play in the firm's strategy. In sum, the management of Thomson-Houston was hardly monolithic, but rather was made up of several groups, each with its own mind-set.

60 ET to S. C. Peck, 25 April 1889, LB 4/89–1/90, p. 101, TP.
61 ET to Robert P. Clapp, 19 April 1890, LB 1/90–11/90, pp. 428–30, TP. Although Passer considered Thomson to be an "imitative" rather than "pioneer" entrepreneur, he did note that Thomson was sensitive to the marketplace, that he emphasized efficiency and reliability in his designs, and that he was good at avoiding patent disputes. In summary, he considered Thomson to be "an outstanding electrical engineer, and he could usually design equipment superior to that already on the market." See *The Electrical Manufacturers*, p. 192.

Technological innovation at Thomson-Houston: the ac lighting system, 1885–90

Having outlined the marketing strategy and the functional structure of Thomson-Houston, let us now consider how Thomson pursued product innovation within the firm. As a case study, I shall narrate how Thomson developed an ac system for incandescent lighting. That system was vital to the company's marketing strategy because it permitted Thomson-Houston to compete directly with Westinghouse and Edison for a new segment of the central-station market, namely, small cities and towns. In the course of telling the story of this system, we shall see how the process of innovation at Thomson-Houston was strongly influenced by its organizational structure; in particular, we shall see how the design of the system was determined by the interactions of the three groups within the firm.

As described in Chapter 2, Thomson had been fascinated by alternating current from the outset of his career as an inventor. In 1878, Thomson had built, with Edwin J. Houston, a set of arc lights and a dynamo that employed alternating current and induction coils. The purpose of the induction coils was to render each lamp in a series circuit independent. In that way, Thomson and Houston solved the problem of subdividing the electric light; previously, electrical inventors had been able to run only one large arc light from a single dynamo, but they were able to use their dynamo to power several smaller lights. The two men drew up patent applications for that series arrangement in November 1878, as well as for a similar circuit using induction coils in parallel in January 1879 (see Figure 2.23). Because of others' prior work with induction coils, however, their November patent application was rejected by the Patent Office, and they never bothered to file their January application. More important, though, Thomson and Houston soon set their ac system aside when Garrett and McCollin offered to fund a dc lighting system similar to Brush's successful version.

After beginning work at the Lynn facility, Thomson found time to review his work with induction coils and to sketch several new systems. At first, Thomson planned to use induction coils with arc lamps to render each lamp independent and to save power when a nonworking lamp was shunted out of the circuit. However, because Coffin and Barton were anxious to market an incandescent system to compete

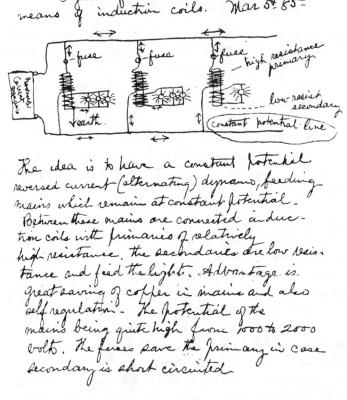

System of Electric Distribution by
means of induction coils. Mar 5th 85 -

The idea is to have a constant potential
reversed current (alternating) dynamo, feeding
mains which remain at constant potential.
Between these mains are connected induction coils with primaries of relatively
high resistance, the secondaries are low resistance and feed the lights. Advantage is.
great saving of copper in mains and also
self regulation. The potential of the
mains being quite high from 1000 to 2000
volts. The fuses save the primary in case
secondary is short circuited.

Figure 5.15. Sketch by Thomson showing induction coils with primaries in parallel, March 1885. From W. J. Foster, "Early Days in
Alternator Design," *General Electric Review,* 23:80–90 (February
1920), p. 80.

with Edison, Thomson began thinking about using induction coils
with incandescent lamps instead of arc lights. Like other inventors, he
sensed that it would be desirable to develop a system of distribution
whereby power could be transmitted to incandescent lights over distances greater than one or two miles, then the physical limit for existing dc systems. Because of that limitation, incandescent dc stations
were erected only in towns and cities with sufficient population density
to pay for the costs of installing large copper mains. To overcome those
difficulties, in March 1885 Thomson sketched an ac system using
induction coils with their primary windings in parallel, a system that
would step the voltage down from 1,000 to 110 volts (Figure 5.15).

The advantage of using the higher voltage was that it permitted efficient transmission of power over long distances. Thomson also included several safety devices to minimize the danger of electrocution from the high voltage. On the primary or high-voltage side of the transformer he inserted a fuse, and on the secondary or low-voltage side he added a ground connection. In case of a short circuit between the primary and secondary coils, that ground connection would conduct the high-voltage current away from the electric lights. Inclusion of such safety devices was part of Thomson's business-technological mind-set: Build a system that was both reliable and not harmful to the customer.[62]

In designing that system in early 1885, Thomson was not especially concerned with introducing it commercially; rather, he considered the invention as one of several projects that he might pursue in his Model Room. Along with a new constant-voltage dynamo and a distributor box for putting incandescent lamps on arc circuits, the induction-coil scheme was one of several plans Thomson had for introducing incandescent lights to the firm's product line.

Curiously, he did not file a patent application for that parallel circuit, but instead filed for a series arrangement[63] (Figure 5.16). He may have chosen such a circuit because two inventors in England, John Gibbs and Lucien Gaulard, were testing a series system at that time, but he seems to have been unaware of their work. Similarly, Thomson had not learned of the ac system being built by Zipernowsky, Blathy, and Deri (ZBD) in Hungary. Unlike the Gaulard-Gibbs circuit, the ZBD system featured transformers whose primary coils were connected in parallel to the generator. Those developments, however, did

62 W. J. Foster, "Early Days in Alternator Design," *GE Rev.*, 23:80–90 (February 1920), especially p. 81; "System of Electric Distribution by means of induction coils, Mar 5. 85," Exhibit No. 12, "Testimony on behalf of Elihu Thomson and Edwin J. Houston . . . ," Patent Interference No. 13,761 (subject: transformer distribution systems), Hall of History Collection, p. 307; ET, "Induction Apparatus Interf. with Gravier" (July–August 1884); and ET to H. C. Townsend, 10 April 1885, LB 5/83–8/85, pp. 65–7 and 110–12; ET to J. A. Fleming, 12 October 1885, LB 8/85–3/86, pp. 82–3; ET to Townsend & MacArthur, 6 January 1887, LB 9/86–3/87, p. 223; all in TP.

63 [ET], "System of Electric Distribution," 7 April 1885, and "Improvements in Systems of Electric Distribution," 9 April 1885 (patent applications); ET to H. C. Townsend, 20 April 1885, LB 5/83–8/85, pp. 90–109 and 150–4, TP; "Elihu Thomson's System of Electric Distribution," *Telegraphic Journal and Electrical Review*, 17:366–8 (31 October 1885).

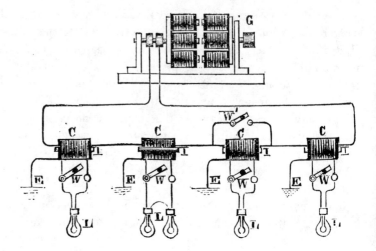

Figure 5.16. Drawing depicting Thomson's plan for using transformers in series, 1885. From "Elihu Thomson's System of Electric Distribution," *Telegraphic Journal and Electrical Review,* 17:366–8 (31 October 1885), p. 366.

impress Coffin, who saw the ZBD system on display in Europe during the summer of 1885. Although Coffin always claimed that he knew nothing of the intricacies of electrical technology, he quickly learned from the ZBD system that alternating current could be used to build central stations in smaller cities and towns. On his return, he urged Thomson to pursue his work with induction coils and to file additional patent applications for parallel circuits as soon as possible.[64]

Through late 1885 and early 1886, Thomson designed and tested an ac system (Figure 5.17). He directed his efforts toward developing a system of self-regulating transformers with their primaries in parallel.

64 For a discussion of the work of Gibbs and Gaulard and Zipernowsky, Blathy, and Deri, see Hughes, *Networks of Power,* pp. 86–98. For an early description of the ZBD system, see "Alternating Electric-Current Machines," *Electrical World,* 3:173–4 (31 May 1884). For Coffin's interest in European developments, see ET to G. Cutter, 7 October 1885, LB 8/85–3/86, pp. 76–80, TP; and ET to H. C. Townsend, 23 October 1885, LB 83–11/85, pp. 249–50, TP. On learning of the ZBD system, Thomson wrote to several people and claimed that the ZBD system was a duplicate of the one he had sketched in 1879; see ET to C. J. Wharton, 21 September 1885, ET to EJH [28 September–3 October 1885], ET to Laing, Wharton & Down, 15 October 1885, and ET to EJH, 17 October 1885, LB 8/85–3/86, pp. 35–7, 55–6, 93–4, and 103, TP.

Figure 5.17. Thomson's first ac generator, 1885. This machine was used to light Factory B of the Lynn works in 1886. From the Thomson Collection, General Electric Hall of History, Schenectady.

Because safety was to be an important feature of his system, he continued to improve the designs of the fuses and other safety devices. By June 1886, an experimental ac power line was run between two buildings at the Lynn plant to deliver current to incandescent lamps. By the year's end, the company was advertising ac generators in its catalog, emphasizing that it could furnish power to incandescent lights over long distances using wires that were smaller than those used in dc systems. Although the catalog described four generator models, none had actually been sold or installed[65] (Figure 5.18). From an organizational perspective, work went forward on the ac system because two interest groups agreed that it was a worthwhile project: Thomson's development group had already done preliminary work in the area, and Coffin's marketing group had decided that an ac system would help them reach new customers.

In the meantime, however, George Westinghouse was making progress in developing his own ac system for incandescent lighting. Whereas Thomson-Houston relied on a single inventor and his staff for

65 ET, "Electric Induction Apparatus," 11 June 1886, LB 3/86–2/89, pp. 168–72; ET to CAC, 5 February 1887, LB 9/86–3/87, pp. 334–7; ET to Townsend & MacArthur, 6 January 1887, LB 9/86–3/87, p. 223; ET to Townsend & MacArthur, 1 and 19 March 1888, LB 3/87–4/88, pp. 884 and 921–2, all in TP; "Extracts (or summaries) of testimony in patent infringement suit of General Electric Co vs Butler Company," Hammond File, J457–9; "Catalogue of Parts of Apparatus Manufactured by the Thomson-Houston Electric Co. . . . ," 1886, MIT Archives.

Figure 5.18. Thomson-Houston ac generator, production version, 1886. The smaller dc dynamo to the right was used to excite the field coils of the ac machine. From "Catalogue of Parts of Apparatus Manufactured by the Thomson-Houston Electric Co. . . ." (1886), p. 173. Thomson Collection, M.I.T. Archives, Cambridge.

development, Westinghouse drew from two different sources of innovation. First, with the help of Frank L. Pope, an independent consulting engineer, he purchased the American rights to the Gaulard-Gibbs system. Second, Westinghouse supported William Stanley's research aimed at improving the transformer, which led to a successful demonstration of ac distribution in March 1886 in Great Barrington, Massachusetts. Westinghouse engineers followed up Stanley's success by redesigning the transformer during the summer of 1886. By intensively funding development in that way, Westinghouse was able to install its first ac system in Buffalo in November 1886 in a preexisting Brush station.[66]

66 Frank L. Pope, in discussion of "The Distribution of Electricity by Secondary Generators," *Telegraphic Journal and Electrical Review*, 19:349–54 (15 April 1887), especially p. 349; Hughes, *Networks of Power*, pp. 98–105; E. W. Rice, Jr., "Missionaries of Science," *GE Rev.*, 32:355–61 (July 1929); Bernard A. Drew and Gerard Chapman, "William Stanley Lighted a Town and Powered an Industry," *Berkshire History*, 6:1–36 (Fall 1985), esp. pp. 7–19; George Wise, "William Stanley's Search for Immortality," *American Heritage of Invention and Technology*, 4:42–9 (Spring–Summer 1988).

Westinghouse gained an important advantage over Thomson-Houston by securing a broad patent for an ac distribution system with transformers in parallel. Strangely enough, Westinghouse's claims for that system were based on the series-circuit work of Gaulard and Gibbs. In contrast, all of Thomson's patent applications for ac distribution were rejected in the fall of 1886. That put the Thomson-Houston Company in the defensive position of having to contest or else bypass the Westinghouse patent.[67]

Thomson responded to the Westinghouse patent for ac distribution by filing additional applications based on his early work with induction coils and arc lamps. Thomson submitted those applications not only to claim what he thought he had previously invented but also to "render it inconvenient for rivals to get around them."[68] In addition, he continued to experiment in the Model Room with different circuit configurations, hoping to find a way to circumvent the Westinghouse patent.

Nonetheless, by early 1887 Coffin and the marketing group were beginning to wonder if perhaps the Model Room was not working fast enough. Why was Westinghouse already installing ac equipment, and Thomson-Houston was not? Had not Thomson been working on patent applications for several months before Westinghouse had even ordered a Gaulard-Gibbs transformer from Europe? In February 1887, Thomson admitted to Coffin that work on the ac system was proceeding slowly. First, Thomson explained that although they had been working as rapidly as possible, "the development of the system had outgrown the model room, which is only adapted to producing small models and nothing of very large size." Thomson would have drawn

67 L. Gaulard and J. D. Gibbs, " System of Electrical Distribution," U.S. Patent 351,589 (26 October 1886); Rankin Kennedy, "Electrical Distribution by Alternating Currents and Transformers," *Telegraphic Journal and Electrical Review*, 19:346–7 (15 April 1887); " Specification of Elihu Thomson, Lynn, Mass. Distribution of Electric Currents," 9 October 1886, LB 3/86–2/89, pp. 232–40, TP; ET to T-H Elec. Co., 28 September 1886, ET to Townsend & MacArthur, 19 November 1886, ET to H. N. Batchelder, 8 December 1886, and ET to Townsend & MacArthur, 10 December 1886, LB 9/86–3/ 87, pp. 18–19, 95–6, 133–4, and 141, TP.

68 Quotation is from ET to CAC, 5 February 1887, LB 9/86–3/87, pp. 334–7, TP. See also ET to H. C. Townsend, 9 November 1886, LB 3/86–2/89, pp. 241–3, TP; ET to Townsend & MacArthur, 23 November 1886, ET to Townsend & MacArthur, 21 January 1887, and ET to EJH, 18 February 1887, LB 9/86–3/87, pp. 103, 279–81, and 376–7, TP.

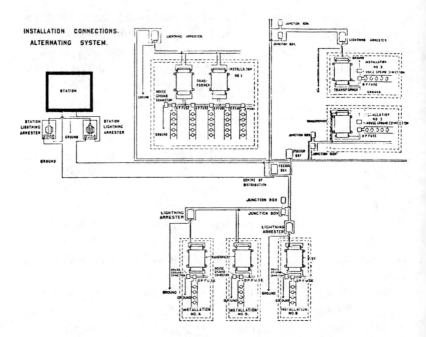

Figure 5.19. Circuit diagram for Thomson-Houston ac incandescent system showing location of various safety components, circa 1889. From "The Thomson-Houston Alternating Current System" (catalog, circa 1889), p. 36. Thomson Collection, M.I.T. Archives, Cambridge.

on the resources of the factory as a whole, but at that point the production department was overwhelmed with filling back-orders. In other words, manufacturing was too busy to help development. But rather than simply blame manufacturing, Thomson offered a second revealing reason: He was determined to introduce a complete ac system, with generators, regulators, lamps, transformers, and safety devices all matched to each other, and designing such a system would take time (Figure 5.19). He believed that an ac system designed as a single entity would be the most reliable; to quote him again, "when we enter this field we wish to . . . be sure of success from the start with a complete and economical system, and the preparatory work that we have done will, we think, tell in the end." [69] Here is a clear statement

69 ET to CAC, 5 February 1887, and ET to E. F. Peck, 22 March 1887, LB 9/86–3/87, pp. 334–7 and 470–1, TP.

of Thomson's belief that the best-designed product will in the long run be the most profitable.

In terms of group dynamics, the situation had progressed to the point that marketing was mistrustful of development, and the development group responded with a statement of its goals. The situation might have deteriorated further, but Thomson improved matters by adjusting his technology to the marketing strategy. Rather than insist that innovation could proceed only in one direction (i.e., toward a technically perfect system), Thomson redirected his efforts so as to improve the company's short-term marketing position.

To reduce the threat of patent litigation, Thomson helped the company arrange a patent-sharing agreement with Westinghouse. During a meeting of the American Institute of Electrical Engineers in March 1887, Thomson met with Pope and discussed the desirability of cooperating rather than competing in the ac field. After several meetings, officials from Thomson-Houston and Westinghouse reached an agreement in August 1887. In return for a license to sell Thomson-Houston arc lighting equipment, Westinghouse allowed Thomson-Houston to manufacture ac systems without fear of infringing the Westinghouse ac distribution patent. Although that agreement was terminated within two years because the Westinghouse patent was ruled invalid in court, it did give Thomson-Houston time in 1887 and 1888 to improve its ac equipment.[70]

Knowing that a patent-sharing agreement could be only a temporary expedient, Thomson next initiated a new patent strategy to bypass the Westinghouse patent. Because Westinghouse controlled the right to the broad principle of using transformers for distribution, Thomson filed for patents on the designs of the most efficient transformers. Thus, the Westinghouse company would be unable to utilize its rights to apply the broad principle, because all of the best transformer designs would be owned by Thomson-Houston. In pursuing that strategy, Thomson filed patents for transformers with laminated cores of different shapes, and he began using an oil insulation bath[71] (Figure 5.20).

70 Frank L. Pope to ET, 23 March 1887, CL; ET to CAC, 24 March 1887, LB 3/87–4/88, p. 1, TP; Passer, *The Electrical Manufacturers,* pp. 145–7.

71 ET to Townsend & MacArthur, 18 January 1887, LB 9/86–3/87, pp. 265–6, TP; ET to CAC, 20 November 1889, LB 4/89–1/90, pp. 729–30, TP; Walter S. Moody to J. W. Hammond, 15 April 1927, Hammond File, L2598–9.

OUT-DOOR TRANSFORMER   STATION TRANSFORMER

Figure 5.20. Thomson-Houston transformers, circa 1889. From "The Thomson-Houston Alternating Current System" (catalog, circa 1889), p. 36. Thomson Collection, M.I.T. Archives, Cambridge.

Still another way in which Thomson directed invention toward short-term marketing needs was through the exploitation of what he called "the principle of induction-repulsion." In 1886 Thomson discovered how a magnetic field created by an alternating current passing through an electromagnet could be used to create rotary motion. Excited by that discovery, Thomson utilized it to develop an ac motor and improved measuring instruments. One especially important product derived by Thomson from the induction-repulsion principle was the recording wattmeter, which allowed for accurate measurement of the electricity consumed by individual customers. In staking out his claims for those inventions, Thomson emphasized that he had discovered a principle, in the belief it could provide the company with general control over the applications derived from it. Over the next two years, Thomson perfected those inventions, giving Thomson-Houston new ac products that helped it gain a share of the market.[72]

72 [ET], "Specification – Alternating Current Motor Device," 22 December 1886, LB 3/86–2/89, pp. 265–76; ET to G. Cutter, 17 December 1886, and ET to CAC, 5 February 1887, LB 9/96–3/87, pp. 163–7 and 334–7, TP; ET, "Novel Phenomena of Alternating Currents," *Electrical Engineer*, 6:211–15 (June 1887); H. G. Hamann and F. G. Vaughen, "Developmental work by Prof. Thomson on Electric Meters," Biographical Materials; [ET], "Specification [for liquid electric meter]," 14 October 1887, LB 3/86–2/89, pp. 19–36; ET to CAC, 12 March 1888, LB 3/87–4/88, p. 913; J. W. Gib-

Thomson began to redirect his development work toward short-term marketing needs in early 1887 and pursued that approach into 1889. Early on, Thomson's efforts began to pay off. In May 1887 the firm shipped its first ac machine to the Lynn Electric Lighting Company, and by the year's end it had installed 22 more systems. The first Thomson-Houston ac systems were installed in smaller cities, such as New Rochelle, Kansas City, Putnam, Connecticut, and Syracuse, New York, where the population density was too low to offset the initial cost of a dc incandescent system. Anxious to show his confidence in the new system and to have a full-scale circuit on which to test new devices, Thomson installed in his home in Lynn one of the new transformers and incandescent lamps. Because of his concern with safety, he employed in his home all of the safety devices he had created – the grounded secondary coils, fuses, and lightning arresters. (To save money, at his home Thomson used bulbs that had been rejected at the factory.) He offered to promote the completed ac lighting system by writing an article for *Electrical World,* but he did so asking "whether my time would be more valuable to the Company employed on new work and in new fields rather than in describing apparatus and arrangements that are comparatively old with us."[73]

As Thomson directed the work of the Model Room to suit the needs and expectations of Coffin and the marketing team, he proposed that marketing help implement some of his ideals. In particular, Thomson was anxious to see that his notions about the safe use of alternating current be implemented. Maintaining that the best system was a safe system, Thomson remarked that "I am a believer in the establishment

boney to S. C. Peck, 26 October 1889, pp. 611–12; all in TP. I am not claiming that Thomson was the first to invent either the ac motor or the wattmeter; other inventors, such as Nikola Tesla and Oliver Shallenberger, may well have preceded Thomson in those areas. My point is simply that Thomson recognized the importance of developing those components and that he worked on them so as to give Thomson-Houston a strong position in the ac field.

73 13 June 1887, LB 3/87–4/88, pp. 163–4, TP. The first Thomson-Houston ac incandescent plants are from "List of T-H Plants." Descriptions of ac lighting used in Thomson's home can be found in ET to Chas. C. Fry, 7 October 1887, and ET to Prof. S. W. Holman, 21 October 1887, LB 3/87–4/88, pp. 522–3 and 572–5, TP; ET to Lynn Elec. Lighting Co., 8 May 1888, LB 4/88–4/89, pp. 13–14, TP; J. A. McManus, memorandum, 6 March 1936, Hall of History Collection; ET, "Systems of Electric Distribution," *Scientific American Supplement,* No. 603 (23 July 1887), pp. 9632–4.

of all safeguards which conduce to the good working of a system, especially when they do not add greatly to the cost of making the installation." More than just fulfilling his technological idealism, Thomson was confident that his safety inventions should be part of the marketing strategy used to fight Westinghouse. Once Westinghouse's broad patent for transformer distribution had been ruled invalid, Thomson suggested that all central stations using Thomson-Houston ac equipment be fitted with the latest safety devices. The company should then emphasize in its advertisements how safe its installations were in comparison with the Westinghouse plants. As a result of adverse publicity, Westinghouse would then be forced to install safety equipment as well. Because Thomson-Houston controlled the patents for the best safety features, Thomson believed that such a strategy would block Westinghouse from acquiring a larger share of the market for alternating current.[74]

As Thomson soon learned, the difficulty with his plan was that it presumed that Thomson-Houston would encourage its customers to install safety devices. Unfortunately, that was hardly the case in 1889. Instead, it appears that Thomson-Houston customers frequently ignored safety equipment and careful installation procedures in the rush to get "on line." Pushed by investors to begin selling electricity as soon as possible in order to make a return on the capital invested, utility operators were forced to keep their construction and installation costs to a minimum. Utilities did not always purchase all the necessary safety accessories; they used poorly insulated wire, and their linemen often were careless and indifferent to the special requirements of alternating current. To get more lights on circuit, central-station operators often placed two dynamos on the same line, even though the insulation of the conductors was insufficient for handling the increased voltage. Although Thomson realized that such poor practices were influenced by the competitiveness of the electric-lighting field, they nonetheless offended his mind-set. "I do not believe in this kind of economy," he warned Coffin. "Rather it would be better not to have the business than incur the risks which are thus involved."[75] As an inventor, Thom-

---

74 Quotation is from ET to T. F. Gaynor, 7 March 1888, LB 3/87–4/88, pp. 900–1, TP. See also ET to CAC, 11 December 1888, LB 4/88–4/89, pp. 547–50, TP.
75 Quotation is from ET to CAC, 13 February 1889, LB 4/88–4/89, pp. 761–6, TP. See also ET to CAC, 16 February 1889, LB 4/88–4/89, pp. 780–2; ET to John J. Moore, 19 October 1889, LB 4/89–1/90, pp. 594–6; ET to Narra-

son would have liked to have had control of his creations from the initial conception to the final installation, but he soon realized that the marketing group was unwilling or unable to help him accomplish that. In that situation, although Thomson and the development group had adjusted their efforts to suit marketing's short-term interests, marketing failed to reciprocate by promoting development's ideas about safety.

In failing to endorse Thomson's ideas about safety, the marketing group soon discovered that it had lost a key ally needed for fighting in the ac–dc controversy. Lasting from 1886 to 1895, that controversy involved the question whether or not ac systems should supplant dc systems, and it was a debate that soon included not simply technical matters but political and emotional issues as well. The controversy became particularly heated in 1888 as it became clear that ac systems could be used to supply incandescent lighting to small cities and towns lacking the population density needed to support a low-voltage dc system. Unable to compete with Westinghouse and Thomson-Houston for that market, the Edison Electric Light Company decided to challenge the ac system by questioning its safety. The higher voltages required for efficient transmission by alternating current, argued the Edison Company, were more likely to cause injury and death. To demonstrate the danger of ac systems, the Edison interests allied themselves with Harold P. Brown, who electrocuted animals in public demonstrations and wrote articles denouncing ac systems. Brown's greatest coup was in arranging for alternating current to be used in the first public execution by electricity in 1890. Prior to securing surreptitiously a Westinghouse generator to power the electric chair, Brown had tried to purchase from Thomson-Houston a 1,000-volt ac generator. Although Coffin was willing to sell Brown the machine, Thomson warned against it. Thomson not only was concerned about the negative publicity of the sale but also was worried that 1,000 volts would not be enough to kill a person quickly and "humanely."[76]

gansett Elec. Light Co., 22 April 1890, LB 1/90–11/90, pp. 443–4; all in TP; ET, "Insulation and Installation of Wires and Construction of Plant," *Electrical Engineer*, 7:90–1 (March 1888).

76 Hughes, *Networks of Power*, pp. 106–9; Passer, *The Electrical Manufacturers*, pp. 164–75; Roger Neustadter, "The Murderer and the Dynamo: Social Responses to the First Legal Electrocution in America" (paper presented to the Popular Culture Association, 1984); [Harold P. Brown] to Spencer Aldrich, 6 February 1889, LB 4/88–4/89, pp. 771–4, TP; ET to CAC, 16 May 1889, Collected Letters, TP.

Along with their willingness to sell to Brown, by the summer of 1889 Coffin and the marketing group were anxious to participate in the ac–dc debate. In all likelihood, they saw it as an opportunity to surpass their two rivals, Edison and Westinghouse. Defensively, they also may have been concerned that the publicity about "deadly" alternating current might harm sales, and they wanted to reassure customers that it was safe to buy Thomson-Houston equipment. Because the company was already manufacturing safety equipment, all that would be necessary for a strong position in the debate would be to have a leading authority promote the general use of alternating current. Given his established interest in electrical safety, Thomson was the obvious choice for that public-relations effort.

In October 1889, Coffin asked Thomson to write an article titled "How to Make Electricity Safe." Along with addressing the general issue of the safety of alternating current, Coffin wanted Thomson to provide a defense for ac power in the wake of an accident that had recently occurred at a utility in New York City. The utility had been using a Thomson-Houston ac system, and it was short-circuited when a telephone wire fell across the 1,000-volt power lines. Much to Coffin's dismay, Thomson turned down the assignment. The utility had done a poor job of installing its ac equipment, and Thomson felt that he could not personally defend such work. Unsafe installation was unacceptable to Thomson, and what was more, Thomson-Houston would not have been in that unfortunate defensive position had they listened to Thomson some months earlier.[77]

At first, Thomson simply suggested that he should remain quiet rather than be "a stumbling block in the way of the Company's business transactions." However, when Coffin pressed for a general endorsement of alternating current, Thomson exploded. In anger, he informed Coffin that he felt like quitting, because "my position with the Company has no attractions for me if my ideas of what is needed to constitute good substantial work are not followed but personally neglected." In a letter written on Christmas Eve 1889, he advised Coffin that the firm would have to recognize that he was primarily an inventor and would not be distracted by writing articles for publicity purposes. With respect to the safety of alternating current, he refused to give a blanket endorsement. "I have no method," he wrote,

77 [A. C. Bernheim] to CAC, 16 October 1889, and ET to CAC, 6 November 1889, LB 4/89–1/90, pp. 589 and 658–61, TP.

I have no panacea – for all the ills which may follow the use of high potential currents under conditions usually found in large cities. I can no more say how to make electricity safe in such cases than I can say how to make railroad travel safe, or how to make steamship travel safe, or how to make the use of illuminating gas safe, nor the use of steam boilers safe. No improvement of our modern civilization has ever been introduced but that involved considerable risk.[78]

Because he had designed the ac system, Thomson knew well the risks involved in using it. He had made it one of his principles that the best system was a safe system. But when he found that the marketing group was interested only in promoting safety as a short-term, defensive measure, he refused to cooperate. They had not been willing to adapt marketing policy to his technological goals, and so he was unwilling to compromise his principles about safety. As a result, the Thomson-Houston Company took no public position in the ac–dc controversy, leaving the debate to be settled by Edison and Westinghouse.[79]

Viewed in terms of the clashing of group interests, it is easy to see why Thomson and the development group refused to help Coffin and marketing. Yet why did Thomson fail to subordinate his ideas about safety for the greater good of the company? Had he not done that earlier in 1887 with his notion of a complete system? The answers to these questions involve several additional developments that informed his relationships within the firm.

First, Thomson was finding it difficult to work with the manufacturing and engineering groups. Previously, although they had been unable to help him with the development work in early 1887, they had, for the most part, been willing to manufacture ac equipment according to Thomson's designs. However, by 1889 the firm's business was rapidly growing and expanding into the new field of electric trolleys; as a result, the factory mushroomed in size, and the tasks of coordinating production became immense. In particular, manufacturing was overwhelmed by the challenge of building and installing equipment for the West End Railway in Boston, the largest electrical construction project

78 First quotation is from ET to CAC, 19 October 1889; second quotation from ET to CAC, 20 December 1889; third quotation from ET to CAC, 24 December 1889; in LB 4/89–1/90, pp. 579–83, 867–78, and 903–8, TP.

79 Thomson-Houston's nonparticipation in the ac–dc controversy is sometimes credited to Coffin, who chose not to enter the public debate and instead concentrated on selling systems. See, for example, David O. Woodbury, *Beloved Scientist: Elihu Thomson, A Guiding Spirit of the Electrical Age* (New York: Whittlesey House, 1944; reprinted Cambridge, Mass.: Harvard University Press, 1960), pp. 173–4.

undertaken up to that time. To fill that $3-million contract, Rice and his staff had to erect several new factory buildings. Such major changes made the production engineers quite cautious about modifying and improving other products, because that would mean more confusion in the factory. Modifications might well mean that manufacturing costs would go up and reduce profits. Production's conservative outlook soon became apparent to Thomson, as when he tried to introduce an improved transformer design in mid-1889. Manufacturing turned it down on the grounds that the new form would cost more to make than the old version, an argument with which Thomson had to agree. Nonetheless, he was disturbed by the event in that it signaled that it was becoming more difficult to introduce the minor improvements that would ensure that the company was manufacturing the best possible system.[80]

A second issue that concerned Thomson was that patent litigation was distracting him from working on new inventions. By 1889, Thomson had filed 375 patent applications, but that output had also led to a sizable amount of litigation. By the end of that year, he had been named in over 60 interference cases, many of which required extensive testimony. In addition, Thomson-Houston was actively suing firms that had infringed Thomson's automatic-regulator patent, making it necessary for him to testify frequently. Thomson became so disgusted with the regulator suits that, in an outburst, he remarked that "I almost wish that I had never seen the regulator at times, especially as there seems to be no limits to the demands on my time and opportunities which may follow out of it." Accustomed to having Thomson assist them with the infringement litigation, the Thomson-Houston lawyers soon began using him as an expert witness in other cases. Although Thomson understood the importance of defending his patents, he came to question his participation in litigation, as it took him away from invention. Eventually he informed Coffin that he

---

80 Thomson summed up his difficulties in introducing new inventions as follows: "The more our facilities grow the harder it seems to be to get through any special work of a new character, simply because we have no department that is absolutely set aside for this kind of work outside of the model department." From ET to S. C. Peck, 30 August 1889, LB 4/89–1/90, p. 422, TP. See also ET to J. S. Bell, 21 January 1888, LB 3/87–4/88, pp. 791–2, TP; ET to T. C. Martin, 16 August 1889, and ET to F. P. Fish, 1 October 1889, LB 4/89–1/90, pp. 363–5 and 502–4, TP; "Recollections of L. G. Banker," Hammond File, J677–83.

would no longer testify. "If I am to act as *inventor* for the Company," he wrote,

> I shall not hold myself in readiness to be called upon as patent expert and handy man ... for the more I invent, the more will my inventions ... embarrass me in the future. ... [It] is simply wasting my time to have to do ... patent expert work.[81]

More than his difficulties with manufacturing or the troublesome patent litigation, Thomson was troubled by a third issue in 1889: his role within the company. As the preceding quotation indicates, Thomson saw himself as the firm's chief inventor. Many of Thomson-Houston's products were his handiwork, and his creative efforts had yielded handsome profits for the firm. Yet, there were signs that Thomson might be losing his position as chief innovator. Beginning in 1888, Thomson was joined in the Model Room by other inventors who came to Lynn as their companies were bought out by Thomson-Houston. Although Thomson was nominally in charge of their work, he may have been worried that his own inventions would no longer be highly valued by management.[82]

In addition to the output of those new inventors, Coffin and the marketing group began to purchase more outside patents in 1888. As mentioned earlier, Thomson intensely opposed that policy, and in 1888 and 1889 he approved the purchase of only a few patents. His opposition appears to have been based on fear that such a policy would jeopardize his control over innovations within the firm. Not only might the company no longer need him, but also it was allowing others to dilute the firm's product line with worthless items. One questionable patent purchased by the company in 1889 was for "electric water." When he learned that the company planned to test that substance, Thomson was enraged. He wrote the Boston office: "If our Company should go seriously to work to expend any money in making tests ... I should feel like resigning on the spot. I have plenty of

---

81 Quotations are from ET to CAC, 24 December 1889, LB 4/89–1/90, pp. 903–8, TP. See also ET to Capt. E. Griffin, 9 October 1888, LB 4/88– 4/89, p. 374; ET to Ernst Thurnauer, 26 October 1889, and ET to T-H International Electric Co., 4 January 1890, LB 4/89–1/90, pp. 613 and 945; all in TP.

82 Along with Thomson, Rice, A. L. Rohrer, Wightman, Lemp, Van Depoele, and Priest filed patents in 1889; see J. W. Gibboney to Bentley & Knight, 6 June 1890, LB 1/90–11/90, p. 597, TP.

material which I do not have the opportunity to work up."[83] The purchase of outside patents and the arrival of other inventors must have suggested to Thomson that other members of the firm were implicitly challenging his control over innovation.

Disappointed with the production group, tired of the patent litigation, and worried about his position as chief innovator, Thomson was in no mood to compromise his business-technological mind-set in the fall of 1889, especially as it related to the subject of safety. He had cooperated fully in the rapid introduction of the ac system and other products, only to find that other groups did not respect his efforts and authority. In fact, he even perceived them as undercutting his "power base" within the firm.

Even after his angry Christmas Eve letter, it took some time for Thomson-Houston managers to realize that Thomson expected to be treated better. During the first months of 1890, the inventor refused to evaluate any outside patents or to serve as an expert witness in court. Furthermore, Thomson expressed his anger by not writing to Coffin for nearly two months, even though previously they had corresponded nearly every day. Instead of coming in early and staying late at the Model Room, he spent more time at home and worked only half-days. Using those tactics, Thomson communicated how he wanted his role within the firm to change.

Sensing Thomson's unwillingness to handle certain kinds of work, the Boston office assigned routine product improvement to the engineering staff in the manufacturing group, and they established a legal department in 1891 for handling patent matters.[84] In the summer of 1890, Thomson replaced his contract with an informal agreement with Coffin by which he was permitted to work on projects of his own choosing, as well as those needed by marketing or production. Under that agreement, Thomson continued to develop products, but he also looked for opportunities to direct his work toward scientific and professional goals. Although he filed for patents for improved transformers and

83 Quotation is from ET to Robert C. Clapp, 23 October 1889, LB 4/89–1/90, pp. 602–3, TP. See also ET to Fish, 1 October 1889, and ET to Capt. E. Griffin, 21 February 1890, LB 1/90–11/90, pp. 185–7, TP.
84 See ET to Robert P. Clapp, 11 January 1890, LB 4/89–1/90, pp. 991–2; ET to Capt. E. Griffin, 3 March 1890, and ET to Robert P. Clapp, 29 April 1890, LB 1/90–11/90, pp. 220–2 and 468, TP. For the absence of letters from Thomson to CAC, see the first 175 pages of LB 1/90–11/90, TP. For the new patent department, see "Testimony for Thomson," Intf. 15,511, p. 99.

electric welding equipment, Thomson also conducted research and published articles on high-frequency and high-voltage phenomena. Professionally, Thomson began to take a more active part in the affairs of the American Institute of Electrical Engineers, and he was elected president of that society in 1889 and 1890. To express his concerns about the safety of electric lighting systems, he served on the National Electric Light Association's subcommittee for overhead wiring, and he presented a paper on "Safety Devices in Electrical Installations" at their annual meeting in 1890.[85]

In redefining his position, Thomson knew that he was relinquishing his role as the firm's chief inventor; other inventors and engineers were becoming responsible for improving the company's products. However, he must have sensed that only by shifting his interests could he overcome the dissatisfaction he had felt so sharply in the fall of 1889. As he observed at the height of his unhappiness,

> the numerous and differing demands on my time have simply been such as to take away much of my interest in my work and destroy my growth in the direction of science, which after all is the thing I work for and care more for than all else besides, having in view at some not too distant day the devotion of my entire energies to what seems to me to be the only thing after all that can make one possessing my tendencies comfortable, that is the study of truth and the search for truth unmodified by any business considerations.[86]

Thomson's anger over the ac–dc controversy seems to have signaled to Coffin and others that the innovation function was neither fully understood by the firm nor completely integrated into the firm. Only

85 For Thomson's informal agreement with Coffin, see J. A. McManus, confidential memorandum, 12 September 1935, Hall of History Collection. For his new research projects, see ET, "Phenomena of Alternating Current Induction," *Electrical Engineer*, 9:212–14 (9 April 1890); and "Notes on Alternating Currents at Very High Frequency," *Electrical Engineer*, 11:300 (11 March 1891). Because of the demands placed on him by the company, Thomson was angry that he was not able to be more active as president of the American Institute of Electrical Engineers. As he complained to T. C. Martin, "this state of affairs is indeed very galling to me, and I hope to take steps to have the condition remedied sometime in the near future." From ET to T. C. Martin, 13 January 1890, LB 1/90–11/90, pp. 3–4, TP. For Thomson's efforts to promote safety, see ET to Capt. Eugene Griffin, 27 December 1889, LB 4/89–1/90, p. 902, TP; ET to E. R. Weeks, 13 January 1890, LB 1/90–11/90, p. 2, TP; and ET, "Safety and Safety Devices in Electrical Installations," *Electrical World*, 15:145–6 (22 February 1890).

86 ET to CAC, 24 December 1889, LB 4/89–1/90, pp. 903–8, TP.

after pushing Thomson to the brink did the firm realize that innovation involved a variety of areas – such as patenting, giving expert testimony, engineering, and inventing – and that those activities needed to be institutionalized in separate departments. Furthermore, by buying outside patents and bringing in additional inventors, Coffin had wanted to expand the firm's sources of innovation, but he did so at the cost of upsetting the firm's original innovator. As a result of that experience, Coffin was much more circumspect about bringing in additional "star" inventors; for instance, Charles Steinmetz came to the Lynn factory in 1892 only after he had been carefully interviewed by Thomson and Rice.[87]

Putting Thomson-Houston into perspective

Thomson-Houston became a leading firm in the electrical field because it brought together marketing strategy, business organization, and technology. Led by the astute Charles Coffin, the firm committed itself to selling electrical equipment to a customer it helped invent: the central-station utility. To help create that new class of customers, Coffin organized Thomson-Houston along functional lines. He personally supervised the marketing function and built a strong organization for sales and finance. At the same time, Rice built a large factory in Lynn for manufacturing dynamos and lights. Significantly, Coffin realized that to develop the central-station market fully, it would be necessary to offer a range of electrical products; in order to sell equipment to central stations in every town and city, he would have to offer dynamos in a variety of sizes and develop lights, motors, and distribution networks suitable to a range of needs. That realization led Coffin to diversify the Thomson-Houston product line and to encourage Thomson to invent new devices and systems. Illustrative of how Thomson developed new products suited to the central-station strategy was the ac incandescent lighting system, a product that permitted Thomson-Houston to compete with Edison and Westinghouse for the town and small-city markets.

It is well known among business historians that Thomson-Houston built a managerial structure in order to provide the special services required by electrical technology; that observation was first made by

87 Woodbury, *Beloved Scientist*, pp. 202–3; Ronald R. Kline, unpublished biography of Charles Steinmetz, 1990, chap. 4, "General Electric," Program in the History and Philosophy of Science and Technology, Cornell University.

Glenn Porter and Harold Livesay and then amplified by Alfred D. Chandler, Jr., in *The Visible Hand*.[88] However, what is new in this story is that Thomson-Houston's marketing strategy embraced product diversification and innovation. Unlike other machinery firms, which reached national markets by mass-producing a single good, Thomson-Houston penetrated the national market by selling a range of electrical products. Thomson-Houston's success was not based on the cost advantages deriving from the use of high-volume, high-speed production machinery, but rather was due to a strong distribution network that used a single marketing strategy to sell a variety of electrical machines. Because of Coffin's organizational ability, the firm enjoyed economies of scope by using the same sales force to sell and install different systems. It was not until the 1920s that other machinery firms (such as Remington Rand and IBM) diversified their product lines to capitalize on their established distribution networks.[89] Put another way, whereas one might have expected that as a machinery firm Thomson-Houston should have evolved much like a steel firm, instead it followed a pattern similar to the Sears department stores and other mass distributors.

Throughout this chapter I have emphasized that the company functioned more as a coalition of groups than as a formal hierarchy of departments. Although the central-station strategy led the firm to organize groups in order to perform the essential functions of marketing, manufacture, and invention, Thomson-Houston was unable to develop its organizational structure further. Because of strong competition, rapid growth, and a changing product line, the firm formally differentiated its functions, but the coordination of those activities remained informal. At no point in that period of rapid change can we discern one or more managers whose specific task it was to coordinate all of the functions undertaken by the firm. Instead, coordination of marketing with invention or manufacture with invention was handled informally by key leaders within the firm. As we have seen in the

---

88 On Thomson-Houston as an example of a firm whose product had special marketing requirements, see Glenn Porter and Harold C. Livesay, *Merchants and Manufacturers: Studies in the Changing Structure of Nineteenth-Century Marketing* (Baltimore: Johns Hopkins University Press, 1971), pp. 184–91; and Chandler, *The Visible Hand*, pp. 309–10.

89 For examples of other companies that diversified their product lines in the 1920s, see Alfred D. Chandler, Jr., *Scale and Scope: The Dynamics of Industrial Capitalism* (Cambridge, Mass.: Belknap Press of Harvard University, 1990), pp. 194–234.

case of the ac system, Coffin played an important role in linking marketing opportunities to Thomson's inventions, and Thomson even adjusted his research-and-development efforts to accommodate the firm's short-term marketing goals. In certain cases, informal coordination can be appropriate for a rough-and-tumble period of rapid growth, but that will depend entirely on the personalities of the leaders. Should they be unable or unwilling to understand the functions and mind-sets of other groups within the firm, then progress on key projects can be limited; such was the case with Thomson and the ac system. Furthermore, if demand for products is decreasing while competition is intensifying, then a firm may be obliged to formalize management structures to ensure coordination. As we shall see in the next chapter, that was exactly what occurred in the electrical industry in the 1890s, and Coffin and Rice struggled to create the mechanisms needed to coordinate production, marketing, and innovation.

Finally, this chapter has revealed that product innovation at Thomson-Houston was a social process. Rather than seeing a process by which a heroic inventor single-handedly designed and pushed inventions through the organization, we have seen how the timing and design of new products were shaped by the interactions of different groups. For the ac system, its design was shaped by a mixture of Thomson's desire for perfection and safety, marketing's need for a product to capture a new segment of the central-station market, and the production group's wish not to upset factory operations. Whereas Thomson wanted to introduce a complete system, pressure from marketing forced him to curtail his efforts and rush accessories into production. Likewise, the attitude of the manufacturing group forced Thomson to "freeze" the design and not add the improvements that he wanted. The system's timing was shaped by the moment at which Coffin identified the marketing opportunity and by Thomson's mind-set of technological perfectionism; if Coffin had seen the potential for an ac system earlier than 1885, or if Thomson had been willing to speed up his efforts, then Thomson-Houston might have introduced the product sooner. Thus, the design process at Thomson-Houston was not just an intellectual activity occurring in Thomson's mind; it was also a social process involving several groups. Overall, innovation was not a straightforward or orderly activity, but rather a highly contingent process dependent on how different individuals and groups responded to each other.

6. Maintaining the organization: product development at General Electric, 1892–1900

Elihu Thomson emerged from the 1880s well situated in the electrical industry. During the preceding 10 years, he and his business associates had created a powerful firm, the Thomson-Houston Electric Company, by linking innovative hardware with an appropriate business organization and marketing strategy. Beginning with the invention of an arc lighting system in Philadelphia, the identification of the central-station strategy in New Britain, and the establishment of a strong marketing and manufacturing organization in Lynn, Thomson, Coffin, and Rice had converted electric lighting from a lecture-hall curiosity to a profitable product.

In coordinating technology, organization, and marketing, Coffin, Thomson, and Rice brought together the necessary resources and knowledge. As we have seen, these included capital, plants, machines, and labor, as well as leadership, engineering knowledge, salesmanship, and skill in manufacturing. Isolated, such resources and knowledge were worth little, but Coffin, Thomson, and Rice made them useful by combining and coordinating them within Thomson-Houston. Once they have been coordinated in an organization, economists and business historians refer to such resources and knowledge as a firm's organizational capability. According to Alfred D. Chandler, Jr., and William Lazonick, firms succeed by assembling and managing the resources and knowledge necessary to exploit the economies of scale and scope inherent in a particular set of business activities.[1] Although economies of scale arising from building larger or faster production facilities were not particularly significant in electrical manufacturing,

---

1 On the concept of organizational capability, see Alfred D. Chandler, Jr., *Scale and Scope: The Dynamics of Industrial Capitalism* (Cambridge, Mass.: Harvard University Press, 1990), pp. 24–34; and William Lazonick, "Organizational Capability and Technological Change in Comparative Perspective" (paper presented to Business History Seminar, Harvard Business School, March 1987).

economies of scope were crucial; Thomson-Houston was effective because it coordinated the functions of inventing, manufacturing, marketing, and financing central-station systems. Moreover, once it had established this capability for arc lighting, the company was able to diversify quickly into new systems of lighting and traction.

Having created their organizational capability for electric lighting and street railways, Thomson and Coffin had every reason to look forward to continued growth and expansion in the early years of the 1890s. These years, however, proved to be the most competitive and tumultuous period in the history of the electrical manufacturing industry. During that era, Thomson-Houston found itself confronted by two formidable adversaries, the Edison General Electric Company and the Westinghouse Electric Company, both of which had achieved a similar integration of technology, organization, and strategy in the central-station field. These three firms fought each other on a variety of fronts, including technical, legal, and marketing, only to discover that relentless competition threatened their limited capital and overall organizational capability. It soon became clear to Coffin and the other industry leaders that this brand of competition would have to give way to some form of cooperation and consolidation, and as a result, two of the firms, Thomson-Houston and Edison General, merged in 1892.

Capitalized at $50 million and employing nearly 10,000 workers, the General Electric Company from the outset dominated the electrical manufacturing industry. Led by Coffin, Rice, and other Thomson-Houston managers, General Electric continued to promote the creation of central stations for both lighting and street railways. Yet within two years of its formation, the mighty General Electric was nearly bankrupt, a victim of the financial panic of 1893 and the ensuing depression. The principal problem for General Electric was that the depression prevented its core customers – the utility companies – from expanding their operations and buying new equipment. The central-station strategy assumed both readily available local capital and a willingness among small manufacturers and shopkeepers to install electric lights, but the depression negated both assumptions.

Previously, historian Leonard S. Reich has argued that General Electric responded to the hard times of the 1890s by pursuing a conservative strategy combining fiscal restraint with a reluctance to introduce new products.[2] But as the history of Thomson-Houston suggests, such a policy would have been a sharp departure from the strategy used by Coffin during the 1880s. Because product innovation had permitted Coffin to build up Thomson-Houston, he continued to use innovation to adapt to the difficult circumstances of the depression of the 1890s. Consequently, in this chapter I suggest that rather than avoiding technological innovation, Coffin and Thomson strove to use it in new ways to maintain General Electric's organizational capabilities. Moreover, when Thomson, Rice, and others found that the existing structure of General Electric impeded product innovation, they created a new institution: the research laboratory.

From Thomson-Houston to General Electric

Just as the strategy and structure of Thomson-Houston informed his work with alternating current, so the organization of the General Electric Company influenced Thomson's work with x-rays, engines, and automobiles. Thus, it is important to understand how and why the new company emerged. To do so, we need to place into context some of the business developments at Thomson-Houston discussed in the preceding chapter and to examine the conditions leading up to the creation of General Electric in 1892.

By 1889, three firms had emerged as dominant players in the industry: Thomson-Houston, Edison General Electric, and Westinghouse Electric. Each of these firms promoted central stations, and each had made the investment necessary to implement that strategy; they had developed large-scale production facilities, national and international distribution networks, and expertise in engineering and invention. Armed with such organizational capability, each firm was determined to exploit its potential, through either economies of scale (such as utilizing their large factories) or economies of scope (such as expanding into related product areas).[3]

---

2 Leonard S. Reich outlined GE's conservative strategy in *The Making of American Industrial Research: Science and Business at GE and Bell, 1876–1926* (Cambridge University Press, 1985), pp. 42–61.

3 My thinking about the key characteristics of the three leading firms has been influenced by Chandler's discussion of a first-mover firm in *Scale and Scope*, pp. 34–5.

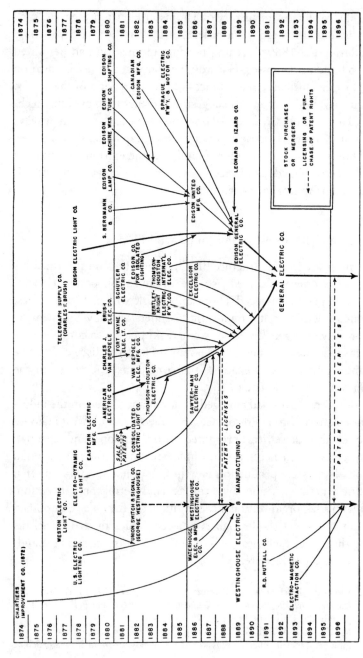

Figure 6.1. Evolution of General Electric and Westinghouse companies, 1872–96. Reprinted with permission of Macmillan Publishing Company from *The Electric Lamp Industry: Technological Change and Economic Development from 1800 to 1947*, by Arthur A. Bright. Copyright 1949 The Macmillan Company; copyright renewed 1975 Evelyn F. Hitchcock.

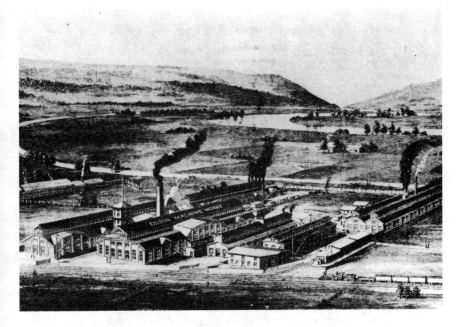

Figure 6.2. Schenectady works of the Edison General Electric Company, 1891. Courtesy of the General Electric Company.

As Chapter 5 revealed, Thomson-Houston clearly had the capability to implement the central-station strategy. Under Coffin's leadership, it had a large plant in Lynn producing a diversified product line of arc lighting, incandescent lighting, and street-railway systems. To market and distribute those systems, Thomson-Houston had a sales and engineering force to help local businessmen develop utility and traction companies. Likewise, to coordinate production and distribution, Coffin had developed a managerial staff organized along functional lines. And to provide a steady stream of new products and improvements, the firm employed Thomson, Charles Van Depoele, and Hermann Lemp.

Although Edison and his associates had been major players in the electrical industry throughout the 1880s, it was only in April 1889 that their significant resources were brought together in the Edison General Electric Company. Organized by financier Henry Villard, Edison General was a consolidation of Edison's various electrical manufacturing concerns (Figure 6.1). Drawing on his connections with major German banks, Villard capitalized the new company at $12 million. J. P. Mor-

Figure 6.3. Harrison Lamp Works of the Edison General Electric Company. Courtesy of the General Electric Company.

gan and his partners, Edison's bankers, also invested in the new company. Once established, Villard took the title of president, but left day-to-day management to Samuel Insull, Edison's personal secretary. With the help of Edison, Insull formed a management team of the best men from the Edison Electric Light Company and Edison's laboratory staff. To improve distribution, Insull created a national sales organization with seven regional districts, all of which reported to a sales vice-president. Insull also established an intelligence department at the company's New York headquarters that collected and analyzed sales data. For production, Edison General had the enormous machine works at Schenectady, a lamp factory at Harrison, New Jersey, and a plant in New York City (Figures 6.2 and 6.3). Although the company continued to focus on dc incandescent lighting systems, it contracted with Edison's new laboratory at West Orange for the development of better lamps, a multipolar dynamo, and a new meter. Insull hoped that Edison would develop an ac lighting system and a street railway, but Edison instead threw his energies into developing his phonograph and ore-milling ventures.[4] Edison General had access to the "wizard" and

4 On the formation of Edison General Electric, see Forrest McDonald, *Insull* (University of Chicago Press, 1962), pp. 39–42; Dietrich G. Buss, *Henry Villard: A Study of Transatlantic Investment and Interests, 1870–1895* (New York: Arno, 1978), pp. 207–10; and Harold C. Passer, "Development of Large-Scale Organization: Electrical Manufacturing Around 1900," *Journal*

his laboratory, but it had no guarantee that Edison would put the needs of the company ahead of his own goals. Thus, unlike Thomson-Houston, Edison General had not fully integrated the innovation function into its organization.

By 1889, Westinghouse had also emerged as a leading firm in the electrical manufacturing industry. Westinghouse had established its reputation by pioneering ac incandescent lighting, but the company had moved quickly into new product areas, including ac industrial motors and street railways. Through a patent-sharing agreement with Thomson-Houston, Westinghouse secured a foothold in the arc-lighting field. To develop its products, Westinghouse employed several inventors, including Nikola Tesla, William Stanley, and Oliver Shallenberger. In terms of production facilities, the company had plants in Pittsburgh (Garrison Alley) and Newark, New Jersey (formerly the United States Electric Lighting Company). For distribution, Westinghouse depended on a small sales force working on commission out of offices in six or seven major cities. Unlike its rivals, Westinghouse lacked a managerial hierarchy; instead, George Westinghouse supervised factory operations, participated in product design, and negotiated many of the major contracts.[5]

As we have seen with the growth of Thomson-Houston, it required substantial capital, technical expertise, and entrepreneurial effort to

of Economic History, 12:378–95 (Fall 1952), especially pp. 380–1. Edison's role in organizing the management of Edison General is suggested by an undated list of men, titles, and assignments in 1886 electric lighting, Edison United Manufacturing Co. folder, ENHS. During the late 1880s, Edison raised the efficiency of his dc system by developing a new multipolar dynamo, a five-wire distribution network, high-voltage dc distribution using a rotary converter, a new meter, and a 200-volt incandescent lamp for street lighting. See Edison General Electric Company, "Central Station Lighting," February 1892, Trade Catalog Collection, Archives and Library, Henry Ford Museum, Dearborn, Mich.; Edison, [notes on multiwire systems], 5 October 1889, notebook N870902, ENHS; A. E. Kennelly, [notes on dial meters], notebook N910430, ENHS; Edison, [alternating meter caveat], 5 August 1890, notebook N900803, ENHS; Edison, [notes on rotating converters], 21 September 1888, notebook N880703, ENHS; A. E. Kennelly, "Calculation for the dimensions of a Commutating Continuous Transformer of 100 light capacity," notebook N880828, ENHS; Edison, "Induction-Converter," U.S. Patent No. 534,208 (filed 21 May 1888, granted 12 February 1895); and "The New Edison Municipal Lamp," Electrical World, 11:74 (18 February 1888). On Edison's plans for a street railway, see J. C. Henderson to Villard, 27 June 1890, box 63, folder 473, Villard Papers.

5 Passer, "Development of Large-Scale Organization," pp. 389–92.

become a major player in the electrical manufacturing industry. Consequently, once the three firms had assembled their factories, sales forces, and inventors, they fought hard to maintain and expand their market shares. Even though the market for electric lighting and power was substantial in the United States, the need to sustain their established capabilities led those firms to keen competition in the early 1890s.

Competition among the three firms took several forms. First, they competed vigorously for contracts to supply complete lighting systems and street-railway systems to towns and cities. For example, in 1890, Thomson-Houston, Edison General, and Westinghouse bid $25,000, $60,000, and $70,000, respectively, to provide equipment to electric companies in Ironwood and Bessemer, Michigan.[6] Although Edison General was known to cut prices on individual components, such as incandescent lamps and streetcar motors, the other two firms generally did not follow suit.[7] Instead, Thomson-Houston and Westinghouse offered utility companies low prices for complete systems, hoping that the profits would come by way of expansion and sales of replacement equipment. As Coffin explained, "once we have [brought] our system into use [in a town or city], other companies may offer prices twenty-five percent lower, but the users willingly pay our price as they cannot afford to change the system."[8] However, as utility companies sought to lower the unit costs of lighting and power by expanding their service

6 These bids came from a telegraph message Villard sent to Coffin. In that message, Villard accused Coffin of submitting an "unreasonably low" bid and proposed that if Thomson-Houston withdrew its bid, then Edison General would give it one-third of the contract's net profits. See Villard to Clark, Dodge & Co., 21 May 1890, box 127, LB 167, p. 235, Villard Papers.

7 Edison was quite adamant that his manufacturing companies cut component prices in order to gain market share; see "Mr. Edison's Reply to Thomson-Houston Memoranda of March 23d, 1889," box 63, folder 472, Villard Papers. As examples, the Edison organization reduced the price of incandescent lamps from $1.00 in 1886 to $0.44 in 1891, and it sold streetcar motors for under $1,500 when manufacturing costs would have dictated a price over $1,600. See McDonald, *Insull*, p. 42; and Arthur Pound and Samuel Taylor Moore, eds., *More They Told Barron: Conversations and Revelations of an American Pepys in Wall Street* (New York: Harper, 1931), p. 38.

8 Coffin's quotation is from Pound and Moore, *More They Told Barron*, p. 37. For an informed discussion of the economics of network technologies, see Paul A. David, "The Hero and the Herd in Technological History: Reflections on Thomas Edison and the 'Battle of the Systems'," publication No. 100, July 1987, Center for Economic Policy Research, Stanford University, especially pp. 9–13.

territories, they demanded that the electrical manufacturers install larger generating plants and distribution networks. Although the electrical manufacturers could reap handsome profits on a large installation, they also knew that they could lose a great deal if they had to submit an extremely low bid to secure the contract. Consequently, as systems grew in complexity and cost, the risk involved in competitive bidding became a mounting concern to the managers of the leading firms.

In competing for contracts for complete systems, Thomson-Houston and Edison General employed a second tactic of integrating forward into the construction and operation of central stations. Although Thomson-Houston had a large force of salesmen and field engineers who reported directly to headquarters, in 1887 it established a subsidiary, the Northwest Electric Construction and Supply Company (also known as Northwest Thomson-Houston), which specialized in the promotion and construction of central stations. Headquartered in Saint Paul, Minnesota, Northwest Thomson-Houston sold electrical equipment to the growing cities and towns of the upper Midwest and Pacific Northwest. With its own salesmen and construction engineers, Northwest Thomson-Houston could move into a city, organize a central-station company with local capital and management, market the company's bonds in Boston, sell a full line of equipment, and build a complete plant. In providing all those services, Northwest Thomson-Houston took advantage of economies of scope to meet the vigorous competition for contracts. Northwest Thomson-Houston was the logical next step in Thomson-Houston's overall strategy of central-station development, and that subsidiary captured a large portion of the market, at least in Wisconsin.[9]

In connection with Edison General, Villard established the North American Company in June 1890 to promote Edison central stations in the Midwest. North American was capitalized at $50 million, with backing from both the German banks and Morgan. With ample capital at hand, North American took over and enlarged the Edison lighting companies in Cincinnati, Saint Paul, and Minneapolis. In Milwaukee, Villard used North American to consolidate the existing street-railway

9 Forrest McDonald, *Let There Be Light: The Electric Utility Industry in Wisconsin, 1881–1955* (Madison, Wisc.: American History Research Center, 1957), pp. 21–2; T. Commerford Martin and Stephen Leidy Coles, *The Story of Electricity* (New York: Story of Electricity Company, 1919), p. 137.

and lighting companies into a single $5-million utility company. Unlike Thomson-Houston, which accepted utility bonds as partial payment for equipment, North American accepted as much as four-fifths of the stock of an Edison utility as payment. Villard further insisted that Edison General sell central-station equipment only to North American "at factory prices, free of all royalty or profits, direct or indirect." By controlling such large blocks of stock and being the sole source of Edison central-station equipment, Villard hoped to use the North American Company to gain complete control of incandescent lighting in the United States.[10]

Not only did the major firms integrate vertically and create subsidiaries, but as a third tactic they integrated horizontally and took over smaller firms in the field (Figure 6.1). As mentioned earlier, Thomson-Houston spent $4 million between 1888 and 1891 purchasing control of seven firms in the arc-lighting and street-railway fields. At the same time, Westinghouse bought out the United States Electric Lighting Company and the Consolidated Electric Light Company for their incandescent-lamp patents and the Waterhouse Electric Light Company for its arc lighting system. In creating Edison General, Villard brought in two non-Edison firms, Leonard & Izard (a small central-station construction firm) and the Sprague Electric Railway & Motor Company. In all cases, the leading firms absorbed those minor concerns in order to gain market share and to prevent valuable patents from falling into the hands of rivals. However, they were also anxious to secure the services of inventors, reminding us again that knowledge of the new technology was embodied in individuals, not books or theories. Although Thomson-Houston continued to operate the large Brush works in Cleveland, the smaller factories were closed, and their inventors were transferred to the major plants at Lynn, Schenectady, and Pittsburgh.[11]

As a fourth tactic, electrical manufacturers used patents in a variety of ways. Not only did they purchase smaller rivals to acquire their

10 On the formation of the North American Company, see Buss, *Villard*, pp. 215–17. The quotation is from McDonald, *Insull*, p. 42. For a description of its operations in Milwaukee, see McDonald, *Let There Be Light*, pp. 51–5.
11 ET to CAC, 20 December 1892, LB 1/1/92–3/29/93, pp. 775–9, TP; Harold C. Passer, *The Electrical Manufacturers: A Study in Competition, Entrepreneurship, Technical Change, and Economic Growth* (Cambridge, Mass.: Harvard University Press, 1953), pp. 52–7, 103, 147; Arthur A. Bright, Jr., *The Electric-Lamp Industry: Technological Change and Economic Development from 1800 to 1947* (New York: Macmillan, 1949), pp. 80–3.

patents, but they also used patents to shape their relationship with their customers, the central-station utilities. Patents allowed the manufacturer to exert influence over its customers; by requiring them to become licensees, the manufacturer could attempt to force its customers to buy equipment exclusively from it. At the same time, patents were necessary to attract central-station customers, because they conveyed to central-station officials the hope of monopoly power. In order to convince local businessmen to invest heavily in a new utility, frequently each electrical manufacturer would claim that it alone held the key patents for a particular type of system (arc, incandescent, or railway) and that it would prosecute all patent infringers. In making such promises, the manufacturer wanted the local businessmen to believe that they would face little or no competition in the utility field.[12]

As competition increased in the late 1880s, the three leading firms did not hesitate to use patent litigation as a means of attacking and draining the resources of their rivals. As we saw in Chapter 5, in 1887, Frederick Fish, chief counsel for Thomson-Houston, launched a comprehensive attack against all who had infringed the patent for Thomson's dynamo regulator. That campaign helped wear down several of Thomson-Houston's major arc-lighting competitors and facilitated the acquisition of those firms by Thomson-Houston. Similarly, Westinghouse sued Thomson-Houston in 1887 for infringing its Gaulard-Gibbs transformer patent, leading to a patent-sharing agreement with Thomson-Houston.[13]

Of the major firms, the Edison organization was the most energetic in licensing its central-station customers and proclaiming the strength of its patents. As early as 1885 the Edison group began suing both nonlicensed utility companies and competing lamp manufacturers for patent infringement. As competition with Westinghouse and Thomson-Houston increased in the late 1880s, the Edison organization increased

---

12 To the best of my knowledge, no historian has analyzed the role of patents in the relationship between electrical manufacturers and utility companies. In narrating the problems GE encountered in the early 1890s with former Edison licensees, George Wise suggested that the licensees expected that the patents would convey monopoly power to them; see his "History of General Electric" (unpublished ms.), chap. 3, "Shoemakers," pp. 104–7. Additional information about the relationship between the Edison organization and its licensees can be found: A. Michal McMahon, *Reflections: A Centennial Essay on the Association of Edison Illuminating Companies* (New York: Association of Edison Illuminating Companies, 1985), pp. 13–17.

13 Bright, *The Electric-Lamp Industry*, pp. 86–7; Passer, *The Electrical Manufacturers*, p. 144.

the intensity of its legal actions. Edison's lawyers instituted proceedings against a hundred or more infringers, but they devoted most of their energy to trying a single case against the United States Electric Lighting Company, concerning incandescent-lamp filaments. (Because Westinghouse subsequently purchased U.S. Electric, this case was effectively against Westinghouse.) After a long and involved trial in federal court, in July 1891 Judge William Wallace ruled in favor of Edison, sustaining his claim to have invented the first incandescent lamp with a high-resistance carbon filament in a sealed bulb.[14]

It often has been thought that the 1891 patent victory gave Edison General a decisive edge over Westinghouse and Thomson-Houston and permitted Edison General to force Thomson-Houston to submit to the merger that formed General Electric.[15] Yet the court decision had sustained only one claim of the original lamp patent, and both Westinghouse and Thomson-Houston found ways to work around that patent. Westinghouse avoided further infringement by developing a "stopper lamp," which was used in the elaborate incandescent-lighting displays at the 1893 Chicago World's Fair.[16] Thomson-Houston welcomed the decision, because Coffin was confident that he could negotiate a patent agreement with Edison General. As Coffin wrote to Henry L. Higginson,

> we believe the decision [sustaining Edison's patent] to be better for our interests than it would be to have the invention thrown open to the public, as we can far better afford to arrange with the Edison Co. than to compete with the fifty or more smaller manufacturers.[17]

Rather than giving one firm a decisive advantage over the others, patent litigation among the major firms served other purposes. It permitted them to weaken and absorb smaller firms, and it allowed one

14 Bright, The Electric-Lamp Industry, pp. 87–8; John Winthrop Hammond, Men and Volts: The Story of General Electric (Philadelphia: Lippincott, 1941), pp. 180–7.

15 For examples of how historians have interpreted the lamp decision as giving Edison General the decisive edge, see McDonald, Insull, p. 48; and Hammond, Men and Volts, p. 192.

16 On the Westinghouse stopper lamp, see Passer, The Electrical Manufacturers, pp. 142–3. According to Thomson, although those lamps avoided conflict with the Edison patent, they worked very poorly, and Westinghouse used as few of them as possible in the lighting displays at the Chicago fair; see ET to CAC, 19 June 1893, LB 3/93–4/95, pp. 132–3, TP.

17 CAC to Henry L. Higginson, 15 July 1891, Higginson Papers, box XII-3, folder 1891, CAC.

firm to force short-term changes on another. Most important, litigation demanded substantial amounts of time and money; by attacking Thomson-Houston and Westinghouse, the Edison organization hoped to force its competitors to divert resources away from further improvements in their organizational capabilities.

Along with patent litigation, the leading firms mounted publicity campaigns attacking each other. One example of this fifth tactic is how Westinghouse interfered with Thomson-Houston's efforts to secure a revised corporate charter. In late 1888, Thomson-Houston decided to amend its charter in order to enlarge its authorized capitalization and secure the right to manufacture and sell street-railway equipment. Because the company was chartered in Connecticut, Thomson-Houston had to petition the state legislature for a special act. In the course of that effort, pro-Westinghouse interests vigorously opposed the bill, with the goal of preventing Thomson-Houston from entering the railway field and competing with Westinghouse. During the legislative struggle, Edward H. Johnson of the Edison organization wrote to Coffin, stating that he considered the Westinghouse action unfair and offering to help Thomson-Houston fight Westinghouse on the matter. With this assistance, Thomson-Houston secured its revised charter in 1889.[18] Clearly, this episode reveals the range of tactics that the major firms were willing to employ to prevent competitors from gaining any advantage.

By far the most significant publicity campaign was that mounted by the Edison organization attacking Westinghouse and alternating current.[19] Although Edison and his laboratory staff at West Orange were capable of designing ac lighting and power systems, Edison chose not to do so because he believed that power losses in the available trans-

18 Untitled lecture on the history of T-H and General Electric, Hammond File, 6290–392, especially 6350–1.

19 Among the more useful accounts of the "battle of the systems" are the following: Passer, *The Electrical Manufacturers*, pp. 164–75; Thomas P. Hughes, *Networks of Power: Electrification in Western Society, 1880–1930* (Baltimore: Johns Hopkins University Press, 1983), pp. 106–39; Paul A. David and Julie Ann Bunn, "The Economics of Gateway Technologies and Network Evolution: Lessons from Electricity Supply History," *Information Economics and Policy,* 3:165–202 (1988); W. Bernard Carlson and A. J. Millard, "Defining Risk within a Business Context: Thomas A. Edison, Elihu Thomson, and the AC–DC Controversy, 1885–1900," in V. Covello and B. B. Johnson, eds., *The Social and Cultural Construction of Risk* (Boston: D. Reidel, 1987), pp. 275–93.

formers would render such a system uneconomical.[20] Instead, Edison concentrated on improving the efficiency of his dc system, in the belief that the Edison organization would attract more customers as the cost of lighting decreased.[21] However, as both Westinghouse and Thomson-Houston began installing high-voltage ac plants, the Edison organization found itself unable to secure contracts in towns and cities with low population densities. (Because of the high cost of copper mains, the Edison system was economical only in populous urban

20 Despite the claims of various Edison biographers, Edison's notebooks and caveats reveal that he did understand alternating current and that he sketched a number of ac generators, transformers, and distribution networks. See Edison, "New Idea – The whole system is a transformer" (sketch), 22 November 1887, notebook N87115, ENHS; and caveat No. 117, 2 November 1889 (Cat. 1141), ENHS. Edison also encouraged Arthur E. Kennelly and his other experimenters to test ac machinery at West Orange; see Kennelly Notebooks, vol. 1, ENHS. On the basis of that research, Edison filed for several patents for ac systems; see "System of Electrical Distribution," U.S. Patent No. 438,308 (filed 6 December 1886, granted 14 October 1890); "System of Electrical Distribution," U.S. Patent No. 524,378 (filed 6 December 1886, granted 14 August 1894); "Alternating Current Generator," U.S. Patent No. 470,928 (filed 25 August 1891, granted 15 March 1892).

   However, as Edison studied alternating current, he grew suspicious. He was troubled by power losses in transformers, which he found to be at minimum 7% to 12%. "Evidently this results in a great diminution of the profits of the business," he observed in "System of Electrical Distribution," U.S. Patent No. 382,415 (filed 27 December 1887, granted 8 May 1888). See also Edison to Villard, 8 February 1890, box 63, folder 473, Villard Papers. Furthermore, Edison was concerned about the costs of building ac generating stations. Westinghouse claimed that a major advantage of ac was that one could erect a large plant that could generate cheap power on the outskirts of a city. Familiar with the difficulties of raising capital to build his own dc stations, Edison believed that large ac plants would cost too much money to construct and that the interest charges on the investment would eliminate any operating profits. See Edison to H. Villard, 11 December 1888, LB 881112, p. 354, ENHS. Finally, Edison was distressed by the problem of properly insulating ac wires. He and his men were having enough difficulty finding good insulation for their low-voltage system, and he doubted that he could find insulation for a 1,000-volt line and its transformers. See Edison, "Reasons against an alternating converter system," notebook N860428, pp. 261–5, ENHS. For all those reasons, Edison concluded that "the use of the alternating current is unworthy of practical men." See Edison to H. Villard, 24 February 1891, box 63, folder 475, Villard Papers.

21 Edison summed up his competitive philosophy when he advised a central-station manager: "Try everything you can towards economy. No one is safe in the cold commercial world that can't produce as low as his greatest competitor. No matter how much money you are making never for an instant let up on economizing." From Edison note, 10 May 1895, Meadowcroft Papers, box 84, ENHS.

districts where copper costs could be spread across a large customer base.) Edison managers became especially frustrated in the late 1880s when they came to believe that Westinghouse had beaten them on major contracts in Denver and Minneapolis by submitting unrealistically low bids.[22] Feeling that Westinghouse had already acted unethically, Francis S. Hastings, treasurer of the Edison Electric Light Company, launched a publicity campaign depicting ac as the "death current."[23] In doing so, he enlisted several allies who had already begun to question the safety of ac systems. Those allies included Harold P. Brown, a consulting electrical engineer who had already tangled with Westinghouse, and a group of New York City physicians who were investigating electrocution as an alternative form of capital punishment. Working through Brown and the physicians, the Edison organization whipped up public hysteria about the dangers of alternating current and surreptitiously arranged for it to be used in the first electrocution at Sing Sing prison in 1890. The Edison group also tried to convince several state legislatures to limit the maximum voltage of electrical systems to 300 volts, and they came very close to securing such legislation in Ohio and Virginia.[24]

The "battle of the systems" between Edison and Westinghouse gradually ended as Thomson, Charles Steinmetz, and other engineers improved the safety of ac systems, increased the efficiency of trans-

22 For information suggesting that the Edison organization lost contracts in Denver and Minneapolis to Westinghouse, see "A Warning from the Edison Electric Light Company," circa 1888, Electricity, box E-5, Warshaw Collection of Business Americana, National Museum of American History, Washington, D.C. This is the famous red-covered pamphlet in which the Edison organization attacked the safety of ac systems. For a description of the technical and financial troubles of the Westinghouse plant in Denver, see W. P. Hancock, "Report on Westinghouse Plant of Colorado Electric Company," 1888 Electric Light–Westinghouse folder, ENHS.

23 Documents in the Edison archives strongly suggest that it was Francis S. Hastings, not Edison himself, who mounted the attack on Westinghouse and ac systems; see Hastings's letters to A. E. Kennelly, 6 August 1888, 20 November 1888, and 26 November 1888, in 1888 Edison Electric Light Co., July–December, folder, and 1888 Electrocution folder, as well as Hastings to Edison, 21 January 1889, in 1889 Electricity-Use folder, ENHS.

24 On Harold P. Brown, see Thomas P. Hughes, "Harold P. Brown and the Executioner's Current: An Incident in the AC–DC Controversy," *Business History Review*, 32:143–65 (1958). On the role of the New York physicians in promoting ac electrocution as an alternative to hanging as capital punishment, see Roger Neustadter, "The Murderer and the Dynamo: Social Response to the First Legal Electrocution in America" (paper presented to the Popular Culture Association, April 1984).

formers, and introduced rotary converters to link ac and dc systems.[25] In addition, many central-station customers installed ac systems because it allowed them to distribute electricity over greater areas and thus serve more consumers. Yet the battle was significant as another facet of the struggle among leading firms to maintain their organizational capabilities.

Through these five tactics – competing for contracts, integrating forward into central-station development, absorbing minor firms, patent litigation, and publicity attacks – the major players struggled to sustain and improve their positions in the industry. Notably, when considered together, these five tactics suggest differences in the levels of organizational capability of the leading firms. As we have seen, Thomson-Houston and Westinghouse concentrated on improving their organizational capabilities by adding resources (such as buying minor firms or enlarging factories) and by making special efforts to coordinate these resources (such as arranging for in-house inventors to work on key products). Of course, Thomson-Houston went even further than Westinghouse in terms of organization-building by developing a national sales network and a managerial hierarchy. In contrast, Edison General appears to have focused its efforts less on building its organizational capability and more on shaping the marketplace. Rather than improve the internal coordination of resources, Edison General chose to engage in price competition, patent litigation, and, ultimately, a major publicity attack on Westinghouse. To some extent, Edison General may have pursued these tactics because they appealed to Edison, but in general, the key decisions in this company were made by Insull, Hastings, and other professional managers. Although it may seem obvious to us that a policy of building organizational capability will lead to long-term growth and success, we must keep in mind that the Edison managers were among the first managers to be faced with the challenge of building a large, well-coordinated manufacturing firm, and they did not necessarily see what is obvious to us in hindsight. Instead, they framed a policy that made sense to them, based on their own business experience.

Another important point is that these tactics required substantial amounts of capital, especially the acquisition of small firms, as well as patent litigation. Yet, as we have seen, electrical manufacturing was

25 Hughes, *Networks of Power*, pp. 121–9.

quite a capital-intensive business, requiring enormous amounts of money to develop full product lines, build major factories, and establish national sales networks. As Villard wrote to Drexel, Morgan & Co. in March 1890,

> the general business of the Edison General Electric Company is growing at a rate that is equally surprising and gratifying. This growth has rendered the provision for working capital made upon the organization of the Company entirely inadequate. Instead of one million, several millions are imperatively wanted to meet the current demands of the several manufacturing departments.[26]

Already a capital-intensive business, these tactics made the electrical industry even more unstable financially in the early 1890s.

The major electrical manufacturers found themselves in precarious positions because they had become capital-intensive enterprises prior to the development of capital markets suited to large-scale industrial expansion. Before 1890, individuals tended to invest surplus capital in real estate, and the stock exchanges in New York and other cities dealt only in railroad securities. Most manufacturing enterprises were private partnerships that did not offer stocks or bonds for sale to the general public. The exceptions to this pattern were the New England textile mills, which marketed securities through two Boston brokerage houses (Lee, Higginson & Co., Kidder, Peabody). As a result, many manufacturers found it difficult to secure capital for expansion. Frequently, their only recourse was to borrow short-term money from commercial banks for long-term investment in plant and repay the loans out of large immediate earnings. Such a strategy was adequate in a period of economic expansion, but it often led to bankruptcy when business conditions worsened. Partly in response to the lack of available capital, firms in other capital-intensive industries (e.g., sugar refining, whiskey distilling, lead smelting), developed "trusts" in the late 1880s as a means of pooling capital and ownership.[27]

Thomson-Houston secured ample capital for expansion and competition by allying itself with the Boston brokerage house of Lee, Higginson & Co. Headed by Henry L. Higginson (Figure 6.4), the firm had

---

26 Villard to Drexel, Morgan & Co., 13 March 1890, syndicate book 2, pp. 159–60, Archives of The Pierpont Morgan Library, New York.
27 Thomas R. Navin and Marian V. Sears, "The Rise of a Market for Industrial Securities, 1887–1902," *Business History Review*, 29:105–38 (June 1955), especially pp. 106–16, 125.

Figure 6.4. Henry L. Higginson (from an engraving). From the Higginson Papers, Baker Library, Harvard University Graduate School of Business Administration, Boston.

made its fortune through the promotion of the Calumet & Hecla copper mines of northern Michigan. Building on that experience, Higginson specialized in the development of industrial securities. Higginson probably became associated with Thomson-Houston when the firm introduced its "trust series" for reselling central-station bonds. In 1889, Higginson helped Thomson-Houston offer one of the first industrial issues of preferred stock. (Preferred stock issues were popular with conservative investors, because dividends were paid on preferred shares before common shares.) By the early 1890s, Higginson was assisting Thomson-Houston in raising money for takeovers, selling large blocks of Northwest Thomson-Houston stock, and financing street-railway companies. To facilitate these financial efforts, Coffin corresponded regularly with Higginson, sharing market data and consulting with him about strategy.[28]

Neither Edison General nor Westinghouse had a similar alliance with a powerful investment house that could have provided a steady flow of capital. In building up the Schenectady works for Edison General, Insull doubled the value of the plant from $750,000 to $1.5 million, but only by juggling numerous short-term loans and operating with a cash holding of less than $10,000. Drexel, Morgan & Co. did lend money to Edison General, but the Morgan partners tended to be more interested in investing in Edison central stations in New York and Boston than in long-term returns accruing from improving the factories.[29] Insull and Villard probably intended to expand operations by plowing back profits, but that proved difficult because Edison General accepted so much utility stock as payment for central-station equipment. In the fall of 1890, with the passage of the Sherman Silver Purchase Act and the failure of the London brokerage house of Baring Brothers, the German bankers lost confidence in Villard and recalled their loans. These developments weakened Edison General and completely crippled the North American Company. In response, Villard ordered Insull to sell equipment only for cash or short-term credit, and

28 On the history of Lee, Higginson, see Navin and Sears, "The Market for Industrial Securities," pp. 116, 125. The relationship between that brokerage house and Thomson-Houston is revealed in various letters in the Higginson Papers. In particular, see the following letters from CAC to Henry L. Higginson: 18 April and 24 September 1890, box XII-2, folder 1890 General; 13 July and 5 October 1891, box XII-3, folder 1891 CAC; 25 February 1892, box XII-3, folder 1892 CAC. See also the following letters between Charles Fairchild and Higginson: 23 January 1890, box XII-2, folder 1890 Fairchild; 14 April and 28 December 1891, box XII-3, folder 1891 Fairchild.

29 On Insull's efforts to juggle short-term loans, see McDonald, *Insull*, p. 38. In September 1891, Drexel, Morgan & Co. loaned Edison General $1 million by selling Edison General's six-month notes to a syndicate of a dozen banks and investors. See J. P. Morgan to H. Villard, 9 September 1891, and J. P. Morgan to Unger, Smithers & Co., 11 September 1891, LB 1887–93, pp. 600–2, The Pierpont Morgan Library, New York. See also Vincent P. Carosso, *The Morgans: Private International Bankers, 1854–1913* (Cambridge, Mass.: Harvard University Press, 1987), n. 166, p. 775. Morgan's role in promoting Edison central stations is discussed in "Personal Recollections. Edward H. Johnson. Mr. Morgan's Contribution to the Modern Electrical Era," November 1914, Herbert Satterlee Papers, box 3, folder A10, The Pierpont Morgan Library, New York.

in January 1891 he decided to raise $3 million through a new stock issue.[30]

Westinghouse also faced the problem of earning enough to pay off its short-term loans, and in this case the problem nearly bankrupted the company. Thanks to the company's innovative ac equipment, Westinghouse annual sales jumped from $800,000 in 1887 to $4 million in 1890. As sales boomed, though, Westinghouse had to develop an engineering staff and enlarge its factories. At the same time, Westinghouse joined the other major firms in buying out smaller companies and engaging in vigorous patent litigation. Amazed by his rival's bold and rapid growth, Edison commented in 1889 that

> [George Westinghouse's] methods of doing business lately are such that it cannot be accounted for on any other grounds than the man has gone crazy over the sudden accession of wealth, or something unknown to me, and is flying a kite that will land him sooner or later in the mud.[31]

Westinghouse partly financed this expansion by advancing the company $1.2 million of his own money, but he also borrowed heavily. By mid-1890, the firm was carrying $3 million in short-term liabilities, when its total assets were $11 million and its current assets $2.5 million. As with Edison General, disaster struck in November 1890 with the failure of Baring Brothers, as Westinghouse's creditors called in their loans. In response, Westinghouse proposed to reorganize the company and double its capital stock, but investors failed to take up the new issue. Westinghouse next asked Pittsburgh bankers for an immediate loan of $500,000; however, they insisted that Westinghouse relinquish some control of the company, and Westinghouse refused. In desperation, Westinghouse turned to the New York broker-

30 On Villard's fall in 1890, see Henry Villard, *Memoirs of Henry Villard, Journalist and Financier, 1835–1900*, 2 vols. (Westminster: Archibald Constable, 1904), Vol. 2, pp. 342–3, 357–8; and Buss, *Villard*, p. 217. On the Baring crisis, see Charles P. Kindleberger, *Manias, Panics, and Crashes: A History of Financial Crises* (New York: Basic Books, 1978), pp. 153–6. On Villard's new policies for Edison General, see McDonald, *Insull*, p. 49. In response to the failure of North American, Fairchild recommended that Thomson-Houston "disregard the Edison Competition so far as to decline to give special credits in any shape or to take bonds & stocks of local [companies]"; see Fairchild to Higginson, 11 November 1890, box XII-2, folder 1890 Fairchild, Higginson Papers.
31 Passer, *The Electrical Manufacturers*, p. 279. Quotation is from Edison note on Edward D. Adams to Edison, 2 February 1889, box 63, folder 472, Villard Papers.

age house of August Belmont. With the help of Higginson, Belmont set up a committee of powerful investors who reorganized the firm. Viewing Westinghouse as "a bright & fertile mechanic" who lacked both tact and an understanding of high finance, the committee initially tried to circumscribe his power. However, drawing on his friendship with committee member Charles Francis Adams, Jr., Westinghouse persuaded the committee to permit him to continue as president.[32]

Concerned about their continuing problems in raising capital, the top management of the electrical companies concluded that relentless competition might well be fatal for all of their firms. Consequently, Villard early on investigated the possibility of cooperation among the three firms. Perhaps drawing on his extensive experience in Wall Street maneuvers, Villard shrewdly established relationships with both Westinghouse and Coffin. At first, Villard simply exchanged information on production, sales, and earnings with each man, but soon he was attempting to negotiate a patent agreement with Westinghouse and fix contract bids with Coffin. For instance, in February 1889, Villard and Coffin agreed that Sprague would not bid on a street-railway contract in Washington, D.C., provided that Thomson-Houston not compete for the Richmond railway contract. Similarly, in 1891, Villard sent an Edison General manager to meet with Coffin to negotiate the bids that Edison General and Thomson-Houston would submit for four street-railway contracts. Charles Fairchild, a Higginson partner, estimated that those negotiations saved the two companies $1.5 million, leading him to conclude that "the Co[mpanie]s in harmony get that much more than they would in Competition."[33] Although Villard had little

32 For an overview of the financial difficulties encountered by Westinghouse, see Passer, *The Electrical Manufacturers*, p. 279; and Francis E. Leupp, *George Westinghouse: His Life and Achievements* (Boston: Little, Brown, 1918), pp. 157–61. The negotiations between Westinghouse and Belmont are described in letters sent by Charles Fairchild to Higginson; in particular, see letters dated 30 December 1890, 4 February (or March?) 1891, and undated items in box XII-2, folder 1890 Fairchild, and box XII-3, folder 1891 Fairchild, Higginson Papers. Quotation is from Fairchild to Higginson, 6 May 1891, box XII-3, folder 1891 CAC, Higginson Papers. On the relationship between Charles Francis Adams, Jr., and Westinghouse, see Fairchild to Higginson, 19, 24, and 26 July 1891, box XII-3, folder 1891 CAC, Higginson Papers; and Edward C. Kirkland, *Charles Francis Adams, Jr. 1835–1915: The Patrician at Bay* (Cambridge, Mass.: Harvard University Press, 1965), pp. 175–6.

33 Villard's efforts to cooperate with Coffin and Westinghouse are described in the following letters from Villard: to Westinghouse, 16 December 1889, box 126, LB 64, p. 500; to Westinghouse, 20 February 1890; to CAC, 5 March

success in cultivating a relationship with Westinghouse, such behind-the-scenes negotiations appealed to Coffin and helped establish rapport between Edison General and Thomson-Houston. As Villard pursued a policy of cooperation, Coffin boldly proposed consolidation. In March 1889, just as Edison General was being organized, Coffin outlined a possible merger, arguing that continued competition and patent litigation would ruin both companies. Coffin also might have suggested that a larger consolidated company could work with Higginson to secure ample capital. Although Villard politely declined the proposal on the grounds it would be difficult to convert Edison General's stock to match that of Thomson-Houston, he let Edison demolish Coffin's plan. Enraged by the audacity that Thomson-Houston would even think of taking over his company, Edison attacked Thomson-Houston as "amateurs" who had "boldly appropriated and infringed every patent we use." As far as Edison was personally concerned, a merger would mean that "my usefulness as an inventor is gone. My services wouldn't be worth a penny. I can only invent under powerful incentive. No competition means no invention." Instead, Edison believed that the best policy for Edison General would be to strive to reduce the cost of electric lighting through more efficient products and better manufacturing techniques.[34]

1890; to Westinghouse, 10 March 1890; and to CAC, 25 and 28 March 1890; all in box 127, LB 66, pp. 74, 111, 144, 299, and 341, respectively, Villard Papers. See also John Muir to Villard, 31 March 1890, box 127, LB 66, pp. 360–2, Villard Papers; and Charles Fairchild to Higginson, n.d., box XII-3, folder 1891 CAC, Higginson Papers. On the Washington and Richmond deal, see Villard to CAC, 18 February 1889, box 126, LB 61, p. 161, Villard Papers. In that deal, Villard got the better contract, because Thomson-Houston was unable to secure permission from the authorities in Washington to use overhead trolley wires and was forced to use expensive storage-battery cars; see CAC to Higginson, 29 June 1891, box XII-3, folder 1891 CAC, Higginson Papers. Although Sprague encountered a number of difficulties in Richmond, his success there established his reputation in the traction field; see Harold C. Passer, "Frank Julian Sprague: Father of Electric Traction, 1857–1934," in William Miller, ed., *Men in Business: Essays in the History of Entrepreneurship* (Cambridge, Mass.: Harvard University Press, 1952), pp. 212–37. Quotation is from Charles Fairchild to Higginson, n.d., box XII-3, folder 1891 CAC, Higginson Papers.

34 I have not been able to find Coffin's 1889 merger proposal; consequently, the terms of his proposal must be inferred from "Mr. Edison's Reply to Thomson-Houston Memoranda of March 23d, 1889," 1 April 1889, box 63, folder 472, Villard Papers. See also Villard to CAC, 15 March 1889, LB 76, p. 381, box 130; and Villard to CAC, 3 April 1889, LB 62, pp. 3–4, box 126, Villard Papers.

Although Edison still believed in competition, Higginson and the other investors came to agree with the managers that consolidation offered the only means of protecting their substantial investment in the electrical companies. J. P. Morgan was especially concerned with how much capital was required by the electrical manufacturers, but at the same time he was uncertain as to how Edison General and Thomson-Houston might be joined. As he observed to Higginson in February 1891,

> regarding Thomson-Houston, I do not think it worth while to run two establishments. The Edison system affords us all the use of time and capital that I think desirable to use in one channel. If, as would seem to be the case, you have the control of the Thomson-Houston, we will see which will make the best result. I do not see myself how the two things can be brought together, certainly not on any such basis as was talked about a year or more ago.[35]

Just as railroad leaders and financiers had concluded a few years earlier that competition and cooperation had to give way to consolidation, the electrical manufacturers and their financiers were coming to realize that the competitive tactics of takeovers, patent litigation, and creation of central-station subsidiaries were proving costly and ineffective. It seemed obvious to both the managers and bankers that the only way to manufacture and market electrical equipment profitably was to concentrate the necessary resources in a single firm. "What we all want," wrote Charles Fairchild, a Higginson partner, in July 1891, "is the union of the large Electrical Companies." Accordingly, during the reorganization of Westinghouse, Belmont and Fairchild attempted to arrange for Thomson-Houston to take control of the troubled Pittsburgh firm. That merger attempt failed not only because Westinghouse persuaded the committee that he should remain as president but also because Coffin antagonized the reorganization committee by letting it be known that he preferred to see Westinghouse fail.[36]

---

35 Quotation is from J. P. Morgan to Higginson, 3 February 1891, LB 1887–93, pp. 532–3, The Pierpont Morgan Library, New York. I am grateful to Jean Strouse for calling this letter to my attention.

36 Alfred D. Chandler, Jr., provided an overview of the consolidation of American railroads in *The Visible Hand: The Managerial Revolution in American Business* (Cambridge, Mass.: Harvard University Press, 1977), pp. 145–71. Quotation is from Fairchild to Higginson, 24 July 1891, box XII-3, folder 1891 CAC, Higginson Papers. On Coffin's antagonistic attitude toward Westinghouse, see Fairchild to Higginson, 5 May 1891; and CAC to Higginson, n.d.; both in box XII-3, folder 1891 CAC, Higginson Papers.

Unable to bring Thomson-Houston and Westinghouse together, Higginson and Fairchild encouraged Coffin and Villard to investigate combining their two companies. Villard and Coffin continued to exchange information on street-railway contracts and technology, and in February 1891 Villard visited the Thomson-Houston factory in Lynn. During the next eight months, little progress was made toward consolidation, perhaps because Villard may have felt more confident after winning a favorable decision in the litigation over the lamp patent in June. In the meantime, though, Thomson-Houston was beating Edison General in the marketplace, or, as Coffin boasted, "he is knocking the stuffing out of them all along the line." For 1891, Thomson-Houston had total sales of $10 million, and $2.7 million in profits, whereas Edison General had sales of $11 million and profits of only $1.4 million.[37]

Such marketplace performance may finally have brought Edison General to the bargaining table. Perhaps the major stockholders realized that although Edison General possessed substantial resources – large factories, a national sales network, and access to Edison's laboratory – Insull and the firm's top managers had not succeeded in creating an effective organization. Consequently, in early 1892, Coffin and Fish began negotiating a merger with Hamilton McKay Twombly, a Morgan associate who represented Edison General. The negotiations focused on the issue that Villard had raised in 1889, namely, an exchange of Edison and Thomson-Houston shares. Even though Thomson-Houston had earned 50% more per share than Edison General in 1891, Fairchild recommended that Coffin offer to assign a higher value to the Edison shares because "for the sake of union T-H can afford to give them a good trade." Coffin proposed that three common shares of Thomson-Houston be converted to five shares of the new company, with Edison General shares being converted one-to-one. That offer was accepted in February 1892, and a committee consisting of Twombly, J. P. Morgan, D. O. Mills, Frederick L. Ames, T. Jefferson Coolidge, and Higginson was organized to handle the ex-

37 Fairchild to Villard, 23 and 25 February 1890, box 63, folder 473, Villard Papers; Passer, *The Electrical Manufacturers*, p. 322; McDonald, *Insull*, pp. 48–9. Quotation is from Fairchild to Higginson, 29 December 1891, box XII-3, folder 1891 Fairchild, Higginson Papers; profits and sales figures are from "Committee on Stock List. New York Stock Exchange. General Electric Co. 31 May 1892," syndicate book 3, 1890–2, p. 127, The Pierpont Morgan Library, New York.

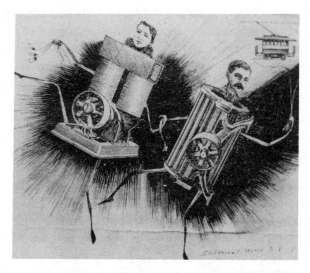

Figure 6.5. Cartoon celebrating the formation of General Electric in 1892. The cartoonist placed Edison and Thomson's heads atop their respective dynamos. From *Electrical World* (13 February 1892).

change of stock and the creation of the new company. That committee met in March, and at Coffin's suggestion it secured a charter from the state of New York creating the General Electric Company on 15 April 1892[38] (Figure 6.5).

38 Thomson recalled that Twombly was initially asked by the Morgan interests to reorganize Edison General and that in doing so he decided that Edison General and Thomson-Houston should be merged; see ET to John W. Howell, 7 January 1930, Woodbury's notes, CL, TP. The course of the negotiations can be gleaned from letters from CAC to Higginson, 1 and 7 February 1892, and two undated notes, box XII-3, folder 1892 CAC, Higginson Papers. Quotation is from Fairchild to Higginson, 29 January 1892, box XII-3, folder 1892 Fairchild. J. P. Morgan does not appear to have played a significant direct role in the negotiations; his principal contribution was in securing the support of a majority of Edison General stockholders. See his letter to Higginson, 1 March 1892, box XII-3, folder 1892 General, H-Q, Higginson Papers. The terms of the stock trade and the organization committee are from "Stockholders' Agreement Appointing Committee," 8 February 1892, syndicate book 3, 1890–2, The Pierpont Morgan Library, New York. The March meeting of the organization committee is mentioned in J. P. Morgan to Higginson, 1 March 1892, folder 1892 General, H-Q; and C. H. Coster to Higginson, 22 March 1892, folder 1892 Coster; both in box XII-3, Higginson Papers. The charter is discussed in CAC to Higginson, 2 March 1892, box XII-3, folder 1892 CAC, Higginson Papers.

The General Electric Company (GE) was capitalized at $50 million; after U.S. Leather, it was the second largest merger prior to the financial panic of 1893. GE's board of directors consisted of six bankers, two Thomson-Houston men, and two Edison men, with Twombly as the chairman. The bankers included Morgan and his associates Charles H. Coster and Mills, and Higginson was joined by Boston financiers Coolidge and Ames. Representing Thomson-Houston were Coffin and Eugene Griffin, and they were balanced by Edison and Hastings. Thomson was also offered a directorship, but he declined it because he believed that it would keep him from his technical work. Coffin was named president of the new company, and he selected most of his top managers from Thomson-Houston. The only Edison man to receive a major post was Insull, who was offered the position of second vice-president; however, he chose to move to the presidency of Commonwealth Edison in Chicago.[39]

There were several reasons why GE was dominated by Coffin and Thomson-Houston men, not by Edison and his associates. First, at the time of the merger, Thomson-Houston was the more successful firm; in 1891, Thomson-Houston earned a return on capital of 26%, while Edison General earned only 11%. Anxious to see such profits continue, Higginson and Morgan decided that Coffin and his associates should run the new company. Second, the other likely candidate for the presidency of GE, Villard, was not acceptable to the bankers. Involved in several business ventures (including the presidency of the Northern Pacific Railroad), Villard had had little to do with the management of Edison General. Moreover, his credibility had been severely damaged by the collapse of North American in the fall of 1890. Preoccupied with troubles on the Northern Pacific and campaigning for repeal of the Sherman Silver Purchase Act, Villard resigned as president of Edison General in February 1892. Thus, contrary to the claims of other historians, Villard played no part in the GE merger.[40] And finally, it had been Coffin, Higginson, and Fairchild —

---

39 GE's board of directors and top management: Navin and Sears, "The Market for Industrial Securities," p. 118; Passer, *The Electrical Manufacturers*, p. 322; David O. Woodbury, *Beloved Scientist: Elihu Thomson, A Guiding Spirit of the Electrical Age* (New York: Whittlesey House, 1944; reprinted Cambridge, Mass.: Harvard University Press, 1960), p. 205; McDonald, *Insull*, pp. 51–4.

40 Perhaps impressed with how Villard had organized Edison General, several historians have assumed that he played a part in the creation of GE, only to

not Villard or Morgan – who had pushed through the merger. They had been seeking such a consolidation since 1889, and they took the lead in the negotiations. Consequently, Coffin and the Boston investors reaped the rewards of the consolidation.

One might well ask why Westinghouse was not included in the merger of Edison General and Thomson-Houston. Higginson and Fairchild had participated in the reorganization of Westinghouse in 1891 and had hoped at that time to combine all three firms. It appears that such a merger was not possible because of the personal characteristics of George Westinghouse. Although the Boston bankers admired him as an engineer and entrepreneur, they questioned his understanding of finance and his ability to negotiate. As Fairchild explained,

> whatever power Westinghouse has, and I grant that it is great, is mechanical. His forté is the arrangement & control of a factory & in dealing with the practical problems. He is not a financier & he is not a negotiator. . . . What we all want is the union of the large Electrical Companies, and to bring this about will require skill & tact in the management of competing business as well as able negotiations when

be squeezed out at the last moment by Coffin and Morgan; see Matthew Josephson, *Edison: A Biography* (New York: McGraw-Hill, 1959), pp. 362–3; and McDonald, *Insull*, pp. 49–51. As evidence that Coffin and Morgan conspired to eliminate Villard, these scholars cited an unpublished Edison biography, "The Old Man," by Hugh Russell Fraser, in the Edison archives that described the Edison General and Thomson-Houston negotiations and a meeting between Coffin and Morgan. I have examined the relevant portion of this manuscript (pp. 362–72) and found that it does not mention the famous Coffin-Morgan meeting and that Fraser attributed a quotation to a Thomson-Houston executive (C. W. Dean) whom I have never seen mentioned anywhere else. A careful reading of letters in the Villard, Higginson, and Morgan papers reveals nothing to suggest that Villard was involved in the negotiations. In fact, according to the memoirs prepared by Villard's son, Villard advised his German banking friends to sell off their Edison General holdings in early 1892, and he strongly disapproved of the GE merger; see Villard, *Memoirs*, Vol. 2, p. 326. Both Morgan and Higginson were quite aware that Villard could be a stumbling block to creating a consolidated company; as Morgan wrote to fellow banker T. Jefferson Coolidge on 24 March 1892, "I entirely agree with you that it is desirable to bring about closer management between the two companies. Mr. Villard's resignation will take effect on the 1st [of] April, and I think the best way would be for Mr. Coffin to be then elected President of the Edison General Co." See LB 87–93, p. 676, The Pierpont Morgan Library, New York. Villard's resignation can be found in his letter to the board of trustees of Edison General Electric, 18 February 1892, LB 76, p. 318, box 130, Villard Papers. For a discussion of his activities in 1891–2, see Villard, *Memoirs*, Vol. 2, pp. 358–63; and Buss, *Villard*, pp. 224–43.

the time comes to trade. The final step will be to build up a disposition to trade – a willingness – Westinghouse cannot possibly do this. He irritates his rivals beyond endurance.

Westinghouse particularly irritated his rival Coffin. Like the Edison managers, Coffin did not like the Westinghouse Company's "attitude of bitter and hostile competition" – an attitude reflected in the Pittsburgh firm's low bids on equipment contracts. Further, during the 1880s, when Thomson-Houston and Westinghouse shared the Sawyer-Man patents through the Consolidated Electric Light Company, Coffin felt that Westinghouse had been obstinate and difficult. At the same time, Westinghouse had little love for Coffin. Anecdotal evidence reveals that Westinghouse saw Coffin as an aggressive wheeler-dealer who "will make a man about ten different propositions in ten minutes." Westinghouse had built up his business on the basis of engineering and manufacturing, and he had little respect for Coffin's understanding of marketing, finance, and organization building. Consequently, Westinghouse made it quite clear that he would not work with any electrical combination headed by Coffin.[41] Knowing of the animosity that had arisen between the two men, Higginson and Morgan probably decided that it was best not to attempt to include Westinghouse in the GE merger.

From another perspective, the Westinghouse Company may have been left out because it lacked a managerial hierarchy. Both the Edison and Thomson-Houston organizations had managerial and engineering staffs whose members could talk to each other. Ostensibly in competition, these managers had been known to cooperate at times. As we have seen, Edison managers helped Thomson-Houston fight off Westinghouse and secure a revised corporate charter in 1888–9. Under Villard's encouragement, Edison General and Thomson-Houston managers and salesmen had exchanged information about street-railway contracts. Although communications between the staffs of the two companies certainly did not cause the merger, such communications may have signaled to Higginson and Twombly that the combination of Edison General and Thomson-Houston would be feasible. In contrast, because George Westinghouse made most of the key decisions, the

41 First quotation is from Fairchild to Higginson, 24 July 1891, box XII-3, folder 1891 CAC, Higginson Papers. Second quotation is from CAC to Higginson, 7 May 1891, box XII-3, folder 1891 CAC, Higginson Papers. Third quotation is from Pound and Moore, *More They Told Barron,* p. 38.

Westinghouse Company lacked a similar cadre of managers and engineers who might have interacted with their peers at Edison General or Thomson-Houston. Thus, there was no communications or managerial momentum to encourage the inclusion of Westinghouse in the merger.[42]

In his study of the electrical industry, Harold C. Passer argued that the formation of GE could be attributed to the patent situation and the desire of Thomson-Houston and Edison General to diversify their product lines.[43] As the foregoing narrative reveals, neither factor was as significant as Passer suggested. Although the ongoing patent litigation was costly, it had not created an impasse that could be resolved only by consolidation. Even though the court had found in favor of Edison in the incandescent-lamp case, both Westinghouse and Thomson-Houston had found ways to work around the Edison patent. Likewise, product diversification was not a major issue. To be sure, Edison General had focused on dc incandescent lights and motors, whereas Thomson-Houston had specialized in arc lighting and ac systems. However, through takeovers, patent agreements, and in-house research, both firms had taken steps to diversify their full product lines prior to the merger. Although it is not generally known, Edison's associates at West Orange experimented extensively with alternating current, high-voltage dc transmission, and rotary converters, all for the purpose of developing an alternative to their competitors' ac systems. Thus, neither patents nor incomplete product lines determined the creation of GE.

Instead, GE was the result of three other factors: the desire to eliminate competition, the problem of raising sufficient capital for a capital-intensive industry, and the efforts of managers and investors to maintain organizational capability. As we have seen, Thomson-Houston, Edison General, and Westinghouse competed fiercely between 1889 and 1892. Using a variety of tactics – new products, integrating forward into central-station construction and management, publicity campaigns, and patent litigation – each firm tried to expand its share of the market and increase its profits. However, whereas Edison and George Westinghouse firmly believed that such competition would lead to the survival of the fittest, Coffin, Villard,

---

42 I am grateful to Alfred D. Chandler, Jr., for suggesting this point about managerial hierarchies. He briefly discussed this problem for Westinghouse in *Scale and Scope*, pp. 215–16.
43 Passer, *The Electrical Manufacturers*, pp. 324–6.

and their financial supporters soon realized that over the long run, competition was a poor use of resources and would lead to diminishing returns. Although the three firms could have continued to attack each other in the marketplace, the courts, and the technical and popular press, such attacks would have consumed capital and resources that could be better spent developing new products and improving manufacturing techniques. Well aware of the problems of competition, Coffin and Higginson chose to minimize it by merging with their chief rival, Edison General.[44]

The problem of competition in the electrical industry was compounded by the difficulties of raising capital for industrial enterprises in the late 1880s and early 1890s. The electrical manufacturing industry was created just as investors and bankers were developing the mechanisms for providing large amounts of risk capital for industry. Indeed, both Edison General and Westinghouse were caught in the dilemma of trying to build organizations appropriate for the scale and scope of electrical technology while employing the existing financial practice of borrowing short-term money. In my opinion, Higginson and Coffin saw this dilemma, solved it for Thomson-Houston, and then decided that the long-term solution was to create an even larger company. A large firm would be more profitable because it could take advantage of economies of scale (such as larger factories) and economies of scope (by having larger factories manufacture several closely related products). By exploiting such economies, the large firm should have a higher rate of return than several smaller firms and hence be more attractive to investors. Thus, the creation of GE was partly a response to the problems of raising sufficient capital in a capital-intensive industry.[45]

44 In his study of the electrical industry, Passer is cautious about claiming that the desire to eliminate competition was a factor in the formation of GE. In his view, one could only draw this conclusion if the merger had included Westinghouse and thus completely eliminated competition. See *The Electrical Manufacturers*, pp. 326–7. However, as the many letters from Coffin, Higginson, and Fairchild reveal, these men believed that competition was problematic and that it should be minimized or eliminated. Furthermore, they had tried to merge all three firms during the Westinghouse reorganization, only to find it difficult to deal with Westinghouse personally. Consequently, given the severity of the competition and the views expressed by the leading actors in their correspondence, I would conclude that the desire to eliminate competition contributed to the GE merger.

45 My specific discussion of how problems in mobilizing capital influenced the creation of GE supports Lance Davis's general conclusions about the relation-

Closely related to the problem of raising capital was the third factor of maintaining organizational capability. As the industry's pioneers, Coffin, Villard, and Westinghouse had struggled to build large factories, organize sales forces, develop full product lines, and create managerial hierarchies to coordinate production and distribution; in short, they had brought together the resources necessary to compete effectively. Once they had assembled their resources, those managers were loathe to let anyone or anything harm their organizational capability; indeed, they were anxious to utilize and expand their resources in pursuit of greater profits and market share. Of course, to build organizational capability, managers had to borrow heavily, and thus financiers such as Higginson and Morgan came to have a significant stake in those companies. Consequently, whereas the three firms competed and tried informal cooperation, eventually it became clear to both the managers and their bankers that the most promising way to sustain organizational capability was through consolidation.

The structure and strategy of General Electric

Once the merger was completed in the spring of 1892, Coffin set about organizing the new company (Figure 6.6). In doing so, Coffin duplicated the functional organization he had developed at Thomson-Houston. To cover each key function, Coffin appointed a vice-president. Eugene Griffin, who had been a vice-president at Thomson-Houston and had concentrated on street-railway sales, became the first vice-president for sales. A second vice-president was responsible for financial matters; initially that post was offered to Insull, but after his resignation it was filled by a Morgan man, Joseph P. Ord. To handle manufacturing and engineering, Coffin appointed Rice as technical director and promoted him to third vice-president in 1895. To support his top management, Coffin added a secretary to the corporation, as well as a legal department, headed by Frederick P. Fish, former chief counsel for Thomson-Houston. With the exception of Fish, who stayed with his Boston law firm, all of those top managers worked out of the company's new headquarters in Schenectady.[46]

ship between capital markets and the rise of big business in the United States; Davis, "The Capital Markets and Industrial Concentration: The U.S. and U.K., a Comparative Study," *Economic History Review*, 19:255–72 (1966).
46 Brief biographies of GE's top managers in 1892 can be found in "Organization of the General Electric Company," *Electrical World*, 19:331 (14 May

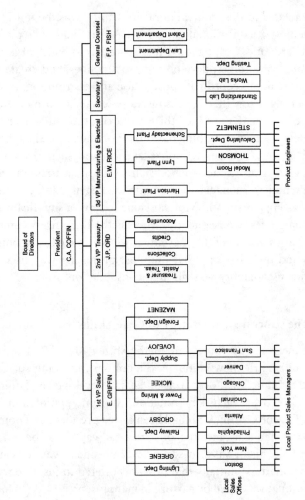

Figure 6.6. Organization of General Electric in the 1890s. Source: *Annual reports of the General Electric Company*, 1892–1900.

Like top management, GE's sales organization resembled that of Thomson-Houston. Again, individual departments were set up for the major product areas of lighting, railways, and power and mining. In addition, a supply department was established to handle switches, wire, and various small items, and after 1894 a foreign department was created to promote overseas sales. To reach customers, those departments worked through district offices in major cities. Within each district office, local sales managers each specialized in one product area; such a scheme made sense because customers tended to buy products from only one line. To coordinate sales efforts, Griffin headed a Sales Committee consisting of the product sales managers. That committee met monthly to set policy and approve sales contracts between $5,000 and $25,000. (Smaller sales could be approved by the local sales managers, but larger sales had to be approved by an Executive Committee of the board of directors.)

To control manufacturing and engineering, Rice had the superintendents of the three plants report to him. Decisions concerning product design and manufacture were made by a Manufacturing Committee, which was an outgrowth of the Factory Committee that Rice had used to run the Lynn works. That committee met monthly and included Rice, the factory managers, product engineers, and several other executives. Each factory began to specialize in the manufacture of selected products. Incandescent-lamp production was concentrated at Harrison, power equipment was produced at Schenectady, and smaller standard products such as arc lights, meters, and motors were made in Lynn.[47] Product engineering was decentralized, with engineers working on a particular product assigned to the plant where it was produced. To support the engineering staff, Rice established at Schenectady a Works Laboratory for testing materials purchased by the company and a Standardizing Laboratory for maintaining electrical measuring instruments. For new product development, Rice looked to Thomson and the Model Room at Lynn, as well as to Steinmetz and the Calculating Department in Schenectady.[48]

1892). George Wise mentions Ord's connection to Morgan in chap. 3, "Shoemakers," of his unpublished history of GE, p. 97.

47 Passer, "Development of Large-Scale Organization," pp. 382–6.

48 Reich, *The Making of American Industrial Research*, pp. 57–8; John Anderson Miller, *Workshop of Engineers: The Story of the General Engineering Laboratory of the General Electric Company, 1895–1952* (Schenectady, N.Y.: General Electric, 1953), pp. 1–5.

Through 1892 and 1893, GE continued the marketing strategy of Thomson-Houston and promoted the creation of new lighting and street-railway companies. In the eight-month period June 1892 to January 1893, sales totaled nearly $12 million, and profits were close to $3 million; converted to an annual basis, those figures would be $18 million and $4.5 million[49] (Table 6.1).

However, the new company was soon tested by the financial panic of 1893 and the ensuing depression. For 1893, sales were $15 million, and profits over $2 million, giving GE a profit rate of only 13%. As the panic limited the sources of capital available to industry, GE faced an immediate cash-flow problem. GE had inherited the large portfolio of utility securities that Thomson-Houston and Edison General had accepted as partial payment for equipment. In prosperous times, Thomson-Houston had remarketed some of these securities through its trust series and the Electric Securities Company. But during the panic, the utilities were doing poorly, and GE was unable to sell these securities to raise money to meet the payroll and interest payments on GE bonds. The problem was further compounded by the fact that customers were slow to make payments on equipment delivered. By July 1893, GE's debt had swelled to $10 million, and the company had only $1.3 million in cash on hand.[50]

In response, Coffin assembled a portfolio of the best utility securities, and with the help of Higginson and Morgan he established a special trust series. The approximate par value of the portfolio was $12.2 million, and Coffin offered the securities to the stockholders for 33 cents on the dollar. The stockholders could buy the securities outright once the panic was over; in the meantime, they were deposited with a special group of trustees. Morgan and Higginson underwrote the sale and advanced $4.5 million to GE. (Although Morgan was anxious to see GE survive, he did not like the terms of the trust, and he referred to it as a "Boston idea.") With that extra cash, Coffin was able to avoid declaring bankruptcy.[51]

49 Adjusted figures for 1892 are from Passer, *The Electrical Manufacturers*, p. 328.
50 Hammond, *Men and Volts*, pp. 220–2.
51 Details of the stock syndicate can be found in syndicate book 3, pp. 240–2, The Pierpont Morgan Library, New York. Coffin himself contributed $272,000 of the $4.5 million. In addition, GE's financiers and directors contributed the following: Drexel, Morgan, $945,000; Lee, Higginson, $600,000; T. J. Coolidge, $556,000; F. L. Ames, $556,000; H. M. Twombly, $780,000. Morgan's comment on the syndicate comes from his letter to Higginson, 31 July 1893, LB 87–93, p. 947, Higginson Papers.

Table 6.1. *Income, expenses, and profits of General Electric, 1892-1900 (thousands of dollars)*

Year	Income		Expenses			Profit or Loss			Accumulated Surplus or Deficit[d]
	Sales	Other[a]	Cost of Goods	Losses Written Off[b]	Other[c]	Total	Dividends	Retained in Business	
1892[e]	11,728	2,157	10,529	118	242	2,996	1,971	1,025	1,025
1893	15,645[f]	510	12,455[f]	14,587	938	-11,825	1,655	0	-12,455
1894	12,540	723	9,557	2,360	932	414	0	414	-14,795
1895	12,730	1,006	9,860	661	2,337	878	0	878	-15,306
1896	12,541	786	9,691	729	1,947	960	0	960	-13,917
1897	12,396	649	9,242	413	2,159	1,231	0	1,231	-12,957
1898	15,679	1,581	11,276	0	4,184	1,800	1,610	190	157
1899	22,379	2,168	16,437	2,000	2,913	3,197	1,001	2,196	2,353
1900	28,783	1,046	23,585	0	240	6,004	1,728	4,276	6,629

[a]Includes royalties, sundry profits, dividends and interest on securities owned, interest and discounts, and profits on sales of securities.
[b]Includes reduction of the valuation of securities held, plant inventory, and patents.
[c]Includes general expenses, taxes, and interest on debentures.
[d]From 1894 to 1898, GE liquidated and wrote down various assets. Consequently, the deficit for a given year is not necessarily reduced or increased by the surplus retained in the business for that year.
[e]Figures for April to December 1892.
[f]Estimated; the *Annual Report* for 1893 does not give these figures.
Source: Annual Reports of the General Electric Company, 1893-1901.

Once the immediate crisis passed, Coffin and his top managers took steps to streamline the organization and ride out the storm of the depression of the 1890s. Griffin tightened the sales organization and curtailed the power of the district offices, which previously had operated autonomously. Ord increased GE's efforts to collect accounts receivable and instituted a policy of selling most products on a cash basis. Ord also wrote down the value of the company's various assets (see the losses column in Table 6.1). Just as the depressed state of the securities markets reduced the value of the utility stocks held by GE, so generally depressed prices meant that the company's inventories of raw materials and finished goods were worth less. The value of patents held by the firm was also reduced. Rice and the engineers actively sought "to increase the efficiency of manufacture and reduce the cost of the manufactured product." They did so by enlarging the factories, installing special-purpose machines, and redesigning products to simplify manufacture. Thomson assisted in those efforts in a variety of ways, such as by evaluating a special machine for winding meters and by reworking his arc-lamp designs. Overall, Rice's efforts to improve manufacturing efficiency paid off; for 1895, Rice estimated that such steps resulted in a 30% increase in factory output over the previous year.[52]

Although such efforts to improve the organization were crucial to weathering the depression, GE officials realized that the company could no longer exclusively pursue the central-station marketing strategy. In the depths of the depression, GE found it difficult to get local businessmen and investors to put up the capital to create new lighting and street-railway companies. As the company admitted in its annual report for 1893,

52 The various efforts to streamline GE's organization are outlined in the second, third, and fourth GE annual reports (1893–5). Those reports are available on microfilm in the Cole Room, Baker Library, Harvard Business School. Quotation is from the *Third Annual Report of the General Electric Company* (1894), p. 3. To reduce production costs further, the company investigated consolidating all manufacturing in a single new plant in Cranford, New Jersey; see Charles H. Brush & Co. to CAC, 10 January 1896, box XII-5, folder 1896 GE, Higginson Papers. Thomson's efforts to help increase production are mentioned in ET to Manufacturing Committee, 14 October 1893, GE Transfile, Factory Notes, LB 1/93–12/94; W. C. Fish to Baker, 15 July 1897, GE Transfiles, Factory Notes, LB 12/94–12/98; ET to CAC, 31 January 1899, LB 1/98–4/99, pp. 790–2; all in TP. The statistic for 1895 is from *Fourth Annual Report* (1895), p. 5.

your directors do not believe that it will be possible for some time to come to do as large a business as was done by the company prior to the panic. . . . The street railway business, which to a considerable extent was done through syndicates and promoters, many of whom have become embarrassed, promises to be smaller than during the previous year. Arc lighting business is also reduced, largely because of the inability of local companies to secure capital with which to extend their business for the purpose of carrying out municipal contracts. The business of the company, with respect to incandescent lighting, which is to a great degree, performed by strong and conservatively managed companies, is in a more healthy condition, and has not suffered so severely.[53]

Because it prevented them from promoting the creation of new lighting and street-railway companies, the depression posed a vexing challenge to Coffin and the GE managers. Within both Thomson-Houston and GE, they had created the organizational capability specifically required to promote central stations. Once that market had disappeared, what strategies should the company pursue to protect and utilize its plants, sales force, and management team? How could Coffin and his managers redirect the firm's capabilities and survive the depression?

In response, GE pursued different strategies in all of its major product areas. In the lighting and central-station field, the company manufactured products that helped existing utilities increase operating efficiency and diversify their customer load. As Coffin observed in the 1896 annual report, "the disturbed financial and political conditions . . . have curtailed . . . the establishment and extension of Power and Lighting plants, and have enforced the practice of great economy on the parts of its customers."[54] To help utilities operate more efficiently, GE engineers designed large-capacity generating units that produced electricity at lower cost by taking advantage of the thermal efficiency of large steam engines. In 1892, the largest generator manufactured by GE was rated for 275 horsepower, but by 1899 the firm was building 5,000-horsepower units.[55] In many cases the new generators were compact and could fit into existing powerhouses, thus saving a utility the expense of constructing new buildings.

53 On the disappearance of the central-station market: *Second Annual Report of the General Electric Company* (1893), printed in *Electrical World*, 23:512– 15 (14 April 1894), quotation on p. 513.
54 *Fifth Annual Report of the General Electric Company* (1896), p. 5.
55 *First Annual Report of the General Electric Company* (1892), p. 2; *Eighth Annual Report of the General Electric Company* (1899), p. 10.

GE engineers complemented that increase in electrical output by offering central stations new interconnection devices for expanding and diversifying their load. Using a rotary converter, an ac utility could provide dc power for street railways and older incandescent-lighting circuits. Similarly, Thomson developed a constant-current transformer that permitted dc arc lights to be connected to ac networks. Thomson and Steinmetz also worked to develop an ac arc light.[56] Significantly, those efforts to help utilities diversify their load represented a sharp departure from the old central-station marketing strategy, for previously both Thomson-Houston and GE had encouraged businessmen to set up separate utility companies for arc lighting, incandescent lighting, and traction.

GE also offered utilities more efficient lighting devices. Through a variety of modifications, the company improved the quality of its incandescent lamps; whereas in 1893 lamps had burned at their rated candlepower for less than 20% of their life, by 1895 the standard lamps retained 80% of their rated power for more than 50% of their life. Similarly, GE introduced the enclosed arc lamp in 1893; by enclosing the arc carbons in a glass globe and restricting the flow of oxygen, that lamp increased the life of carbons 10-fold. Through the 1890s, GE produced 50,000 of those lamps annually.[57]

While helping central stations to increase their efficiency, GE pursued a second strategy: promoting the use of electric power in mining and industry. In moving into that field, GE built on the efforts of its two predecessor companies; while Sprague at Edison General had pioneered the use of dc motors for elevators and other industrial applications, Thomson-Houston engineers had used motors designed by Thomson and Charles Van Depoele to develop a line of mining equipment. Through the 1890s, GE actively marketed electric motors

56 On rotary converters, see ET to CAC, 15 October 1893, LB 3/93–4/95, p. 279, TP; *Fourth Annual Report of the General Electric Company* (1895), p. 15; and *Fifth Annual Report of the General Electric Company* (1896), pp. 13–14. On Thomson's constant-current transformer, see his letter to Steinmetz, 10 October 1898, LB 1/98–4/99, pp. 490–4, TP. On the ac arc light, see Rice to W. C. Fish, 28 January 1896, GE Transfile, Factory Notes, LB 12/94–12/98; and ET to Rice, 3 January 1898, LB 11/96–1/98, p. 978, TP.
57 Hammond, *Men and Volts*, pp. 261–3; ET to F. P. Fish, 8 March 1898, LB 1/98–4/99, pp. 134–8, TP.

for use in mines and textile mills, and it convinced the U.S. Navy to employ motors to turn gun turrets on battleships.[58]

Closely related to the introduction of motors to industry was the development of three-phase ac transmission. Following up his previous work with ac systems, in 1892 Thomson built at the Lynn factory a small demonstration system in which a small three-phase generator distributed power to motors, incandescent lamps, and arc lights using both transformers and rotary converters.[59] Like others in the electrical industry, Thomson was impressed with the potential of three-phase ac systems for permitting one plant to provide "universal" electric service, but further development of three-phase ac systems would be centered on the problems of power transmission in the western United States. In California, large-scale mines and rapidly growing cities demanded increasing amounts of power, but their expansion was limited because of the high cost of shipping coal for steam power. Local entrepreneurs recognized that such demand could be met by harnessing waterfalls, and they approached GE for new equipment that could transmit large amounts of power from remote mountain locations to mines and cities. During the 1890s, GE engineers designed and installed a number of pioneering long-distance three-phase power plants. In 1893, an installation in Redlands, California, used 10,000 volts to transmit power 21 miles, and by 1898 a system in Los Angeles was operating at 33,000 volts over 80 miles. Thanks to installations such as these, the power and mining department was the only sales department to enjoy steady growth during the depression.[60]

In its third major product area, electric railways, GE also had to seek new customers. Just as new lighting companies could not be formed, so GE managers found it difficult to promote the creation of new street-

58 A. R. Bush, "Re: Power & Mining Department," 1 September 1923, Hammond File, L1176–82; *Fourth Annual Report of the General Electric Company* (1895), pp. 11, 15; Hammond, *Men and Volts*, pp. 209–12, 251–3.
59 ET to CAC, 5 January 1898, LB 1/92–3/93, pp. 804–7, TP.
60 On the development of three-phase power transmission, see General Electric Company, Power and Mining Dept., Circular No. 2, *Three-Phase Transmission Plants*, circa 1894, MIT Archives; *Seventh Annual Report of the General Electric Company* (1898), pp. 7–8; and Hammond, *Men and Volts*, pp. 231–2, 250–1. The three-phase power plant installed by GE at Folsom is now a California state historical landmark. For data on the steady growth of this department, see *Sixth Annual Report of the General Electric Company* (1897), p. 11.

car or trolley lines. Consequently, they looked for new applications for electric-railroad technology. That included developing large locomotives to pull passenger and freight trains through tunnels, as well as electrification of the branch lines of major railroads. Working with Sprague, GE engineers also developed a new electric traction system with a third-rail contact and separate motors in each car. During the 1890s, GE installed variations of that system as elevated railroads in Chicago and New York, and it became the technological base for the modern rapid transit systems of those cities.[61]

Its efforts in lighting, power and mining, and electric traction permitted GE to hold its own during the depression. From 1894 to 1897, sales hovered just over $12 million, and the profit rate remained below 10% (Table 6.1). Such flat sales figures must have been disappointing to Coffin and the other managers who had experienced the phenomenal growth of Thomson-Houston only a few years earlier. Clearly, GE's lackluster performance reflected the decreased demand for capital goods and the deflation caused by the depression, but one wonders if performance was also limited by the difficulties of creating one of the first giant managerial hierarchies in manufacturing. Coffin and his associates streamlined the organization and strove to coordinate manufacturing and marketing, but the sheer size of the company may have made it difficult to control costs and achieve a reasonable level of operating efficiency.[62] Moreover, although the strategies to diversify central stations and find new customers for motors and power transmission protected the firm's organizational capability, at the same time these strategies did not fully utilize the company's resources. In particular, GE managers were worried that they were not using their factories to full capacity. Thus, Coffin encouraged the company's engineers and inventors to develop entirely new products that might utilize the firm's existing plants.

61 *Fourth Annual Report of the General Electric Company* (1895), p. 10; *Fifth Annual Report of the General Electric Company* (1896), p. 10; *Sixth Annual Report of the General Electric Company* (1897), pp. 14–15.
62 Chandler cites GE as one of the first machine-making firms to acquire a managerial hierarchy, in *The Visible Hand*, pp. 426–33. Louis Galambos emphasizes that the managers of many of the new giant companies faced substantial challenges in creating new organizational arrangements, in "The American Economy and the Reorganization of the Sources of Knowledge," in A. Oleson and J. Voss, eds., *The Organization of Knowledge in America, 1860–1920* (Baltimore: Johns Hopkins University Press, 1979), pp. 269–84.

Although Thomson participated in the company's efforts to improve its existing product areas, much of his energy in the 1890s was devoted to investigating entirely new products. In doing so, Thomson was continuing his role as the company's chief innovator, and he chose areas that allowed him to blend his scientific interests with the firm's commercial needs. Yet, in contrast to his previous experiences, in which he had created products that had gradually forced the firm to change, Thomson had to begin to develop inventions that would enhance the existing organization. To appreciate how Thomson directed new product development toward maintaining the organization, let us turn now to one of his major projects of the 1890s: the development of x-ray equipment.

Developing x-ray equipment

An x-ray is a form of electromagnetic radiation produced when a stream of fast electrons hits a metallic target in an evacuated glass tube. Located beyond ultraviolet light on the electromagnetic spectrum, x-rays were discovered by the German physicist Wilhelm Conrad Roentgen while studying the phenomena associated with Crookes tubes. A Crookes tube is a highly evacuated glass bulb in which a pale greenish glow, called cathode rays, can be observed passing from the cathode (negative terminal) to the anode (positive terminal). To excite a Crookes tube, one can employ an electrostatic generator, an induction or Ruhmkorff coil, or a high-frequency, high-voltage transformer.

Roentgen made his fundamental discovery in November 1895 while investigating the properties of cathode rays. In the course of one experiment, he was surprised to find that a barium platinocyanide screen fluoresced in the presence of a Crookes tube enclosed in a lightproof cardboard shield. Roentgen deduced that the fluorescence was caused by invisible radiation, which he termed X *Strahlen,* or x-rays, to indicate its unknown nature. In exploring the new radiation, he soon found that various materials were transparent to the rays, but that photographic plates were sensitive to them. Roentgen combined those two observations to make a shadowgram of the bones in his wife's hand. Roentgen announced his sensational discovery at a meeting of the Physical-Medical Society of Würzburg in December 1895. By early

January 1896, reports of Roentgen's discovery had reached American newspapers and electrical journals.[63] The announcement of rays capable of penetrating opaque bodies provoked a flurry of research in the United States. During the first six months of 1896, nearly every scientist, inventor, and doctor having access to a Crookes tube and an electrostatic generator or Ruhmkorff coil tried to produce the rays.[64] Thomson was one of the early investigators of x-rays; he had a Crookes tube and an induction coil readily available in the Model Room. More than that, however, he was drawn to the phenomenon because it was an opportunity to conduct experiments and do research that was more scientific than commercial.

Thomson entered into the flurry of x-ray activity in February 1896 by publishing two short papers commenting on the new rays. In the first paper, he was the skeptical scientist; he commented that both Heinrich Hertz and Phillip Lenard had previously noted that cathode rays could pass through opaque bodies. Thomson concluded his first report and devoted most of his second paper to proposing forms for x-ray tubes. In particular, he suggested using a glass vessel with an aluminum window on one side by which the rays could emanate and an aluminum coating on the other side to serve as an electrode. Borrowing from his experience in using oil to cool transformers, Thomson advocated immersing the tube in an oil bath to prevent overheating.[65]

63 A. E. Woodruff, "William Crookes and the Radiometer," *Isis*, 57:188–98 (Summer 1966); Eugene W. Caldwell, "A Brief History of the X-Ray," *Electrical Review*, 38:78–9 (12 January 1901); E. R. N. Grigg, *The Trail of the Invisible Light: From X-Strahlen to Radio(bio)logy* (Springfield, Ill.: Charles C. Thomas, 1965), pp. 3–4, 9–10.

64 J. W. Howell to E. W. Rice, 20 March 1896, GE Transfile, Letters to Officers of the Company, 1896, TP (hereafter cited as GE Officers 1896); Ruth and Edward Brecher, *The Rays: A History of Radiology in the United States and Canada* (Baltimore: Williams & Wilkins, 1969), p. 30; Grigg, *The Trail of the Invisible Light*, pp. 12–14; Nancy Knight, " 'The New Light': X Rays and Medical Futurism," in J. J. Corn, ed., *Imagining Tomorrow: History, Technology, and the American Future* (Cambridge, Mass.: MIT Press, 1986), pp. 10–34.

65 ET, "The Phenomena of the Cathode Rays. – Suggested Apparatus for their Production," *Electrical Engineer*, 21:134–5 (5 February 1896); ET, "Cathodographic Experiments," *Electrical Engineer*, 21:161–2 (12 February 1896). Aluminum was not a practical material for x-ray tubes, as it is difficult to fashion a tube that will hold a vacuum; see Benjamin Davies, "New Form of Apparatus for the Production of Roentgen Rays," *Electrical Engineer*, 22:320–1 (30 September 1896).

During the next two months, Thomson explored the rays in a wide-ranging manner. He did not allot specific time to x-ray research, but squeezed in a few experiments between his other tasks for the company. In the course of that unstructured research, Thomson speculated that x-rays were ordinary ether waves with a very high pitch and a small amplitude, such that they could pass through the spaces between the molecules of most materials. Using a Wimshurst-Holtz electrostatic machine to excite his tube, he examined the internal structures of starfish and sea urchins, and he noticed that the rays could be used to identify different kinds of coal. He also found that not all of the rays were absorbed by a single photographic plate and that multiple copies could be made by simultaneously exposing several sheets of photographic paper. In another experiment, Thomson discovered that he could make stereoscopic images by placing his x-ray tube in two slightly different positions above the object being exposed. He periodically communicated his results to the electrical trade journals as short articles or letters to the editor. Thomson continued those experiments until he had burned out all of his Crookes tubes through overuse. Because GE had centralized the production of incandescent lamps to Harrison, Thomson did not have access in his Model Room to the vacuum pumps and glassblowers necessary for producing additional tubes.[66]

Thomson's various x-ray experiments were followed closely by Rice. Because of his training in science and his years of association with Thomson, Rice, too, was curious about x-rays. In February and March of 1896, he arranged for the Harrison factory to construct tubes for both himself and Thomson, and he published a brief article in *Electrical Engineer* on his own x-ray experiments.[67]

66 See ET to Edward S. Chapin, 11 February 1896; ET to Dr. T. J. Harman, 14 February 1896; ET, "A New Use for Roentgen Rays," circa February 1896; and ET to T. C. Martin, 20 February 1896; all in LB 4/95–11/96, pp. 391–2, 395, 407–10, and 483, TP. See also ET, "The Source of the X-Rays," "Stereoscopic Roentgen Pictures," and "Manifolding by Cathode Rays," *Electrical Engineer*, 21:236 and 255–6 (4 and 11 March 1896); ET, "Stereoscopic Roentgen Shadow Pictures," *J. Franklin Inst.*, 141:381–3 (May 1896); and ET, "Producing Stereoscopic Pictures by Roentgen Rays," U.S. Patent No. 583,956 (filed 5 January 1897, granted 8 June 1897).

67 ET to J. W. Howell, 7 February 1896; and ET to E. W. Rice, 9 March 1896; both in LB 4/95–11/96, pp. 388–9 and 422–3; E. W. Rice to ET, 25 February, 3 March, and 10 April 1896, GE Officers 1896, TP; and E. W. Rice, Jr., "X-Ray Photographs from the Wimshurst Machine," *Electrical Engineer*, 21:410 (22 April 1896).

Although he appreciated the importance of x-rays as a scientific discovery, Rice was equally interested in seeing them put to use commercially. Noting the number of articles on x-rays in the electrical journals and the volume of unsolicited requests for x-ray equipment, Rice and other managers at GE became convinced in early March that there was a significant market for x-ray tubes and apparatus. As A. D. Page, sales manager for incandescent lamps, told Rice, "I have had it in mind ever since the first rumors of the new method of photography were cabled from Europe that there might be considerable business in selling Crookes tubes."[68] To Rice and the other GE executives, x-ray apparatus must have seemed especially promising because the manufacture of tubes and excitation equipment would utilize idle plant capacity. The x-ray tubes could be made using the glassblowing and vacuum equipment at the Harrison Lamp Works, and the excitation apparatus (consisting of transformers and induction coils) could be produced by the Lynn factory. Furthermore, it was assumed that the apparatus could be marketed through GE's existing sales network. In July 1896, Rice estimated that GE could do annual sales of $100,000 in x-ray equipment and that the markup on such goods would be nearly 100%. Given GE's flat sales, the income from x-ray apparatus would be especially welcome.

Page suggested that engineers at the Harrison Lamp Works should experiment with and design an x-ray tube, but Rice realized that the ongoing work to improve lamp production would prevent them from devising a satisfactory tube. Under the leadership of John W. Howell, the engineers at Harrison had just finished introducing the squirted-cellulose process for making carbon filaments, and they had just begun to install a new vacuum process purchased from an Italian engineer, Arturo Malignani. Judging that the design of a tube and excitation apparatus required further research and careful testing, Rice turned to Thomson. His former teacher was already experimenting with the new rays, and he had had nearly 20 years of experience in developing new products. In March 1896, Rice asked Thomson to design a practical tube, as well as a high-frequency coil for exciting the tube. Rice proposed that Thomson design and test new tubes in his Model Room at Lynn, but that he have the Harrison Lamp Works construct the tubes.

68 Quotation is from A. D. Page to E. W. Rice, 6 March 1896; see also J. W. Howell to E. W. Rice, 5 and 20 March 1896; T. H. Soren to ET, 4 April 1896; and E. W. Rice to F. P. Fish, 22 July 1896; all in GE Officers 1896, TP.

Admittedly an inconvenient arrangement, Rice wanted to capitalize on both Thomson's expertise and the glassblowing facilities at Harrison.[69]

It is interesting to note that Rice deliberately chose Thomson, rather than Thomas Edison, to develop GE's new line of x-ray apparatus. Through the Harrison Lamp Works, Edison still had some connection with GE, and in October 1895 he contracted with the company to experiment with lamp filaments.[70] Edison had been working on x-rays since early February, with a great deal of journalistic fanfare, but no consistent results. After speculating about an x-ray bulb for general lighting purposes, Edison had experimented with a few tube designs and had conducted an extensive search for the material that would fluoresce best in response to the rays. Finding that barium fluoride responded strongly to the x-rays, Edison designed a viewing box, or what he called his fluoroscope, which permitted him to view x-rays directly without having to use photographic plates. In March 1896, Edison offered his tube designs to GE, proposing that he and the company split the profits. Rice was surprised by Edison's offer, because it seemed unlikely that any patents could be secured that would assure profits or royalties for Edison. Rather than deal with Edison, Rice preferred to have Thomson develop x-ray apparatus. Thomson had been producing inventions for the company for years and had never demanded a share of the profits arising from any of his inventions. Furthermore, Rice knew that Thomson had the ability to work within the GE organization in designing a practical tube. Thomson could be relied on to consult with company engineers, give clear instructions for the construction of apparatus, and eliminate the problems of manufacturing such a complex item; Thomson knew how to push an invention through the organization. Although Edison had utilized the same skills in introducing his electric lighting system, by the 1890s he had become highly independent and unwilling to cooperate consistently with managers and engineers outside his personal circle. Despite Edison's personal reputation and advertising value, Rice probably judged that the development of x-ray equipment was too

69 Paul W. Keating, *Lamps for a Brighter America: A History of the General Electric Lamp Business* (New York: McGraw-Hill, 1954), pp. 44–6; E. W. Rice to ET, 11 and 23 March 1896, GE Officers 1896, TP.
70 [Agreement between GE and Edison], 1 October 1895, Harry F. Miller file, ENHS.

important for the company to permit it to be jeopardized by Edison's capricious style. Edison subsequently turned his designs over to the Edison Manufacturing Company, which produced Edison x-ray tubes and fluoroscopes for several years.[71]

Charged with the development of commercial x-ray apparatus for GE, Thomson undertook a formal research program. Some years later, he described that program:

> Early in 1896, I examined these Crookes tubes to discover, if possible, which form was best suited for Roentgen-ray examination, and further, the more important knowledge of what part of or in what condition the interior of the tube was favorable as a source of rays.[72]

Because so little was known about Crookes tubes and the conditions necessary for generating the rays, Thomson engaged in what might be termed "fundamental" research; he was gathering the data necessary to develop a new technological innovation. Such an approach must have been appealing to Thomson because it would allow him to conduct scientific experiments while at the same time fulfilling the needs of the company. Drawing on his years of experience of working on new products, Thomson was able to restrict his "fundamental" investigations to only what was required for commercial development; in that way, he balanced the intellectual curiosity of the scientist and the creative urge of the inventor.

In free moments during his busy days, Thomson sketched a variety of tube designs that the lamp works made up for him. In experimenting with different tubes, he quickly came to the conclusion that the x-rays originated from the anode (Figure 6.7). Some researchers, including Roentgen himself, had suggested that the rays emanated from the glass wall of the tube, whereas others assumed that they came from the cathode. To Thomson, that meant that x-rays were not the same as

71 On Edison's lack of organizational ability in the 1890s, see W. Bernard Carlson, "Edison in the Mountains: The Magnetic Ore Separation Venture, 1879–1900," *History of Technology*, 8:37–59 (1983). For the Edison Manufacturing Company, see Andre Millard, *Edison and the Business of Innovation* (Baltimore: Johns Hopkins University Press, 1990), p. 168; Grigg, *The Trail of the Invisible Light*, p. 49; and advertisement in *Electrical World*, 22:xviii (7 November 1896).

72 ET, "Work in the First Decade of Roentgenology," *American Journal of Roentgenology and Radium Therapy*, 28:385–8 (September 1932); quotation on p. 385. On the general confusion concerning how Crookes tubes produced x-rays, see Brecher and Brecher, *The Rays*, p. 44.

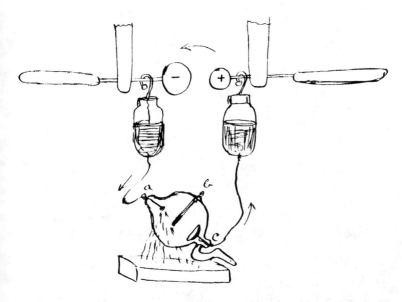

Figure 6.7. Sketch by Thomson showing x-rays emanating from anode: (a) anode, (b) large platinum target, (c) cathode. The tube was connected to terminals of an electrostatic machine. From E. Thomson, "Roentgen Rays from the Anode Terminal," *Electrical Engineer*, 21:281 (18 March 1896).

cathode rays, but instead were "anodic" rays. Anxious to obtain professional and scientific recognition, Thomson rushed to publish a report of his discovery in *Electrical Engineer*. Following publication, Thomson was pleased to learn that the prominent physicist Henry Rowland had earlier come to the same conclusion. Although he regretted that he had not been the first to publish that scientific discovery, Thomson speculated about how the two kinds of rays corresponded to positive and negative charges.[73]

According to modern theory, x-rays do not emanate from the anode, but from whatever target happens to be in the path of the electron

73 ET to E. W. Rice, 14 and 16 March 1896; ET to C. R. Cross, 14 March 1896; all in LB 4/95–11/96, pp. 452–5, 458–61, and 456–7, TP; ET, "Roentgen Rays from the Anode Terminal," and "Roentgen Rays 'Anodic' not 'Cathodic'," *Electrical Engineer*, 21:281 and 305–6 (18 and 25 March 1896); H. A. Rowland et al., "Notes of Observations on the Roentgen Rays," *American Journal of Science*, 151:247–8 (March 1896).

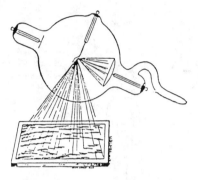

Figure 6.8. Single-focus x-ray tube. The cathode is on the right, the anode to the left, and the target is in the center. From W. H. Meadowcroft, *The ABC of the X-Rays* (New York: 1896), p. 119.

stream or cathode rays. Depending on the configuration of the Crookes tube, the electron stream impinged either on the anode or on the glass wall of the tube, making it understandable that the early researchers had confused them as the source of the x-rays. In conducting his early experiments, Thomson employed a tube with an especially large platinum target directly in front of the anode, leading him to conclude that the rays came from the anode rather than from the target. In early April, he realized his error and published a short article revising his original observations.[74]

Though his large-target tube failed to yield a genuine scientific discovery, it did lead to a practical tube design. Through prolonged use, the platinum target had melted from the heat of the x-rays, so that it was at an angle to the electron stream. Known as the single-focus tube, that particular design was discovered by several different x-ray researchers in early 1896, but usually it is credited to the Scottish engineer A. Campbell Swinton (Figure 6.8). Thomson found that the tube produced an abundance of x-rays, and on seeing a version of it illustrated in *Electrical Engineer*, he advised the lamp works to begin production of the design. Knowing the importance of getting the new product into production quickly, Thomson strongly recommended

74 ET, "Roentgen Ray Source," *Electrical Engineer*, 28:178 (8 April 1896).

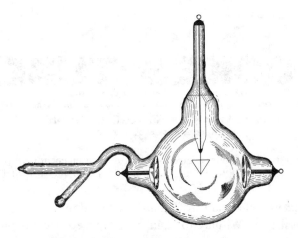

Figure 6.9. Production model of Thomson's double-focus tube, 1896. From "Thomson X-Ray Induction and Double-Focus Tube," *Electrical Engineer,* 22:404 (8 October 1896).

that design, remarking that "the sooner we get down to a form of tube which is the best for practical purposes the more business can be done."[75]

Not completely satisfied with the single-focus tube, Thomson sought to develop his own unique design. Within a week he asked the lamp works to blow a double-focus tube. In the tube were two concave aluminum electrodes and a single, wedge-shaped platinum target (Figure 6.9). Both concave electrodes had a radius of curvature such that they focused the cathode rays on a small area of the platinum target, thus producing a strong stream of x-rays. When excited by an alternating current from a Ruhmkorff coil or high-frequency transformer, each electrode became alternately the anode and the cathode, causing the rays to emanate from either side of the target. In addition to using ac power sources, the double-focus tube could be excited by a dc Holtz electrostatic machine by connecting one electrode to the positive and the other to the negative. Because the tube could be utilized with all

75 Quotation is from ET to W. H. Meadowcroft, 4 April 1896, LB 4/95–11/96, pp. 521–4, TP; see also "A New X-Ray 'Focus' Tube," *Electrical Engineer,* 21:340 (1 April 1896); and Brecher and Brecher, *The Rays,* pp. 44–6.

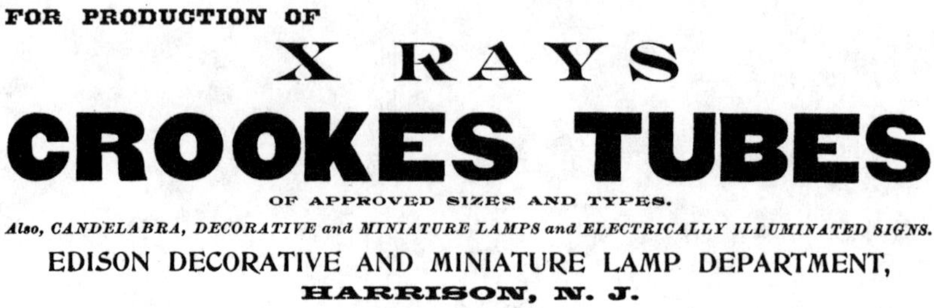

FOR PRODUCTION OF

X RAYS

CROOKES TUBES

OF APPROVED SIZES AND TYPES.

Also, CANDELABRA, DECORATIVE and MINIATURE LAMPS and ELECTRICALLY ILLUMINATED SIGNS.

EDISON DECORATIVE AND MINIATURE LAMP DEPARTMENT,

HARRISON, N. J.

Figure 6.10. General Electric's first advertisement for x-ray equipment, April 1896. From *Electrical Review*, 28:viii (8 April 1896).

types of excitation apparatus, Thomson referred to it as his standard or universal tube. Wishing to claim that unique design as his own, Thomson promptly published descriptions of the new tube in the electrical journals in April 1896. Unfortunately, it was not until August that Thomson got around to filing the patent application for his design.[76]

With Thomson's recommendation of the single-focus tube in early April, the Edison Lamp Works of GE began to place large advertisements in electrical trade journals (Figure 6.10). With the development of the Thomson standard tube, sales managers supplemented the advertisements with a formal announcement of GE's entry into the x-ray field:

> Although the General Electric Company commenced very early in the present year to experiment on the making of Crookes tubes for producing Roentgen rays, it is only after a long series of careful observations that the company has decided that it was ready to put Crookes tubes on the market. As will be seen in our advertising columns, the Edison Decorative and Miniature Lamp Department is now ready to supply Crookes tubes of approved sizes and types. We are informed that very successful results have been obtained with the tubes already furnished by them. Experiments are being continued in

76 ET to J. W. Howell, 8 April 1896, LB 4/95–11/96, pp. 544–5, TP; ET "A Proposed Standard Tube for Producing Roentgen Rays," *Electrical World*, 27:426 (18 April 1896); *Electrical Engineer*, 21:377 (15 April 1896); *Electrical Review*, 28:191 (15 April 1896); Brecher and Brecher, *The Rays*, p. 47; ET, "Roentgen Ray Tube," U.S. Patent No. 575,772 (filed 21 August 1896, granted 26 January 1897). Notably, this was the first American patent issued for x-ray apparatus.

order that the most improved forms may be within reach of the public constantly.[77]

At the time GE made that announcement, it appears that there were only three other firms engaged in the manufacture of x-ray apparatus.[78] Although the field would soon be crowded with small manufacturers, it was relatively wide open when GE decided to enter.

With the universal tube design in hand, Thomson turned his attention to the problems of manufacture. As a methodical inventor and engineer, Thomson demanded a high standard of workmanship in the construction of the tube, and he devoted much energy to overcoming the tendency of the lamp works to produce mediocre tubes. Working closely with William H. Meadowcroft, an engineer at the lamp works, Thomson tackled the problem of regulating the vacuum within the tube. For a Crookes tube to produce cathode rays, it was necessary that a small amount of gas remain inside the tube. However, as the tube was used to produce x-rays, the rays tended to break down the gas molecules, thus increasing the vacuum, or making the tube "harder." To remedy the problem, Thomson proposed that the tube be constructed with a small side chamber containing potash. If periodically heated by an outside source, that chemical would give off enough gas to reduce the vacuum. By extending the working life of the tube, that feature helped make the Thomson standard tube practical and commercially feasible.[79]

77 "Crookes Tubes," *Electrical Engineer*, 21:423 (22 April 1896); and *Electrical World*, 27:470 (25 April 1896).

78 According to advertisements and stories in the electrical journals, GE's competitors in April 1896 consisted of an incandescent-lamp manufacturer, the New York and Ohio Company of Warren, Ohio, which was producing Crookes tubes, and J. A. Le Roy, of New York, who was selling "a complete x-ray outfit, consisting of coil, tube, and fluoroscope which is perfect in every respect." A fluoroscope was also being marketed by the chemists Aylsworth and Jackson, of Orange, New Jersey. In addition, the electrical firm Siemens & Halske and four other European companies were selling x-ray devices in Europe, but it is not clear whether they marketed their products in America. See *Electrical Review*, 28:192 (15 April 1896); "Le Roy's Portable X-Ray Apparatus," *Electrical Engineer*, 21:423 (22 April 1896); "Prof. Elihu Thomson on the Fluoroscope," *Electrical Engineer*, 21:448 (29 April 1896); and Grigg, *The Trail of the Invisible Light*, pp. 27, 32, 42.

79 On Thomson working with Meadowcroft to eliminate production problems, see ET to W. H. Meadowcroft, 14, 22, and 28 April and 24 June 1896, LB 4/95–11/96, pp. 563, 587–9, 601–3, and 825–7; W. H. Meadowcroft to

As he attended to those manufacturing details, Thomson experienced having x-rays used on himself for diagnostic purposes. In early May, Thomson broke his leg while riding a tandem bicycle, and he arranged to have the doctor set his leg using one of his new x-ray tubes and a fluoroscope. During the operation, Thomson held a fluoroscope and undoubtedly gave his doctor extra advice on how to set the bone. Even while convalescing at home in bed, Thomson continued to experiment with different x-ray tubes and advise Meadowcroft at the lamp works about their feasibility.[80]

By mid-May 1896, GE was moving ahead with its x-ray product line. Thomson had designed an original tube for the company and was helping the Harrison factory eliminate production "bugs." To power the tubes, he had constructed a special induction coil and had begun to develop a powerful yet portable electrostatic machine. As production problems were worked out, the Manufacturing Committee decided to market the universal tube at 12 dollars, a price calculated to bring a fair profit, as well as permit substantial discounts for preferred customers. GE managers expected that the company salesmen would sell x-ray equipment directly to hospitals, doctors, and university physics departments.[81]

Unfortunately, GE was not moving fast enough in developing its x-ray tube. While still convalescing, Thomson noted that a small Boston firm, the L. E. Knott Company, was already producing a copy of his double-focus tube. That firm primarily manufactured scientific instruments, but it also had made glass mantles for gaslights, giving it some glassblowing capability. Unlike GE, with its extensive bureaucracy, Knott appears to have been the typical entrepreneurial firm of the late nineteenth century whose survival depended on flexibility and adaptation (see Chapter 3). In producing the universal tube, Knott had relied primarily on Thomson's published article on the tube, but Knott

E. W. Rice, 15 April 1896; all in GE Officers 1896; and W. H. Meadowcroft to ET, 15 May 1896, CL, TP. On the vacuum regulator, see ET, " Work in the First Decade of Roentgenology," p. 388; Grigg, *The Trail of the Invisible Light*, p. 53; and Brecher and Brecher, *The Rays*, p. 47.

80 J. W. Gibboney to E. W. Rice, 5 May 1896; ET to W. H. Meadowcroft, 11 May 1896; both in LB 4/95–11/96, pp. 632 and 647–50, TP.

81 W. H. Meadowcroft to ET, 26 May 1896, CL; ET to F. H. Soren, 8 April 1896; ET to Rice, 5 June 1896; ET to W. H. Meadowcroft, 16 and 25 June 1896; all in LB 4/95–11/96, pp. 541–2, 762, 792–3, and 829–33, TP; F. H. Soren to ET, 13 April 1896, GE Officers 1896, TP.

officials may have seen a prototype during a visit to the Lynn factory. Just as he had not seen the market potential for x-ray apparatus in February, so Thomson was not particularly concerned about Knott as a competitor. Likewise, Meadowcroft was not especially concerned about Knott, even after he learned that it was selling its double-focus tube for eight dollars.[82]

Rice, however, saw the situation differently. How could GE, with its tremendous engineering and production capacity, allow itself to be beaten out by an obscure manufacturer of scientific apparatus? Enraged, Rice wrote Meadowcroft demanding an explanation. "I think this is a matter of great regret," he wrote, "as the Knott people had no assistance from Prof. Thomson other than the description which he published in the electrical journal, whereas you have had the benefit of personal interviews and letters from him and me on the subject." Rice saw GE's lag as simply a problem of being unable to do high-grade glasswork, and he felt that Meadowcroft should be able to solve the problem at once. Rice ordered Meadowcroft to secure a Knott tube surreptitiously to determine its quality. "We certainly cannot afford," he insisted, "to have a small manufacturer excel us in a matter of this kind."[83]

Knott's entry into the x-ray field had the important effect of speeding up GE's development work. Without the threat of competition, the GE bureaucracy might have taken months to decide what kind of excitation apparatus to manufacture and how the marketing campaign should be conducted. Instead, under the leadership of Rice, GE moved quickly and made effective use of its engineering, production, and marketing capabilities. Rice arranged for several vacuum pumps to be installed in Thomson's Model Room so that he would not have to depend on the lamp works to make his experimental tubes. He also had the legal department begin preparing patent applications for Thomson's universal tube and other x-ray inventions. With Rice's approval, the Sales Committee and Manufacturing Committee met to set production levels and prices. A catalog was printed, and additional

82 ET to W. H. Meadowcroft, 11 May and 12 September 1896, LB 4/95–11/96, pp. 647–50 and 744–5; W. H. Meadowcroft to ET, 26 May 1896, CL, TP; "New Coil for Roentgen Ray Work," Electrical World, 28:113 (25 July 1896); " Knott X-Ray Apparatus," Electrical Review, 29:261 (25 November 1896); Grigg, The Trail of the Invisible Light, pp. 50–1. I am grateful to Nan Knight for sharing with me the information she has uncovered about this firm.
83 E. W. Rice to W. H. Meadowcroft, 20 June 1896, GE Officers 1896, TP.

advertisements were placed in the electrical journals during the summer of 1896. On his own, Meadowcroft wrote a short book, *The ABC of the X-Rays,* in which he described the operation and use of GE x-ray products. In coordinating the necessary resources and personnel, Rice exhibited the managerial skill and vision essential to get a large organization to take up an innovation.[84]

Of special concern to Rice and other GE managers was the matter of patents. Through their experience in the electric-lighting field, they had learned that patents could be utilized to eliminate rivals and establish barriers to entry. Consequently, Rice decided in July to approach Roentgen and ask him to take out American patents with their assistance. The strategy behind the move, as explained by C. D. Haskins, a manager in the incandescent-lamp division, was to control the entire x-ray field: "To my mind, it means all the difference between a practical monopoly of a very large and commercial enterprise on the one hand and quite severe competition on the other from a large number of small concerns who can manufacture cheaply." To negotiate with Roentgen, Rice asked Fish, GE's chief counsel, to visit Roentgen during his summer vacation. Assuming that as a man of science Roentgen would be concerned with priority and quality, Thomson suggested that Fish assure Roentgen that he would receive full credit for his work and that the company would be producing high-quality apparatus, thus discouraging the "cheap clap-trap work which is being undertaken" elsewhere in America.[85] However, Roentgen chose to give his discovery of x-rays freely to the world; he never tried to patent it.[86]

84 See E. W. Rice to ET, 20 June 1896; E. W. Rice to G. R. Blodgett, 20 June 1896; C. D. Haskins to ET, 23 and 29 June and 1 July 1896; and C. D. Haskins, [memorandum], 29 June 1896; all in GE Officers 1896, TP. See also J. W. Gibboney to G. R. Blodgett, 25 June and 17 September 1896, LB 4/95–11/96, pp. 828 and 860–1, TP; "Roentgen-Ray Apparatus," *Electrical World,* 28:234 (22 August 1896); *Electrical Review,* 29:ix (19 August 1896); and W. H. Meadowcroft, *The ABC of the X-Rays* (New York: Excelsior, 1896). A copy of GE's first catalog of x-ray apparatus can be found in Medical, X-Ray [series], box 46, Warshaw Collection of Business Americana, National Museum of American History, Washington, D.C.
85 First quotation is from C. D. Haskins to J. R. Lovejoy, 29 June 1896, GE Officers 1896, TP; second quotation is from ET to F. P. Fish, LB 4/95–11/96, p. 847, TP. See also E. W. Rice to F. P. Fish, 22 July 1896, GE Officers 1896, TP.
86 When offered large sums of money by different firms for his x-ray discoveries, Roentgen is said to have "rejected indignantly all 'commercial offers'." See Grigg, *The Trail of the Invisible Light,* p. 42. However, Thomson suggested

As a result of those efforts, GE was selling a full line of x-ray products by the end of August 1896. Besides the Thomson universal tube, the line included several forms of excitation apparatus, interrupters, fluoroscopes, and accessories. Although he had a hand in designing many of those items, Thomson was especially interested in the machines used to excite x-ray tubes. In the early years of x-ray research, such tubes generally were powered by electrostatic generators, Ruhmkorff coils, or high-frequency "Tesla" coils, and Thomson studied each of those machines. Drawing on his experience in designing an improved Holtz machine as a young man (see Chapter 1), Thomson designed a portable yet powerful electrostatic machine that generated high potentials by rotating several large glass disks simultaneously. He also designed a special Ruhmkorff or induction coil that could step up 52- or 104-volt alternating current to 7,000 volts, thus producing six-inch sparks. For the high-frequency or Tesla coil, Thomson wound a special transformer that he used in conjunction with an induction coil; with that arrangement, he secured voltages as high as 75,000 volts. Though it was powerful, Thomson found that the high-frequency coil did not generate sharply focused x-rays. Consequently, Thomson preferred to use an electrostatic machine to excite tubes in his Model Room, and GE tended to emphasize the induction coil in its advertisements.[87]

Just as he had designed complete systems for arc lighting and alternating current, so Thomson strove to create an integrated system of

that another reason that Roentgen was unwilling to negotiate was that he might not have been able to secure a patent for his discovery. With Crookes's original research on the cathode-ray tube and Lenard's observation of cathode rays outside the tube, Thomson believed that there had been sufficient prior work to prevent Roentgen from securing a broad patent on x-ray apparatus. At best, Thomson thought that Roentgen could have gotten a patent for a method of disclosing the interior structure of opaque bodies and organisms. With limited patent options, Roentgen may have had no choice but to forgo patenting and donate his discovery to the world. See ET to F. P. Fish, LB 4/95–11/96, p. 847, TP.

87 ET to C. D. Haskins, 18 June and 23 July 1896; and C. D. Haskins to ET, 29 June and 18 July 1896; all in GE Officers 1896, TP; ET to E. P. Thompson, 6 August 1896, LB 4/95–11/96, pp. 855–6, TP; ET, "Electrostatic Influence Machine," U.S. Patent No. 583,957 (filed 5 January 1897, granted 8 June 1897); ET, "Some Recent Roentgen-Ray Work," *Electrical World*, 28:415–16 (10 October 1896); "Thomson X-Ray Inductorium and Double-Focus Tube," *Electrical Engineer*, 22:404 (21 October 1896); Meadowcroft, *The ABC of the X-Rays*, pp. 76–83; Grigg, *The Trail of the Invisible Light*, p. 41.

Figure 6.11. Thomson's x ray system with double-focus tube and high-frequency transformer. Note the fluoroscope on the left, used to view the x-rays. Courtesy of the General Electric Company.

x-ray apparatus in which each component would complement the others (Figure 6.11). He tried, for instance, to develop excitation apparatus that would secure the best results from the double-focus tube, and his interrupters were engineered so as to provide the best effects with the induction coil. Finding that the lamp works was still having difficulty in manufacturing tubes with the proper vacuum, Thomson continued to experiment with vacuum adjusters and argued that the adjuster was vital to the system. To ensure that the x-ray products would perform as promised, Thomson advised GE to sell only complete systems and insist that apparatus be used as specified in the instructions. In selling individual components, the company would run the risk of having customers complain about unsatisfactory performance. Furthermore, in light of the incident with the Knott company, Thomson was also concerned that the "inductorium" should not be sold to other manufacturers, who might either use it incorrectly or steal GE's design. In advocating that his x-ray devices be marketed as a system, Thomson was again following his business-technology mind-set that a high-quality product would prove to be the most profitable in the long run.[88]

Despite Thomson's continuing development of x-ray equipment in the summer and fall of 1896, GE had lost its initial market position; GE was no longer the single large firm dominating the new field. The market for x-ray apparatus had become divided among a number of competitors. To complement its double-focus tube, Knott came out with an electrostatic machine, an induction coil, and a high-frequency coil. To differentiate itself from GE, Knott featured in its advertisements the high-frequency coil, an item that GE did not carry. Knott was joined in the field by several other scientific instrument makers, most of which were located in New York or Boston. Judging from advertisements in *Electrical Review*, by December 1896 there were at least eight firms selling x-ray apparatus. Notably, the Edison Manufacturing Company and GE were the only firms in the x-ray field that were not instrument manufacturers.[89]

GE continued to manufacture x-ray apparatus for several years, but eventually dropped the product line at some time in the mid-1900s. Most likely, as its regular business in selling generating and power equipment improved after 1898, the company no longer needed special products to boost sales and profits. In addition, the firm may have been unwilling to support further development of the new x-ray devices that would have been necessary to remain competitive in such a rapidly changing field. In particular, GE would have had to introduce a new tube design to replace the double-focus tube. It was found that over time, the double-focus tube became difficult to regulate and blackened as the platinum target was vaporized with use. Because the double-focus tube did not provide the high resolution achieved with the single-focus tube, it was eventually used for therapeutic rather than photographic purposes. And finally, one cannot help but wonder how effective was the match between the x-ray products and the existing sales organization. Accustomed to selling large pieces of capital equip-

88 ET to W. H. Meadowcroft, 11 November 1896, LB 4/95–11/96, pp. 967–9, TP; ET to M. P. Rice, 11 December 1896, LB 11/96–11/97, pp. 50–2, TP; William Allen Pusey and Eugene Wilson Caldwell, *The Practical Application of the Roentgen Rays in Therapeutics and Diagnosis* (Philadelphia: Saunders, 1903), pp. 329–30.
89 See advertisements in *Electrical Review*, 29:ix (23 December 1896).

ment to utilities and industrial firms, it seems likely that the local sales managers would have lacked the contacts necessary to sell a small product such as x-ray equipment to doctors and hospitals. In summary, as prosperity returned, and as technical problems remained with the universal tube, GE chose to drop that product line. Only with the discovery of the hot cathode tube by William D. Coolidge in 1914 did the company reenter the field, and it remained a major manufacturer of x-ray equipment until recently.[90]

The coming of the research laboratory

Thomson's efforts to develop x-ray equipment in 1896 reveal much about new product development at GE. Viewed from the perspective of Thomson as an individual innovator, several trends are apparent. Once again, Thomson needed guidance in identifying the market potential for a new technology. Just as Garrett and Coffin had previously helped him to understand the potential customers for arc lighting and ac systems, so Rice suggested to Thomson the market potential for x-rays. Yet once the market was defined, he moved quickly and delivered a practical product. In working with x-rays, Thomson balanced fundamental research with development; he did just enough research into the basic phenomena of x-rays to design a unique double-focus tube. Thomson also placed his personal stamp on the project by insisting that GE market a complete x-ray system, with tubes, excitation apparatus, and accessories carefully matched.

From an organizational perspective, Thomson's x-ray work reinforced the tradition of product innovation within GE. At Thomson-

---

90 Indicative that the company was finished with the development of x-ray equipment was that Thomson's assistant, Hermann Lemp, was assigned to work on arc-light rectifiers and steam vehicles; see E. W. Rice to S. D. Greene, 3 October 1896, GE Officers 1896, TP; and E. W. Rice to ET, 26 January 1897, CL, TP. For Thomson's later x-ray inventions, see the following U.S. patents: "Regulating Roentgen Ray Tubes," No. 591,899 (filed 4 August 1897, granted 19 October 1897); "High Potential Apparatus," No. 645,675 (filed 26 December 1899, granted 20 March 1900); with R. Shand, "Current Interrupter," No. 649,015 (filed 8 March 1900, granted 8 May 1900); and "Current Interrupter," No. 669,291 (filed 26 December 1899, granted 5 March 1901). On problems with the double-focus tube, see Pusey and Caldwell, *Practical Applications*, pp. 54–5. On the Coolidge hot cathode-ray tube, see Grigg, *The Trail of the Invisible Light*, pp. 77–9; and Hammond, *Men and Volts*, pp. 355–6.

Houston, Thomson had demonstrated that it was possible to develop new products within the firm that would combine the latest breakthroughs in science and engineering with the marketing and manufacturing capabilities of the company. Familiar with Thomson's inventive ability, Coffin and Rice readily looked to him to develop products that would help the firm weather the depression. Because Thomson was able to focus his research efforts on creating a practical x-ray system, he showed that product innovation was not necessarily a risky activity that would drain the company's limited resources. Instead, working with Rice, Thomson ensured that the x-ray project would make effective use of the underutilized plants at Harrison and Lynn. Thus, although the depression may have tempted Coffin, Rice, and other GE managers to forgo the development of any new products, the x-ray episode shows how Thomson sustained a tradition of product innovation within the firm.

Even though a firm may have achieved economies of scale and scope and may have invested heavily in the necessary managerial hierarchy, it may not have the organizational arrangements, decision-making procedures, or knowledge base to innovate effectively. Rice and Thomson had the will to introduce x-ray apparatus, but the firm lacked the organizational arrangements to do so in a timely fashion and thus was beaten to the marketplace by the more nimble Knott company. Within a firm as large as GE, it was difficult to bring together the personnel and equipment needed to create a new product. In part, that was because Coffin had structured the firm to optimize manufacturing and marketing, not product innovation. Whereas Thomson and his assistants had the expertise and equipment to develop the excitation apparatus in Lynn, the glassblowing apparatus needed for x-ray tubes was in Harrison. Although Thomson worked closely with Meadowcroft, his efforts were nonetheless hampered by having to wait for experimental tubes to be shipped from Harrison to Lynn. Thus, although GE possessed tremendous resources for innovation, the existing organizational arrangements required substantial efforts on the part of Thomson and Rice to combine the men and machines necessary to bring out even a small new product like x-ray apparatus. As this suggests, product innovation was a particularly difficult function for a large corporation to perform – even for a pioneering firm like GE.

The organization of GE affected not only the allocation of resources in the x-ray project but also decisions related to the project. Whereas

Thomson designed his new tube and excitation apparatus with a general sense of how the product might be manufactured and marketed, the specific decisions regarding pricing, production, and advertising were made by the Manufacturing Committee and Sales Committee, and those groups failed to expedite the introduction of the new product. Meanwhile, decisions regarding patent coverage were made separately by Thomson and the Legal Department. Of course, the authority for those different matters had been delegated to the various groups to ensure that they would be handled correctly for the existing product lines, but such compartmentation meant that it could be difficult to coordinate those same activities as they related to a new product. In failing to coordinate product design, patent coverage, and marketing considerations, the GE managers lost the chance to create a technological barrier to the entry of other firms into the new field of x-ray equipment. Although Rice was able to use the sudden appearance of Knott to force better coordination of design, production, and marketing, that experience may have shown him that the existing decision-making procedures did not facilitate the introduction of new products.

The x-ray episode also may have raised questions in the minds of Thomson and Rice about the skills and knowledge required to create a new product such as x-ray equipment. On the one hand, Thomson's craft skills permitted him to conduct experiments and design a distinctive tube. On the other hand, Thomson lacked the necessary advanced understanding of physics and chemistry that would have allowed him to recognize and correct the problem of the blackening of the tube. In a relatively new field (such as electric lighting), often a firm can establish itself with a product that basically works and is moderately different from those of its competitors. However, as an industry matures and competition intensifies, the search for a more clearly differentiated product may require that the firm exploit more subtle features of the basic phenomena underlying a product. Although craftsmen and mechanics often possess detailed and intuitive understanding of devices, by the close of the nineteenth century it was the scientists who were able to see the most promising ways of dealing with the increasing complexities of new products. In the case of x-rays, though Thomson possessed the skills for getting a product out quickly, he was not particularly well prepared intellectually for sustained investigation and improvement of x-ray tubes. Consequently, the x-ray episode may have set Thomson, Rice, and others to thinking about what kind of expertise was needed for competitive product development.

Those various problems annoyed and disappointed Thomson. In February 1897, as he completed work on the x-ray product line, he told Frederick Fish that

> my opportunities for work with the General Electric Co. are and have been, since the removal to Schenectady, so restricted in various ways that there is little satisfaction to me in continuing my present relations, and I feel too that it may be that the Co. cannot afford to have me do so. In fact, I have been for some time past on the point of writing a statement to the Company setting forth the situation as I see it. . . . My regret is that under present conditions, I can only be useful in a limited way. New work in new fields is not to be attempted at Lynn on any considerable scale as the tendency is to let manufacture at lowest cost absorb all facilities.[91]

Despite such feelings, Thomson never wrote his statement to the company, and instead investigated two other new products: high-efficiency engines and automobiles. Thomson studied engines in the mid-1890s as part of GE's strategy to help central stations increase their efficiency. GE sought to improve not only its generators but also the engines used to drive them. By far, GE's most important project in that area was the development of a steam turbine, from 1896 to 1903, by Charles G. Curtis, but the firm also asked Thomson to investigate a simple engine that could be used in smaller central stations and isolated plants. Again, GE officials hoped that the manufacture of engines might utilize idle plant capacity.[92]

Thomson's engine work soon came to be linked to the development of an automobile. Thomson and other GE engineers realized that a road vehicle would be an excellent means to test a small engine. For an engine to be successful in an automobile, it would have to be light-weight, simple, and easy to operate. If he could produce an automobile

91 Quotation is from ET to F. P. Fish, 12 February 1897, CL, TP. Unlike most of the documents in the collected letter file, this letter was a draft written by Thomson in pencil, which suggests that Thomson may not have sent this letter to Fish.

92 For GE's interest in small engines, see ET to CAC, 14 December 1895 and 20 and 25 January 1896, LB 4/95–11/96, pp. 288–9, 327–8, and 355–8, TP. On the development of the Curtis turbine, see Hammond, *Men and Volts*, pp. 275–84. Thomson was not especially impressed with the Curtis turbine when it was under development at Schenectady and instead urged the company to concentrate on developing his smaller engines; see ET to Rice, 13 August 1898, LB 1/98–4/99, p. 411, TP.

engine with those characteristics, then Thomson figured that the same engine would be excellent for powering generators in small stations lacking highly trained attendants. In addition, Coffin wanted to consider an automobile as a possible new product that could utilize excess plant capacity. In August 1895 he asked Thomson to advise him on the possibility of manufacturing bicycles, but Thomson instead recommended that the company consider automobiles. Like other inventors and engineers in the mid-1890s, Thomson and some of his fellow GE engineers were intrigued by the challenge of the automobile. With the growing popularity of the bicycle as a form of individual transportation, it seemed highly desirable to create a self-propelled vehicle. Along with Edison, Elmer Sperry, Hiram Maxim, and others, Thomson and Coffin sensed that the success of the bicycle indicated a huge market for a horseless carriage.[93]

In response to those developments, Thomson studied both engines and automobiles. As an electrical inventor, he had great faith that electricity could be used to solve nearly all of the practical problems of modern society, but he nonetheless concluded that an electric vehicle was not practical because of the weight of the batteries and the need for a network of charging stations. "It's like a calf," explained Thomson to his associate Hermann Lemp. "If you move it, you have to take the cow along too."[94] Instead, Thomson concentrated his efforts on a variety of nonelectric engines. They included internal-combustion engines using both oil and gasoline, engines employing powdered coal, and even a liquid-air motor. At Coffin's request, Thomson carefully examined the Diesel engine and recommended against GE securing the

93 ET to CAC, 6 July 1895 and 2 May and 12 September 1899, LB 4/95–11/96, pp. 94–6, and LB 4/99–7/1900, pp. 76–7 and 371–4, TP. On the early development of the automobile industry, see John B. Rae, *The American Automobile: A Brief History* (University of Chicago Press, 1965); Hiram Percy Maxim, *Horseless Carriage Days* (New York: Harper, 1937); and Thomas P. Hughes, *Elmer Sperry: Inventor and Engineer* (Baltimore: Johns Hopkins University Press, 1971), pp. 80–8.

94 On Thomson's rejection of an electric vehicle, see ET to CAC, 23 September 1895 and 25 January 1896, LB 4/95–11/96, pp. 173 and 351–5, TP; David O. Woodbury, "Inventor's Progress" (on Hermann Lemp), *Technology Review* (May–June 1944), pp. 419–21, 436, 438, 491–3, 500, 502; quotation on p. 492. Despite Thomson's rejection, GE Lynn built two electric vehicles in 1894 and 1897; see Beverly Rae Kimes and Henry Austin Clark, Jr., *Standard Catalog of American Cars, 1805–1942* (Iola, Wisc.: Krause, 1985), p. 579.

Figure 6.12. Thomson-Lemp steam automobile, circa 1897. Courtesy of the General Electric Company.

American patent rights to it, arguing that the engine's high compression would require too much expensive precision machining. Although he was impressed with the power-to-weight ratios of the available gasoline engines, Thomson was troubled by their exhaust fumes and rough running. Consequently, he experimented with kerosene-fired engines and developed a high-efficiency motor that he called his transfer engine.[95]

At the same time he was investigating engines, Thomson worked with Lemp on a steam-powered vehicle (Figure 6.12). For that vehicle, Thomson designed his "uniflow" engine, which achieved improved thermal efficiency by exhausting cool steam at the end of the stroke through a special set of exhaust ports.[96] Lemp complemented that engine by using his knowledge of electric welding to build a high-

95 ET to CAC, 14 December 1892, 20 September and 4 December 1895, 25 January, 11 February, and 3 June 1896, and 21 February and 7 April 1898, LB 1/92–3/93, pp. 754–8, LB 4/95–11/96, pp. 168, 252–6, 355–8, 390, 755–8, and 761, and LB 1/98–4/99, pp. 20–2 and 212–13, TP.
96 J. A. McManus, "Memorandum – Re: Thomson Uniflow Engine," 24 November 1919, Hall of History Collection; E. M. Shealy, *Steam Engines* (New York: McGraw-Hill, 1919), pp. 112–13.

pressure, coiled-tube flash boiler. In addition, Lemp developed improved steering and braking mechanisms. By August 1898 the steam vehicle was operational, and Thomson wrote to Rice that "I have just come from the room where the steam carriage is being put together by Mr. Lemp, and he has been running around the room at the rate of 6 or 8 miles an hour – running into things on occasion."

Lemp demonstrated the vehicle's practicality by driving from Lynn to Newburyport and back, a distance of 25 miles. Coffin also came to Lynn for a test ride, and though the vehicle did not perform perfectly, Coffin was sufficiently impressed that he encouraged Thomson and Lemp to begin planning for production. In May 1899 they began work on a new and lighter design that was to be "complete and perfect in all parts; in other words to reduce the carriage to a standard article, as if we were building an arc lamp or dynamo for reproduction."[97]

GE, however, chose not to put the Thomson-Lemp steam automobile into production. After consulting with Thomson, Coffin and the company's patent attorneys concluded that they would not be able to secure adequate patent coverage. Although Thomson and Lemp had filed patent applications for details of the vehicle and its engine, it became clear that the company would not be able to assemble a group of patents that would prevent other firms from entering the automobile field. Full-fledged production of vehicles would require a substantial investment by the company, and Coffin believed that it was too risky to make that investment if the company could not control the field. Equally important, beginning in 1898 GE's core business had recovered. The company was receiving new orders from utility companies for equipment, thus eliminating the immediate need for a new product to employ the underutilized plants. Thomson and Lemp assigned their automobile patents to the company, and they were subsequently sold by GE to other automobile manufacturers.[98]

In the course of that project, Thomson was again frustrated with how the company handled new product development. In part, he believed that he had failed to get strong patents on his steam engine

97 First quotation is from ET to Rice, 13 August 1898, LB 1/98–4/99, p. 411; second quotation is from ET to CAC, 11 May 1899, LB 4/99–7/1900, p. 107, TP. See also ET to CAC, 13 March 1897 and 22 August 1898, LB 11/96–1/98, p. 278 and 1/98–4/99, p. 429, TP.

98 ET to CAC, 30 December 1898, 10 June 1899, and 11 October 1899, LB 1/98–4/99, pp. 677–8, and LB 4/99–7/1900, pp. 223–31 and 445–6, TP; Woodbury, "Inventor's Progress," p. 492.

because the Patent Department had not assigned a lawyer to concentrate on filing automobile applications. The Patent Department had been unwilling to push the company's automobile patent cases because GE officials had yet to decide whether or not the company was going to move into the new field.[99]

But more important, Thomson realized that the engine and automobile work had gone slowly because of the existing organizational arrangements and lack of expertise. By December 1899, Thomson concluded that what was needed was an organizational change, and he wrote to Coffin

> that it has grown upon me strongly within the last four or five months that what is needed is a department at the Works especially for the development of this kind of machinery [i.e., engines]. We should have men and machinery wholly devoted to work in this field – together with the automobile field – and they should be separated out as it were in a building or department by themselves. As it is, the work is scattered and partly done in one place and partly in another, and it is almost impossible to force it along at the rate required. I find it extremely difficult with the work scattered as it is, to impress upon the men the necessity of saving time or to get a proper appreciation of the value of time in the development of new work. Things move at an exasperatingly slow rate, and the only cause for it that I can discover is the lack of concentration in one place of draftsmen, men and tools.[100]

Thomson was proposing what today we would call a research-and-development (R&D) laboratory. What he wanted was a department isolated from manufacturing operations, staffed by specialists, and equipped with the necessary machine tools. Although he did not suggest that scientists be hired, what is more important is that he wanted individuals "wholly devoted to work in this field," that is, specialists. Significantly, Thomson proposed a research department as a way of coordinating resources and expediting the innovation process. He had shown that new products could be developed at GE, but because it was such a large organization, he was not able to control the innovation process and deliver new products in a timely fashion. If the firm was to succeed in using new products to gain a competitive advantage, Thomson realized that it would need a new institution: the R&D department or industrial laboratory.

99 ET to G. R. Blodgett, 5 March 1897, LB 11/96–1/98, p. 252; ET to CAC, 4 December 1899, LB 4/99–7/1900, p. 598, TP.
100 ET to CAC, 12 September 1899, LB 4/99–7/1900, pp. 371–4, TP.

Figure 6.13. Thomson and Charles Steinmetz in Lynn in the mid-1890s. From the Thomson Papers, American Philosophical Society, Philadelphia.

Although GE did not go into the fields of automobiles and engines, and hence did not create the proposed special research department, Thomson knew that his concerns about the organizational arrangements for new product development were shared by the company's other innovator, Charles Steinmetz (Figure 6.13). Working first in the Calculating Department at the Schenectady plant, and then in a laboratory at his boardinghouse, Steinmetz had applied his mathematical skills to raising the efficiency of ac generators, transformers, and motors. By the late 1890s, Steinmetz had become especially concerned that GE's carbon-filament lamp was about to be overtaken by several new and more efficient lighting devices – the Welsbach gas mantle, the Hewitt mercury-vapor lamp, and the Nernst metallic-filament lamp. Aware that those devices had been invented by men familiar with electrochemistry, in July 1897 Steinmetz proposed that the company establish a special chemical laboratory where those devices could be investigated. Although his first proposal was ignored by GE officials, Steinmetz repeated his request in early 1899, and he began assiduously courting Rice and chief patent attorney Albert G. Davis.[101]

101 Several historians have recounted how Steinmetz pushed for the creation of the research laboratory; see Reich, *The Making of American Industrial Research*, pp. 62–7; George Wise, *Willis R. Whitney, General Electric, and the*

Steinmetz kept Thomson abreast of his plans and indicated that he thought that any new laboratory should work in consultation with Thomson. In September 1900, Steinmetz, Thomson, Rice, and Davis succeeded in convincing the company that a research laboratory should be established to investigate and develop new products.[102] To create that new institution, the four men pulled together several key issues. First, the company was in a position to consider a special department for product innovation because Thomson and Steinmetz had established a tradition of product innovation. Because of his numerous inventions at both Thomson-Houston and GE, Thomson had amply demonstrated to GE officials the potential of new products for capturing new markets and enhancing the firm's capability. Second, Thomson's recent experiences with x-rays and automobiles had revealed that the existing organizational arrangements of the company impeded product innovation, thus suggesting that a new department was needed. As Rice knew from the x-ray case, it was difficult to coordinate men and resources across a large organization. In order to develop new competitive products in a timely fashion, it would be necessary to concentrate resources in a single department. Third, all four men had felt the frustration of the manner in which decisions had been made about new products. Clearly, each new product needed an individual who could orchestrate decisions about patenting, production, and marketing. Davis, in particular, was aware how difficult it was to create coherent patent coverage when engineers and inventors worked at scattered locations, and he hoped that a central R&D facility might work more closely with the Patent Department.[103] Fourth, although the scale of the GE organization indicated that a special laboratory was needed to coordinate resources and personnel, it was the competitive situation that suggested that the laboratory

Origins of U.S. Industrial Research (New York: Columbia University Press, 1985), pp. 74–9; and Ronald R. Kline, unpublished biography of Charles Steinmetz, 1990, Chap. 7, "New Settings for Research," Program in History and Philosophy of Science and Technology, Cornell University.

102 Steinmetz indicated that he thought the proposed laboratory should work in consultation with Thomson, in his "Review of Engineering Work during the Year 1898," Hammond File, L5458–67. I am grateful to Ronald Kline for sharing this document with me. The efforts of Rice, Steinmetz, and Thomson to establish the laboratory in September 1900 are revealed in the following letters: Steinmetz to ET and to Rice, 21 September 1900, Hall of History Collection.

103 "Interview with A. G. Davis," 14 November 1927, Hammond File, L2992.

should be staffed by specialists. In all three cases – x-rays, automobiles, and incandescent lamps – Thomson and Steinmetz realized that GE's competitors were gaining the edge by understanding and exploiting subtle features of products. Had the company gone ahead with the automobile research department, it would have hired inventors and engineers with automotive experience; however, because the immediate commercial problem in 1900 was incandescent lighting, GE staffed the laboratory with chemists possessing the necessary expertise to understand and build new lamps. In short, the industrial research laboratory was created not only in response to the immediate competitive threat to GE's lighting business but also because of a gap between the tradition of product innovation and the existing organizational arrangements.

In his proposal for the new laboratory, Steinmetz emphasized that a chemist should be hired to apply chemical theory and laboratory techniques to the development of new lighting devices, but it was Thomson who suggested that the laboratory might have a broader mission of pursuing fundamental research; as he wrote to both Steinmetz and Rice,

> it does seem to me that a company as large as the General Electric Company should not fail to continue investigating and developing new fields; there should, in fact, be a research laboratory for commercial applications of scientific principles, and even for the discovery of those principles.[104]

In espousing both the application and discovery of scientific principles, Thomson was implementing the ideology that he had acquired from the Philadelphia scientific community 30 years earlier. In his high-school valedictory address, Thomson had waxed eloquently on how science might help the manufacturers of Philadelphia. Having come to a position of authority with a major manufacturer, he had helped create an institution that embodied the marriage of science and industry.

Pleased as he was with the creation of the research laboratory, Thomson must have sensed that its appearance signaled the end of his role as chief innovator for the firm. GE would no longer look to him to develop new products, but instead would turn to a team of scientists led by Willis R. Whitney at the laboratory. Moreover, although

104 ET to Steinmetz, 24 September 1900, Hall of History Collection.

product development still required individuals with the same hands-on experimental skills possessed by Thomson, the laboratory was built around specialists, not the generalist that Thomson had been. Thomson had succeeded as an inventor because he knew a little about everything and had used his craft skills to integrate ideas and information into new inventions. In the twentieth century, the synthesis required for a new invention would be that of combining scientific theory with team management.

Thomson was not bitter about relinquishing his role of chief innovator to the laboratory, and he served on the research laboratory's advisory committee for nearly a decade. In part, Thomson was comfortable with such changes because the laboratory did reflect his vision of science helping industry. Equally, he had grown tired of working exclusively on practical problems for the firm, and he preferred to investigate new topics in pure science. During the first two decades of the new century, Thomson took up research in astronomy, focusing in particular on the development of new telescopes.[105] But most of all, Thomson accepted the coming of the laboratory because it permitted the interweaving of technological innovation, organization, and marketing strategy. Throughout his career he had helped create a balance among those three factors, and it must have been a source of deep satisfaction to see the creation of an institution that explicitly coordinated product innovation with the structure of the company and its marketing strategy.

105 For Thomson's participation on the laboratory's advisory council, see Reich, *The Making of American Industrial Research*, pp. 72–3; and Woodbury, *Beloved Scientist*, p. 251. Thomson's scientific activities in the twentieth century are recounted in Woodbury, *Beloved Scientist*, pp. 256–328, and documented in Harold J. Abrahams and Marion B. Savin, *Selections from the Scientific Correspondence of Elihu Thomson* (Cambridge, Mass.: MIT Press, 1971).

Epilogue and conclusion

The establishment of the industrial research laboratory at General Electric marked the end of Thomson's career as an inventor. With the laboratory, GE shifted its commitment to technological innovation away from the individual and craft knowledge and began instead to look to groups of scientists and engineers. Through the first two decades of the twentieth century, Thomson continued to serve as a consultant to the company, and he maintained his Model Room at the Lynn factory. But rather than work on the problems posed by the company's organization and strategy, Thomson largely investigated scientific problems of his own choosing.

Thomson chose scientific problems in part because he had grown tired of the hassles of pushing a new product through the organization; however, he also took up science because he had never abandoned the ideals of his youth. The scientific community had helped Thomson give order and meaning to his life at a formative age, and so when he gave up the role of GE's chief innovator, it was not surprising that he returned to science. "My ambition," he wrote in 1897, "has been to be able to devote more and more of my time to scientific work, not necessarily with any hope or prospect of pecuniary benefit." Thomson looked to science not for public acclaim but for personal and intellectual legitimation; he planned to write more papers on pure science in order "to secure the good opinion of those whose opinions I value."[1]

During the next two decades, Thomson focused his renewed interest in science on astronomy and published short papers on eclipses, meteors, comets, and the craters of the moon. Intrigued by Percival Lowell's claims that the planet Mars was inhabited by intelligent life forms who had constructed the "canals" visible on the planet's surface, Thomson made his own study of the red planet. In response, Thomson proposed that the lines on the planet were the result of vegetation advancing and

1 ET to F. P. Fish, 12 February 1897, CL, TP.

340

falling back because of seasonal temperature changes.[2] Thomson was equally intrigued by Meteor Crater in Arizona, and he worked for over a decade with Daniel M. Barringer in an attempt to prove that the crater had indeed been created by a giant meteorite striking the earth.[3]

Complementing his investigations of such spectacular astronomical phenomena, Thomson also worked to improve telescopes. As a young man, he had derived a great deal of pleasure from grinding lenses and mirrors, and in the early 1900s he built a telescope and observatory at his home in Swampscott, Massachusetts. Drawing on his craft skills, Thomson became quite proficient in grinding telescope mirrors, and he was soon corresponding with leading astronomers, such as George Ellery Hale, about the construction of major telescopes. For the mirrors of those new telescopes, Thomson advocated using fused quartz instead of glass. Using an electric resistance furnace he had invented, Thomson had been able to melt and work quartz, and he had studied the material as a possible high-voltage insulator. Because fused quartz was clearer, stronger, and less susceptible to temperature changes than optical glass, Thomson was confident that it could be used to construct 100- or even 200-inch mirrors. In 1928 and 1929, at the GE plant in Lynn, Thomson attempted to cast a 200-inch blank for the Palomar telescope, only to fail because he was unable to control the temperature in the 40-ton mass and prevent bubbles from spoiling the disk's optical surface. Eventually, the Palomar mirror was cast by Corning Glass engineers using Pyrex.[4]

2 David O. Woodbury, *Beloved Scientist: Elihu Thomson, A Guiding Spirit of the Electrical Age* (New York: Whittlesey House, 1944; reprinted Cambridge, Mass.: Harvard University Press, 1960), pp. 257–8. The idea that the canals or dark areas were vegetation was widely accepted until the 1950s. Astronomers then began to suspect that Mars was lifeless and that the canals were caused when light-colored dust was blown by winds off dark rock formations. Observations from the Mariner flights further revealed that the canals are not continuous, but are chance alignments of dark patches. See Brian G. Marsden, entry for Percival Lowell, *Dictionary of Scientific Biography*, ed. C. G. Gillespie (New York: Scribner, 1973), Vol. 8, pp. 520–3.

3 Harold J. Abrahams, ed., *Heroic Efforts at Meteor Crater, Arizona: Selected Correspondence between Daniel Moreau Barringer and Elihu Thomson* (Rutherford, N.J.: Fairleigh Dickinson University Press, 1983); William Graves Hoyt, *Coon Mountain Controversies: Meteor Crater and the Development of Impact Theory* (Tucson: University of Arizona Press, 1987).

4 A selection of Thomson's correspondence with Hale has been published: Harold J. Abrahams and Marion B. Savin, eds., *Selections of the Scientific Correspondence of Elihu Thomson* (Cambridge, Mass.: MIT Press, 1971),

Just as he had been active in the Franklin Institute and the American Philosophical Society in the 1870s, Thomson was prominent in professional organizations in the second phase of his scientific career. During his years as an inventor, he had participated in the work of the American Institute of Electrical Engineers (AIEE); in 1884 he had signed the "call" for its first meeting, and in 1889 he served as its president. As a leader of the AIEE, Thomson was especially active in promoting safe use of electricity in lighting and power installations. In the twentieth century, he continued that work through the International Electrotechnical Commission, which established worldwide standards for electrical measurements. In 1908, Thomson succeeded Lord Kelvin as head of that commission. During World War I, Thomson was appointed to the National Research Council, and he helped develop submarine detection devices, apparatus for nitric acid production, optical glass, and improved gunfire control for warships. Especially concerned about engineering education, Thomson had close ties to the Massachusetts Institute of Technology (MIT). Beginning with his appointment as a lecturer in electrical engineering in 1894, Thomson served on the Visiting Committee to MIT's Electrical Engineering Department, as a member of the institute's governing corporation, and eventually as acting president, from 1920 to 1923. In addition, Thomson served on visiting committees to the Harvard Observatory and the National Bureau of Standards.[5]

Thomson's contemporaries recognized and rewarded his technological and scientific accomplishments. His peers named him, before Edison, a member of the National Academy of Sciences. (Thomson was one of a handful of inventors in the academy.) He was also a

pp. 251–98. Thomson discussed his investigations of fused quartz and his high hopes for that material in "Silica Glass or Fused Quartz," *GE Rev.*, 26:68–74 (February 1923). Thomson's efforts to cast the first Palomar mirror are recounted in David O. Woodbury, *The Glass Giant of Palomar* (New York: Dodd, Mead, 1939), pp. 124–45.

5 For Thomson's professional affiliations, see Woodbury, *Beloved Scientist*, pp. 164, 175, 253, 260, 264–5, 307, 312–13; and Rexmond C. Cochrane, *Measures for Progress: A History of the National Bureau of Standards* (n.p.: National Bureau of Standards, 1966), p. 557. His technical projects during World War I are listed in Abrahams and Savin, *Scientific Correspondence*, pp. 388–9. In recognition of his years of service, MIT sponsored an elaborate dinner for Thomson's eightieth birthday; see *Elihu Thomson Eightieth Birthday Celebration at the Massachusetts Institute of Technology* (Cambridge, Mass.: MIT Press, 1933).

fellow of the American Academy of Arts and Sciences and the American Association for the Advancement of Science. The American engineering societies awarded Thomson the John Fritz Medal, their highest honor. An internationally renowned figure, Thomson was given the Hughes Medal by the Royal Society, the Lord Kelvin Medal by the British engineering societies, and the Grashof Medal by the Verein Deutscher Ingenieure. He was named Officier et Chevalier de la Légion d'honneur by the French. Thomson came to enjoy some popularity in the American press; whenever leading scientists and inventors were discussed in popular magazines in the 1910s and 1920s, Thomson was frequently mentioned.[6]

After a full and active life in science and technology, Thomson died in 1937 at the age of 84. His career was best summed up by MIT president Karl T. Compton, who wrote in Thomson's National Academy of Sciences Memoir:

> Perhaps no inventor save Edison has brought so much renown to our country or contributed so much to its recent progress. His life encompassed the development of the electrical industry, and he will long be remembered as one of those who brilliantly extended and applied the primary discoveries of Faraday and the other pioneers in the science of electricity.[7]

Scientific values and craft knowledge

I have attempted to show that Thomson was a gifted inventor who made important contributions to electrical technology. One need only look at his spherical-armature dynamo or his arc-lighting regulator to appreciate his technical talent. Yet what is significant about Thomson is that he invented within business organizations. Instead of being the heroic inventor who went it alone, he was the original corporate engineer who prided himself on developing efficient and profitable products that helped his companies grow. Thomson did not invent either arc lighting or ac distribution, but he performed the crucial work that permitted those artifacts to become commonplace. And although many have made the easy assumption that bureaucracy is inimical to

6 Karl T. Compton, "Biographical Memoir of Elihu Thomson, 1853–1937," *National Academy of Sciences Biographical Memoirs*, 31:143–79 (1939), especially p. 159.
7 Ibid., p. 162.

creativity, Thomson's career reveals that an individual can with imagination and effort work effectively within an organization and to match technology to the company's strategy and structure, and even reshape the large organization's ability to sustain innovation over the long term.

But my purpose has not been simply to glorify Thomson. Rather, I have used his story to investigate two themes: how modern technology involves both scientific and craft knowledge, and how technological innovation is a social process. I have looked carefully at the ideas, skills, and values inventors such as Thomson brought to their creative endeavors. Although it is tempting to assume that all inventors had equal access to all ideas and facts available at any given time, the reality is that each was familiar with only a portion of the information available. In economics, scholars such as Giovanni Dosi have underscored the constraints on knowledge by referring to "bounded rationality."[8] The knowledge that inventors and other individuals possess is very much circumscribed by their personal preferences and needs and by their social contacts. Consequently, inventions are partly manifestations of how technological knowledge is valued, organized, and distributed.

These aspects of technological knowledge are amply demonstrated by Thomson's experience. Thomson developed his inventions using a combination of scientific values and craft knowledge. He secured his particular combination as a result of his emotional needs, his education and friendships, and his institutional ties in Philadelphia. Deeply impressed with the orderliness and power of science, Thomson strove to participate in the Philadelphia scientific community as a young man. In doing so, he absorbed the values of the scientific community, including objectivity and the importance of publication. At the same time, his work as a chemistry teacher stimulated his skills in building and manipulating apparatus. Drawing on those values and skills, Thomson entered the electric-lighting field in the late 1870s and soon developed an original arc lighting system. Perhaps the most telling sign of how the scientific community influenced Thomson was that he designed his first lighting system to impress his scientific colleagues.

Once Thomson embarked on a career of invention, he gradually complemented his scientific values with a growing body of knowledge

8 Giovanni Dosi et al., eds., *Technical Change and Economic Theory* (London: Pinter, 1988).

about electrical technology. Significantly, Thomson did not organize or utilize that knowledge in terms of formal theories or mathematical relationships; instead, it was based on intimate familiarity with specific objects and circuit configurations. Like the laser physicists that Harry Collins studied, Thomson learned about electrical machines by "rubbing" up against them.[9] Thomson's understanding of electricity was action-oriented, in that it came through direct, hands-on manipulation, rather than passive observation. And finally, although he could represent his electrical knowledge both verbally and visually, he preferred to use sketches and models. To highlight those characteristics, I have referred to his understanding of electricity as craft knowledge.

Whereas other scholars have observed that craft or "fingertip" knowledge often is difficult to describe and analyze, I have tried to indicate the content of that knowledge and the processes by which it was utilized. Early on, Thomson acquired his craft knowledge of electricity through direct contact with machines. As a young man, he studied electrical machines firsthand and then built duplicates. Thomson also tested several dynamos at the Franklin Institute, and that experience taught him how to analyze the complex relationships embodied in electrical machines. Through his direct involvement with artifacts, Thomson came away with two kinds of knowledge. First, he acquired a mental model of how mechanical motion and a magnetic field could be combined in a dynamo to produce an electric current. Whereas other electrical inventors chose not to make explicit what they knew about the interplay of such forces, Thomson's scientific background stimulated him to articulate and publish some of those relationships. Second, by observing and testing dynamos, he acquired a series of specific arrangements or mechanical representations that he could use in building such machines. For instance, for his early dynamos, Thomson borrowed the idea of using four separate field coils from Edward Weston's dynamo.

In his study of Robert Fulton and Samuel F. B. Morse, Brooke Hindle emphasized that apprentice craftsmen learn by copying or emulating the work of a master.[10] In doing so, the apprentice seeks not only

9 Harry M. Collins, "The TEA Set: Tacit Knowledge and Scientific Networks," *Science Studies*, 4:165–86 (1974); Harry M. Collins and R. Harrison, "Building a TEA Laser: The Caprices of Communication," *Social Studies of Science*, 5:441–5 (1975).
10 Brooke Hindle, *Invention and Emulation* (New York: Norton, 1981).

to duplicate the mechanical representations but also to learn something of the thought processes required to design an artifact. Such was the case with Thomson; once he had secured a general familiarity with dynamos, he began a deliberate process of imitating Brush's dynamo and arc light. He was encouraged to do so by his patron, Garrett, in the hope of quickly securing a lighting system that could be readily marketed. However, in order to patent his system, Thomson could not simply duplicate the work of Brush; he had to seek novel arrangements. His effort to surpass Brush led Thomson to investigate how to control his system and resulted in a superior dynamo regulator. Thus, along with direct observation and manipulation of models, another activity directly related to craft knowledge is emulation.

Later in his career, Thomson developed other skills. In New Britain, he learned how to use obstacles, such as the lack of machine tools and poor raw materials, to define his problem space. Thomson also learned how to substitute a variety of mechanical representations in an invention such as his arc light, not just to secure additional patents, but to hone his mental model of how such devices worked. In Lynn, Thomson took that heuristic of trying different mechanical representations and raised it to a high art, and in the late 1880s he produced a remarkable array of ac devices.

Thomson's craft skills and knowledge permitted him to continue to develop new products, such as x-ray apparatus, into the mid-1890s, but gradually he realized that future product developments would depend on a better theoretical understanding of phenomena, as well as the more advanced craft skills taught in the physics and chemistry laboratories of universities. Consequently, Thomson encouraged GE to hire the university-trained scientists who would have those new skills.

In sum, Thomson's use of scientific values and craft knowledge demonstrates that modern technology is strongly based in science, as well as another form of knowledge, and that it is possible to describe and analyze that other knowledge. By using concepts such as mental models and mechanical representations, and by looking carefully at the skills used by inventors to acquire and utilize their knowledge, we can understand the craft component of technology. Not only are relatively simple artifacts such as shoes manufactured on a basis of craft knowledge and skill, but Thomson's story shows that complex artifacts such as electric lighting systems are grounded in the same sorts of skills and knowledge.

Thomson's career clearly reveals how the electrical industry in the nineteenth century was created using both scientific knowledge and craft knowledge. Yet as the twentieth century has progressed, that industry has come to be seen as the paradigm of science-based industries. Why, in particular, did GE come to view itself as being science-based? Was science brought into the corporation simply because it led to better inventions, or were there other compelling organizational reasons? Although such questions are just beyond the scope of this study, Thomson's story does suggest some answers.

First, although GE did hire more university-trained scientists and engineers in the 1890s and 1900s, it did so more to secure special skills than for their theoretical expertise. GE employed Willis R. Whitney, William D. Coolidge, and other chemists in the belief that their state-of-the-art experimental techniques in physical chemistry would permit them to devise a new metallic-filament lamp. In the same way, American Telephone and Telegraph (AT&T) hired Ph.D. physicists in the 1900s because it needed individuals with firsthand experience in developing vacuum tubes.[11] Hence, on one level, it would appear that the electrical industry in the early twentieth century continued to depend on craft knowledge for new product development. Of course, once employed, these scientists applied not only their experimental skills but also their theoretical understanding to improvement of products. In doing so, they reshaped the organizations that had hired them and provided large corporations with the ability to remain innovative over the long term.

A second reason that GE may have emphasized science over craft knowledge concerned the size of the organization. Throughout this study we have seen how electrical technology required the coordination of different functions, including product design, manufacture, marketing, and finance. Initially, Coffin and Rice coordinated those activities informally, but as the scale of operations grew, they created an elaborate organization and employed large numbers of engineers.

11 That GE and AT&T hired scientists more for their laboratory skills than for their theoretical expertise is a conclusion I draw from information presented by George Wise, "Ionists in Industry: Physical Chemistry at General Electric, 1900–1915," *Isis*, 74:7–21 (March 1983); George Wise, *Willis R. Whitney, General Electric, and the Origins of U.S. Industrial Research* (New York: Columbia University Press, 1985); and Leonard S. Reich, *The Making of American Industrial Research: Science and Business at GE and Bell, 1876–1926* (Cambridge University Press, 1985).

To ensure that hundreds of engineers could work smoothly within the bureaucracy, GE had to create a corporate culture.[12] In part, GE managers accomplished that through a series of training programs for engineers and other employees.[13] Equally important, however, was the creation of a discourse within the company that could provide engineers a common language and standard concepts with which they could discuss a variety of technical problems. Anxious to have that discourse transcend individual differences, be applicable to a range of problems, and provide intellectual legitimacy, the engineers framed their discourse as a science. By far the most prominent example of the scientific discourse that grew up within the corporate context of GE was Charles Steinmetz's theory and design rules for ac motors and transformers. Thus, GE became science-based as engineers created a discourse that permitted effective communication and coordination of ideas about electricity across the organization.[14]

Third, GE came to emphasize its scientific roots because of the capital-intensive nature of its business. To develop and introduce electrical technology required substantial capital, and in fact the drive for capital was one of the reasons that Thomson-Houston and Edison General joined together to form GE. To ensure that the capital and resources invested in GE would be adequately utilized, Coffin continued to support new product development, and he looked to Thomson and Steinmetz to provide those innovations. Thomson's innovations were strongly based on his personal, hands-on knowledge, and although he tried to deliver new products in a timely fashion, he could not always control the process by which his craft skills led to an

12 Louis Galambos has argued that Theodore Vail encouraged technological innovation and systems engineering as ways of creating an effective corporate culture at AT&T; see his unpublished essay: "Theodore N. Vail and the Role of Innovation in the Modern Bell System," History Department, Johns Hopkins University.

13 George Wise, " 'On Test': Postgraduate Training of Engineers at General Electric, 1892–1961," IEEE Transactions on Education, E-22:171–7 (November 1979); Charles M. Ripley, Life in a Large Manufacturing Plant (Schenectady, N.Y.: General Electric Company Publication Bureau, 1919).

14 Ronald Kline, "Science and Engineering Theory in the Invention and Development of the Induction Motor, 1800–1900," Technology and Culture, 28:283–313 (April 1987), esp. pp. 305–12. I suspect that an examination of the in-house technical journal, General Electric Review, would yield further examples of the engineers' scientific discourse. For a discussion of the Review, see David E. Nye, Image Worlds: Corporate Identities at General Electric (Cambridge, Mass.: MIT Press, 1985), pp. 60–70.

innovation. As we saw in the development of his ac lighting system, Thomson had difficulty in delivering the system as quickly as Coffin and the marketing group wanted it. Because of experiences such as that, GE managers came to see product development by inventors as being unpredictable and difficult to control. Although they could tolerate the idiosyncrasies of inventors during the early phases of the company's growth, the unpredictability of inventors became more of a problem as capital investment grew. Once GE came to have substantial organizational capability, its managers were increasingly reluctant to look to a few individuals such as Thomson and Steinmetz to undertake product development. It was simply too risky to bet the company on the personal and craft knowledge possessed by Thomson. Instead, GE managers wanted an institution to perform the function of innovation that was as reliable, as controlled, as their new manufacturing and marketing institutions. Consequently, they turned to scientists for new product development because in their rhetoric those scientists spoke of being able to predict and control the forces of nature. Along with Rice, Davis, and Steinmetz, Thomson certainly knew the symbolic power of science, and he strongly urged that the company create a scientific laboratory. Thus, a final reason that GE came to emphasize scientific research was that science appeared to offer more reliable sources of new products than could inventors, and such reliability was needed to protect the firm's capital and human resources.

One further implication of this discussion of craft knowledge in modern technology is that it suggests that historians of technology need to look at a wider range of actors. If craft knowledge informed the creation of complex artifacts such as electric lighting systems, then it seems appropriate that scholars investigate the sources and contributors of that knowledge. It is not enough to focus on how professional scientists and engineers create new technology; we also need to look at the roles played by craftsmen and technicians who help build new artifacts, as well as the installers, operators, and consumers who use them. Although these craft-oriented actors may not establish the overall configuration of a new technology, they certainly participate by selecting the particular devices – the mechanical representations – that influence the performance of the technology. For instance, Walter Vincenti has shown how the technique of flush riveting to assemble metal aircraft was developed on the shop floor and how that technique permitted aircraft manufacturers to realize their design ideals.[15] Similarly, one of the first programmable computers was developed not by International Business Machines (IBM) researchers but by IBM customers; anxious to acquire a high-speed machine to perform calculations of missile trajectories, engineers at Northrop Aircraft crudely joined an IBM punchcard machine to an electronic tabulator to create a "poor man's ENIAC" in 1948.[16] Historians might refine the notion of craft knowledge and apply it to twentieth-century examples such as these, with the result that we might better understand how a particular technology acquires all of its characteristics. Moreover, by including a wider range of participants in the analysis of the innovation process, a consideration of craft knowledge can allow at least a portion of the history of technology to be written "from the bottom up."

Innovation as a social process

A second theme of this study has been technological innovation as a social process. To do so, I have argued that the creation of a complex technology such as electric lighting required not simply the invention of new hardware, but deliberate linkage of that hardware to particular organizational arrangements and marketing strategy. Thomson and his associates made electric lighting a widely available commodity and a profitable business because they matched new lighting systems with a functional business organization and the strategy of central stations.

Significantly, the linking of technology, organization, and marketing strategy did not take place automatically, driven by inexorable technical or economic forces. Rather, individuals and groups forged those links gradually as they interacted on several levels, making mistakes, changing their approaches, and ultimately developing an appropriate match between the hardware and the business system.

Most directly, those links evolved as Thomson worked with other individuals. Unlike previous studies of inventors, this book has depicted innovation not as the act of a lone individual but rather as an activity in which the inventor interacts with a variety of people. Many

---

15 Walter G. Vincenti, "Technological Knowledge without Science: The Innovation of Flush Riveting in American Airplanes, ca. 1930–ca. 1950," *Technology and Culture*, 25:540–76 (July 1984).

16 Charles J. Bashe et al., *IBM's Early Computers* (Cambridge, Mass.: MIT Press, 1986), pp. 69–71.

biographies of Edison have mentioned that he worked with a team of experimenters, but then have narrated how he alone performed the creative act.[17] In contrast, here we have seen how Thomson created and refined his inventions by communicating and working with business partners and assistants. Although Americans like to celebrate a romantic myth of the heroic inventor tinkering alone in his garage or basement, it is important to realize that an invention becomes an established product only when the inventor is able to work with other people.

For Thomson, the key relationships were those with his backers and managers. Throughout his career, Thomson depended on his business associates to identify the commercial potential of his inventions. In Philadelphia, it was Garrett who helped him see the need to increase the number of lights powered by his dynamo; at Thomson-Houston, it was Coffin who urged him to develop an ac system; and at GE, it was Rice who saw the commercial potential of x-ray apparatus. Although one might use those examples to argue that Thomson was a "hired gun" who applied technology to whatever business opportunity his employers chose, that interpretation would miss the subtlety of the social process. As each episode reveals, the process of matching the technology to the marketing opportunity involved significant give-and-take; often Thomson would have the technology in hand before the backer had identified the commercial potential, and subsequently they would work together to modify both the technology and the marketing. Those negotiations were especially important in the case of the ac system, where Coffin had to adjust his expectations of when the product would be delivered, and Thomson had to compromise his wish to create the perfect system. On an initial level, then, innovation was a social process for Thomson in that his inventions were shaped by interactions with his backers and managers.

As an inventor works to bring a technological artifact to the marketplace, frequently he or she not only must work with other individuals but also must help shape an organization around the artifact. Consequently, a second way in which innovation is a social process has to do with making the connection between the physical systems created and

17 For examples of Edison biographies that juxtapose the team approach with heroic moments of invention, see Matthew Josephson, *Edison: A Biography* (New York: McGraw-Hill, 1959); and Robert Conot, *A Streak of Luck* (New York: Seaview, 1979).

the appropriate business organizations. Like other students of the social construction of technology, I believe that it is a mistake to separate the artifact from its organizational setting. Something important is lost when we consider a technological artifact such as the Model T without thinking about the Ford Motor Company with its moving assembly line, its five-dollar-a-day pay scale, and Henry Ford's style of management. Likewise, we would fail to appreciate completely why Thomson designed his electric lighting systems the way he did without considering the business organizations in which he worked.[18]

In Thomson's story we see how his inventions and the business organizations mirrored each other, growing together in size and complexity. In Philadelphia, Thomson's arc lighting system could power but eight lights, required little custom machine work in its manufacture, used one type of lamp and few accessories, and cost only a few thousand dollars; consequently, Thomson and Garrett created an informal partnership and employed only a few workmen. In contrast, Thomson's ac lighting system produced in Lynn a decade later powered hundreds of incandescent lamps, used special lamps for interior lighting and street lighting, required special safety devices and regulators, required special insulating materials and careful construction, and cost tens of thousands of dollars. Appropriately, the Thomson-Houston Electric Company had a huge plant, employed thousands of workers, and developed an elaborate organization, with departments for invention, manufacture, and marketing. Just as Tracy Kidder described in *The Soul of a New Machine* how computer engineer Tom West could see the corporate organization of a rival company in the layout of its minicomputer, so the characteristics of Thomson's systems and the structures of his companies reflected each other.[19]

Although Thomson's electrical systems and the ambient business organizations mirrored each other, it is important to realize that the technology itself did not determine the structure of his companies.

18 For another example of linked social and technological innovations, see Robert Frost's discussion of how electrical household appliances and the role of the housewife evolved together in France between the world wars: "Semiotics, Narrative, and the Technological Artifact: Hardware Meets the Software Script (and They Contend Endlessly Thereafter)" (paper presented at the Society for the History of Technology meeting, Wilmington, Del., October 1988).

19 Tracy Kidder, *The Soul of a New Machine* (New York: Avon, 1981), pp. 30–2.

Indeed, the needs and dynamics of each firm did far more to shape the design of his systems and his process of inventing. This is clear at Thomson-Houston, especially as the innovation process evolved from being an interaction between Thomson and other individuals to being a group dynamic. As different individuals took up the tasks of marketing, manufacturing, and invention, they acquired distinctive mind-sets that highlighted their particular functions. Thomson, Coffin, and Rice strove to coordinate these functions, but they nonetheless clashed at times, and these conflicts informed the specific features of Thomson's ac system. Likewise at GE, the needs and characteristics of the company influenced Thomson's choice of project. Anxious to maintain the organization during the depression of the 1890s, Coffin and Rice encouraged Thomson to develop products that could be manufactured in idle plants. One such product was an x-ray system, and we have seen how Thomson's efforts to develop this product in a timely fashion were limited by the dispersion of the necessary equipment (such as lamp-blowing machinery) and decision-making power throughout the firm. In general, Thomson's experiences reveal that neither the technology nor the business organization determined the other; rather, Thomson, Coffin, and Rice shaped both at the same time to achieve goals that were a blend of business and technological factors.[20]

Not only did Thomson and his associates have to match electrical technology and business organization, they also had to implement an effective marketing strategy. To accomplish this required a third level of social interaction; Thomson and others had to interact with a group

20 In making this point about how inventors and entrepreneurs simultaneously shape both technology and business organizations, I am trying to warn business historians of the trap of treating technology as a "black box." Following the lead of economists, business historians frequently have treated technology as a "given" in the development of modern corporations in nineteenth- and twentieth-century America. As Alfred D. Chandler, Jr., has argued, changes in transportation and manufacturing, as well as the invention of new products, were prerequisite for the rise of big business, but he did not inquire as to how entrepreneurs and managers actively shaped these technological changes to match the business organizations they were creating. See his book *The Visible Hand: The Managerial Revolution in American Business* (Cambridge, Mass.: Belknap Press of Harvard University, 1977). In my opinion, an analysis of the origins of managerial capitalism without a detailed examination of the corresponding technologies is only half the story; to understand fully the profound changes that occurred in the American economy between 1880 and 1920, we must understand how individuals shaped technology to sustain and reinforce new business arrangements.

outside the firm, the customers for electric lighting. Indeed, they could not assume that electric lighting would sell itself; instead, they had to work with the customers to create the central-station marketing strategy.

Like other arc-lighting inventors in the late 1870s, Thomson and his partners in Philadelphia and New Britain believed that they could sell electric lighting equipment simply as a capital good. Customers would pay cash for the equipment, install it themselves, and use it as they wished. However, like Brush, Thomson soon realized that there were few customers able to purchase such isolated electric lighting plants; electrical equipment was too expensive and too complex for most customers. Yet because electric lighting was seen from the outset as modern, progressive, and desirable, local businessmen were willing to experiment with different arrangements whereby they could make money from the new technology. One arrangement that local businessmen tried was to sell not lighting equipment but rather the service of lighting. In doing so, those local entrepreneurs reduced the cost of electric lighting by spreading the cost of the equipment across a large number of end users, and thus they invented the concept of the central-station utility. Consequently, whereas previously historians have seen the central station as a creation of Edison, actually it was a bottom-up development, pioneered by businessmen in San Francisco. Rather than being passive recipients of the new technology, local businessmen were active participants in shaping how electric lighting would be marketed.

Once the strategy had been identified, the Brush, Edison, and Thomson-Houston companies all seized the idea of central stations and promoted them. Of those firms, Thomson-Houston was the most active, and by 1891 it had installed more stations than its competitors. Thomson-Houston was successful with that strategy because it effectively matched its technology and organizational structure to the central-station strategy. To penetrate the central-station market, Thomson improved his regulator and increased the capacity of his arc-lighting dynamo by adding his air-blast device. He also designed new systems of dc and ac incandescent lighting so that the company would have systems appropriate for towns and cities of different sizes. Likewise, Coffin developed a sales force that could market the technology to those different cities, and he worked out new ways by which the utility companies could finance their equipment purchases.

In promoting central stations, Thomson-Houston entered into complex negotiations with groups of businessmen in numerous towns and cities. In building the first central stations, Thomson-Houston salesmen and engineers often had to work closely with local capitalists, helping them raise capital, organize a utility company, secure the necessary licenses, and design and install the plant. All of those activities had to be handled with an awareness of the local conditions, such as population density and geography, in order to ensure that the central station would operate profitably. Those efforts at local coordination meant that whereas the system might use standard dynamos and lights, the station itself would be custom-designed to fit the community. By necessity, it was a product of negotiation between the manufacturer and the local businessmen.

More than simply matching the technology to the local conditions, the Thomson-Houston Company had to grapple with the cultural implications of electric lighting. The company had to convince local capitalists to risk money in a new and unproven enterprise. Although today we consider electric lighting a necessity, we must remember that there was no obvious need for electric lighting in the late nineteenth century, especially because it was more complex and more expensive than the existing alternatives of gas or kerosene. In order to be able to convince local businessmen to invest money in a central station, Thomson had to design simple and rugged systems that would make central-station entrepreneurs feel confident about their undertaking. Coffin and his associates had to develop arguments to show how electric lighting could be a lucrative business, and they also strove to link their technology to positive cultural values.[21] By emphasizing that electric lighting was scientific, modern, and progressive, the company helped persuade businessmen that it would be appropriate to risk money on the new technology. Thus, the invention of electric lighting was a social process in the sense that inventors and manufacturers had to negotiate with local businessmen regarding the cultural and economic implications of the new technology.

21 For other studies investigating the cultural implications of electric lighting, see Carolyn Marvin, *When Old Technologies Were New: Thinking about Electric Communication in the Late Nineteenth Century* (Oxford University Press, 1988); Wolfgang Schivelbusch, *Disenchanted Night: The Industrialization of Light in the Nineteenth Century,* trans. A. Davies (Berkeley: University of California Press, 1988); and David E. Nye, *Electrifying America: Social Meanings of a New Technology* (Cambridge, Mass.: MIT Press, 1990).

Thomson's experience demonstrates that technological innovation was thus a social process on several levels. Innovation involves the interaction of individuals, the creation of business organizations, and the implementation of new marketing strategies that grow out of negotiations between producers and customers. At these different levels, neither the technology nor the set of social factors determined the other; rather, inventors and entrepreneurs together shaped the technology, the organizations, and the strategies.

Content and context, individuals and organizations

In its essence, Thomson's story is one of how individuals introduced a new technology by interweaving hardware, business organizations, and marketing strategy. I believe that this central lesson has methodological implications for both the history of technology and business history.

As John Staudenmaier has suggested, the most important methodology in the history of technology has been the contextual approach. In many of their studies, historians of technology have combined a detailed understanding of a technical design with an awareness of how various contextual factors – political, social, economic, and religious – influenced the design. "Genuine contextualism," wrote Staudenmaier,

> is rooted in the proposition that technical designs cannot be meaningfully interpreted in abstraction from their human context. The human fabric is not simply an envelope around a culturally neutral artifact. The values and world views, the intelligence and stupidity, the biases and vested interests of those who design, accept, and maintain a technology are embedded in the technology itself.[22]

According to Staudenmaier, the contextual approach is vital to the history of technology as a means of refuting the commonplace notions of autonomous technological progress. By showing how technological artifacts are not value-free, but are very much products of a particular time and place, historians of technology are demonstrating that the contours of human culture and experience are not dictated by technology.

As important as contextualism is to the history of technology, however, practitioners have not fully developed or refined the approach. As

---

22 John M. Staudenmaier, S.J., *Technology's Storytellers: Reweaving the Human Fabric* (Cambridge, Mass.: MIT Press, 1985), p. 165.

Merritt Roe Smith and Steven C. Reber have observed, contextual approaches fall across a spectrum. At one end of the spectrum are Thomas P. Hughes and David A. Hounshell, who have written histories depicting technology as a body of expanding knowledge for which contextual factors form a backdrop. In those studies, contextual factors occasionally influence technological design, but the evolution of technology is more or less "its own sweet beast." At the other end of the contextual spectrum are scholars such as David F. Noble and Ruth Schwartz Cowan, for whom the cultural context is central, and technical factors are secondary. For those scholars, technology is a social product, shaped by culture and society in response to a variety of factors, including class relations and gender roles.[23] This perspective has been further developed by sociologists Trevor Pinch and Wiebe Bijker; taking a social-constructivist stance, they have argued that social groups appropriate and design artifacts to suit their needs and values.[24] Together, these social historians and sociologists have provided important insights into how technology can be socially determined.

Yet absent from both contextualism and the social-constructivist approach is a thoroughgoing integration of the technological and the social. Whether centered on the technology or its cultural ambience, contextualism embodies a dichotomous causal relationship in which the cultural and social are seen as behind and separate from the technology. The cultural and social are assigned to the environment, where they can influence technological change, but where they cannot be shaped by historical actors. In the social-constructivist approach, groups design artifacts in response to needs and values, but this model does not suggest that groups reorganize themselves or create new organizations and values in order to exploit the artifacts they choose.

23 Merritt Roe Smith and Steven C. Reber, "Contextual Contrasts: Recent Trends in the History of Technology," in S. H. Cutcliffe and R. C. Post, eds., *In Context: History and the History of Technology* (Bethlehem, Pa.: Lehigh University Press, 1989), pp. 133–49.
24 Trevor J. Pinch and Wiebe E. Bijker, "The Social Construction of Facts and Artifacts: Or How the Sociology of Science and the Sociology of Technology Might Benefit Each Other," in W. E. Bijker, T. P. Hughes, and T. J. Pinch, eds., *The Social Construction of Technological Systems: New Directions in the Sociology and History of Technology* (Cambridge, Mass.: MIT Press, 1987), pp. 17–50.

Yet if Thomson's case is indicative, what successful inventors and entrepreneurs do is create both technological artifacts and social artifacts, such as business organizations and marketing strategies. Content and context are to a considerable extent both made, and inventors and entrepreneurs struggle to have them reinforce each other. This is not to say that there are no external factors influencing the actions of inventors and businessmen; certainly Thomson's story reveals how factors such as the availability of capital or the preferences of customers shaped his inventions and companies. Rather, it is crucial to realize that historical actors responded to these factors by social inventions. Moreover, it is in linking technological and social artifacts that inventors and entrepreneurs irrevocably change the patterns of society and culture.

The need to investigate how historical actors simultaneously create technological and social artifacts has been anticipated by other scholars. In a theoretical essay, Hughes suggested that historians should study systems that include both physical components and organizations, but he did not discuss in detail the organizational elements.[25] In contrast, Bruno Latour, Michel Callon, and John Law have shown in their work how scientists and technologists actively combine technical and social artifacts in "actor networks." In particular, in a study of fifteenth-century Portuguese navigation, Law has argued that technologists are in the business of building (and holding together) networks of technical and nontechnical artifacts, an activity that he terms "heterogeneous engineering."[26]

In this study, I have followed the path proposed by Hughes, Latour, Callon, and Law; I have explicitly narrated how the hardware and the organizations evolved together. Thomson and his cohorts certainly were "heterogeneous engineers," struggling to get their technological and social inventions to fit together. However, I decided not to use the concept of either a system or network in this book because I felt that

25 Thomas P. Hughes, "The Evolution of Large Technological Systems," in Bijker, Hughes, and Pinch, *The Social Construction of Technological Systems*, pp. 51–82.

26 Bruno Latour, *Science in Action: How to Follow Scientists and Engineers Through Society* (Milton Keynes: Open University Press, 1987); Michel Callon, "Society in the Making: The Study of Technology as a Tool for Sociological Analysis" and John Law, "Technology and Heterogeneous Engineering: The Case of Portuguese Expansion," both in Bijker, Hughes, and Pinch, eds., *The Social Construction of Technological Systems*, pp. 83–103 and 111–34.

neither was appropriate for this book. Both are broad analytical categories imposed by the scholar on the historical record in an effort to create order, and I was worried that such categories would fail to capture the subtleties and nuances of an individual such as Thomson. Nevertheless, I would agree with these scholars that the next step for the history of technology is to examine deliberately and effectively how individuals create both technological artifacts and the supporting organizational and cultural ambience. Just as Thomson and his cohorts wove hardware, organizations, and strategy together, historians of technology should seek to integrate them into their narratives, noting the manner in which they interact to shape historically particular organizational and technological settings.

Thomson's story also has implications for the field of business history. Just as contextualism has come to mark the history of technology, so a managerial approach has come to dominate business history. This approach has been developed largely by Alfred D. Chandler, Jr., who emphasizes that the central challenge for business historians is to comprehend the rise of large business organizations in which managers determine economic destiny. For Chandler, the rise of managerial capitalism was a response to technology and markets. Anxious to capitalize on new processes and products and to penetrate national and international markets, farsighted businessmen created hierarchical organizations in which managers coordinated the various functions related to production and distribution. Although the first managerial hierarchies appeared in the United States, Chandler has recently described how firms in Britain, Germany, and Japan developed similar functional organizations.[27]

In this study, I have drawn heavily upon Chandler's paradigm: Thomson and his associates moved from an informal partnership to the complex functional structure of GE partly in response to the requirements of technology and the desire to reach new markets. However, although this pattern of organizational evolution conformed to the Chandler paradigm, it also involved a powerful drive to quell the forces of competition, a drive that became linked to the search for capital and the effort to preserve organizational capability. Rather than being the result of inexorable and autonomous forces of technol-

27 Alfred D. Chandler, Jr., *The Visible Hand,* and *Scale and Scope: The Dynamics of Industrial Capitalism* (Cambridge, Mass.: Belknap Press of Harvard University, 1990).

ogy and markets, the rise of GE was a contingent process in which specific individuals played key roles in determining the outcome.

This process was individualistic and contingent in several ways. First, it was simply good fortune that Thomson was able to progress from one set of business partners to another just at the moment he needed more capital or marketing expertise. Had he not met Garrett, Churchill, and Coffin in the sequence that he did, Thomson undoubtedly would have failed as an inventor, or at the very least created different inventions. Thomson was especially fortunate that he teamed up with Coffin, for this shoe manufacturer possessed remarkable abilities in marketing, organization building, and finance. It was largely through the partnership of Thomson and Coffin that Thomson-Houston and GE achieved their syntheses of technology, organization, and marketing.

A second illustration of contingency is related to the central-station marketing strategy. What if the tiny American Electric Company had not received the Kansas City order that forcefully demonstrated to it the potential of central stations? What if the firm had gotten the order, but Thomson and Skinner had failed to appreciate its significance? What if Coffin had lacked the skills needed to create the organizational arrangements necessary to exploit this strategy? Clearly, success in developing this marketing strategy depended on the fortuitous joining of information with the right people.

A third example of contingency concerns the availability of capital. The evolution of the electrical industry was very much shaped by the state of the capital markets, and as suggested earlier, Coffin formed GE as a way of overcoming limitations on his sources of capital. Had capital been readily available to Edison, Westinghouse, and other electrical firms in the late 1880s, the process of change would have been altered. It is possible that more firms would have competed vigorously and perhaps generated a wider range of alternative business structures and electrical systems.[28] However, because electrical manufacturers had to coordinate the functions of innovation, production, and distribution, it is likely that the industry still would have become an oligopoly, dominated by the few large firms that were able to create

---

28 Lance Davis explored the relationship between the availability of capital and the number of firms in a particular industry in "The Capital Markets and Industrial Concentration: The U.S. and U.K., a Comparative Study," *Economic History Review*, 19:255–72 (1966).

effective managerial hierarchies. The central point here is that although the creation of modern business enterprise was shaped by the nature of technology and the availability of national and international markets, the timing of the emergence of such firms in a particular industry was contingent on the availability of capital.

Finally, the origins and early development of GE add contingency to the Chandlerian paradigm in one other important regard. Within Chandler's framework, we might expect that managers in the electrical and chemical industries would have quickly and effectively rationalized and institutionalized the innovation function within their firms; because the exploitation of new scientific or engineering knowledge could give them a competitive advantage, it would seem probable that these managers would have established research departments or laboratories as an essential step in creating strong, well-coordinated firms. Yet, as the x-ray episode indicates, large firms such as GE found it difficult to innovate and moved slowly to create new institutional arrangements for innovation. Struggling to create an effective management team and survive the depression of the 1890s, Coffin and GE's top managers were not in a position to think through and plan carefully the role that innovation should play in the organization.[29] Indeed, GE's modern R&D laboratory emerged only after Thomson, Rice, and others became disgusted with the problems of coordinating resources and personnel across the huge organization. The laboratory that did appear in 1900 was thus shaped by the same array of individual, organizational, and technical factors that were at work in other aspects of the early history of GE. The process by which the innovation function was institutionalized was contingent and shaped to a considerable extent by individual inventors, scientists, and managers. Thus, reflecting on the story of Thomson and GE, it is important that we add individuals and contingency to the Chandler paradigm. Only by look-

29 Louis Galambos has suggested that large corporations in the early twentieth century were slow to establish industrial research laboratories because their managers "were preoccupied with the need to consolidate their firms and stabilize their companies' position in their respective markets. From our vantage point, the difficulties of stabilizing market shares, prices, and profits do not look very great – the outcome seems assured. We have forgotten the combines that failed." See "The American Economy and the Reorganization of the Sources of Knowledge," in A. Oleson and J. Voss, eds., *The Organization of Knowledge in America, 1860–1920* (Baltimore: Johns Hopkins University Press, 1979), pp. 269–84, esp. p. 275.

ing closely at the individual actors and their decisions can we come to appreciate the complexity of the process by which modern business enterprise evolved.[30]

What Thomson's story reveals is that the study of individuals is essential to the historical enterprise. As shown here, an emphasis on individuals need not be simply biographical or overly heroic, with individuals changing the course of history by force of character or intellect. Rather, by examining the thoughts and actions of a key individual, such as Thomson, we are able to put the larger forces of culture, technology, and business into perspective and to probe in detail how individuals react to and shape those forces. Knowing Thomson's experience does not tell us how to design and manage technology step by step toward future goals, but it does provide a framework in which we can analyze the interplay of technology and culture.

30 Harold Livesay has called for a reintegration of the entrepreneur into business history in "Entrepreneurial Dominance in Businesses Large and Small, Past and Present," *Business History Review*, 63:1–21 (Spring 1989).

Index

Weston, 102
Wilde-Ladd, 68–9, 81
dynamo armatures
  Brush, 70f, 116–17
  closed-coil, 117, 118f
  drum-wound (Siemens), 69
  Gramme ring, 69
  open-coil, 117, 118f
  Thomson, spherical, 138
  Thomson, three-coil, 118, 120f
  Thomson and Houston, combination
    drum and bobbin windings, 99
dynamo regulator, infringement litigation, 216, 243, 245, 264, 281
  see also automatic current regulator
dynamometer, 159

economic conditions, U.S. (1875–1900),
  110–13
economies of scale and scope, 216, 269,
  273, 279, 300, 329
economies of speed, 112, 113, 131
eddy currents, 84, 99, 104
Edison, Thomas Alva, 1, 3, 6, 11, 13, 16,
  17, 147, 153, 156, 173, 186, 187,
  195, 203, 207, 233, 236, 240, 342,
  343, 351
  ac research, 276, 283–5, 299
  assessment of Thomson-Houston, 292
  assessment of Westinghouse, 290
  belief in competition, 278n, 284n 292,
    299
  carbon microphone, 79–80
  central-station marketing strategy, 133,
    175, 354
  Edison General Electric, 275–6, 286
  etheric force controversy, 57–64
  on GE's Board of Directors, 296
  incandescent-lighting system, 133, 144,
    175, 277n, 282, 284
  as independent inventor, 191
  interest in automobiles, 332
  opposes alternating current, 283–5
  ore milling, 276
  phonograph, 276
  telegraph inventions, 57
  ties with GE, 315–6
  West Orange laboratory, 276, 283,
    299

x-ray research, 315–16
Edison Electric Light Company, 144, 194,
  274f, 276
  ac–dc controversy, 261–2
  see also Edison organization
Edison General Electric Company, 272,
  273, 299, 300, 304, 308, 348
  business organization, 276
  cooperates with Thomson-Houston,
    291
  formation, 275–6
  forward vertical integration, 279–80
  horizontal integration, 280
  incandescent-lamp litigation, 282
  need for capital, 287, 289, 300
  North American Company, 279–80
  performance (1891), 294, 296
  predecessor firms, 274f
  pricing strategy, 278
  strategy, 286
  see also Edison organization
Edison Manufacturing Company, 316,
  327
Edison organization, 249, 268
  ac–dc controversy, 285
  cooperates with Thomson-Houston,
    283, 298
  fails to develop diversified product line,
    217
  infringement litigation, 243, 281–2
  problems selling central stations,
    217–18
  sales force, 223–5
  see also Edison Electric Light Com-
    pany; Edison General Electric Com-
    pany
Edson, Tracy R., 144
Eiffel Tower, 245
electric automobiles, 332
electric lighting
  as capital good, 128, 134, 172, 354
  conservative attitude of businessmen
    toward, 131
  cultural meanings, 355
  early development in France, 88
  subdivision, 86, 88
  see also arc lighting; central-station
    marketing strategy; central stations;
    incandescent lighting
electric welding, 236, 267, 333